SPECIALIZED ETHNOGRAPHIC METHODS

ETHNOGRAPHER'S TOOLKIT
Second Edition

Jean J. Schensul, Institute for Community Research, Hartford, Connecticut
Margaret D. LeCompte, University of Colorado, Boulder

PURPOSE OF THE ETHNOGRAPHER'S TOOLKIT

The second edition of the **Ethnographer's Toolkit** is designed with the novice field researcher in mind. In this revised and updated version, the authors of the **Toolkit** take the reader through a series of seven books that spell out the steps involved in doing ethnographic research in community and institutional settings. Using simple, reader-friendly language, the **Toolkit** includes case studies, examples, illustrations, checklists, key points, and additional resources, all designed to help the reader fully understand each and every step of the ethnographic process. Eschewing a formulaic approach, the authors explain how to develop research questions, create research designs and models, decide which data collection methods to use, and how to analyze and interpret data. Two new books take the reader through ethical decision-making and protocols specific for protection of individual and group participants in qualitative research, and ways of applying qualitative and ethnographic research to practical program development, evaluation, and systems change efforts. The **Toolkit** is the perfect starting point for students and faculty in the social sciences, public health, education, environmental studies, allied health, and nursing, who may be new to ethnographic research. It also introduces professionals from diverse fields to the use of observation, assessment, and evaluation for practical ways to improve programs and achieve better service outcomes.

    1. *Designing and Conducting Ethnographic Research: An Introduction, Second Edition*, by Margaret D. LeCompte and Jean J. Schensul
    2. *Initiating Ethnographic Research: A Mixed Methods Approach,* by Stephen L. Schensul, Jean J. Schensul, and Margaret D. LeCompte
    3. *Essential Ethnographic Methods: A Mixed Methods Approach, Second Edition*, by Jean J. Schensul and Margaret D. LeCompte
    4. *Specialized Ethnographic Methods: A Mixed Methods Approach*, edited by Jean J. Schensul and Margaret D. LeCompte
    5. *Analysis and Interpretation of Ethnographic Data: A Mixed Methods Approach, Second Edition*, by Margaret D. LeCompte and Jean J. Schensul
    6. *Ethics in Ethnography: A Mixed Methods Approach,* by Margaret D. LeCompte and Jean J. Schensul
    7. *Ethnography in Practice: A Mixed Methods Approach* by Jean J. Schensul and Margaret D. LeCompte

SPECIALIZED ETHNOGRAPHIC METHODS
A Mixed Methods Approach

Edited by
Jean J. Schensul and Margaret D. LeCompte

A division of
ROWMAN & LITTLEFIELD PUBLISHERS, INC.
Lanham • New York • Toronto • Plymouth, UK

Published by AltaMira Press
A division of Rowman & Littlefield Publishers, Inc.
A wholly owned subsidary of The Rowman & Littlefield Publishing Group, Inc.
4501 Forbes Boulevard, Suite 200, Lanham, Maryland 20706
www.rowman.com

10 Thornbury Road, Plymouth PL6 7PP, United Kingdom

British Library Cataloguing in Publication Information Available

Library of Congress Cataloging-in-Publication Data

Specialized ethnographic methods : a mixed methods approach / edited by Jean J. Schensul and Margaret D. LeCompte.
    p. cm. — (Ethnographer's toolkit v.4)
  Includes bibliographical references and index.
  ISBN 978-0-7591-2205-5 (pbk. : alk. paper) — ISBN 978-0-7591-2206-2 (electronic)
  1. Ethnology—Methodology. I. Schensul, Jean J. II. LeCompte, Margaret Diane.
  GN345.S628 2013
  305.80072'4—dc23

                                                                    2012025784

∞™ The paper used in this publication meets the minimum requirements of American National Standard for Information Sciences—Permanence of Paper for Printed Library Materials, ANSI/NISO Z39.48-1992.

Printed in the United States of America

CONTENTS

LIST OF TABLES AND FIGURES

LIST OF EXAMPLES

INTRODUCTION

The *Ethnographer's Toolkit,* a mixed methods approach to ethnography, is a series of texts on how to plan, design, carry out, and use the results of applied ethnographic research. Ethnography, as an approach to research, may be unfamiliar to people accustomed to more traditional forms of research, but we believe that ethnography will not only prove congenial but also essential to many researchers and practitioners. Many of the investigative or evaluative questions that arise in the course of answering basic questions about ongoing events in a community or school setting or in the context of program planning and evaluation cannot be answered very well with other approaches to research, such as controlled experiments or collection of quantifiable data. Often there are no data available to quantify or programs whose effectiveness needs to be assessed! Sometimes the research problem to be addressed is not yet clearly identified and must be discovered. In such cases, ethnographic research provides a valid and important way to find out what *is* happening and to help research-practice teams plan their activities.

NEW IN THE SECOND EDITION OF THE *ETHNOGRAPHER'S TOOLKIT*

In this second edition of the *Toolkit,* we have updated many sections of the books and, based on feedback from our colleagues, we have clarified many of the concepts and techniques. Book 1 of the *Ethnographer's Toolkit* remains an introduction and primer, but it includes new material on data collection, definition, and analysis as well as new chapters on research partnerships and using ethnography for a variety of applied purposes. In Book 1 we define what ethnographic research is, when it should be used, and how it can be used to identify and solve complex social problems, especially those not readily amenable to traditional quantitative or experimental research methods alone. Book 2 now is devoted to the process of developing a conceptual basis for research studies and to more detailed questions of research design, modeling, and preparing for the field experience. Books 1 through 4 emphasize the fact that ethnography is a peculiarly human endeavor; many of its practitioners have commented that, unlike other approaches to research, the *researcher* is the primary tool for collecting primary data. As we demonstrate in these books, ethnography's principal database is amassed in the course of human interaction: direct observation, face-to-face interviewing and elicitation, audiovisual recording, and mapping the networks, times, and places in which human interactions occur. Further, the personal characteristics and activities of researchers as human beings and as scientists become salient in ethnography in ways not applicable in research that permits the investigator to maintain more distance from the persons and phenomena under study. Interpretation of ethnographic research results emerges only from the process of engaging researcher understanding with direct, face-to-face field experience.

Book 4, a collection of individually authored chapters, now includes new chapters on cutting-edge approaches to ethnography. Books 6 and 7 also are entirely new to the *Toolkit*. The former provides extensive detail on the burgeoning field of research ethics and the latter approaches the dissemination and application of ethnographic research in new ways.

We have designed the *Toolkit* for educators, service professionals, professors of applied students in the fields of teaching, social and health services, communications, engineering and business, and students working in applied field settings who are interested in field research and mixed methods ethnographic research. The examples we include throughout the books are drawn from these fields as well as our own research projects and those of our colleagues.

INTRODUCTION TO BOOK 4: SPECIALIZED ETHNOGRAPHIC METHODS

Book 4, *Specialized Ethnographic Methods*, complements the basic inventory of ethnographic data collection tools presented in Book 3 with a number of important additional approaches to the conduct of ethnography. These include defining and collecting cultural artifacts, collecting secondary and archival data, cultural sorting and comparing methods, spatial research and analysis, network research and analysis, the use of multimedia approaches for the collection of ethnographic data, ways to recruit and study "hidden populations," and participatory ethnographic video production. We have termed these data collection strategies "enhanced ethnographic methods" because each of them parallels and enhances a strategy first presented in Book 3.

Chapter 1 addresses an often-overlooked area of ethnographic research, the collection, organization, archiving, and making sense of cultural artifacts. This chapter defines cultural artifacts as text (two-dimensional print), semitext (partial text plus other materials), and three-dimensional material objects. The authors describe why items in these domains are called "artifacts," why they are important in ethnographic research, and how they can be collected, organized, carried back from the field, and used for a variety of different purposes, from illustrating dimensions of community culture and patterning that cannot be displayed in other ways, to using artifacts as forms of unobtrusive measures of changes in purchasing patterns. Text documentation of artifacts and analysis of artifactual data complete the chapter. It should be read in conjunction with Book 3, chapters 3, 4, 5, and 6 on entering the field, exploratory research, key informant interviews, and additional exploratory tools.

Chapter 2 also explores an underdescribed area of ethnographic work, the collection of secondary and archival data on the issue of concern and the study community. Most researchers will try to collect some information about the study area before proceeding with field research. In this chapter, the author argues that such data provide important insights into the current context, the historical record, and contemporary culture of study communities and groups. He shows that there are multiple, often unconsidered sources of both qualitative/ethnographic and quantitative data that can be accessed quite readily and rapidly and how and why their use can enhance field research and study proposals. Using these secondary sources is an important part of preparing for fieldwork. This chapter should be read in conjunction with Book 2, *Initiating Ethnographic Research: Models, Methods, and Measurement,* especially chapters 1 and 2 and Book 5 on analysis.

Chapter 3, on cultural consensus modeling, shows how simple listing, sorting, and comparing strategies are used to learn more about the ways people organize their thinking about cultural domains such as games, animals, risk behaviors, and rituals or holidays. The chapter outlines different approaches for understanding these specifically cultural-level phenomena that help to clarify how people think about and organize perceptions of their cultural worlds. Finally, it provides suggestions for types of software and procedures that can be used for analysis of these data. The chapter should be read in conjunction with chapters 4, 5, and 6 of Book 3 that address basic observational, interviewing, and mapping approaches to the collection of preliminary and cultural-level data in the field.

Chapter 4, "Mapping Spatial Data," is concerned with the relationships among individuals or other objects located on the earth's surface, in particular those relationships that vary when the locations of the objects change. The chapter argues that spatial data analysis and mapping are essential tools in the ethnographer's toolkit. It focuses on the spatial context of daily, weekly, monthly, and annual activities of people living in local geographic communities and the geographic dimensions of organizations with respect to how they function to provide services or otherwise relate to residents of the communities in which they are located. The chapter's final two sections address critical issues in sampling and producing spatial data that illustrate or test hypotheses regarding the relationships among people, places, and events.

The collection, organization, and analysis of network data is the subject of chapter 5, titled "Conducting Ethnographic Network Studies: Friends, Relatives, and Relevant Others." Over the past fifteen years, network research has come to constitute a central component in the set of research approaches, methods, and strategies used to understand how people, places, and events are connected to each other, socially as well as spatially. This chapter describes why network research is important, how it has been used, and different approaches based on personal networks, people connected to each other in "bounded spaces" such as buildings or classrooms, and people and sites connected in open systems that do not have fixed boundaries. It provides examples of tools for data collection as well as a summary that provides a set of questions that ethnographers typically need to answer that can be addressed through network research. This chapter should be read in conjunction with Book 1, chapter 6; Book 3, chapters 7 and 9; Book 6 on ethical considerations in the field; and Book 7 on interventions.

Many ethnographers are involved in research with people who, from others' point of view, may be unfamiliar, may reside in places that are unfamiliar, or may be, for various reasons, difficult to reach. Chapter 6, titled "Studying Hidden and Hard-to-Reach Populations," addresses the many methodological, ethical, and other challenges involved in identifying, reaching, and doing research with such populations. It describes sampling procedures and staffing considerations, and it outlines the variety of reasons why groups of people may be difficult to find because their behavior is marginalized, stigmatized, or hidden from the general public. This chapter is essential reading for any researchers planning to do research with people whose behaviors are considered to be illegal (such as drug users or drug dealers, political dissidents, or undocumented immigrants), or outside of normative social behaviors for the community within which they are living (such as school dropouts and people living with AIDS in communities where HIV is stigmatized). It should be read in conjunction with Book 1, chapters 6 and 10; Book 3, chapters 9 and 10; and Book 6, on ethical considerations in ethnographic research.

Multimedia data collection techniques involve recording behavior and speech using electronic equipment. They expand the capacity of ethnographers to observe and document individual-level behaviors and meaning by creating a more complete and permanent record of events and coexistent linguistic and nonverbal behavior of respondents. These can be used for discourse analysis as well as other linguistically based analyses. Ethnographers, however, do not always have the benefit of a good review of the ways in which these technologies can be used, what options are available, and how data collected through the use of photography and digital video can be analyzed and interpreted. The author of chapter 7, titled "Using Multimedia Techniques in Ethnographic Research," provides such a guide for aspiring visual researchers. She covers conceptual, methodological considerations and applications of multimedia techniques to the collection of multimedia data in the field. In addition, she provides a guide to the types of software for mixed-methods data analysis that include the use of photographs and digital video without which reduce the complexity and cost of "text/visual" analysis of multimedia data. This chapter should be read in conjunction with Book 1, chapters 6 and 7 on approaches to data collection and analysis; Book 4, chapter 8, on participatory video production; and Book 5 on analyzing ethnographic data.

Many ethnographers find that the creation of audiovisual or multimedia materials calls for close collaboration with members of the study community. Collaboration can lead to the development of participatory ethnographic video productions that illustrate the community perspective. In chapter 8, "Creating Participatory Ethnographic Videos," the author, an experienced participatory videographer, describes in detail the history of and rationales for participatory videography, and all of the steps required for the production of videos created in collaboration with, and for the benefit of, the study community. The chapter describes the many benefits of participatory film making as a form of participatory action research, as well as the challenges ethnographers face in making difficult film-editing decisions. It concludes with strategies for sharing video productions with sectors of the community before release and approaches to utilization for education, norms change, and advocacy purposes. This chapter should be read in conjunction with Book 1, chapters 6 and 7; Book 4, chapter 7; Book 5 on data analysis and interpretation; Book 6, on ethical issues faced by users of video recording; and Book 7, which includes chapters on team and participatory research methods in applied ethnography. It is important for the reader to recognize that the essential ethnographic methods described in Book 3 can be used alone, but the enhanced ethnographic methods covered in Book 4 help ethnographers strengthen their data collection procedures and provide a more fully rounded picture of cultural life in a community, organization, work group, school, or other setting. Thus, we would recommend that researchers use the methods described in both Book 3 and Book 4. Doing so adds dimensions of depth and accuracy to the cultural portrait constructed by the ethnographer.

Jean J. Schensul
Margaret LeCompte
Editors

1 ❖•❖•❖

DEFINING, COLLECTING, CATALOGING, AND ANALYZING ARTIFACTS

Margaret D. LeCompte and Sheryl A. Ludwig

WHAT IS AN ARTIFACT? WHEN IS AN ARTIFACT "CULTURAL"?

Artifacts are things made, used, or given special meaning by human beings, and sometimes by other animals, and they usually are displayed publically. Artifacts become cultural when they acquire meaning or significance because of how they relate to the history, behavior, practices, and the values and beliefs of the groups that produce and use them. The use of artifacts can be particularly important in research among groups that normally privilege oral, rather than text-based, communication, and in situations where the written texts, test scores, interviews, surveys and questionnaires, and various instruments that are the stock in trade of quantitative researchers might not be available. Ethnographers discover artifacts as they live in and become familiar with the sites and participants they have chosen to investigate. Material objects, then, become "artifacts" because researchers define them as such in the course of their observations, interviews and residence in the site; such

1

artifacts help researchers describe more fully the phenomenon under study.

CHARACTERISTICS OF CULTURAL ARTIFACTS

Artifacts usually are smaller objects: tools, utensils, clothing, artworks, pottery shards, sacred items, books, toys; they are not houses, bridges, vehicles, or factories. They can be carried, displayed, and used. They often are mundane, as common as kitchen utensils, artists' brushes, a computer, the tools used by weavers, souvenirs that frequent travelers bring home with them on a trip, or the furniture and decorations in someone's home. They are given meaning by particular colors, shapes, building materials, the people who make or use them, and the rituals in which they are used. The origins, composition, and uses of artifacts vary widely, depending on resources available and how those resources are adapted to human needs. Whatever they may be, they often are collected by researchers as souvenirs of the field, but they are

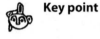 **Key point**

less often collected and used as data. *It is important for ethnographers to make serious efforts to use cultural artifacts in their investigations because artifacts—items representing material culture (Johnson 1980)—evoke and illustrate important concepts about how people live and what they believe.* Objects become data for researchers when the following characteristics are evident.

An **artifact** is:

- Usually produced by human beings
- Often publically displayed in a home or community setting
- Sometimes a natural object that has been given cultural meaning
- Sometimes a natural object that is represented in human-made objects to evoke a cultural meaning
- Usually part of the material culture of a group, something that is made or constructed by human beings
- An object used in everyday life or for rituals or special occasions

- Any item to which cultural (rather than personal) meaning has been ascribed

Most critical is the last characteristic.

Cultural meaning cannot simply be inferred. Rather, researchers must observe the artifacts in use and painstakingly ask the users and creators of artifacts many questions about the significance of each before a clear picture of their function and meaning emerges. ***Any object to which cultural meaning has been ascribed can serve as a cultural artifact for researchers if that object helps to explain how people live and experience their world. This explanation emerges through the researcher's observations and interviews with participants.*** In order to determine whether items or objects can be considered artifacts, researchers must ask the following questions:

Key point

Key point

- What kinds of items or objects are associated with the phenomenon of interest?
- Do any of the items or objects help explain anything important about the phenomenon?
- What additional information might be needed to create an authentic story about the items or objects?
- Is there a relationship between them and where or with whom they were found?
- What objects are collected and displayed by people as markers of their own status or experience?
- What kinds of status or experience do the objects document or represent?
- In which venues are such objects displayed?
- Can any inferences be made about the culture from the objects that have been defined as artifacts? If so, what kinds?
- What kind of supporting evidence is needed to substantiate and corroborate the researcher's inferences?

In the pages that follow, we provide examples of artifacts and what researchers did to construct them as such.

Figure 1.1　Classroom in the Southwestern United States. Photo by Sheryl Ludwig

EXAMPLE 1.1　

EVERYDAY ARTIFACTS: ESMERALDA'S CLASSROOM

Figure 1.1 shows a classroom for elementary school children in the U.S. Southwest, who are taught by a teacher who is a former immigrant from Mexico. It depicts an environment full of artifacts and thus rich in material culture. Some artifacts are commercially produced; others were made by the teacher, students, or people from the local community. The artifacts include furniture and tools such as tables, chairs, desks, curtains and window shades, small filing boxes, a bulletin board, and an easel. They also include student work mounted on walls and bulletin boards; weavings from Guatemala, the country of origin of many of the children; commercially produced cards depicting letters of the alphabet; teacher-made posters depicting vowels pinned to the wall; and paper cutouts of numbers hanging from the light fixtures. Having been a teacher for thirty years, Sheryl Ludwig, the researcher, was familiar with most of what was in the room. But she did not know what they meant to Esmeralda, the teacher, and her students, or how they used them. That information could only be ascertained when Ludwig interviewed the teacher and students and observed them in action.

> **Cross Reference:** See Book 3 for a discussion of the kind of good observation and interviewing that ethnographers must do to document material culture such as that depicted in Figure 1.1

Figure 1.2   Blanca Peak. Photo by Margaret LeCompte

◄►•◄►•◄►   **EXAMPLE 1.2**

BLANCA PEAK IN SOUTHERN COLORADO

Figure 1.2 depicts Blanca Peak in southern Colorado, a part of the natural environment in southern Colorado. To white people it is just one of many beautiful peaks in the Sangre de Cristo Mountain range. To mountain climbers, it is one of the fifty-four challenging "fourteeners"—mountains higher than fourteen thousand feet—in Colorado. To the Navajo, an indigenous group in the Southwestern United States, Blanca Peak is sacred. It is one of four mountains that mark the north, south, east, and west boundaries of their traditional lands. Navajo people identify with their landscape, seeing in its physical features evidence of past battles between their Holy People and ancient enemies, places where their ancestors originated and lived, and the location where resources that enable them to survive exist. Many Navajo wish to live no place other than within the boundaries marked by the four sacred mountains. In order to understand the depth of Navajo culture, researchers must know what Blanca Peak and the other three sacred mountains represent.

Researchers could use this photo to invite Navajo people to speak about what is meaningful in their lives. It could stimulate both Navajo and non-Navajo researchers to tell others about Navajo religion and culture, or be helpful in eliciting stories and meanings about it from Navajo people. The painting in Example 1.3 (Figure 1.3) below can serve the same purpose, as it includes an image of Blanca Peak.

EXAMPLE 1.3

PAINTING OF BLANCA PEAK AND SACRED SYMBOLS

The painting in Figure 1.3, done by Navajo artist, Robert Yazzie, is an artifact that depicts not only Blanca Peak and the other three sacred mountains but also the colors of the north, south, east, and west; the eagle feathers; wedding basket; lightning, rainbow, wind, and clouds; and other symbols associated with each of the mountains. This painting could elicit even richer explanations from Navajo people than the photograph because it places Blanca Peak in its entire symbolic context.

Figure 1.3 Painting of Blanca Peak. Photo by Margaret LeCompte

For the researcher who owns the painting, it serves as a momento of fieldwork and an attractive representative of an interesting period in her life, as well as representing one aspect of her growing knowledge about the Navajo people. However, it remains simply an artwork unless the painter or other Navajo can explain what the symbols and colors, fundamental to the religious life of the Navajo people, mean. The painting is more evocative of meaning than words and text alone and even more than the photo in Example 1.2. To "read," or to understand the underlying cultural meanings of, this painting requires eliciting from the painter and members of the Navajo Nation the meaning of each symbol. With the addition of colors and symbols, the painting's content is more culturally laden than a photograph of the mountain by itself.

As Example 1.4 illustrates, objects can have multiple functions and meanings. Artifacts that serve a specific purpose for one group can be given other purposes or meanings by members of other groups.

EXAMPLE 1.4

WHEN IS TRASH SOMETHING ELSE?

"The empty glassine packets can be found in Manhattan, Brooklyn, and beyond, scattered on streets and sidewalks with only obscure slogans or graphic images to suggest their former use. At one time they contained heroin, and the markings stamped on the packets were meant to differentiate strains of varying purity or provenance. To some they are crime evidence. Addicts may see them mainly as a vehicle to fulfill a dangerous urge. For a group of artists who have been collecting them they are cultural artifacts that are equally unsettling and compelling. On Wednesday, a weeklong show called 'Heroin Stamp Project' open[s] . . . on the Lower East Side. The show, which includes 150 packets picked off city streets . . . is meant to examine the intersection of advertising and addiction and provoke questions about how society addresses dependence and disease. [It also illuminates] the relationship between HIV and drug use . . . the images on the glassine envelopes served as advertisements . . . marketing heroin. 'Even something so forbidden, so demonized, can be branded.'" (Sociologist Pedro Mateu-Gelabert, quoted in Moynihan 2010)

Thus, a simple item can be defined as street litter or trash, a cellophane wrapper, a simple container, a quality control marker, an advertisement, crime scene evidence, a locational marker for illicit behavior, an art work, a cultural artifact, part of a social commentary, or data for analysis of social problems—depending on whether the viewer is a drug dealer, an addict, a law enforcement officer, a social worker, an artist, a gallery owner, or a sociologist. How an object is defined or used depends on the background and motives of the user. How an object is viewed, understood, and interpreted also depends on the intentions of the viewer and the viewer's ability to observe, interview, and document the way in which that object is defined, perceived, and used. In each and every case, researchers must elicit this information through interviews and observations, and then document it.

WHY RESEARCHERS SHOULD USE CULTURAL ARTIFACTS

People surround themselves with artifacts; they make, wear, use, and talk about artifacts. Even if they are just utilitarian objects, artifacts often are decorated and consequently 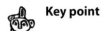 **Key point** expressive of the values and beliefs people hold. *Artifacts evoke the identities, concepts, and values to which individuals and members of a culture adhere.* People use them as markers to communicate information about how they see themselves and want themselves, their homes, and their communities to be seen by others. In everyday life, people rely on both visual and auditory markers to identify and **Definition:** categorize the people around them so that they can figure An "identity out how they can and should interact with each other. How kit" consists of to behave and interact with people holding different status markers of behavior, and cultural positions involves understanding and credibly dress, cosmetics and enacting socially recognized behaviors, expectations, and hair style, stance, beliefs associated with particular positions in a social struc-voice quality and ture. Goffman (1959) has argued that enactment of social register, and behavior roles is enhanced by markers that people adopt and "put that people adopt on" to signify their identity and enhance their performance to enhance role of a given role. He called these markers an "**identity kit**," performance and to which consists of and is expressed in types of clothing, jew-signify to others their elry, cosmetics and hair styles, housing and interior decora-identity

tions, tools people use, the leisure activities and foods they prefer, their modes of movement, speech codes and styles, the proxemics and kinesics of their interaction, and even personal tastes that they practice by associating with others who share the role they desire to occupy (Goffman 1959; Hall 1966). Much of what constitutes the identity kit is part of the material culture with which people surround themselves; it can be useful to researchers in creating a portrait of their lives. Ludwig (2006), for example, notes that Guatemalan women weavers can change from being perceived as ethnically Maya to being seen as assimilated Ladinas simply by changing their clothes from handwoven *traje*, or outfit, to T-shirts and blue jeans and switching from Mayan to Spanish language.

Artifacts do not have to be exotic. The identity kit of the U.S. tourist—athletic shoes, drip-dry shorts or pants, T-shirts, and waterproof parkas—as clearly identifies where they are from as their passports. *Such artifacts tell us about the every day, taken-for-granted cultural meanings that people value, give to their surroundings and to the things they make and use, and how they adapt the resources they have to their needs.* Most of the objects that researchers collect as artifacts are common, easily obtained, and generally in the public domain, especially if they are paid for. Artifacts are important, however, no matter how common, because they can be "read" as a way to determine what people think about themselves and their environment. They also can serve as data points that illuminate important research questions. Perhaps most important, artifacts can serve as "unobtrusive measures" (Webb et al. 1966) of phenomena that are otherwise difficult to observe.

Key point

EXAMPLE 1.5

ELICITING INFORMATION ABOUT NAVAJO CONSUMPTION PATTERNS AND PARTICIPATION IN THE CASH ECONOMY FROM SALES RECEIPTS

Donna Deyhle was trying to assemble a portrait of the subsistence economy of the Navajo community she studied, and in particular, how dependent the inhabitants were on goods imported from off the reservation. She assessed as unreliable interviews that asked people to recall what they consumed. So she systematically collected the sales receipts from the only food store in the community where she worked. Each receipt was a piece of paper displaying what was purchased and how much was paid for each purchase. From these receipts, and from making observations in the family gardens in the community, she was able to construct a picture of what people ate and consumed and what they couldn't make or grow themselves. This created a powerful measure of the economy in her research site (Deyhle 1998, personal communication).

Thus, artifacts can be any objects that help a researcher tell an authentic story. Researchers should be as creative as possible in identifying artifacts that offer alternative pathways to the improvement of data collection—as Deyhle was in using the store receipts to help her portray the economy of the town.

DISTINGUISHING CULTURAL ARTIFACTS FROM OTHER KINDS OF DATA

We have argued that artifacts can constitute kinds of data. This means that like other data, they can serve as part of the body of evidence accumulated in a research project. Strictly speaking, a **datum** can be thought of as a single piece of evidence; **data**, the plural form, then, constitute the body of evidence used by researchers and other professionals to support an argument, make a case, describe a phenomenon, explain a process or occurrence, or establish a warrant. Data come in all forms, shapes, content, and sizes, and some disciplines are more comfortable with specific forms than others. In disciplines that privilege numeric or numeric-like data, these may be seen as the only legitimate form of data. This is, however, a limited notion of data or evidence. The kinds of data used by ethnographers and qualitative researchers usually are not initially numeric, with exceptions such as the sales receipts mentioned earlier. In this chapter, we focus primarily on data that may not even be found initially in written form. Most researchers tend to focus primarily on what people say and do. Because qualitative researchers tend to privilege meanings found in the spoken word or the observable event, they can overlook the meanings embedded in objects created by

Definition: Data are the body of evidence used by researchers and other professionals to support their claims and arguments

Cross Reference: See Book 1, chapter 5, for a detailed discussion of the characteristics of data

and surrounding the people whom they study—in particular, objects of use, veneration, or derision. These objects, or cultural artifacts, are of particular importance to ethnographers. As noted, a cultural artifact is created, given meaning by, and used by a particular group of people.

Being curious about artifacts can open unexpected avenues or sources of information for the researcher. Artifacts are important to people; being curious about what people make and use provides opportunities for conversation. Questions such as "What is this?" "What's it used for?" and "How long did it take for you to make it?" can be taken by respondents to mean that researchers care about them and their cultural practices. Such questions are answered in the course of interviews and observations, but the interviews and observations alone, as we shall explain, do not constitute all of the "data." The object, or artifact, still is of primary importance. Thus, the paper texts of interviews and field notes may include information about items that have been designated as cultural artifacts, but documenting an artifact so as to transform it into data used in a field report requires focus on the artifact itself. Whether or not any object becomes an artifact depends on the researcher's questions and purposes.

CATEGORIES OF ARTIFACTS

We identify three categories of artifacts: text-based artifacts, semi-text-based artifacts, and physical objects. Although physical objects are most commonly what is thought of in a discussion of artifacts, we begin with text-based artifacts, as these are often the easiest to collect.

Text-Based Artifacts

Text-based artifacts exist mostly on paper, and they consist of written texts. They include letters, diaries, student essays, newspapers, magazines, minutes from meetings, committee reports, curriculum guides, and project proposals. Some have symbolic meaning by themselves—such as sacred texts—while others have meaning because they provide information about the phenomenon under study.

Cross Reference:
See Books 3 and 5 and the text below for details of content analytic approaches

Some text-based artifacts can be analyzed with ordinary content analytic techniques (discussed later in this chapter) that permit the researcher to elicit meaning directly from the text itself. Others, however, have additional meaning as objects themselves, and in the context of their use. For example, sacred or holy books have special rules about how, by whom, and when they can be used and even how they are held and treated; they are considered to have power apart from what is written within them. Furthermore, the "how," "by whom," and "when" rules concerning such books can change over time. Such information has to be obtained through direct contact and discussion with the users.

EXAMPLE 1.6

A NEWSPAPER FROM GUATEMALA

This newspaper article (Figure 1.4), whose translated title reads "Rite to 'cleanse' Iximche: Maya elders seek to return a spiritual balance following the visit of Bush," and the photographic representation of this article is an artifact providing evidence of the unhappiness indigenous people in Guatemala felt about United States foreign policy. After President Bush and his wife visited their country, Guatemalan shamans

Figure 1.4   Clipping from Guatemalan newspaper. Photo by Sheryl Ludwig

performed a ceremony to cleanse the land wherever the president's party walked in the Iximche area, the ancestral home of the Kakchiquel Maya. Ludwig used it to show the extent to which Maya people resented U.S. policies in Central America, especially the ways in which globalizing economics were adversely affecting the resources and markets available to Maya craftspeople.

EXAMPLE 1.7

"BIG BOOK" MADE BY IMMIGRANT CHILDREN

This "big book" made by Mayan-speaking Guatemalan immigrant children in a U.S. elementary school describes events in their daily life (Figure 1.5). The teachers wanted the students to read and write in Spanish but had no textbooks with which to work. So they had the children write their own books. The students drew the pictures and created the text with the help of their teachers.

The book might be considered an object, textbook, or work of art created by a collective, but the information in it could also be treated as a text documenting how much vocabulary children had acquired, the activities in their daily lives, or how immigrant children felt about living in their new country.

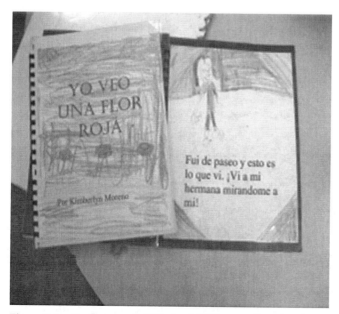

Figure 1.5   Student-created "big book." Photo by Sheryl Ludwig

Semi-Text-Based Artifacts

Semi-text-based artifacts exist primarily on paper, but they do not contain much, if any, text. They include photographs, drawings, murals, maps, web pages, and posters. They communicate much information, but like physical objects, the exact meaning of the information often must be inferred. Thus researchers also must ask participants to explain what actually is depicted and its meaning, as well as what the items depicted are used for. The children's book depicted in Figure 1.5 was, in fact, treated as an artifact emblematic of the teacher's resourcefulness. In interviews, the teachers in this school said that they did not have many materials in Spanish to use with Mexican immigrant children, and none for use with Q'anjob'al-speaking Maya immigrant children. To remedy this deficit, and at the same time to support language and literacy learning in three languages (English, Spanish, and Q'anjob'al), teachers created literacy instruction that engaged the children in writing their own stories in all three languages. The children gained literacy practice and developed reading, writing, and oral fluency. Further, when the teachers then bound their stories into books, the children became "authors." The children were proud of being able to read and write in three languages, and they were extremely pleased to be "authors" who contributed to a growing library of bilingual books for the next year's classes. Further, when coupled with the children's explanations of what they had depicted, the illustrations in the book provided indicators of what was occurring in the children's daily lives, and how they felt about them.

EXAMPLE 1.8

WALL MURALS IN GUATEMALA

Figures 1.6, 1.7, and 1.8 show part of a semi-text-based mural painted along a wall near the entrance of the Maya city of San Juan Comalapa, Guatemala. It includes both text and painting. The figures illustrate how data from various sources must be triangulated to elicit the full meaning of an artifact. At the beginning of the mural (Figure 1.6) the goddess Ixchel, patron saint of weavers and the moon, is shown with her vision of what is important in order to maintain the Maya cosmology and culture. Later sections depict the story of traditional Kakchiquel Maya life in San

Figure 1.6 Guatemalan wall mural *Vision of Ixcel*. Photo by Sheryl Ludwig

Juan Comalapa (Figure 1.7), including the years of "La Violencia," (Figure 1.8) when thousands of Mayan people simply disappeared or were openly killed in this region. In the final section of the mural, Maya artists from Comalapa depict their belief that the genocide was an effort by the state of Guatemala to destroy the Maya culture.

Figure 1.7 Guatemalan wall mural *The Maya Ideal*. Photo by Sheryl Ludwig

Figure 1.8   Guatemalan wall mural *La Violencia*. Photo by Sheryl Ludwig

A researcher hoping to use this mural as an artifact first would have to study the history and cosmology of the Maya people to learn about their religion and the actual events in "La Violencia, and then would need to find out both what the artist's intentions were and how various sectors in the contemporary community feel about it. The murals could be viewed as community artwork, a political statement, an historical depiction, or a way to beautify a barren piece of landscape, and the depictions could be viewed as a positive portrayal of Maya culture, a way to portray cleavages in the community, or as a treasonable critique of the current government, depending on the person providing the interpretation.

These, and the examples that follow, illustrate

- How much a researcher must know in order to be able to attribute cultural meaning to an item
- The complexity of the meaning, in terms of how different meanings can be attributed by different people to the same artifact
- How the actual and potential uses of the artifact in the setting can vary

Figure 1.9   Poster. Photo by Margaret LeCompte

●─●─●─●   **EXAMPLE 1.9**

POSTER ADVERTISING A CAMPUS PRESENTATION ON ENVIRONMENTAL CONTAMINATION

This poster (Figure 1.9) was collected on a university campus in a very environmentally conscious town. It has very little overt information on it. The name of the sponsor of the event indicates that it is an environmental coalition, and the subtitle of the talk is "Threats to Our Health and Safety." To find out what the poster really evokes, a researcher would have to find out that this speech was part of a campaign against serious environmental pollution of the local water supply, which had caused deformities in fish and deaths of migratory ducks. A close look at the poster reveals something peculiar: the littlest duck has three eyes. The fact that the littlest duck is defective evokes deformities found in other ducks and fish species, and it is why the title of the speech asks if people, too, are about to become "dead ducks."

●─●─●─●

Such a poster can have several meanings, but the researcher must clarify what they are through further research. It could be used in a description of or to illustrate the type of activism the environmental coalition engaged in on campus, or it could become part of the documentation of the depth of environmental understanding and commitment among people in the community. It also could raise all kinds of questions in the minds of researchers or observers about who the sponsors were, who was speaking, what other kinds of activities were going on, what the environmental hazards were, and what the history of environmental activism in the community was. In the process of participant observation, researchers would take note of such a poster and use it as stimulus to ask more ethnographic questions about the whole situation behind it—the "back story."

EXAMPLE 1.10

TOURIST MAP OF BOULDER, COLORADO

This map (Figure 1.10) is a semi-text-based artifact containing graphics, text, and pictures. It was commissioned by the Chamber of Commerce of Boulder, Colorado, a mountain town with a strong tourist presence in addition to its resident state university. At one level, maps such as this simply help visitors learn how to navigate the area. However, they also communicate a great deal about what the community wishes others to know about it. For example, the map shows where museums, art galleries, restaurants, churches, and points of geological interest are located. If one understood what the symbols meant, one could look at it and infer that this area is a place where many artists live and work, that it is proud of being home to the state university, and that it is a good place to go for a vacation because it shows where to eat typical meals and where to stay in places that reflect the traditional cultural heritages of the town. A critical analysis of the map might also reveal how the map promotes commodification of the local environment and history.

Physical Objects

Physical objects are concrete three-dimensional "things" that have depth, weight, and shape. They include everything from tools and sculptures to kitchen utensils, jewelry, and religious relics. While every ethnographer collects physical objects as souvenirs of the field, most of these objects do not constitute a key focus for data collection, nor are they data. Usually, they end up decorating the ethnographer's house and attesting to her/his many travels or identification with a specific ethnic/cultural community or location. However, avoiding the use of

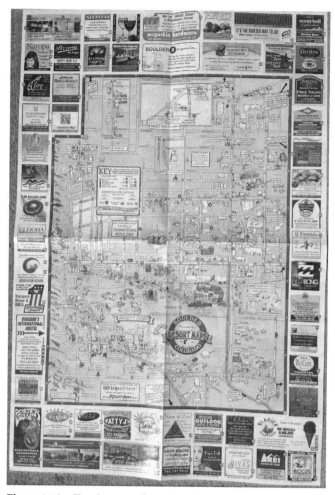

Figure 1.10 Tourist map of Boulder, Colorado. Photo by Margaret LeCompte

physical objects as data is not just carelessness or an oversight. Physical artifacts are hard to work with. They can be difficult to interpret, and they cannot be easily crunched and analyzed like field notes, interviews, or surveys. They cannot be sent via an electronic file or pasted into research reports, and they can be difficult to carry and hard to ship home. Some, such as buildings or mountains, can only be "collected" in the form of representations—like photographs or drawings—no matter how important they might be. Regardless, for artifacts to be useful, they must be documented. In other words, their cultural identity *and* meaning must be elicited by researchers from participants and documented, thereby transforming them into data, as we describe later in this chapter.

EXAMPLE 1.11

USING STUDENTS' SELF-PORTRAITS TO EXPLORE SELF-ESTEEM

Martinez (1998) thought that the meanings of self-portraits he collected of elementary Latino/a immigrant children in the school he studied were self-evident. Martinez noted that the portraits differed starkly by group. White children drew themselves with smiling faces, under sunny skies and next to nice houses with flower gardens. Latino/a children portrayed themselves as sad or unsmiling, with very dark skin—much darker than their actual skin color. The Latino/a faces were unaccompanied by any of the bucolic surroundings produced by white children.

Martinez photographed the self-portraits because he inferred that they depicted how the children actually felt about themselves in their new home; his inference was based on his sense that the sad, dark faces the children drew were a reflection of unhappiness deriving from the racism and marginalization immigrants experienced in the community. Considered together with supporting evidence from interviews, observations, and news media, the paintings served as an unobtrusive measure (Webb et al. 1966) of student self-esteem because the student artists and their artifacts were clearly related. They also were easy to access because teachers had mounted them in the school hallways.

EXAMPLE 1.12

A CONTEMPORARY PROFESSIONAL WOMAN WITH HER IDENTITY KIT

Figure 1.11 illustrates what the "identity kits" of various types of people might be. The woman is dressed in rather formal clothing that denotes her professional status, and she is surrounded with markers of the kind of work she does. To many people, a computer is simply a tool for getting work done. However, to researchers, the computer may also be a symbol of their own identity and an adjunct to their brains. Additionally, many professionals carry around a laptop computer to signify to others how indispensable they are, in that they are always "at work," even when on vacation. Adding a cell phone, iPad, iPhone, or other new electronic communication medium may signify that individuals think they should never be out of touch or unreachable by friends, business contacts, or the world in general. However, these meanings attributed to clothing and objects cannot be confirmed until further research is done to understand how people actually use, display, and

Figure 1.11 Professional identity kit. Photo by Margaret LeCompte

think about these objects, and what meanings are associated with them. Further, inferring that the use of electronic gadgets means the same across societies may be erroneous. In some countries, a cell phone may be the only means of telephone or electronic communication available, if an adequate telecommunications infrastructure is lacking; it also may also denote that the individual has sufficient economic resources to buy one.

EXAMPLE 1.13

GUATEMALAN *GIGANTES*

In Guatemala, people dressed as *gigantes* (giants) "dance" at festivals and celebrations (Figure 1.12). On the surface, they appear to be mere entertainment, especially to observers who are unfamiliar with Guatemalan history. However, they actually represent entrenched social hierarchies that are dramatized and reenacted through these rituals. Without someone to interpret what is happening, these meanings

Figure 1.12   Guatemalan *gigante* figures. Photo by Sheryl Ludwig

would be missed. The *gigantes* actually represent the Spanish conquerors who were taller and larger than the local Maya. The *gigante* figures, though, are far larger than human beings and as such, they evoke the enormous power that the colonial rulers of the past held and the current Ladino government still holds over the Mayan people. The *gigantes'* representations reflect the still-tense political and status relationships in the country. However, bringing home the *gigante* costumes as artifacts would be nearly impossible for ethnographers, even if they were able to procure them. Therefore, a photograph such as this one, accompanied by explanations derived from fieldwork, must suffice.

Creating a Field Guide for Eliciting Descriptions

Interviewing participants about the artifacts they use or make and observing the artifacts as they are in use or being made in the site enables the researcher to determine what people think about themselves, their environment, and how they live within it. This is of critical importance, because it helps to identify potential problems in how ethnographers relate to both the objects and the people associated with them. The process begins by eliciting participants' descriptions of the artifact to create a text that can then be analyzed; it also provides a way to talk deeply about issues that may be difficult for research participants to discuss otherwise.

EXAMPLE 1.14

USING ARTIFACTS TO ELICIT INFORMATION FROM INFORMANTS ABOUT SENSITIVE OR ABSTRACT CONCEPTS: MAYAN WOMEN IN TRADITIONAL DRESS

Sheryl Ludwig (2006) was interested in why Maya women continued to create and wear traditional Maya dress, even when doing so made them subject to discriminatory behavior. The women in Figure 1.13 are wearing the weavings typical of the village where they live, one known for its fine weavings. Asking the women why they wore this particular clothing elicited statements including that this clothing identifies them as Maya, that they are proud to be Maya, that the clothing denotes the village that they come from, that this village is known for its fine weavers, and as such, that they are skilled weavers and artists who made the weavings themselves. All these ideas were of interest to Ludwig, but they were difficult to explore with the women,

Figure 1.13   Maya women in *guipil* and *corte*. Photo by Sheryl Ludwig

who were not accustomed to discussing abstract ideas such as "identity" and "self-concept" or to responding to questions such as "How do you define yourself?" and "What does it mean to be Maya?" So Ludwig used the weavings and weaving tools as stimuli for discussions that answered her questions indirectly. When faced with questions about what the symbols and colors in their weavings and the tools used to make them signified, and how they felt when they wore their best weavings, the women were quite able to discuss ideas that depicted clearly the strength and importance of their cultural identity.

A PLAN FOR ELICITING INFORMATION ABOUT ARTIFACTS

To accomplish these interviews, Ludwig had to formalize her questions, creating a plan or field guide for interviews and observations that could determine:

- What documentary material (archives, books, journal articles) already existed about the artifacts?
- What kinds of questions needed to be asked about artifacts in conversations and interviews and of whom should they be asked?
- What kinds of observations involving artifacts should/could be carried out, where, when, and with whom?
- What member checks and other safeguards were needed to assure valid and reliable descriptions?
- What triangulation was necessary?

These are, of course, the same sorts of plans or field guides created for other aspects of a study, but the focus here was specifically on the artifacts of interest—the weavings. Once she had collected data as described, Ludwig could then infer important characteristics of the culture and its meaning by understanding the meaning embedded in the women's weaving and how they described their clothing.

PROBLEMS IN COLLECTING AND USING ARTIFACTS IN RESEARCH

We have mentioned that the initial problem in using artifacts as data involves defining what constitutes an artifact—that is, what kinds of physical objects and documents constitute objects of culturally assigned veneration, use, or derision that can help shed light on the culture of a people. However, there are less complex, but no less knotty, problems in *using* artifacts for data. Representation or reproduction of physical objects is one problem. Transport is another. Objects cannot be copied electronically and sent via the Internet. Many artifacts are large, lumpy, difficult to carry, and expensive to ship home. As we have noted, some, such as buildings or mountains, can only be "collected" in the form of representations—like the photographs or drawings depicted earlier. Further, most artifacts cannot be pasted into research reports, though their photographs can.

Another problem is that collecting or possessing some artifacts is illegal or tabooed. While it may not be illegal to *possess* drug paraphernalia, possession of such objects may lead to suspicion by authorities that researchers not only possess, but also *use* drugs, which could put the researchers at risk for arrest. Collection of other objects may be prohibited because of taboos or religious beliefs. Even collecting representations can be problematic; for example, some religious groups prohibit taking photographs of people. Some cultures even proscribe photographing religious sites or antiquities, as well as sacred objects or ritual paraphernalia. Taking pictures of women, politicians, or religious figures also may be forbidden. Finally, it may be against the law to remove some archeological artifacts from their home countries.

The next example illustrates some of the sensibilities that must be considered in collecting artifacts. In this case, the object desired by LeCompte had multiple meanings to the Somalis beyond simply being a "writing tablet," which is how the ethnographer had defined it.

Figure 1.14 Korani board. Photo by Margaret LeCompte

EXAMPLE 1.15

A KORANI WRITING BOARD FROM A SOMALI *MADRASSA*

A Korani writing board (Figure 1.14) is a "book" used by children in the religious schools in Somalia, where Margaret LeCompte served in the Peace Corps. Made of wood, it typically would have had verses of the Koran written on it with a soot-and-water ink. LeCompte, a budding educational anthropologist, was interested in the differences in how children learned and were taught in the United States and other countries. In contrast to the textbooks and paper tablets used in the United States, Somali children memorize the Koran verses written on the board, then wash the ink off and reuse the board for another verse to be memorized. The Somalis would not let LeCompte purchase a Korani board with the original verses written on it; Somalis do not believe that non-Muslims should own the holy words. However, the people in LeCompte's village knew that she was a teacher. They were sympathetic to her explanation that she wanted a Korani board to use when she returned to the United States as an example of the kinds of learning materials Somali teachers and children used. The villagers erased the verses and replaced them with some alphabet characters in Arabic on the board, which they then agreed to sell to her.

Researchers, then, must learn which items they can own or photograph in the local cultural situation, and be wary of the kinds of inferences they make based on the appearance of specific objects or the researchers' knowledge of the sources and history of such objects. Such inferences always should be backed up, as Martinez did, with data from fieldwork, and preferably, with data from multiple sources.

CATEGORIZING AND CATALOGING ARTIFACTS

For an item to be defined as an artifact, it must be identified and categorized as culturally relevant. As Donna Deyhle's use of grocery receipts illustrates, the most ordinary of items can shed light on a cultural issue. Once identified as important, artifacts have to be collected and/or documented. Then they have to be categorized and cataloged.

Particularly if they are text documents, photographs, or scanned materials, many artifacts can be collected, copied, categorized, and filed just like any other document. Researchers should group them by specific type—minutes from meetings, proposal documents, photographs of home interiors, maps—and file them separately both in hard copy and electronically—if possible. Indexes then should be created for each grouping so that individual items can be retrieved easily.

Physical objects pose another problem. Researchers may have assembled various artifact collections—musical instruments, drug paraphernalia, masks, videotapes of ceremonies, kitchen utensils, or weavers' tools—that are relevant to their research but which cannot be filed easily. Such collections should be treated more or less as if they were part of a museum collection. In the best-case scenario, each item should be photographed individually with proper lighting and from all sides to be sure that any relevant aspects of it are recorded and visible to the viewer. The photographs should then be categorized. A description of each object's origins, composition, functions, and history should then be attached to the photograph. The photographs and descriptions should be filed as documents would be, under indexed categories, while the actual items should be stored in boxes or curatorial drawers. These, too, must be labeled and indexed, and matched to the photographs and descriptions. In this way, both the text data and the item itself can be retrieved easily if needed. The researcher then must assess the completeness of the collection and what kinds of objects might have been omitted or missed, and why.

Next, we describe how ethnographers transform artifacts into usable data.

Cross Reference: See Book 3, chapter 10, for a discussion of organizing and managing qualitative data and artifacts

CONVERTING ARTIFACTS INTO DATA VIA TRANSCRIPTION

Once they are identified and categorized, artifacts or their representations must be turned into usable data. As we have explained in Book 1, artifacts must be transformed into data by being "**transcribed**." This means that a text must be created about them so that they can be "read." Some of this text is created in the field, during the process of collection and fieldwork—and contained in field notes, interviews, and observations. Other text materials are created out of the field; these text materials amplify what was collected in the field, and they systematically include answers to questions about the function, manufacture, and composition of the artifacts, their history, the types of people who make and use them, and their symbolic as well as actual meaning. We categorize these topics as follows:

Definition:
Converting an artifact to data requires transcription, or creation of a text explaining its provenance, composition, meaning, and use

- Origins of the artifact
- Material description—what the artifact is made of, how, and why
- Functional description—how it is used, by whom, when, and how
- Symbolic description—What its meaning is, both connotative and denotative
- Historical description—When it originated and why, as well as changes in the above over time

Cross Reference:
See Book 1, chapter 5; also the discussion earlier in this chapter

A text containing the above information "converts" an object into data, because while artifacts themselves cannot be read easily, the text about them can be. It also can be coded or analyzed just like field notes or other texts, and the results can then be interpreted. The text accompanying the artifact is, of course, categorized and cataloged with its artifact or representation as described above. Even in research reports, representations—drawings or photographs or even recordings—cannot simply be inserted into a report without field-based explanations as to their function, meaning, and provenance. Doing so assumes—perhaps unwisely—that the reader will know exactly what the researcher meant to convey by the artifact.

Cross Reference:
See Books 1, 3, and 5 for further information on coding, analysis, and interpretation of data

Creating a Descriptive Text

The next stage in transcribing an artifact involves creating a description, including the following areas:

- *Origins*—Were the artifacts made by people for their own use—such as clothing, tools? Were they made by people for the use of others? Or in response to requests by superiors, such as students' work? Were they made in response to a researcher's request, such as diaries, journals, samples of toys? Were they created as an object of admiration or veneration, as in artwork or religious items? How long did it take to make the object? What kind of person made this? Why did this particular person(s) make it and not another person?

- *Material description*—What is the object made of? Why was it made from that substance? What are its shape, color, size, and form? Is it decorated? How? Why is it decorated? Are other similar objects similarly decorated? If not, why not?

- *Functional description*—Who uses the object? What for? Is it used just for specific purposes? Is it used only by certain individuals? Who are they, and what limitations are placed on its use by others? If it is old, are things like this still made? Are they still used in the same way, or do they have new uses? Can other objects serve the same purposes? If so, under which circumstances are substitutions made?

- *Symbolic description*—What does it mean to use, wear, or create this object? What else could it mean? What would happen if someone else made, used, or wore it? Do the components or pieces of the object carry meanings in themselves? What about the color? Do the specific materials used to make it have significance? What importance do the designs have?

- *Historical description*—How old is it? Are these things still made? Have the above changed over time? If so, how have they changed in use, production, or meaning over time? Have similar objects been used in other times/regions by this particular or another group of people?

As mundane as they may seem, systematically answering these questions creates a text that researchers can use to link objects and artifacts to other forms of data in an overall process of analysis. The text, in addition to repeatedly examining and reexamining the artifacts themselves, enables the ethnographer to "make sense" of why people present and re-present themselves publicly as they do. In the process of "making sense" of artifacts, ethnographers can learn a great deal about the ways in which people construct, maintain, and even transform their identities. It is important, however, to remember that what researchers are analyzing is not the artifact itself, but a text written about it. The objects themselves also could be coded in various ways and analyzed for meaning not based on the text, but on the item itself. To that end, the text should be interrogated for biases, exaggerations, and omissions, just as any other form of data would be, and corroborated by triangulation with information collected from a number of sources.

Definition:
Content analysis is a method social scientists use for studying the content of various forms of communication. Usually, that communication is recorded in writing; it includes writings as disparate as books, websites, paintings, film scripts, newspapers, legal decisions, and anthropological field notes

CONTENT ANALYSIS OF TEXTS REPRESENTING ARTIFACTS

Analysis of texts, including those which are artifacts themselves and those which are transcriptions about artifacts, involves the same procedures discussed elsewhere in the *Ethnographer's Toolkit* for analysis of any texts, including field notes, narrative descriptions, letters, diaries and other personal documents, project proposals, published works and archives, and research reports. We call this approach **content analysis.**

What Is Content Analysis?

Content analysis is a method social scientists use for analyzing the content of written texts; it can be used on writings as disparate as books, websites, paintings, film scripts, newspapers, legal decisions, and anthropological field notes. Content analysis can proceed both qualitatively and quantitatively; ethnographers make more use of the former than the latter. Here, we define them both.

Quantitative Content Analysis

Quantitative content analysis often begins with the assumption that words and phrases mentioned most often are those reflecting the important concerns in a communication. This assumption often guides the initial analysis of languages, where it is important to systematically identify linguistic properties such as the frequencies of most used keywords (e.g., KWIC, "Key Word in Context"), or in analysis of coded materials or newspapers, where content analysis can locate the more important structures of the communicative content.

For example, content analysis was used to analyze newspapers in the early 1900s to assess the strength of political parties and opinions; the analysis was done manually by physically measuring the number of lines and amount of space given a subject. Because frequency of use is so important in understanding a message, politicians have adapted and still use this as a strategy for measuring support.

Content analysis of media also has been used to measure trends; Betty Friedan's seminal book, *The Feminine Mystique*, used content analysis of popular women's magazines to illustrate the changing role and status of women in the mid-twentieth century, and John Naisbitt's *Megatrends* (1982) was based on content analysis of the U.S. media. Since the 1980s, content analysis has become an increasingly important tool for measuring success in public relations, notably media relations programs, and for the assessment of media profiles. In these circumstances, content analysis is an element of media evaluation or media analysis. In analyses of this type, data from content analysis is usually combined with data about the medium, such as circulation, readership, number of viewers and listeners, and frequency of publication.

While knowing the *structures* does permit inferences to be made about what is written most often, to whom, and where the communicators are located, it does not always reveal the *content* of the communication. Hence, content analysis extends far beyond plain word counts. Answers to open-ended questions, newspaper articles, political party manifestoes, medical records, or systematic observations in experiments and many other forms of text now can all be subject to machine-assisted systematic analysis. In the example below, researchers used theoretical number crunching to reveal interesting patterns that could then be explored using other means.

EXAMPLE 1.16

THE TOR NETWORK STUDY: IN WHICH THE NUMBER AND COUNTRY OF ORIGIN OF EMAILS SENT SERVES AS A MEASURE OF "TRAFFIC" (HTTPS://WWW.TORPROJECT.ORG/ABOUT/OVERVIEW.HTML)

Dissidents throughout the globe find it necessary, but dangerous, to communicate with one another and to provide the world outside their communities with news about events inside. To facilitate this communication, a network of private computers has been established by volunteers. To prevent information from leaking from the network, passwords change rapidly, and neither content nor identifying information about the senders and receivers can be retrieved by individuals not in the TOR network. However, researchers who were interested in just how much the TOR network was being used did study its traffic. They could determine how many messages were being sent as well as the countries of origin and destination of the messages. While this information could not be traced back to individual computers or users, and it also could not indicate who was using the network or what kind of information was being transmitted, it still gave a measure of how much the network was being used by which countries.

The Qualitative Content Analytic Process

Qualitatively, content analysis can involve any kind of analysis where communication content (speech, written text, interviews, images, narratives) is categorized and classified. In the social sciences, it is commonly used by researchers to analyze observational field notes and recorded transcripts of interviews with participants. However, it also can be used to analyze the texts ethnographers create about artifacts—the transcriptions. They can be analyzed as text, just like observational notes and long interviews. The analysis can proceed deductively with a coding frame or system derived from a preexisting conceptual framework, or it can be inductive, using a more mundane process of playing with ideas. These strategies are discussed in Book 5, chapter 5; they include:

Cross Reference:
See chapter 5 in Book 5 for a discussion of "playing with ideas"

- Constantly comparing items against one another
- Contrasting like and unlike items to refine, modify, and generate new items and categories
- Looking for negative cases
- Looking for co-occurrences and sequences of events and units
- Examining emerging concepts for additional items, units, and patterns to be discovered

The content analytic process begins as researchers or their machine surrogates read the text over and over, examining its content for similarities and dissimilarities, the frequency with which items or ideas are mentioned, patterns of consistency and inconsistency, patterns and linkages to other data and patterns, and overall themes. Themes are identified, the items and units are noted and coded, and then they are assembled into patterns and factors and subsumed within structures and domains. This process can begin early in data collection and continue on through the development of a fully realized coding system such as the one that Holloway and LeCompte (2000) were developing for the Arts Focus program. Only after multiple iterations of this process have been accomplished does the full "story" about an artifact emerge. It then can be written up and integrated with other information from different data sources in the site.

Cross Reference:
See chapter 10 in Book 5

Characteristic of artifacts are that the information about them comes from various sources, all of which must be considered and triangulated in creating an accurate portrayal of the object. Information may include photographs and drawings, stories told and recorded about them, video and audio recordings of the objects in use or field notes and drawings made during use, and historical material on uses in the past and changes in manufacture over time. Sometimes, the process will result in a consensus on or a composite sense of the artifact; other times it will produce several stories because creating a consensus or identifying a uniform "truth" about it may not be possible—as might be the case for the murals in San Juan Comalapa. However, identifying those several perspectives may illuminate cleavages and other important features of the culture under study in ways that conventional interviewing and observation could not.

The story told can even include information showing how and why a single object's meaning and purpose changes over time. The following example shows how triangulation of information from a variety of sources and users/creators of an object can build an overall portrait of changes in use and meaning over time.

EXAMPLE 1.17

SANDPAINTINGS: EVOLUTION FROM COMPONENT OF CEREMONIES OF WORSHIP AND HEALING TO ART OBJECT AND REFRIGERATOR MAGNET

In the twenty-first century, sandpaintings are still made for ceremonies among indigenous people in the U.S. Southwest. They are created by hand-dribbling colored sand and ground stone onto a smooth piece of soil, then are destroyed as soon as the ceremonies are ended, even if they are extraordinarily complex and took days to make. However, parts of some sandpaintings now serve as artworks. Like the forty-five-year-old sandpainting in Figure 1.15, they are made by sprinkling the colored sand onto wood covered with wet glue. When the glue dries, they can be sold as artworks to tourists and art collectors. Some of these sand paintings are very complex, but increasingly, they consist of simple designs or parts of designs put on small wooden blocks by children in a family. These become key chains and refrigerator magnets and are sold cheaply for souvenirs. They thus change in function from religious object to saleable art to knickknacks, but they remain important in augmenting a family's income. Such changes can be a measure of changes in the economic base of a community as well as in family structures and responsibilities.

Researchers must be aware that both the presence and absence of artifacts tell a story. Sometimes the absence is that of something one expected to find but did not; in other cases, the absence becomes obvious in comparison with the abundant presence of other items or factors.

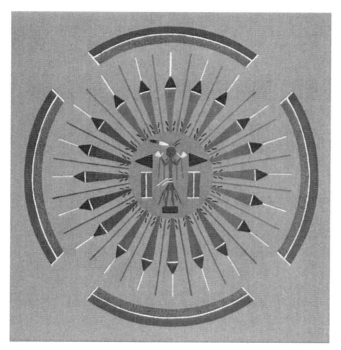

Figure 1.15   Navajo sandpainting. Photo by Margaret LeCompte

EXAMPLE 1.18

WHEN ABSENCE OF ARTIFACTS SPEAKS MORE LOUDLY THAN THEIR PRESENCE

In her studies of schools and classrooms, LeCompte typically collected artworks of students, student essays, photographs of the classroom and the natural environment, instructional materials, curriculum guides, and photographs—all of which reflected the cultural meanings and the material culture of the classroom. Usually that culture also reflected the community in which the school was located. However, in one of the schools LeCompte studied, located deep in a very traditional area of the Navajo Nation, absolutely nothing relevant to Navajo culture was hung on the walls, portrayed in the artwork, exhibited in the language, or discussed in the curriculum. The material culture completely contradicted the stated educational priority given by the district to valuing and preserving the Navajo language and culture; in fact, in appearance and curriculum, the schools could have been anywhere in the United States—not in the unique, culturally rich Navajo homeland. This particular school differed from others in the region that had Navajo rugs hanging in offices, murals depicting the history of the Navajo people lining the hallways, and many other indications of the special culture in the area. Given that the principal of this school strongly believed that Navajo students had to move into the mainstream to achieve academic success, LeCompte inferred that the absence of Navajo cultural artifacts in the school represented the heavy pressure Navajo students experienced to assimilate; it was symbolized by the material environment of their schools, which displayed only white, middle-class, European American cultural icons and language.

Sometimes, analysis of cultural artifacts will result in consensus on or a composite sense of the artifact; at other times it will produce several stories because consensus may not exist. Nonetheless, identifying those several perspectives may illuminate cleavages and other important features of the culture under study in ways that conventional interviewing and observation would not. For example, conversations with Guatemalan Maya villagers about the meaning and purposes of wall murals in their village produced narratives quite different from the upper-class non-Maya administrators and officials in the town (see Example 1.8). Maya villagers thought the murals accurately depicted contrast between their ideal pastoral lifestyle and the genocide inflicted upon them for centuries by the Spanish. By contrast, the officials and administrators simply viewed the paintings as a way to decorate empty walls and capitalize upon the appeal of Maya culture to tourists.

INTERPRETING ARTIFACTS

In the preceding pages, we have discussed how artifacts are transcribed, coded qualitatively or quantitatively, and rendered amenable to use in research findings. In the remainder of this chapter we use examples from our own work and that of our colleagues to demonstrate how artifacts made possible insights and understandings that could not have been reached without them. The theme that runs throughout these extended examples is the social construction of identity among marginalized people in a variety of settings. In our own work we have particularly studied the process of identity construction in diaspora situations and multicultural settings, and among students who do not easily fit into existing niches in their schools and communities. We draw on this research in the following discussions.

Artifacts as Markers of Identity: An Example

As we have described, artifacts can evoke cultural identity; they have a great deal to "say" about who people are and how they wish to present themselves. Our understanding of these processes is informed by Erving Goffman's (1959) concept of the identity kit—the adornments people put on their bodies and enact in behavior to signify their identity. Military officers, for example, are "decorated" with insignia denoting their rank and the awards they have received; these, in turn, signify where they have served and in what capacity. The insignia are signals to other military personnel about how they should be treated, including the degree of deference that they should be shown and the amount and type of privileges to which they are entitled. They also can serve as markers of status and culture that can be read by ethnographers as well.

EXAMPLE 1.19

USING ONE'S CLOTHING TO SIGNIFY IDENTITY

People in Guatemala are defined as *ladino/a*, or Westernized and assimilated, or Maya, or indigenous and adhering to traditional culture, by the clothing they wear and the language they speak. Often people can transform themselves simply by changing their clothes, as Maya people do when they change to Western clothing and speak Spanish. Even though she lives in a rural, small, poor mountain village, and her *guipile* and *corte* are old and not of fine quality, the woman in Figure 1.16 still chose clothing that clearly discloses her identity. She could have worn less-expensive garments such as used T-shirts from the United States, but she says that she chose to wear her handmade *guipile* instead because it identifies her as a Maya woman rather than a Ladina.

Identity kits are relatively unproblematic when all present in a setting understand what they represent and how they are to be "read" by others. However, when the home place of a group of people is changed by virtue of external factors such as war, or forced migration, or when people change their home place, they must change and adapt their identities

Figure 1.16   Woman and child in traditional Maya dress. Photo by Sheryl Ludwig

as well. In the process of those changes, what they do and how they present themselves to others—their identity kit—may change in ways that become clues for researchers trying to determine how they identify themselves in the new setting.

EXAMPLE 1.20

A TRADITIONAL MUSLIM WOMAN NEGOTIATING MULTIPLE WORLDS

This student at a small western college is managing multiple identities (Figure 1.17). She wears a traditional headscarf and dress to signify that she is an observant Mus-

Figure 1.17   Muslim woman student. Photo by Sheryl Ludwig

lim, but being Muslim does not obviate going to college, attending class with men, working online with a computer, and counting both men and women as friends. In a very real sense, Zenab is establishing what many call a *third space identity* (Franquiz 1995; Lorde 1984), or a synthesis of behaviors, beliefs, and cultural markers from both the home culture *and* the new culture. Zenab says that she refuses to choose between the old and the new; she argues that hers is a new, unique, hybrid and multicultural identity. This identity is symbolized by her traditional dress, headscarf, laptop computer, and iPod. Those aspects of her identity kit provided an inroad to discussions with her about her definition of self.

EXAMPLE 1.21

GUATEMALAN STUDENTS IN THE UNITED STATES PRESENT
THEIR INDIGENOUS CULTURE TO THE MAINSTREAM

In contrast to Martinez's experiences, Figure 1.18 depicts a group of Guatemalan high school students living in the southwestern United States whose dance performances have raised their own self-esteem and enhanced the visibility of their own group. Once lumped together with Mexican Americans and virtually invisible to whites in the community, these Central American immigrant students, who also are indigenous people in their home village in Guatemala, have deliberately revived their customs and traditional dress so as to celebrate their existence and teach the community about their culture. However, interviews and participant observation reveal that the existence of their folkloric dance group did not spring into existence without great effort. Rather, their activities are a symbol of how students were able to add value to how they were

Figure 1.18   Guatemalan students' folklorico dancing. Photo by Sheryl Ludwig

perceived in the local community by learning forms of traditional cultural expression
and by becoming teachers and entertainers themselves.

EXAMPLE 1.22

CONSTRUCTING IDENTITY IN A PUBLIC SCHOOL ARTS PROGRAM

LeCompte's study of a multidisciplinary program of arts for middle-school children
was intended to examine the impact of participation in the arts on the identity
construction of students and teachers. LeCompte soon realized that the artifacts
used in the theater program were critical to students enacting the roles of characters
in the plays and to helping them develop alternative personalities. The costumes,
swords and weapons, the make-up kits, and roles they enacted all allowed the children to practice and enact identities and roles that were alternatives to the gender
and occupational roles they traditionally envisioned for themselves. Talking to girls
about, for example, the impact of learning to fight with real swords while playing
the part of a man in *Romeo and Juliet* made it clear that the swords themselves had
symbolic meaning, representing a power that girls had never felt before. Similarly,
owning a make-up kit made students feel like real actors, allowed them to try on
alternative identities, and opened acting up as an occupational possibility. In visual
arts, students created portraits of themselves and their worlds both as they really
were and as the students imagined them to be. They made masks that were sup-

posed to portray their "hidden personalities." Collecting these artifacts and talking to students about why they portrayed themselves as they did was a vivid window into their lives and thoughts.

LeCompte found that as students in the Arts Focus program began to act out roles and use the skills they had learned to express themselves more eloquently in public meetings, they created artifacts that quite explicitly demonstrated how they were trying on and imaginatively rehearsing different roles and ways of being in the world (Mead 1934; Goffman 1959). An example involved the sets of self-portraits that students created in Visual Arts to represent how students actually looked now and how they would like to look or what they would like to be in a few years.

EXAMPLE 1.23

ARTS FOCUS: SKETCHING FROM A PRAIRIE DOG MODEL

In Figure 1.19 a stuffed prairie dog stands in for the live nude model usually found in arts classes but deemed inappropriate for middle school. The state's Fish and Wildlife Service brought in a variety of stuffed wild animals for students to use as

Figure 1.19 Art student and model. Photo by Margaret LeCompte

models; students studied the habitat of the animals they chose before beginning so as to sketch in an appropriate setting for each animal.

Here, the stuffed animals are artifacts that help to create the authentic experience of being an artist who draws from life. Interviews with the students and teacher indicated that this and other experiences were emblematic of how seriously the Arts Program took the emerging artistic identities of the students.

The Influence of External Forces on Identity Construction

Participation in art forms and arts production is not always benign, however, and the identities expressed by artistic endeavors can be controversial, depending on how the art is interpreted by various audiences and the level of esteem in which the artist is held by the society at large.

EXAMPLE 1.24

MANIFESTING IDENTITY THROUGH THE ARTISTIC PROCESS

While Sheryl Ludwig was interested in the technology of Guatemalan backstrap loom weaving, she was more curious about the strength and persistence of the women's Maya identity despite systematic and long-standing oppression of the Maya people throughout more than five hundred years of colonial subjugation. Profound contradictions existed between the environment of the local public school in which she taught English—devoid of any reference to Maya culture—and the widespread use by the government of Maya cultural icons for tourist advertising. Clearly visible was the disconnect between, on the one hand, celebration of the artifacts that Maya people make, and on the other, the government's simultaneous efforts to subjugate the Maya people themselves. One artifact that displayed this clearly was a touristic billboard portraying Maya people in traditional dress, but with no facial features. Ludwig's inference was that the things the Maya made were important, but the people themselves were not. In searching for literature about Maya weaving before beginning her fieldwork, Ludwig found museum archives with much that already had been published about the symbolic meaning of the weavings themselves, the tools and techniques used to create them, and how they were used, but very little about the women weavers themselves and why they wove and wore their own handmade clothing. Nothing had been written about how the women described themselves and their own identities.

To gain entry into their lives, and because she wanted to learn how to weave herself, Ludwig then became an apprentice to a group of Kakchiquel women weavers to study indigenous ways of knowing in general, and of learning and teaching in particular. This gave Ludwig a window into their world as she worked and talked with the women weavers about what they were weaving, why they chose the designs they used, and what it meant to them to wear their own weavings. The women themselves were not literate, and some were fluent only in the Kakchiquel language. They were not facile in verbally articulating their feelings about their roles and indigenous identities, but Ludwig was able to discuss with the women what and how they were weaving, as well as how and why the textiles were worn. These conversations served as a catalyst to explorations of more inchoate feelings and emotions. Ludwig, for example, discussed what the various colors and motifs meant; one weaver, for example, explained that she used the color blue, the symbol of royalty, because it made her feel powerful and happy; doves, the symbol of rain, because of how beautiful the country became during the rains; and the crayfish design to represent her ancestral links to an area where a lake once existed before being drained by the Spanish colonialists. Such introspection could not have been elicited in any way other than in long-term conversations about weaving with the women—during the time-honored socializing of daily conversations over work. Ludwig also gleaned more from informal interviews conducted and observational field notes made in the cooperative and markets, and from conversations with women in other Guatemalan Highland villages. All of this information was transcribed, triangulated, and used to complete a portrayal of the relationships between self and weaving among the women.

Data such as these, collected in the process of her fieldwork, were critical to understanding what the women's activities meant to them and to interpreting what impact they had on how the women related to externally imposed changes in the global economy of tourism and artistic production.

EXAMPLE 1.25

WOMEN IN CONTEMPORARY *TRAJE* (DRESS)

A collection of the clothing worn by contemporary Mayan women not only provides a vivid glimpse of material culture in Mayan communities but also graphically displays changes in technology and aesthetics, and patterns of exchange and economy (Figure 1.20).

Figure 1.20   Women in Maya handmade *traje*. Photo by Sheryl Ludwig

Ludwig was able to interweave what she learned from weaving herself, and what she recorded in videotapes and in her field notes, with information obtained from repeated examination of the weavings themselves for their use of color and design, as well as historical material on the meanings of and changes in the design. She integrated that with information gleaned in conversations with the women themselves about more contemporary meanings and uses for their work. While Ludwig could have inferred many of these meanings from her own observations, a careful "reading" of the artifacts helped to establish the validity of her research findings. Ludwig learned from the women that Guatemalan women still prefer to wear their own weavings, not only because they are warm and comfortable but also because they identify the weavers as members of specific village communities and the individual weavers by the distinctive motifs they create. Complex *guipiles*, or blouses, though, take as much as a year to make and are expensive; they are prized by art collectors and tourists. She also learned that despite their wishes to the contrary, many Maya women cannot afford to wear their own best weavings because they have to sell them as fast as they can make them. What the women wear, then, with or without indigenous woven clothing, not only is a sign of pride but also a stark reminder of class or economic difference.

➤•➤•➤ **EXAMPLE 1.26**

WOMAN IN A CHEAPER *GUIPIL*—SAME FUNCTION, CHEAPER ALTERNATIVE

Some women compromise by wearing simpler, easier to make *guipiles*, which serve the same purpose of body covering (Figure 1.21).

➤•➤•➤ **EXAMPLE 1.27**

WOMEN WITH T-SHIRTS AND *CORTE*: DIFFERENT ARTIFACT, SOMEWHAT SIMILAR FUNCTION

The same function also is served by even cheaper used clothing from the United States (Figure 1.22). Both keep the women warm and decently clothed. The former does evoke Maya identity, but both the cheap blouse and the T-shirt lack the cultural and aesthetic meaning that *guipiles* of the artist's own design carry. Analysis of weavings enabled Ludwig to enumerate key aspects of what weaving means in Maya communities:

- Weavings are made to wear.
- Weavings are made to use in the home.

Figure 1.21 Maya woman in cheaper machine-made blouse. Photo by Sheryl Ludwig

Figure 1.22 Maya woman in cheapest alternative clothing. Photo by Sheryl Ludwig

- Weavings are made to use for ceremonial occasions.
- Weavings are made to sell.
- Weaving is a way to establish community.
- Weaving is a means of artistic expression.
- Weaving is a sign of talent and intelligence.

Further, the ability of a young Maya woman to weave well is a measure of her self-sufficiency. Selling weavings pays for corn, school fees for children, cell phones, computers, and other modern needs. The weavers say as long as they can weave, they will always be able to support themselves and their families. Weaving also builds community, and it is an important way in which Maya culture is maintained and transmitted. The time spent weaving is when the generations learn from each other. The ancient designs woven into the cloth carry meanings about life and what is valued among the Maya; the children learn because they quite literally grow up on the looms, which are central and active features of the home and community (Ludwig 2006).

EXAMPLE 1.28

THE RISKS OF GENERALIZING FROM ONE SETTING TO ANOTHER

The Mayan backstrap loom is an integral part of rural village life and household architecture, as well as a center for socialization. However, transferring cultural meanings from one setting to another is risky, as Barbara Medina's (1998) study of a Navajo community and school demonstrates. Navajo people still widely engage in weaving as a commercial and personal artistic venture, and Navajo rugs are prized—and priced—even more highly than Mayan weavings. Some of the senior classroom teachers participating in Medina's study created a science and social studies unit on weaving. The teachers, students, and teacher aides all were Navajo. The unit included field trips to collect dye plants; creating a sheep camp where children slept overnight, cared for sheep, and sheared their wool; lessons on making dyes and coloring the wool; and practice in carding and spinning the wool into thread—something the teachers thought would be a culturally relevant unit for the beginning of the school year. The teachers also set up a loom in the classroom so that students could practice weaving. However, none of the teachers could weave. They had to ask their aides—who still wove—to instruct the students. This represented a loss of status for the teachers, so they stopped asking the aides to teach weaving. Thus, once the initial classroom unit was completed, the loom sat unused for the remainder of the year. Medina referred to it as "the silent loom"—eloquent for what it said about the loss of cultural meaning and the status differentials in that community.

Medina's (1998) study showed a loom that symbolized something quite different from the loom in Ludwig's village—something that only became obvious because of Medina's detailed understanding of cultural meanings and social status in the community. Her analysis also serves as a caution against making hasty inferences; Medina could have mistaken the presence of the loom in the classroom for a real enthusiasm among the teachers for traditional culture—and weaving—which it was not at all. Alternative explanations for an artifact's meaning, therefore, must be carefully examined.

CONCLUSION

In this chapter, we have discussed how to define, collect, and catalog artifacts, and how to create texts that facilitate their use as data. We also have outlined the kinds of questions that make it possible to understand the nuanced meanings of objects in the environment of the field site. The most important message in this chapter is that ethnographers should be as creative as possible in thinking about the items in their field sites as possible data sources. They should think of using artifacts to stimulate conversations with informants and to elicit information that otherwise would not be available.

The examples in this chapter provide a way to identify a different and useful strategy for eliciting material about a wide variety of cultural concepts, and they are intended to make researchers more sensitive to the meanings of the signs and symbols, decorations, productions, and all the elements of material culture used by research participants.

REFERENCES

Anzaldua, G. 2007. *Borderlands/la frontera: The new mestiza.* Iowa: Aunt Lute Press.

Collier, John Jr. 1967. *Visual anthropology: Photography as a research method, 2nd edition.* New York: Holt, Rinehart and Winston.

Deyhle, D. 1998. Personal communication.

Franquiz, M. 1995. Transformations in bilingual classrooms: Understanding opportunity to learn within the change process. Ph.D. dissertation, University of California, Santa Barbara.

Garfinkel, H. 1967. *Studies in ethnomethodology.* Malden, MA: Blackwell Publishers.

Goffman, E. 1959. *The presentation of self in everyday life.* New York: Anchor Books.

———. 1961. *Asylums: Essays on the social situation of mental patients and other inmates.* New York: Anchor Books.

Hall, E. T. 1959. *The silent language.* New York: Anchor Books.

———. 1966. *The hidden dimension.* New York: Anchor Books.

Holloway, D. E., and M. D. LeCompte. 2000. Theater arts focus and the creating of identity among middle school girls. *Education and Urban Society.*

Johnson, N. B. 1980. The material culture of public school classrooms: The symbolic integration of local schools and national culture. *Anthropology and Education Quarterly* 11: 173–90.

LeCompte, M. D., and J. Preissle. 1993. *Ethnography and qualitative design in educational research.* New York: Academic Press.

LeCompte, M. D., and J. J. Schensul. 1999. *Analyzing ethnographic data. Book 5, The Ethnographer's Toolkit.* Walnut Creek, CA: Altamira Press.

Lorde, A. G. 1984. *Sister outsider: Essays and speeches.* Berkeley, CA: Ten Speed Press.

Ludwig, S. A. 2006. Making fast the thread: Cultural maintenance and transmission of Mayan women weavers who weave on backstrap looms. Doctoral dissertation, School of Education, University of Colorado.

Martinez, E. L. 1998. Valuing our differences: Contextual and interactional factors that affect the academic achievement of Latino immigrant students in a K–5 elementary school. Doctoral dissertation, School of Education, University of Colorado.

Mead, G. H. 1934. *Mind, self and society: From the standpoint of a social behaviorist.* Chicago: University of Chicago Press.

Medina, Barbara. 1998. Din'e b'hana b'oolta. Unpublished doctoral dissertation, School of Education, University of Colorado, Boulder.

Moynihan, C. 2010. The art of the potentially deadly deal: Marketing heroin on the street. *New York Times,* June 23, C1–C5.

Tatum, B. 1999. *"Why are all the black kids sitting together in the cafeteria?": And other conversations about race.* New York: Basic Books.

Webb, E. J., D. T. Campbell, R. D. Schwartz, and L. Sechrest. 1966. *Unobtrusive measures: Nonreactive research in the social sciences.* Chicago: Rand McNally.

2

USING ARCHIVAL AND SECONDARY DATA IN ETHNOGRAPHIC RESEARCH

Stephen L. Schensul

INTRODUCTION

The collection of primary data is a major effort requiring significant outlay of person power, time, money, equipment, and resources. Any approach to data collection and analysis that can shortcut the process, add important information, and save valuable resources is an advantage for ethnographic researchers. Using data sets and other information collected by others can serve these purposes. At the same time, the use of archival and secondary data sources can further the comprehensiveness of data collection, understanding of results, and the cross-cultural and cross-national comparability and generalizability of a specific study. The purposes of this chapter are to define and describe archival and secondary data sources that are both available and potentially useful in ethnographic research; to identify how to access and analyze these data sources;

and to demonstrate how they can be integrated with other forms of data collection in the ethnographic endeavor.

DEFINING ARCHIVAL AND SECONDARY DATA

Archival and secondary data can be defined as qualitative or quantitative data collected for governmental, research, education, or service purposes and available to researchers in usable "raw" data forms and formats. The term *raw* refers to the fact that these data sets or sources are available in their unanalyzed and uninterpreted formats (case records, questionnaires, applications, forms, or numerical or text data coded and formatted into computer-readable data sets). They are organized and stored in their original sampling frames and units (for example, cases of individuals, households, classrooms, communities, and countries).

Some texts use the terms *archival* and *secondary data* interchangeably. We find it useful to distinguish these terms as follows: **archival data** are materials collected for bureaucratic, service, or administrative purposes and transformed into data for research purposes. **Secondary data** are data collected by other researchers for their own research purposes, which ethnographers can obtain for their own use either through public access or personal negotiation.

We also distinguish between local secondary data and nonlocal secondary data. **Local secondary data** are derived from the work of other researchers on the population under study; they are used to add to the researcher's understanding of the local situation; to help to shape study design and formative theory and research models; and to interpret study results.

Nonlocal secondary data are data obtained from research conducted elsewhere with comparable or different populations on similar topics. A special class of nonlocal secondary data that has implications for local description consists of national or state data sets that permit data to be extracted on local geographic units or social/ethnic communities in which ethnographic research will be conducted.

Definition: Archival and secondary data are qualitative and quantitative data collected for research, service, and other official and unofficial purposes by researchers, service organizations, and others, and stored in the format in which they were collected, or transformed into computer-readable data

Definition: Archival data are materials originally collected for bureaucratic or administrative purposes that are transformed into data for research purposes

Definition: Secondary data are raw data other researchers collect for their own purposes, which ethnographers can access for other uses

Definition: Local secondary data are data gathered by other researchers on the population under study

Definition:
Nonlocal secondary data are data obtained from related research conducted elsewhere on related topics/populations

These data offer researchers the opportunity to enhance their research models, test preliminary hypotheses on related data sets prior to entering the field, and situate their locally available secondary and primary data in the context of comparable populations and larger data sets. They also offer the opportunity for testing new hypotheses emerging from the study and clarifying the idiosyncratic features of single community studies.

The U.S. Census, other national census data, and many other such data sets provide demographic, health, housing, and other important information about the population of a study before entering the field and can be a useful supplement to primary data collection during postfield analysis. Researchers also can find many sources of information about local communities in the form of reports, fact books, and maps. These materials can be found in local libraries, community organizations, and college or university special collections on local cities, communities, or ethnic/racial groups.

EXAMPLE 2.1

LOCATING LOCAL INFORMATION BASED ON SECONDARY DATA

In a city such as Hartford, Connecticut, researchers can obtain a demographic fact book for new residents, a Chamber of Commerce Summary of Business Activity, a report of the status of education in the Hartford Public School System, a Children's Health Report Card, and relatively up-to-date special reports on the status of Hartford's children through the Hartford Health Department. Further, Trinity College, a local private four-year college, has an official archive on the history of Hartford, and Central Connecticut State University has an archive on the area's Polish community. The Institute for Community Research (ICR), a locally based research organization, maintains a website (the Connecticut Cultural Heritage Arts Program, CHAP) and archive on the cultural activities, history, and material culture of over eighty different ethnic/national groups in the Connecticut area. ICR also maintains original data sets derived from government-funded studies that are available upon request for secondary analysis by students, community researchers, and others.

These reports, labeled by librarians as "fugitive" or "grey" literature, often are not available through the usual sources—universities, libraries, informational clearing-houses, and research centers. Researchers usually must locate them through the agency that produced or archived them. Further, these archival sources listings are not located in a single place. Key informants, other researchers working in the area—especially policy and cultural researchers—and legislative aides can sometimes provide information about the availability of such reports. These reports are the products of others' analyses of archival or secondary data, and thus do not fit our definitions of either. Despite the challenges of locating these materials, however, they also are important sources of descriptive information, and ethnographic researchers should make every effort to secure them during the early stages of their research.

LOCAL ARCHIVAL DATA

Local archival data are available on general demographic and socioeconomic characteristics of the research community or area as well as specific aspects of the population of interest to researchers such as health status or educational achievement levels. In the following pages we discuss how to locate and use both forms of local archival data.

Local Archival Data on General Features of Communities

Local archival data that can be used to inventory the population and obtain information about social and geographic features of the community under study include:

- Area and topographic maps, which can identify physical features, roads, and residential and other building structures in rural communities and urban neighborhoods
- Municipal records of births, marriages, deaths, real estate transactions, and ownership of telephones, cars, and property

- Census, tax, and voting lists available in villages and neighborhoods of urban areas, for example, the *gramasevana* (the lowest public official/office in Sri Lanka) has the list of all individuals in the unit over eighteen years of age who are eligible to vote. Municipal officials have similar data in Lusaka, Zambia.
- Specialized surveys of water, soil, weather, agricultural production, and other features
- Service system records from health, social welfare, and education organizations
- Court proceedings and cases

Pelto and Pelto (1978) state that "governments and their agents maintain a variety of records concerning population sizes, births and deaths, crimes, marriages and other social statistics . . . fieldworkers should make every attempt to obtain official archival data wherever possible" (116). These archival data can serve as a means of describing the physical environment, establishing the composition of the study population, selecting samples, establishing observational settings, delineating community and population change through time, and many other population development and dynamics issues.

EXAMPLE 2.2

USING ARCHIVAL DATA IN THE STUDY OF URBAN COMMUNITIES (*PUEBLOS JOVENES*) IN LIMA, PERU

Researchers Schensul, Schensul, and Zegarra initiated a study to explore the association between patterns of pediatric health problems and the evolution of communities in the northwest quadrant of Lima. This study used the community as the unit of analysis. The city of Lima, Peru, expanded dramatically during the past two decades as rural residents from the highlands, jungle, and coastal areas migrated to the city in search of a better life. Limited availability of housing in the central city and the high cost of land and new housing resulted in the organization of *invasiones* (invasions) of open public or private land on the outskirts of the city. Professional organizers work with from fifty to over a thousand families to capture a piece of land during the night and occupy it permanently. These organized "new communities" establish temporary housing and seek official recognition so that they can gain the geographic stability required to invest in the construction of permanent housing. Residents also organize themselves at the

Cross Reference: See Book 1, chapter 7; Book 2, chapters 4 and 5 for a discussion of units of research and analysis

block, block cluster, and community levels to take care of their health, social, and educational needs during the process of advocating for "recognition."

A team from the University of Connecticut Health Center, Institute for Community Research, and Universidad Peruana de Cayetano Heredia conducted research in the northwest quadrant of Lima, in a relatively narrow canyon bordered by the foothills of the Andes. New towns or *pueblos jovenes* were arrayed along the canyon from those closest to central Lima to those farther away. Some communities were located on the more desirable flatlands in the center of the canyon and others along the steep canyon walls. Communities located closer to Lima were officially recognized as municipalities, were older and more developed, and owned title to their own plots. Communities situated at greater distances from central Lima tended to be newer, unrecognized, with temporary housing and no infrastructural amenities. Communities located on the steep sides of the canyon experienced more economic and physical disadvantages than those on the canyon floor.

As a first step, the researchers found two maps in the City Planning Department: a topographic map of the canyon (Canto Grande), and a map that located the boundaries of each of the communities in the area of the canyon in which the research was to be conducted. Key informants added the boundaries of newer communities not included in the official map of Canto Grande as well as official extensions to existing communities that had not yet been added to the official map.

These maps proved crucial in the field in helping the research team to locate communities and to define geographical and other visible variations among the communities that might relate to children's health. The maps also helped the team to understand spatial dimensions of community variation and development. The maps were digitized by the department of geography at the University of Connecticut, producing a three-dimensional view of the canyon showing the elevation of communities in the canyon in relation to one another, and a base map of Canto Grande upon which social, economic, political, and other community-level data could be overlaid for comparative purposes (Schensul, Schensul, and Zegarra 1985).

Cross Reference: See Book 4, chapter 4, on mapping spatial data for a more complete discussion of computerized and computerizing of maps

Local Archival Data on Specific Domains of Interest

Local archival data can also be used to learn about particular domains or areas of interest to researchers. The following three sources illustrate the types of information usually available to researchers involved in health, education, and correctional issues.

Schooling and Education

Local school systems can provide an enormous repository of qualitative and quantitative information on individual students, their families, individual schools in the system, and the school system as a whole. These data include student demographic characteristics, student academic and test performance, student behavior, family economics and demographic characteristics, and teacher performance and behavior.

EXAMPLE 2.3

USING LOCAL SCHOOL-BASED ARCHIVAL DATA TO COLLECT INFORMATION
ON CHILDREN'S ACTIVITIES

Researchers Schensul, Diaz, and Woolley were interested in gathering information from children seven to ten years of age attending two schools in the Hartford Public School system. Children were excluded from the study if they reported taking any form of medication for behavioral or learning problems or if they had asthma. To obtain information about the number, gender, and ethnicity of children with diagnosed behavioral or learning problems that required medication, researchers met with representatives of the Central Board of Education in charge of school records. Although the records for individual children were confidential, these representatives were able to provide aggregate information about the classrooms that included children in the required age level. In this way, the researchers were able to select classrooms that had an adequate number of male and female children, broad ethnic representation, and small numbers of children on medication for "hyperactivity" or asthma (Schensul, Diaz, and Woolley 1996).

The following example illustrates the use of historical documents obtained from schools and newspapers to document parents' attitudes toward education.

EXAMPLE 2.4

USING HISTORICAL DOCUMENTS FROM SCHOOLS AND NEWSPAPERS TO DEMONSTRATE A HISTORY
OF LATINO PARENTS' INVOLVEMENT IN EDUCATION

Ruben Donato is studying the access of Latinos to education in the Colorado area during the first half of the twentieth century, using the minutes of school board meetings, attendance records, census records, curriculum documents, superinten-

dent reports, school board election statistics, and records of expenditures in white and Latino schools. This work follows from research he conducted in a California community (Brownfield) to challenge the idea that Latinos were passive victims who accepted their educational fates. Using newspaper archives, he established that there had been a consistent historical pattern of Latino concern and activism over educational issues in the area (Donato 1997, 2007).

Health Services and Issues

Health care facilities such as hospitals, public ambulatory health centers, and private medical practices, as well as nontraditional health service providers (e.g., Ayurveda, acupuncture, and homeopathic medicine), all maintain patient records. These records are likely to vary greatly in completeness and accuracy. In addition, they include only patients who use the service and thus are not a representative sample of the larger community. They are, nonetheless, an invaluable source of information about the characteristics of those using the service, the frequency of reported illnesses, and the treatments prescribed for these illnesses.

 **EXAMPLE 2.5**

COLLECTING CLINIC DATA FROM PUBLIC CLINICS IN THE SAN JUAN DE LURIGANCHO AREA OF LIMA, PERU

To explore their hypothesis regarding a relationship between the level of community development of new communities in the northern quadrant of Lima and patterns of children's health problems, researchers Schensul, Schensul, and Zegarra obtained data on pediatric illness by community. They initiated a comprehensive review of records in the *Centros de Salud* serving the thirty communities. A program titled *Niño Sano* (well child) kept comprehensive data on the health status of mothers and children including heights and weights, family information, health problems of mother and child, and sociodemographic information on the family. The research team, with the assistance of clinic staff, collected a sample of at least thirty children's records for each *pueblo joven* in the area—a total of approximately one thousand records. In a situation where it would have been impossible to collect primary health data, the clinic records were a vital source of information on the health status of children in the sample communities (Schensul, Schensul, and Zegarra 1985).

Legal, Penal, and Court System

Almost all formal civil and criminal courts in the world keep a qualitative record of their cases. These banks of case data can serve as an important record of community disputes, crimes, sentences, policies, and precedents. Sarah Blaffer Hrdy, for example, used wills and probate records to assess the social value differentially accorded to sons and daughters as reflected in inheritance patterns in the San Francisco Bay area (Hrdy 1995). Police records can also be an important source of data on family disputes, gang violence, drug abuse, commercial sex workers, and other populations and issues.

EXAMPLE 2.6   

OBTAINING INFORMATION FROM POLICE RECORDS FOR USE IN RECRUITING INJECTION DRUG USERS FOR DRUG AND AIDS PREVENTION PROGRAMMING

Researchers Weeks, Singer, and Schensul have been involved in AIDS- and drug-related research for the past twelve years. This research has been based primarily in the city of Hartford. Much of the research has involved recruiting injection or other high-risk drug users and enrolling them in various types of intervention programs, or studies to determine how best to conduct interventions designed to reduce both drug- and AIDS-related risks for themselves and their partners and families.

Cross Reference: See Book 4, chapter 6, "Studying Hidden and Hard-to-Reach Populations," for more information on targeted sampling and recruitment; see also Cromley's chapter 4 in Book 4 for a detailed discussion of mapping in ethnography

Recruiting people from streets, abandoned buildings, and other locations where they spend much of their time is a challenging task. One way to increase the likelihood of recruiting a larger and more representative sample is to identify the geographic areas where they are most likely to concentrate their activities.

While drug use is not recorded in any archives, other information is recorded in different administrative reporting systems and can be combined to create a geographic map of what the researchers termed "high-risk areas." Locational data sources available for this purpose included records of crimes, shootings, homicides, assaults, robberies, arrests for prostitution, arrests for drug sales, and locations of abandoned buildings. Institute for Community Research data managers coded these separate sources of information from police administrative databases and reproduced them in a neighborhood Geographic Information System (GIS), using a desktop computer

mapping system (MapINFO). The neighborhoods that showed the highest concentrations of the above activities were those targeted for recruitment.

USING LOCAL ARCHIVAL DATA

A great deal of local archival information is available in most communities. Researchers can locate these local archival sources by making the proper contacts with institutions and organizations and by conducting interviews with key informants. However, they are not always fortunate enough to find these data already organized into clean and immediately usable quantitative or qualitative databases. Data are often stored—sometimes in disorganized ways—in filing cabinets and folders and must be collected, coded, and even computerized to be useful. The accumulation of such data requires considerable time and effort. It is important for ethnographic researchers to inventory the data and to select the data most likely to be central to the study in order to structure retrieval and sampling operations efficiently. The following examples illustrate two cases where local archival data were collected. In the first, a great deal of time was devoted to the collection of local archival data that did not relate to the research topic. In the second, the archival data collected were directly useful to the study.

   EXAMPLE 2.7

COPYING ARCHIVAL DATA ON LEGAL DISPUTES IN RURAL SOUTHWESTERN UGANDA

Researcher Stephen Schensul undertook a study in rural Uganda to examine the social and economic impact of the migration of rural village residents to the city of Kampala for wage labor. In the initial stages of the research, Schensul learned from one of the local chiefs that the local court kept transcripts of criminal cases and civil disputes. He hypothesized that those individuals who had migrated to Kampala for work might be more likely to be involved in criminal activity and, as a consequence of having more financial and property resources, would be involved in larger numbers of court-adjudicated civil disputes. He had no copy machine available in the isolated community in which he was working, so he had to copy court records of disputes laboriously by hand. After much time and effort, he discovered little evidence that migrants had any greater court involvement than

nonmigrants. While the material was interesting, it turned out to be irrelevant to the central focus of the study (Schensul 1969).

EXAMPLE 2.8

USING LOCAL ARCHIVAL DATA TO OBTAIN INFORMATION
ON NAVAJO FOOD PROCUREMENT PATTERNS

In contrast, Donna Deyhle (1998) found it useful and efficient in her study of dietary consumption practices on the Navajo Reservation to record data on food and nonfood purchases as derived from cash register receipts stored by local grocery stores and trading posts. Deyhle created her own archive of these materials, and then supplemented these data with interview data about what families bought on overnight shopping trips to larger towns off the reservation.

Researchers wishing to access, record, and use local archival data should consider the following issues:

- How to identify useful archival data
- How to identify the shortcomings of the archival data
- Which decisions to make about allocating resources to archival data collection
- What kind of procedures for storing and analyzing the archival data should be implemented

Identification of the Data

The location and content of the data must be identified. This often occurs with the assistance of key informants both within and outside the population under study. Steps in identification involve:

- Establishing who has control over access to the data
- Identifying and carrying out formal and informal procedures necessary for gaining access to the data, which may include meetings, written requests for access, and going through social networks to persuade gatekeepers to provide access
- Obtaining or ensuring informed consent if the data describes individual cases (adults, minors, families)

- Developing a means for recording/copying the data including Xeroxing, PDF prints, speaking the information into a tape recorder or voice-activated computer program, developing a coded format for the data, or scanning data directly into a computer
- Creating a strategy for organizing and storing the data

Identifying the Shortcomings of the Archival Data

Archival data may have many shortcomings for the purposes of the study, since they were or are being collected for entirely different purposes. In order to avoid wasting valuable resources, it is important to identify problems with the data in advance before going to great lengths to record it. Incomplete items and missing documents are a significant shortcoming in archival data. No archival data fully represent the study population. Clinic data, for example, record only those attending the clinic, not all cases of a disease. These same data sources may also record information inaccurately or, at times, not at all. Case records and billing forms for patients may record one diagnosis for purposes of billing rather than the two or three for which the patient is being treated. Or they may subsume a specific illness under a broader domain (for example, sometimes categorizing pneumonia as an upper respiratory infection, or as a cause of death when the underlying cause is cancer). Thus, the data are not reliable for research purposes (although the same recording may be appropriate for administrative purposes). Also, recording systems change. Thus, for example, when the definition of AIDS changed in the mid-1990s, far more cases of AIDS were recorded than previously. It would be easy to misinterpret the data if this shift in definition and reporting were unknown to the researcher.

Making Decisions about Allocating Resources to Archival Data Collection

Once having decided that the archival data of interest are valuable to the study, researchers must make decisions about whether the resources required to capture or record the data are available, and how these resources should be allocated. Decisions about the allocation of time and resources to data retrieval may include determining:

- How long it will take to obtain access to the physical location where the archival information is kept
- How long it will take to record the data
- How much recording the data will cost
- How much archival or other staff cooperation is required to access the data
- Whether to obtain all or a sample of records

Procedures for Storing and Analyzing the Archival Data

Before investing time in recording local archival data, researchers should consider storage and analysis. Often archival data must be copied by hand because of the environmental challenges of the field situation or the limited resources of the researcher. Researchers can save valuable time, however, if they can find ways of recording data directly into a qualitative or quantitative computer data management and analysis program. Decisions about storage, management, and analysis include:

- Selection of text search, text management, or quantitative data management and analysis program
- Which analytical procedures to use
- When to use the data and in what form (for model development, contextual description, triangulation, or post primary data collection hypothesis testing)
- How to triangulate the data with other archival, secondary, and primary qualitative and quantitative ethnographic data

LOCATING AND USING SOURCES OF SECONDARY DATA WITH LOCAL RELEVANCE

Secondary data are original data sets that other researchers have created for their own purposes. Ethnographers can access these data sets with the permission of the original researchers; these sources of data may come from previous studies in the research community, including national studies that have selected the research community as a local site.

Obtaining Data from Previous Studies in the Same Communities

Fortunate researchers may be able to use the qualitative and quantitative data collected from studies previously conducted in the research community. The research carried out by Stephen Schensul and Mary Bymel in Chicago's West Side Mexican American community (1968–1976) initiated two decades of continuous work by anthropologists such as Gwen Stern, which then was available for use by local researchers, students, and community members.

EXAMPLE 2.9

THE *CUARENTENA* AS A POSTPARTUM PRACTICE IN THE
MEXICAN AMERICAN COMMUNITY ON THE WEST SIDE OF CHICAGO

Between 1969 and 1974, the Community Research Unit (CRU) of the Community Mental Health Program at the West Side Medical Complex (University of Illinois, Chicago) documented the role of Mexican traditions in the adaptation of newly arriving Mexicans to Chicago. One such tradition is the *cuarentena*; a forty-day postpartum period in which the new mother is excused from household chores, rarely leaves the house, and devotes herself to taking care of the new baby while relatives, friends, and neighbors take care of the family.

In 1974, the National Institute of Mental Health provided funding that enabled researchers Stephen Schensul and Gwen Stern to study the effects of the *cuarentena* on the health and mental health of Latino mothers during the postpartum period. The West Side Community Research Unit's previous ethnographic research on traditional health practices suggested that the practice of the *cuarentena* would be as important as perinatal health care in producing positive maternal and infant health outcomes.

Research results showed that first-generation Mexican women who had migrated from Mexico were significantly more likely to participate in the *cuarentena* than second- or third-generation Chicago residents. The study also found that those women who *expected* to practice the *cuarentena* had a less problematic pregnancy and fewer physical and emotional problems during the postpartum period than those who did not. Finally, the study showed that actual observation of the *cuarentena* predicted better maternal and child health outcomes. Stern and colleagues used these results to support the formation of a new organization, *Mujeres Latinas en Accion* (Latina Women in Action). The data also provided the basis for developing a program to assist pregnant women (particularly second- and third-generation young women) to construct a social support system and perinatal health practices comparable to the traditional *cuarentena* and appropriate to their lifestyles in urban Chicago. The new program provided the foundation for additional data collection on maternal and child health, adding to a growing corpus of qualitative and quantitative data (Gaviria, Stern, and Schensul 1982) in the community, available to other researchers.

The work of anthropologists Jean and Stephen Schensul, Merrill Singer, and Margaret Weeks has contributed to a similar corpus of health, social, and cultural data on multiethnic communities and neighborhoods. For the past two decades, these anthropologists and their colleagues have been conducting collaborative ethnographic and epidemiologic research in Hartford, Connecticut, through the Hispanic Health Council (1978–2007) and the Institute for Community Research (1987–present). Many of the original data sets from over thirty-five studies on maternal and child health, substance abuse, HIV/AIDS, adolescent health, the health of older adults, and various types of health service utilization are maintained in both organizations and regularly are used to provide the foundation for new studies. Students, new faculty members at local universities, and researchers who have worked in these institutions at some earlier point, or researchers from elsewhere in the country, often contact the directors or principal investigators for access to study data. For example, University of Connecticut faculty member Edna Brown has an interest in health disparities and older adults. With the agreement and collaboration of principal investigator Jean Schensul, she is working on two data sets on older adults in senior housing collected between 2001 and 2007 on exposure to HIV and factors associated with depression.

Health social scientists associated with the University of Peradeniya and the Center for Intersectoral Community Health Studies in Kandy, Sri Lanka, have been generating data on the health and development of urban and rural communities in central and eastern Sri Lanka from 1981 to the present. University and community partnerships such as these yield long-term relationships among social science institutes, university departments, and local communities. The encouragement of funders such as the National Institutes of Health, the Centers for Disease Control, and the World Health Organization in generating these partnerships suggests that the number of local secondary databases will grow dramatically over the next decade, enabling ethnographic researchers to begin their local research with the reanalysis of a substantial amount of previously collected text and numerical data.

NONLOCAL SOURCES OF SECONDARY DATA

In this contemporary survey-oriented world, almost every aspect of human behavior has been surveyed, particularly in the industrialized countries. As a result, the United States and its individual states has hundreds of publicly available data sets starting with the U.S. Census and continuing with surveys of work, education, health, sexuality, adolescence, and many other issues. Similarly, most developing countries have demographic and topical survey data that include censuses, surveys conducted by ministries of health, planning, education, agriculture, and others, and surveys facilitated by the international community (the World Health Organization, UNICEF, the United Nations Development Program) and bilateral arrangements (USAID, the Canadian International Development Agency, GTZ—the German technological assistance agency). One of the largest international survey efforts, supported by USAID and conducted by Macro International, is the Demographic and Health Survey (DHS). DHS data have been collected from sixty-four countries every year since 1987, using the same basic format and questions. The Centers for Disease Control and their counterparts in twenty-four countries have collected cross-national data on reproductive health and contraception for the past thirty years with the Contraceptive Prevalence Survey. In the United States and internationally, demographers have led the way in developing, collecting data, and analyzing large national and cross-national data sets.

Ethnographic researchers frequently underutilize state, national, and even international data sets, not realizing that they are an important source of information on local populations. Most of these data sets include social, economic, employment, health, education, and other sociodemographic and epidemiologic data. National censuses are the most well known and well used of these data sets. Many other specialized national surveys that address specific topics such as AIDS and other sexually transmitted infections (STIs), maternal health, drug use, infant and child health, and agricultural production can be reanalyzed for local use.

Example 2.10 illustrates how a state epidemiological database on sexually transmitted infections can assist in planning for a local-level intervention.

EXAMPLE 2.10

USING STATE SECONDARY DATA SETS FOR INTERVENTION PLANNING

As a part of a project conducted with the Connecticut Department of Health, Steven Schensul and colleagues focused on the factors associated with the rapid rise of STIs in one of the cities in Connecticut. An early step in the process was to "map" the spatial distribution of STI cases in the target city that were reported to the Department of Public Health. By law, all cases of gonorrhea and syphilis must be reported. In practice, however, only a fraction of the cases are reported. Nevertheless, the research team believed that knowing how the cases were distributed geographically in the city would point to areas of high STI concentration, suggesting locations for more intensive ethnographic research.

The results of STI mapping, using the state's Geographic Information System, showed that 55 percent of the cases came from two of the city's census tracts. Focusing on these high-incidence areas permitted researchers to target qualitative and quantitative research to those census tracts and to concentrate planning for intervention in those same geographic areas (Schensul, Eisenberg, Glasgow, and Huettner 1994).

The next example illustrates how national studies on related topics can inform the development of a study's theoretical framework.

EXAMPLE 2.11

USING ANALYSES OF NATIONAL SECONDARY DATABASES TO STRENGTHEN A STUDY'S FORMATIVE THEORY

The formative theory for an AIDS risk study was generated based on the direct knowledge and experience of the administration of the Mauritius Family Planning Association, who had been providing health and family planning services in the industrial zone, and researchers Schensul and Schensul, who were familiar with AIDS risk in industrializing zones elsewhere in the world.

One of the members of the joint research team, Satindur Ragobar, was a faculty member of the University of Mauritius. She recalled the existence of two surveys of workers in the industrial sector conducted by the university. Before the start of the field study, the research team sought and obtained access to the raw data. Such access permitted data analysts to disaggregate from the databases all cases of young women aged fifteen to twenty-five years. Hypotheses were explored examining the associations among work, peer, and family domains, ethnicity, health, and dimensions of the work experience.

In 1989, the University of Mauritius conducted a national survey on Health, Nutrition and Productivity of Workers in the EPZ Industries. The sample size for this survey was 2,500 workers in the Economic Processing Zone (EPZ), of which 1,217 were women and 689 were never-married women between the ages of fifteen and twenty-five. While the focus of the survey was on other health issues, the demographic data allowed researchers to explore hypotheses related to the interaction of ethnicity with family structure and work issues. These analyses allowed identification for the first time of several key differentiating factors in the family organization of young women in the EPZ; it gave the first indication that many of the young women were forced to work in the EPZ because of loss of the male head of household for reasons of death, divorce, separation, and infirmity.

The second survey, the national AIDS Knowledge, Attitudes, Beliefs, and Practices survey, was conducted in 1990 by the University of Mauritius in collaboration with the Ministry of Health and the World Health Organization. The national sample included over two thousand individuals, which, when disaggregated by EPZ employment, marital status, age, and gender, included seventy-nine never-married women, from ages fifteen to twenty-five, employed in the industrial sector. Researchers were able to compare this group with a comparable group of nonemployed women to explore the relationship between work status and AIDS Knowledge, Attitudes, and Behaviors (KAB). The survey instrument also proved to be useful in generating items for AIDS and condom knowledge scales. It was then possible to compare the results of the survey used in this study with results of the national AIDS study.

USING NONLOCAL QUANTITATIVE SECONDARY DATA SETS FOR HYPOTHESIS TESTING AND CROSS-NATIONAL COMPARISONS

The opportunity to "collect locally and compare globally" is a strength of ethnography. However, the diversity of ethnographic methods as well as the locations of ethnographers' research and their commitment to local research and theory development makes such comparisons difficult. One approach, funded by international and bilateral agencies, is to organize multisite research and intervention projects with comparable qualitative and quantitative data collection methodologies (Pelto and Gove 1992). Another more recent example is the NIMH Collaborative HIV/STD Prevention Trial, a five-year study (1999–2004) funded by the National Institute of Mental Health to test a peer-led, venue-based model of intervention that had been successful in the United States with gay men and with heterosexual men recruited from bars and other high-risk locations in sites in five countries (Celentano et al. 2010). Other crossnational studies comparing health problems across countries are increasingly common as health problems are more widely understood as globalized (cf. Latkin et al. 2009). These projects, however, are costly and require much crosssite coordination.

A second approach is to organize ethnographically informed basic and intervention studies on a focused topic such as nutritional status of adolescents, the provision of arts instruction in public schools, or women and AIDS, and compare the results across studies. Examples of this approach include the Women and AIDS studies funded by International Center for Research on Women and summarized in their Phase I (1995) and Phase II (1997) report series (ICRW 1995, 1997), the Getty Foundation's Artists in the Schools program, and the results of a cross-site study of the interaction of newcomers with established residents funded by the Ford Foundation (Lamphere 1992).

Yet another alternative, which ethnographers often underutilize, takes advantage of the increasing number of existing data sets resulting from the administration of a survey instrument to a nationally sampled population. Local data extracted from a national data set can be analyzed to test hypotheses emerging from local qualitative data collection. National data sets can be used to generate questions, hypotheses, and ideas that can guide a local study. The National Household Survey on Drug Abuse, the Adolescent Health Survey, and many other such databases can be used for these purposes in the United States. Internationally, the National Family Health Survey, administered to almost fifty thousand households across India, can be used in this way and can be disaggregated to provide data on specific urban areas, or even "designated slum" areas of cities such as Mumbai. Finally, these data sets are useful in testing hypotheses generated from local research. Below, we describe the steps involved in the use of these national and international data sets for testing locally derived hypotheses.

STEPS IN USING INTERNATIONAL DATA SETS

- Delineation of the key results of local ethnographic research
- Identifying and disaggregating appropriate data sets
- Testing ethnographically informed hypotheses
- Exploring the data sets to seek other associations with the dependent domain
- Developing a new and expanded model

Delineation of the Key Results of Local Ethnographic Research

The results of local ethnographic research produce information limited in time and place and hypotheses that can be tested on populations elsewhere. Large national and international data sets can provide the foundation for testing these locally derived hypotheses.

EXAMPLE 2.12

TESTING HYPOTHESES RELATED TO SOCIAL INEQUALITIES AND SEXUAL INITIATION IN SRI LANKA

In 1997, the Mellon Foundation funded a cross-national study to explore the relationship between social inequality and sexual initiation. Researchers Schensul and de Silva proposed using the Youth and Sexual Risk data set (de Silva et al. 1997) to explore this topic and added to it a substantial number of new interviews on sexual initiation.

In January 1998, researchers Stephen Schensul, de Silva, and Wedisinghe were at the research offices in Kandy, Sri Lanka, reviewing preliminary analyses of their new sexual initiation data and reanalyzing the qualitative and quantitative data sets from the previous study. Results of both studies pointed to a considerable amount of data on unprotected sex during first sexual encounters, and they were considering how to organize the results to reflect and interpret the circumstances under which risks occurred during these encounters. A gender-based analysis was not possible because females reported very limited sexual activity. The research team concluded that "age discordance" (not gender or behavior) was important in accounting for variations in the occurrence of risky behavior.

They defined age discordance as "the relative age difference between the respondent and sex partner in a sexual dyad." Age discordance was a proxy for the power imbalance between older and younger partners in sexual experience, emotional and physical maturity, socioeconomic status, power, and effective risk-prevention communication. Age discordance was defined as positive (respondent **younger** than the partner) or negative (respondent **older** than the partner). Researchers found a large number of examples of both types of age discordance at sexual initiation. The primary hypothesis emerging from the analysis of these data sets was that age discordance at sexual initiation predicted greater exposure to sexual risk later on.

A review of the scientific literature revealed little information on this topic. For this reason the research team decided to conduct a secondary analysis of data on youth and reproductive health behavior based on available national and international data sets. The purpose of the analysis was to test the hypothesis as stated and to identify critical predictors (domains, factors, and variables) for use in a broader study of age discordance and sexual risk in Sri Lanka.

Identifying and Disaggregating Appropriate Data Sets

The next step in testing the generalizability of locally supported hypotheses with large national and international

data sets is to identify those data sets that are likely to be useful. Once these are identified, data analysts must disaggregate them or create subsets within them in terms of the target population (defined by age, gender, ethnicity, income level, or geographic location) and the variables believed to be appropriate for the proposed study. Researchers should recognize that these operations are complex and should not be tackled by novice data analysts. Researchers also should be prepared for there to be gaps in the data records in certain categories, since data collected for one study may not have been collected in other data sets.

EXAMPLE 2.13

PREPARING FOR A STUDY OF AGE DISCORDANCE AND SEXUAL RISK USING RELATED LARGE DATA SETS

To prepare for a study of age discordance, researchers used subsets and selected variables from the following data sets that showed promise in measuring both age discordance and sexual risk behavior:

- **Demographic and Health Survey (DHS)** collected in six Sub-Saharan countries—Uganda, Zambia, Zimbabwe, Benin, Central African Republic, and Cote D'Ivoire—on a variety of health, fertility, mortality, and nutrition topics, also including sexual activity, knowledge, and behaviors regarding AIDS and other sexually transmitted infections. This data set included no information about premarital partners.
- **National Longitudinal Study of Adolescent Health Data UNC, Chapel Hill (Add Health).** The Add Health study (Wave I 1994) was designed to measure the impact of the social environment on adolescent health through the examination of behavioral and demographic factors affecting youth in their communities. The data set contains 6,503 cases; 3,356 females and 3,147 males, from grades seven to twelve. Information is available on age, gender, and other characteristics for three partners so that it is possible to be precise about the difference between the age of the respondent and the age of the partners.
- The **Contraceptive Prevalence Survey (CPS)** has been administered in almost thirty countries but is not as publicly available as the other data sets described. Access to each country's data set has to be negotiated separately either with the specific Ministry of Health or with the individual project officer at the CDC. As a result of working with two participants from Jamaica, researchers at the University of Connecticut Health Center acquired the

Jamaica CPS, from which was then extracted subsets for unmarried young women and men fifteen to twenty-four years old. There were 970 young women and 1,041 young men. The data set for males was more extensive, including sections on sex education, current sexual activity, and knowledge of AIDS, whereas the data for females were limited to demographic and contraceptive use variables.

Testing Ethnographically Informed Hypotheses

A major challenge in using a data set created with purposes only partially related to the research topic at hand is to find the appropriate variables with which to test the main hypotheses. Once these variables are located or created, researchers can seek associations among independent and dependent variables. These processes are described in the following example.

EXAMPLE 2.14

CONSIDERING THE RELATIONSHIP BETWEEN AGE DISCORDANCE AND SEXUAL RISK

Continuing the example cited above on the relationships between age discordance and sexual risk behavior, researchers first created the variables "positive and negative age discordance" in each of the data sets. Next they identified variables in the available data sets related to the major hypothesis to be tested. These included age at first sex and several outcomes related to sexual risks, emotional well-being, conformity to cultural values, and life adjustment.

The data sets generally confirmed the primary hypothesis and related secondary hypotheses. The results are as follows:

- *Perceptions of future sexual risks.* Positive age discordance and earlier age at first sex were related to expectations that one will contract STIs or HIV/AIDS.
- *Contraceptives.* Lower level of knowledge about contraceptives (including condoms) was related to the lower likelihood of using contraceptives/condoms at first sexual experience, early age of initiation into sex, and premarital pregnancy at an early age.
- *Risky sex.* Both age discordance and earlier age at first sex were related to higher levels of sexual risk (more subsequent sexual partners, higher incidence of STIs, and greater likelihood of involvement in coercive sex).

- *Substance abuse.* For both males and females, first sexual experience with older partners was related to the use of several substances, including tobacco, alcohol, cocaine, and other illegal drugs.
- *Emotional problems.* For females, first sexual experience with older males was related to poor self-esteem. For males, early age at first sex was related to poor self-esteem, suicide ideation and attempts, and greater involvement in physical fighting.
- *Premarital pregnancy/fatherhood.* For females, both early age of sexual initiation and negative age discordance (with an older partner) were related to a higher incidence of premarital pregnancy.

Exploring the Data Sets to Seek Other Associations with the Dependent Domain

Large data sets include variables other than those researchers may have considered in the original formulation of the hypotheses to be tested cross-nationally. Thus, an advantage of working with large data sets is the opportunity they provide to explore the associations among domains.

 **EXAMPLE 2.15**

TESTING NEW HYPOTHESES

In the same study, we also explored precursors to age-discordant relationships situated in the domains "family," "work," "school," "peers," and "demographic factors." The results were as follows:

- *Demographic.* Lower age at first sex was related to residence in a rural (versus urban) community, fewer years of education, lower economic status, unemployment, and (for females) working in a setting away from family.
- *Family.* Positive age discordance (i.e., older partner) at first sex was related to unhappy family relationships, a desire to leave home, lack of attention from family members, and low levels of family activity. Living in a single-parent family was related to positive age discordance (for females) and lower age at first sex (for males).
- *Family problems*, characterized by alcohol use in the household, were related to age discordance in first sexual experience. Strict parental discipline and oversight were related to higher age at first sex.
- *Peers.* For males, earlier age at first sex was related to engagement in "negative" activities with male peers. That is, male youth who were initiated into

sex at an early age were more likely to engage, with peers, in high levels of smoking, alcohol use, and visiting commercial sex workers.

- **School.** Both age discordance and early age at first sex were related to school difficulties (e.g., suspension, expulsion) and negative school experiences.

Develop a New and Expanded Model

Large data sets can be used to identify new domains, factors, and variables that can form the basis for a new formative theoretical model, which can take the researcher "back to the field" to conduct additional ethnographic research.

USING QUALITATIVE SECONDARY DATA SOURCES FOR HYPOTHESIS TESTING AND CROSS-CULTURAL COMPARISONS

Archival ethnographic materials, primarily field notes and case studies, exist in two main forms. These are the Human Relations Area Files, a collection of ethnographic case studies that have been coded using a standardized set of codes; and field notes obtained through a number of cross-site ethnographic or mixed-methods studies, including:

- The Whiting and Child studies of socialization across six cultures
- Cross-site school-based ethnographic evaluations conducted in the 1970s to monitor and describe desegregation efforts
- Cross-site mixed-methods studies that include formative or additional ethnographic components. These exist primarily in the health field and are increasingly common
- HRAF files, a coded archive of ethnographic texts for use in cross-cultural analysis

The field of cross-site ethnographic work has evolved sufficiently to result in several publications that discuss team-based ethnography (Davidson and Bresler 1996; Guest and MacQueen 2008; Ouelett et al. 1995). Most federally funded studies in the United States do not require data-sharing plans for qualitative data. Thus protocols and procedures for deidentifying and sharing qualitative/ ethnographic data are in their infancy. And most ethnographers who are not working in a team setting do not leave their field notes for other researchers to use. Individual ethnographers see their text data (observations and informal interviews) as a "personal record" of their field experience and usually do not write field notes for a wider audience. Their notes may vary in quality and completeness, and ensuring confidentiality can be a problem since descriptions of people and places are usually quite detailed, enabling other readers to identify them if special precautions are not taken. Finally, it may be difficult to code personal field notes systematically.

Moving Away from the Individual Researcher to Team-Based Research

With the advent and increasing use of computer-based text coding, management, and search programs, however, this pattern is changing. Establishing, training, and monitoring ethnographic team research is time consuming and requires that ethnographers move beyond their individually oriented training to agree on common themes, coding schemes, and writing topics. In cities such as Hartford, New Haven, Baltimore, Brooklyn, and San Francisco, where team-based ethnographic research is common, there may be multiple studies going on sequentially or at times simultaneously, and where there are agreements to share data, researchers can develop agreements on data-sharing practices that protect confidentiality while allowing for maximum use across projects. These agreements can involve strategies such as assigning code numbers or unique identifiers to key informants and locations and developing a common coding system and code book with unique codes assigned to subprojects. Researchers on any of the participating ethnographic study teams can receive copies of all of the coded field notes from any of the studies and can recode them for their own purposes without tampering with the common coded data set or with each study's commonly

Cross Reference:
See Book 5, chapters 7 and 8, on coding and computer management of text data and with team-based ethnographic research

Cross Reference:
Team-based ethnographic research approaches, methods, and consideration are described in Book 7

coded data set. Members of the research team who wish to use field notes from a particular site for a publication often invite those ethnographers who collected the data to join them as coauthors. These data sets are formatted so that they can be stored and used eventually as secondary qualitative data sets. With properly defined coding categories (conceptual taxonomies) available to them, researchers new to these data sets then could choose to recode the field notes from the perspective of their specific interests. Secondary data analysts could work directly with the author of the notes or independently so long as the authors' contributions were fully acknowledged.

While the technological advances necessary to prepare text data for broader public use are available, to date, there have been few discussions of the ethical aspects of sharing field notes or the effect of making field notes public on the quality and substance of the field notes. These topics remain to be addressed publically in circles that discuss research ethics and will be touched upon in Book 6 of this series, which focuses specifically on ethnographic research and research ethics. In the meantime, ethnographers depend on qualitative archival resources that consist of already processed data. These can be found in the form of ethnographies organized into databases.

Cross Reference:
See Book 6, chapter 6

Three such current databases include a large number of descriptive ethnographies. The units of analysis in these databases are named cultural groups further identified as bands, tribes, kingdoms, and other bounded groups. Databases include the following:

- Atlas of World Cultures—1,264 ethnographies along with a reduced collection of 862 ethnographies assessed as "well described" (Murdock 1967)
- "Standard Ethnographic Sample"—containing 285 societies or cultures (Naroll and Sipes 1973)
- The Human Relations Area Files Sample—360 cultures (Ember and Ember 1998). The HRAF collection is the only one of these databases that provides ethnographic text; the others provide only coded text databases

George Peter Murdock, a leader in cross-cultural research, has led a global effort to compile an organized collection of ethnographies at the Yale Institute for Human Relations, which has allowed scholars to compare cultures of the world. His subject classification (coding) system has been applied not only to ethnographies but also to numerous other studies on cultural topics (1967). Ember and Ember (1998) provide a full description of cross-cultural ethnographic databases, noting that the sources they cite have been available on CD-ROM and the Internet since 1994 (Ember and Ember 1998). Like reports, these ethnographic materials are useful in the preparation of research models and designs as well as in situating the results of local ethnographic research in a global context.

Cross Reference: See Book 5, chapter 6, for an example of the HRAF coding system

SUMMARY

Ethnographic researchers can make good use of secondary and archival data in developing local theory and situating their studies locally and globally. In this chapter we have seen that these data can contribute to initial conceptualization and to the substantive data collection of an ethnographic study. They can provide the opportunity to test field-generated hypotheses at the national and international level.

Ethnographic methodology and perspectives have become an important component of international health and development programs because they deliver the localized, socioculturally specific knowledge essential to appropriate implementation. This in-the-field orientation is an aspect of ethnography that gives "voice" to groups who are marginalized, modifies top-down programs, and contributes to a greater balance between the professionals and the community. At the same time ethnography has been criticized for being too localized, for generating data with limited comparability to other settings, and for lacking comprehensive theories validated by data collection in cross-national settings. The global and comparative ethnology of the past, some would argue, has given way to a utilitarian ethnography devoid of a search for cross-cultural principles and models.

The use of the newly available large national and international data sets may provide a partial answer to this global ethnographic-ethnological dilemma. Almost every country is now committed to a census and other surveys that include contraceptive prevalence, family planning, educational and environmental information, and many other issues. International and bilateral agencies are increasingly promoting the development and use of comparable survey instruments that include core questions and questions tailored to the interests and needs of each participating country.

This approach calls for ethnographers to use the scientific literature and locally conducted ethnographic research to generate hypotheses for testing through the analysis of large data sets. It also requires explaining and interpreting the results of these statistical analyses through the collection of additional qualitative and quantitative data in local field situations. In the future, computer-based text search programs may give us the opportunity to explore and compare large "qualitative" data sets as well. The interplay between local and global primary, secondary, and archival data can produce the national and international comparisons that build on ethnographic traditions and strengths.

REFERENCES

Celentano, D. D., K. H. Mayer et al. 2010. Prevalence of sexually transmitted diseases and risk behaviors from the NIMH Collaborative HIV/STD Prevention Trial. *International Journal of Sexual Health* 22(4): 272–84.

Davidson, J. W., and L. Bresler. 1996. Working in the interpretive zone: Conceptualizing collaboration in qualitative research teams. *Educational Researcher* 25(5): 5–15.

Deyhle, D. 1998. Personal communication with M. D. LeCompte.

Donato, R. 1997. *The other struggle for equal schools: Mexican Americans during the civil rights era.* Albany: SUNY Press.

———. 2007. *Mexicans and Hispanos in Colorado schools and communities, 1920–1960.* Albany: SUNY Press

Ember, C. R., and M. Ember. 1998. Cross-cultural research, in *Handbook of methods in cultural anthropology,* ed. H. R. Bernard, 647–90. Walnut Creek, CA: AltaMira.

Gaviria, M., G. Stern, and S. Schensul. 1982. Sociocultural factors and perinatal health in a Mexican American community. *Journal of the National Medical Association* 74: 983–89.

Guest, E., and K. M. MacQueen, eds. 2008. *Handbook for team-based qualitative research.* Lanham, MD: AltaMira Press.

Hrdy, S. B. 1995. The primate origins of female sexuality, and their implications for the role of nonconceptive sex in the reproductive strategies of women. *Human Evolution* 10(2): 131–44.

International Center for Research on Women (ICRW). 1995/1997. *Women and AIDS research program, Phase I and Phase II research report series.* Washington, DC: International Center for Research on Women.

Lamphere, L., ed. 1992. *Structuring diversity: Ethnographic perspectives on the new immigration.* Chicago: University of Chicago Press.

Latkin, C. A., D. Donnell et al. 2009. The efficacy of a network intervention to reduce HIV risk behaviors among drug users and risk partners in Chiang Mai, Thailand and Philadelphia, USA. *Social Science & Medicine* 68(4): 740–48.

Murdock, G. P. 1967. Ethnographic atlas: A summary. *Ethnology* 6: 109–236.

Naroll, R., and R. G. Sipes. 1973. Standard ethnographic sample, 2nd ed. *Current Anthropology* 14, 111–40.

Ouelett, L. J., W. W. Wiebel et al. 1995. Team research methods for studying intranasal heroin use and its HIV risks, in *Qualitative methods in drug abuse and HIV research,* ed. E. Y. Lambert, R. S. Ashery, and R. Needle, 182–211. Rockville, MD: National Institute on Drug Abuse.

Pelto, G., and S. Gove. 1992. Developing a focused ethnographic study for the WHO Acute Respiratory Infection (ARI) Control and Programme, in *RAP: Rapid Assessment Procedures; Qualitative methodologies for planning and evaluation of health-related programs,* ed. N. S. Scrimshaw and G. R. Gleason, 215–26. Boston: International Nutritional Foundation for Developing Countries (INDFC).

Pelto, P. J., and G. H. Pelto. 1978. *Anthropological research: The structure of inquiry, second edition.* Cambridge: Cambridge University Press.

Schensul, J., N. Diaz, and S. Woolley. 1996. *Measuring activity levels among Puerto Rican children.* Paper presented at the 2nd annual meeting of the Puerto Rican Studies Association, San Juan, Puerto Rico.

Schensul, S. L. 1969. *The impact of industrialization on Northern Minnesotans and Southern Ugandans.* Unpublished doctoral dissertation, University of Minnesota.

Schensul, S. L., M. Eisenberg, J. Glasgow, and J. Huettner. 1994. Translating state data into local health programs: Targeted research for intervention planning. *American Journal of Public Health* 84: 671–72.

Schensul, S. L., J. Schensul, and M. Zegarra. 1985. *Pediatric health and the evolution of urban communities in Lima, Peru.* Paper presented at the 1985 annual meeting of the American Anthropological Association.

Silva, K. T., S. L. Schensul, J. Schensul, M. W. A. de Silva, B. K. Nastasi, C. Sivayoganathan, J. Lewis, P. Wedisinghe, P. Ratnayake, M. Eisenberg, and H. Aponso. 1997. *Youth and sexual risk in Sri Lanka.* International Center for Research on Women. Washington, DC. Phase II Report Series.

3

ELICITATION TECHNIQUES FOR CULTURAL DOMAIN ANALYSIS

Stephen P. Borgatti and Daniel S. Halgin

INTRODUCTION

Definition:
A cultural
domain is a set
of items or things that
are all of the same type
or category

The techniques described in this chapter are used to understand *cultural domains* (Lounsbury 1964; Spradley 1979; Weller and Romney 1988). A cultural domain is a mental category like "animals" or "illnesses." It is a set of items that are all alike in some important way. Humans in all cultures classify the world around them into cognitive domains, and the way they do this affects the way they interact with the world. Not all cultures classify things the same way. For example, English speakers recognize a category called "shrubs," which is different from "trees" and "grasses." But many other cultures do not recognize the "shrub" category at all: they divide up the plant kingdom differently. Even when cultures have the same domains, the contents may be somewhat different. For example, many cultures have a domain called "illnesses," but often these cultures include as illnesses things that most Americans would regard as imaginary, such as "evil eye," or things that Americans regard as symptoms, such as "stomach pains." *Ethnographers often begin their studies by trying to identify and describe the cultural domains that are used by the people they are studying.* **Key point**

The techniques described in this chapter are used to (a) elicit the items in a cultural domain, (b) elicit the attributes and relations that structure the domain, and (c) measure the positions of the items in the domain structure. These techniques, which include free lists, pilesorts, triads, multidimensional scaling, and graph layout algorithms, have been incorporated into two commercially available computer programs called Anthropac (Borgatti 1992) and UCINET (Borgatti, Everett, and Freeman 2002).

Defining Cultural Domains

There are several ways to define a cultural domain. A good starting point is "a set of items all of which a group of people define as belonging to the same type." For example, "animals" is a cultural domain. The members of the domain of animals are all the animals that have been named, such as dogs, cats, horses, lions, and tigers. But there is more to the idea than just a set of items of the same type. Implicit in the notion is also the idea that membership in the cultural domain is determined by more than the individual respondent—the domain exists "out there" either in the language, in the culture, or in nature. Hence, the set of colors that a given individual likes to wear is not what we mean by a cultural domain.

One rule of thumb for distinguishing cultural domains from other lists is that *cultural domains are about people's perceptions rather than people's preferences.* Hence, "my favorite foods" is not a cultural domain, but "things that are edible" is. Another way to put it is that cultural domains are about things "out there" in reality, so that, in principle, questions about the members of a domain have a right answer. Consider, for example, the cultural domain of animals. If asked whether a tiger is an animal, the respondent thinks that she is discussing a fact about the world outside, not about herself. In contrast, if she is asked whether "vanilla" is one of her favorite ice **Key point**

cream flavors, the respondent thinks that she is revealing more about herself than about vanilla ice cream. In this sense, cultural domains are experienced as outside the individual and shared across individuals.

The fact that cultural domains are shared across individuals does not mean that all members of a given population are in complete agreement on which items belong to a given cultural domain. The extent to which a cultural domain is actually shared in any given population is an empirical question—that is, a question that is open to testing.[1] Conversely, simple agreement about a set of items does not imply that the set is a cultural domain. If we ask one thousand randomly sampled informants in our own culture about their ten favorite foods and every one of them happens to give the same list, it is still not a cultural domain because personal preferences are not the kind of thing that *in principle* could be a cultural domain. In contrast, responses to the question, "What foods are preferred in your community?" *could* be a cultural domain.

Another aspect of cultural domains is that they have **internal structure**. That is, cultural domains are systems of items related by a web of relationships. For example, in the domain of animals, some animals are understood to eat other animals. The relation here is "eats," and every pair of animals can be evaluated to see if the first animal eats the second. Another relation applicable to animals, recognized by biologists at least, is "competes with."

Definition: The internal structure of a cultural domain refers to the relationships that exist among the items or things in it

A relation of particular importance, one which seems to be common to all cultural domains, is the relation of similarity. It appears that, for all cultural domains, respondents can readily indicate which pairs of items they consider similar, and which they consider dissimilar. Another relation that seems to apply to most domains is co-occurrence, as in which foods "go with" which others, or which animals live in the same habitats with which others.

Relations among things are a fundamental aspect of how humans think about the world. Lists of "universal" relations have been made by many researchers, including Casagrande and Hale (1967) and Spradley (1979). Spradley's list includes:

- Cause-and-effect (X causes Y, Y is the result of X)
- Inclusion (X is a kind of Y)
- Rationale (X is a reason for doing Y)
- Means-end (X is a way to accomplish Y)
- Sequence (X follows Y)
- Function (X is used for Y)
- Spatial (X is a part of Y), (X is a place in Y)
- Attribution (X is a characteristic of Y)
- Location for action (X is a place for doing Y)

Most of these, however, are not relations among items in the same domain, but rather relate the items from one domain to the items in another domain. For example, "location for action" relates a place, such as "Madrid," with an activity, such as "bullfighting"; places and activities typically belong to different cognitive domains. Similarly, the cause of a given effect is not necessarily a member of the same cognitive domain as the effect. For instance, making love may result in getting AIDS, but most respondents think of these as belonging to different domains. In this chapter we concentrate on only those relations that relate items within a single cognitive domain.

Other largely universal relations are semantic relations among the terms used to label items in a cultural domain. These are relations such as synonymy (same meaning) and antonymy (opposite meaning). For example, in the domain of illnesses, there is often more than one term for a given illness (such as a folk name and a medical term). While the line separating relations among terms from relations among the items themselves may be difficult to draw, in principle our interest here is in the relations among the items rather than among the terms we use to describe them.

An important class of relations among items is the kind that can be reduced to a single attribute. For example, in the domain of illnesses, some illnesses are seen as "more contagious" than other illnesses. This relation is based on a single property of each illness in the domain, which is contagion. This is different from the relation of (perceived) similarity, which is indivisible. We cannot attach a *similarity* score to an individual item—it is always attached to a pair.

For example, we can say that the similarity between "pneumonia" and "flu" is 8 on a scale of 1 to 10, but it doesn't make sense to assign a similarity score to just one of the illnesses by itself (as in, "the flu has a similarity score of 3"). In contrast, it does make sense to assign an individual illness a *contagion* score: we don't have to do it in pairs. The difference between attributes of individual items and relations among pairs of items becomes clearer as we go along in this chapter.

In general, an attribute that makes sense for some items in a cultural domain will make sense for all items. In other words, if "sweetness" is a sensible attribute of fruit, then it is meaningful to ask, "How sweet is ____?" of all fruit in the domain. If the attribute cannot be applied to all items, this is sometimes because not all the items are at the same level of contrast, which in turn means that there are subdomains. For example, if the domain of "animals" contains the items "squirrel," "ant," and "mammal," informants will be confused if asked whether squirrels are faster than mammals. The real test for items of different levels of contrast, however, is to look at the semantic "is a kind of" relation (Casagrande and Hale 1967; Spradley 1979). If any item in a domain is a kind of any other item in the domain (e.g., squirrel is a kind of mammal) then one knows that the latter item is actually a **cover term** (a *gloss*) for a subdomain.

Definition: Cover terms are summary terms encompassing all the items in a domain or subdomain

Even if all the items are of the same level of contrast, however, the inability to apply an attribute to all items is sufficient to suggest that the domain has a hierarchical taxonomic structure and that the attribute belongs to items in one particular class. For example, the attribute "shape of wings" can be applied to some animals, but not to others. This means that the domain of animals contains at least two types—animals with wings and animals without—and within the set of those with wings, we can ask what shape the wings are (Figure 3.1).

ELICITING CULTURAL DOMAINS USING FREE LISTS

The *free list* technique is used to elicit the elements or members of a cultural domain. For domains that have a name or

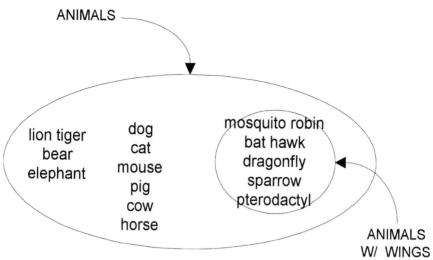

Figure 3.1 Hierarchically structured domain

are easily described, the technique is very simple: just ask a set of informants to list all the members of the domain. For example, you might ask them to list all the names of illnesses that they can recall. If you don't know the name of a domain, you may have to elicit that first. For example, you can ask, "What is a mango?" and very likely you will get a response like "It's a kind of fruit." Then you can ask, "What other kinds of fruit are there?" Note that if a set of items does not have a name in a given culture, it is likely that it is not (yet) a domain in that culture. However, you can still obtain a list of related items by asking questions like "What else is there that is like a mango?"

At first glance, the free list technique may appear to be the same as any open-ended question, such as "What illnesses have you had?" ***The difference between free listing and open-ended questions is that free listing is used to elicit cultural domains, and open-ended questions are used to elicit information about individual informants*** (Table 3.1). In principle, the free lists from different respondents who belong to the same culture should be comparable and similar because the stimulus question is about something outside themselves and which they have in common with other members. In contrast, an open-ended question could easily generate only unique answers.

Key point

Table 3.1 Comparison of Free List and Open-Ended Questions

Type of Question	Example	Objective
Free list question	What illnesses are there?	Learn about the domain (e.g., develop list of named illnesses)
Survey open-end	What illnesses have you had?	Learn about the respondent (e.g., obtain patient history)

Collecting Free List Data

Ordinarily, free lists are obtained as part of a semi-structured interview, not an informal conversation. With literate informants, it is easiest to ask the respondents to write down all the items they can think of, one item per line, on a piece of paper. The exact same question is asked of the entire sample of respondents (see below for a discussion of sample size). We then count the number of times each item is mentioned and sort the items in order of decreasing frequency. For example, I asked fourteen undergraduates at Boston College to list all the animals they could think of. On average, each person listed 21.6 animal terms. The top-twenty terms are given in Table 3.2.

The number of informants needed to establish a cultural domain depends on the amount of cultural consensus in the population of interest—if every informant gives the exact same answers, you only need one—but a conventional rule-of-thumb is to obtain lists from a minimum of thirty lists. One heuristic for determining whether it is necessary to interview more informants, recommended by Gery Ryan[2] (personal communication), is to compute the frequency count after obtaining twenty or so lists from randomly chosen informants, then repeat the count after thirty lists. If the relative frequencies of the top items have not changed, this suggests that no more informants are needed. In contrast, if the relative frequencies have changed, this indicates that the structure has not yet stabilized and you **Key point** need more informants *randomly selected from the population of interest.* If, for example, the domain is illnesses and the first twenty respondents are all nurses, the method might indicate that no more respondents are needed. Yet if the results are intended to represent more than just nurses, more (non-nurse) respondents will be needed.

Table 3.2 Top Twenty Animals Mentioned, Ordered by Frequency

Rank	Item Name	Freq.	Resp. %	Avg. Rank	Smith's S
1	CAT	13	93	4.85	0.758
2	DOG	13	93	3.62	0.814
3	ELEPHANT	10	71	8.20	0.471
4	ZEBRA	9	64	11.11	0.341
5	SQUIRREL	8	57	12.88	0.266
6	TIGER	8	57	5.50	0.440
7	COW	7	50	10.86	0.291
8	FISH	7	50	13.29	0.224
9	BEAR	7	50	7.00	0.366
10	WHALE	7	50	13.86	0.215
11	DEER	7	50	11.29	0.259
12	MONKEY	7	50	10.00	0.293
13	GIRAFFE	6	43	12.00	0.228
14	GORILLA	6	43	14.67	0.146
15	MOUSE	6	43	8.83	0.299
16	SNAKE	6	43	13.33	0.180
17	LION	5	36	11.00	0.199
18	ANTELOPE	5	36	11.00	0.197
19	LEOPARD	5	36	12.40	0.166
20	TURTLE	5	36	7.80	0.238

The frequency of items is usually interpreted in terms of their salience to informants. That is, items that are frequently mentioned are assumed to be highly salient to respondents, so that few forget to mention those items. Another aspect of salience, however, is how soon the respondent recalls the item. Items recalled first are assumed to be more salient than items recalled last. The second column from the right in Table 3.2 gives the average position or rank of each item on each individual's list. With sufficient respondents (more than used in Table 3.2), it is often the case that a strong negative correlation exists between the frequency of the items and their average rank, at least for the items mentioned by a majority of respondents. This means that the higher the probability that a respondent mentions an item, the more likely it is that they will mention it early. This supports the notion of salience as a latent property that determines both whether and when an item is mentioned. In recognition of this, some researchers like to combine frequency and average rank into a single measure.[3]

Once the free lists have been collected and tabulated, it usually becomes apparent that there are a few items that are mentioned by many respondents, and there are a huge number of items that are mentioned by just one person. For example, I collected free list data on the domain of "bad words" from ninety-two undergraduate students at the University of South Carolina. A total of 309 distinct items was obtained, of which 219 (71 percent) were mentioned by only one person (Figure 3.2). As discussed near the end of this section, domains seem to have a core/periphery sort of structure with no absolute boundaries. The more respondents you have, the longer the periphery (the right-hand tail in Figure 3.2) grows, though ever more slowly.

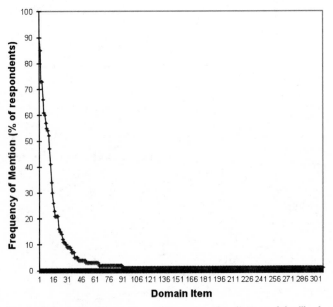

Figure 3.2 Sorted frequency of items in a free listing of the "bad words" domain

From a practical point of view, of course, it is usually necessary to determine a boundary for the domain one is studying.

WAYS TO DETERMINE A DOMAIN BOUNDARY

- Include all items mentioned more by more than one respondent.
- Look for a natural break or grouping.
- Define a boundary arbitrarily.

One natural approach is to count as members of the domain all items that are mentioned by more than one respondent. This is logical because cultural domains are shared at least to some extent, and it is hard to argue that an item mentioned by just one person is shared. However, this approach usually does not cut down the number of items enough for further research. Another approach is to look for a natural break or "elbow" in the sorted list of frequencies.[4] This is most easily done by plotting the frequencies in what is known as a "scree plot" (see Figure 3.2). When such a break can be found, it is very convenient, and it may well reflect a real difference between the culturally shared items of the domain and the idiosyncratic items. But if no break is present, it is ultimately necessary to arbitrarily choose the top N items, where N is the largest number you can really handle in the remaining part of the study. In Figure 3.2, no really clear breaks are present, but there are three "minibreaks" that one might consider. In the sorted list of words, they occur after the twentieth, twenty-sixth, and fortieth words.

One problem that must be dealt with before computing frequencies is the occurrence of synonyms, variant spellings, subdomain names, and the use of modifiers. For instance, in the "bad words" domain, some of the terms elicited were *whore*, *ho*, and *hore*. It seems likely that *whore* and *hore* are variant spellings of the same word, and therefore pose no real dilemma. In contrast, *ho*, which was used primarily by African American students, could conceivably have a somewhat different meaning. (There is always this potential when a word is used more often by one ethnic group than by others.) Similarly, in the domain of animals, the terms *aardvark* and *anteater* are synonymous for most people, but for some (including biologists), *anteater* refers to a general class of animals of which the aardvark is just one. Whether they should be treated as synonyms or not will depend on the purposes of the study. It may be necessary, before continuing, to ask respondents whether *aardvark* means the same thing as *anteater*.

Occasionally, respondents will fall into a response set in which they list a class of items separated by modifiers. For example, they may name *grizzly bear*, *Kodiak bear*, *black bear*, and *brown bear*. Obviously, these constitute subclasses of bear that are at a lower level of contrast than other terms in their lists. Occasionally, these kinds of items may lead respondents to generalize the principle to other items, so that they then list such items as *large dog*, *small dog*, and *hairless dog*. In general this is not a problem because these kinds of items will be mentioned by just one person, and so will be dropped from further consideration.

Analyzing Free List Data

While the main purpose of the free listing exercise is to obtain the membership list for a domain, the lists can also be used as ends in themselves. That is, several interesting analyses can be done with such lists.

Once we have a master list of all items mentioned, we can arrange the free list data as a matrix in which the rows are informants and the columns are items (Table 3.3). The cells of the matrix can contain ones (if the respondent in a given row mentioned the item in a given column) or zeros (that respondent did not mention that item). Taking column sums of the matrix would give us the item frequencies. Taking column averages would give us the proportion of respondents mentioning each item. Taking row sums would give us the number of items in each person's free list.

The number of items in an individual's free list is interesting in itself. Although perhaps confounded by such variables as respondent intelligence, motivation, and personality, it seems plausible that the number of items listed

Table 3.3   Portion of Respondent-by-Item Free List Matrix

		Items							
		Cat	Dog	Ele-phant	Zebra	Squirrel	Tiger	Cow	Fish
Respondents	1	1	1	1	1	1	1	1	0
	2	1	1	1	1	1	0	0	0
	3	1	1	0	1	0	0	0	0
	4	1	1	1	0	1	0	1	1
	5	1	1	1	1	1	1	1	1
	6	1	1	1	1	1	1	1	1
	7	1	1	0	1	1	0	1	1
	8	1	1	1	1	1	1	1	1
	9	1	1	1	1	0	1	1	0
	10	1	1	1	1	1	1	1	1

reflects a person's familiarity with the domain (Gatewood 1984). For example, if we ask people to list all sociological theories of deviance they can think of, we should expect to find that professional sociologists have longer lists than most other people. Similarly, dog fanciers are likely to produce longer lists of dog breeds than ordinary people. Yet, length of list is obviously not perfectly correlated with domain familiarity, as respondents who are relatively unfamiliar with a domain can produce impressively long lists of very unusual items—items with which other respondents would not agree.

To construct a better measure of domain familiarity (or "cultural domain competence"), we could weight the items in an individual free list by the proportion of respondents who mention the item. Adding up the weights of the items in a respondent's free list then gives a convenient measure of what might be called "cultural competence." Respondents score high on this measure if they mention many high-frequency items and avoid mentioning low-frequency items.

Another way to analyze free list data—now focusing on the items rather than the respondents—is to examine the co-occurrences among free listed items. Table 3.4 gives

Table 3.4 Respondent-by-Item Free List Matrix

	A	B	C	D
1	1	0	1	1
2	0	1	0	0
3	1	1	1	1
4	1	1	0	0
5	0	0	1	0
6	1	1	0	0

Table 3.5 Item-by-Item Matrix of Co-occurrences (based on Table 3.4)

	A	B	C	D
A	4	3	2	2
B	3	4	1	1
C	2	1	3	2
D	2	1	2	2

an excerpt from a respondent-by-item free list matrix. There are four items labeled A through D. Consider items A and B. Each is mentioned by four respondents. Three respondents mention both of them. That is, A and B *co-occur* in three of the six free lists. By comparing every pair of items, we can construct the item-by-item matrix given in Table 3.5. This matrix can then be displayed via multidimensional scaling (MDS), as shown in Figure 3.3. In a MDS map of this kind, two items are close together to the extent that many respondents mentioned *both* items. Items that are far apart on the map were rarely mentioned by the same respondents.

Typically, such maps will have a core/periphery structure in which the core members of the domain (i.e., the most frequently mentioned) will be at the center, with the rest of the items spreading away from the core and the most idiosyncratic items located on the far periphery. The effect is similar to a fried egg.[5] This occurs in part because odd items can be odd in so many ways that they tend to be different from each other as well. In contrast, core items are very similar to each other. Another factor is that core items tend to be mentioned so much more often, there is a greater chance of overlapping with other items.

There are a number of other ways to analyze free list data. As Henley (1969) noticed, the order in which items are listed by individual respondents is not arbitrary. Typically, respondents produce runs of similar items separated by visible pauses. Even if we do not record the timing, we can recover a great deal of information about the cognitive

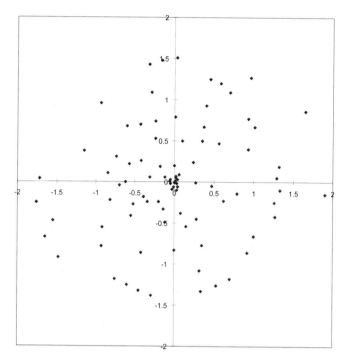

Figure 3.3　MDS of ninety "bad words" based on their co-occurrence in free lists. Core items of the domain are found in the middle of the space. Items mentioned by only a few respondents are on the periphery.

structuring of the domain by examining the relative position of items on the list. Two factors seem to affect position on the list. First, as mentioned, the more central items tend to occur first. When we ask North Americans to list all animals, *cat* and *dog* tend to be at the top of each person's list, and they tend to be mentioned by nearly everyone.

A second pattern is that related items tend to be mentioned near each other (i.e., the difference in their ranks is small). Hence, we can use the differences in ranks for each pair of items as a rough indicator of the cognitive similarity of the items. To do this, we construct a new person-by-item matrix in which the cells contain ranks rather than ones and zeros. For example, if respondent "Jim" listed item *deer* as the seventh item on his free list, then we would enter a "7" in the cell corresponding to his row and the deer column. If a second respondent named "Fred" did not mention an item at all, we enter a special code in Fred's column denoting a missing value (NOT a zero). Then we compute correlations (or distances) among the columns of the matrix. The result is an item-by-item matrix indicating how similarly items are positioned in different people's lists, when they occur at all. This can then be displayed using multidimensional scaling. It should be noted, however, that if uncovering similarities is the primary interest of the study, it would be wiser to use more direct methods, such as those outlined in the next section.

It should also be noted that while we reserve the term *free listing* for the relatively formal elicitation task described here, the basic idea of asking informants for examples of a conceptual category is very useful even in informal interviews (Spradley 1979). For example, in doing an ethnography of an academic department, we might find ourselves asking an informant the following: "You mentioned that there are a number of ways that graduate students can get into difficulty. Can you give me some examples?" Rather than eliciting all the members of the domain, the objective might be simply to elicit just one element, which then becomes a vehicle for further exploration.

It is also possible to reverse the question and ask the respondent if a given item belongs to the domain, and if not, why not. The negative examples help to elicit the taken-for-granted characteristics that are shared by all members of the domain and which therefore might otherwise go unmentioned.

ELICITING DOMAIN STRUCTURE USING PILESORTS

The pilesort task is used primarily to elicit from respondents judgments of similarity among items in a cultural domain. It can also be used to elicit the attributes that people use to distinguish among the items. There are many variants of the pilesort sort technique. We begin with the *free pilesort*.

Collecting Free Pilesort Data

The typical free pilesort technique begins with a set of three-by-five cards on which the name or short description of a domain item is written. For example, for the cultural domain of illnesses, we might have a set of eighty cards, one for each illness. For convenience, a unique ID number is written on the back of each card. The stack of cards is shuffled randomly and given to a respondent with the following instructions: "Here are a set of cards representing kinds of illnesses. I'd like you to sort them into piles according to how similar they are. You can make as many or as few piles as you like. Go!" In some cases, it is better to do it in two steps. First you ask the respondents to look at each card to see whether they recognize the illness. Ask them to set aside any cards representing illnesses that they are unfamiliar with. Then, with the remaining cards, have them do the sorting exercise.

Sometimes, respondents object to having to put a given item into just one pile. They think that the item fits equally well into two different piles. This is perfectly acceptable. In such cases, the researcher can simply take a blank card, write the name of the item on the card, and let the respondent put one card in each pile. As discussed in a later section, putting items into more than one pile causes no problems for analyzing the data, and it may correspond better to the respondents' views. The only problem it creates is that it makes it more difficult later on to check whether the data were entered into computer files correctly, since having an item appear in more than one pile is usually a sign that someone has mistyped an ID code.

Instead of writing names of items on cards, it is sometimes possible to sort pictures of the items (Figure 3.4), or even the items themselves (e.g., when working with the folk domain of *bugs*). However, in our experience, for literate respondents, the written method is always best. Showing pictures or using the items themselves tends to bias the respondents toward sorting according to physical attributes such as size, color, and shape. For example, sorting pictures of fish yields sorts based on body shape and types of fins (Boster and Johnson 1989). In contrast, sorting *names* of fish allows nonvisible attributes to affect the sorting (such as taste, where the fish is found, what it is used for, how it is caught, what it eats, how it behaves).

Normally, the pilesort exercise is repeated with at least thirty respondents,[6] although the number depends on the

ROSE

Figure 3.4 Example of sorting card for the domain of "flowers"

amount of variability in responses. For example, if everyone in a society would give exactly the same answers, you would only need one respondent. But if there is a great deal of variability, you may need hundreds of sorts to get a good picture of the modal answers (i.e., the most common responses) and to be able to cut the data into demographic subgroups so that you can see how different groups sort things differently.

Analyzing Pilesort Data

Pilesort data are tabulated and interpreted as follows. Every time a respondent places a given pair of items in the same pile together, we count that as a vote for the similarity of those two items (Table 3.6). In the domain of animals, if all of the respondents place *coyote* and *wolf* in the same pile, we take that as evidence that these are highly similar items. In contrast, if no respondents put *salamander* and *moose* in the same pile, we understand that to mean that salamanders and moose are not very similar. We further assume that if an intermediate number

Table 3.6   Percentage of Respondents Placing Each Pair of Items in the Same Pile

	Frog	Salam.	Beaver	Raccoon	Rabbit	Mouse	Coyote	Deer	Moose
Frog	100	96	6	2	2	0	0	2	2
Salamander	96	100	4	0	0	2	0	0	0
Beaver	6	4	100	62	65	56	17	25	13
Raccoon	2	0	62	100	71	58	23	29	15
Rabbit	2	0	65	71	100	75	17	27	15
Mouse	0	2	56	58	75	100	17	15	10
Coyote	0	0	17	23	17	17	100	21	15
Deer	2	0	25	29	27	15	21	100	77
Moose	2	0	13	15	15	10	15	77	100

Note: Data collected by Sandy Anderson under the direction of John Gatewood.

of respondents put a pair of items in the same pile, this means that the items are of intermediate similarity.

This interpretation of agreement as monotonically[7] related to similarity is not trivial and is not widely understood. It reflects the adoption of a set of simple process models for how respondents go about solving the pilesort task.

PROCESS MODELS FOR UNDERSTANDING HOW PEOPLE DO PILESORTS

- They use a similarity metric or measure.
- They "bundle" or clump together items with similar attributes.

One such model is the metric model. Each respondent is seen as having the equivalent of a similarity metric in her head (e.g., she has a spatial map of the items in semantic space). However, the pilesort task essentially asks her to state, for each pair of items, whether the items are similar or not. Therefore, she must convert a continuous measure of similarity or distance into a yes/no judgment. If the similarity of the two items is very high, she places, with high probability, both items in the same pile. If the similarity is very low, she places the items, with high probability again, in different piles. If the similarity is intermediate, she essentially flips a coin (i.e., the probability of placing in the same pile is near 0.5). This process is repeated across all the respondents, leading the highly similar items to be placed in the same pile most of the time and the dissimilar items to be placed in different piles most of the time. The items of intermediate similarity are placed together by approximately half the respondents and placed in separate piles by the other half, resulting in intermediate similarity scores.

An alternative model, not inconsistent with the first one, is that respondents conceptualize domain items as bundles of features or attributes. When asked to place items in piles, they place the ones that have mostly the same attributes in the same piles, and place items with mostly different attributes in separate piles. Items that share some attributes and not others have intermediate probabilities of being placed together, and this results in intermediate proportions of respondents placing them in the same pile.

Both these models are plausible. However, even if either or both is true, there is still a problem with how to interpret intermediate percentages. Just because intermediate similarity implies intermediate consensus does not mean that the converse is true, namely that intermediate consensus implies intermediate similarity. For example, suppose half the respondents clearly understand that *shark* and *dolphin* are very similar (because they are large ocean predators) and place them in the same pile, while the other half are just as clear that *shark* and *dolphin* are quite dissimilar (because one is a fish and the other is a mammal). Under these conditions, 50 percent of respondents would place *shark* and *dolphin* in the same pile, but we would NOT want to interpret this as meaning that 100 percent of respondents believed sharks and dolphins to be moderately similar. In other words, the validity of measuring similarity by aggregating pilesorts depends crucially on the assumption of underlying cultural consensus (Romney, Weller, and Batchelder 1986), a topic we take up in more detail a bit further along.

We can record the proportion of respondents placing each pair of items in the same pile using an item-by-item matrix, as shown in Table 3.6. This matrix can then be represented spatially via nonmetric multidimensional

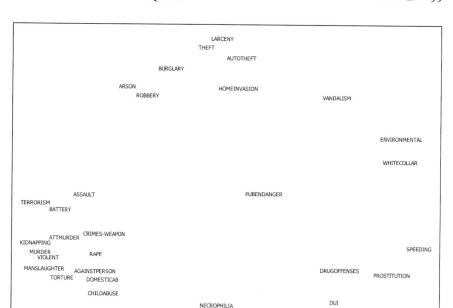

Figure 3.5 Pilesort similarities among thirty crimes, represented by multidimensional scaling

scaling, or analyzed via cluster analysis.[8] Figure 3.5 shows a multidimensional scaling of pilesort similarities among thirty crimes collected by students of Mark Fleisher.[9] In general, the purpose of such analyses would be to:

- Reveal underlying perceptual dimensions that people use to distinguish among the items
- Detect clusters of items that share attributes or comprise subdomains

Let us discuss the former goal first. One way to uncover the attributes that structure a cultural domain is to ask respondents to name them as they do the pilesort.[10] One approach is to ask respondents to "think aloud" as they do the sort. This is useful information but should not be the only attack on this problem. Respondents can typically come up with dozens of attributes that distinguish among items, but it is not easy for them to tell you which ones are important. In addition, many of the attributes will be highly correlated with each other, if not directly synonymous, particularly as we look across respondents.

It is also possible that respondents do not really know why they placed items into the piles that they did: when a researcher asks them to explain, they cannot directly examine their unconscious thought processes and instead go through a process of justifying and reconstructing what they must have done. For example, all native speakers of a language are good at constructing grammatically well-formed sentences, but they need not have conscious knowledge of grammar to do this.

In addition, it is possible that the research objectives may not require that we know *how* the respondent completes the sorting task but merely that we can accurately predict the results. In general, scientists build descriptions of reality (theories) that are expected to make accurate predictions but are not expected to be literally true, if only because these descriptions are not unique and are situated within human languages that use only concepts understood by humans living at one small point in time. This is similar to the situation in artificial intelligence; if someone could construct a computer that could converse in English so well that it could not be distinguished from a human, we would be forced to grant that the machine understood English, even if the way it did so could not be shown to be the same as the way humans do it. What is common to both scientific theories and artificial intelligence is that we evaluate truth (success) in terms of the behavioral outcomes, not an absolute yardstick.

To discover the underlying perceptual dimensions people use to distinguish among items in a cultural domain, we begin by collecting together the attributes elicited directly from respondents. Then we look at the MDS map to see if the items are arrayed in any kind of order that is apparent to us.[11] For example, in the crime data shown in Figure 3.5, it appears that as we move from right to left on the map, the crimes become increasingly serious. This suggests the possibility that respondents use the attribute "seriousness" to distinguish among crimes. Of course, the idea that the leftmost crimes are more serious than the rightmost crimes is based on the researcher's perceptions of the crimes, not the informants'. Furthermore, there are other attributes that might arrange the crimes in roughly the same order (such as violence). The first question to ask is whether respondents have the same view of the domain as the researchers.

To resolve this issue, we then take all the attributes, both those elicited from respondents[12] and those proposed by researchers, and administer a questionnaire to a (possibly new) sample of respondents, asking them to rate each item on each attribute. This way we get the informants' views of where each item stands on each attribute. Then we use a nonlinear multiple regression technique called PROFIT (Kruskal and Wish 1978) to statistically relate the average ratings provided by respondents to the positions of the items on the map. Besides providing a statistical test of independence (to guard against the human ability to see patterns in everything), the PROFIT technique allows us to plot lines on the MDS map representing the attribute so that we can see in what direction the items increase in value on that attribute. Often, several attributes will line up in more or less the same direction. These are attributes that have different names but are highly correlated. The researcher might then explore whether they are all manifestations of a single underlying dimension of which the respondents may or may not be aware.

Sometimes MDS maps do not yield much in the way of interpretable dimensions. One way this can happen is when the MDS map consists of a few dense clusters separated by wide-open space. This can be caused by the existence of sets of items that happen to be extremely similar on a number of attributes. Most often, however, it signals the presence of subdomains (which are like categorical attributes that dominate respondents' thinking). For example, a pilesort of a wide range of animals, including birds, land animals, and water animals, will result in tight clumps in which all the representatives of each group are seen to be so much more similar to each other than to other animals that no internal differentiation can be seen. An example is given in Figure 3.6. In such cases, it is necessary to run the MDS on each cluster separately. Then, within clusters, it may be that meaningful dimensions will emerge.

We may also be interested in comparing respondents' views of the structure of a domain. One way to think about the pilesort data for a single respondent is as the answers

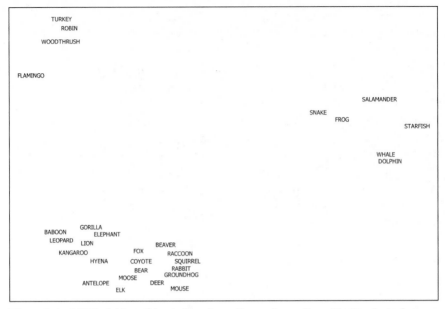

Figure 3.6　MDS of thirty animals, based on pilesort data collected by Sandy Anderson and John Gatewood. Note: The lower-left cluster has been artificially spread out to avoid having labels right on top of each other.

to a list of yes/no questions corresponding to each pair of items. For example, if there are N items in the domain, there are $N(N - 1)/2$ pairs of items, and for each pair, the respondent has either to put them in the same pile (call that a YES) or a different pile (call that a NO). Each respondent's view can thus be represented as a string of ones ("yes's") and zeros ("no's"). We can then, in principle, compare two respondents' views by correlating these strings.

However, there are problems caused by the fact that some people create more piles than others. This is known as the "lumper/splitter" problem. For example, suppose two respondents have identical views of what goes with what. But one respondent makes many piles to reflect even the finest distinctions (he's a "splitter"), while the other makes just a few piles, reflecting only the broadest distinctions (she's a "lumper"). Correlating their strings would yield very small correlations, even though in reality they have identical views. Another problem is that the strings of two splitters can be fairly highly correlated even when they disagree a great deal because both say "no" so often (i.e., most pairs of items are NOT placed in the same pile together). Some analytical ways to ameliorate the problem have been devised, but they are beyond the scope of this chapter.

The best way to avoid the lumper/splitter problem is to force all respondents to make the same number of piles. One way to do this is to start by asking them to sort all the items into exactly two piles, such that all the items in one pile are more similar to each other than to the items in the other pile. Record the results. Then ask the respondents to make three piles, letting them rearrange the contents of the original piles as necessary.[13] The new results are then recorded. The process may be repeated as many times as desired. The data collected can then be analyzed separately at each level of splitting, or combined as follows. For each pair of items sorted by a given respondent, the researcher counts the number of different sorts in which the items were placed together. Optionally, the different sorts can be weighted by the number of piles, so that being placed together when there were only two piles does not count as much as being placed together when there were ten piles. Either way, the result is a string of values (one for each pair of items) for every respondent, which can then be correlated with each other to determine which respondents had similar views.

A more sophisticated approach was proposed by Boster (1994). In order to preserve the freedom of a free pilesort while at the same time controlling the lumper/splitter problem, Boster begins with a free pilesort. If the respondent makes N piles, the researcher then asks the respondent to split one of the piles, making N + 1 in total. He repeats this process as long as desired. He then returns to the original sort and asks the respondent to combine two piles so that there are N − 1 in total. This process is repeated until there are only two piles left.

Both of these methods, which we can describe as *successive pilesorts*, yield very rich data, but they are time consuming for participants and also can potentially require a participant to wait a long time while data are recorded. In Boster's method, because piles are not rearranged at each step, it is possible to record the data in an extremely compact format without making the respondent wait at all. However, it requires extremely well-trained and alert interviewers to do it.

ELICITING DOMAIN STRUCTURE USING TRIADS

An alternative to pilesorts for measuring similarity is the triad test.

> Triads are used for:
>
> - Very small domains (twelve items or fewer)
> - Testing hypotheses where it is important that every respondent make an active judgment regarding the similarities among a certain set of items
> - Getting people to define what attributes they use to distinguish among items

In a triads test, the items in a domain are presented to the respondent in groups of three. For each triple, the respondent must pick out the one she judges to be the most different. For example, one triple drawn from the domain of animals might be:

DOG   SEAL   SHARK

Picking any item is equivalent to voting for the similarity of the other two. Hence, choosing *dog* would indicate that *seal* and *shark* were similar, while choosing *shark* would indicate that *seal* and *dog* were similar. If all possible triples are presented, each pair of items will occur N − 2 times,[14] each time "against" a different item. If a pair of items is really similar it will "win" each of those contests and will be voted most similar a total of N − 2 times. If the pair is extremely dissimilar, it will never win. For example, *oyster* and *elephant* might occur in the following triples:

OYSTER	ELEPHANT	DOG
OYSTER	ELEPHANT	SHRIMP
OYSTER	ELEPHANT	OSTRICH

In the first one, the respondent might choose *oyster* as the most different. In the second, the respondent might choose *elephant*. In the third, the respondent might choose *oyster* again, and so on. Hence, the triad test in which every possible triple is presented will yield a similarity score for each pair of items that ranges from zero to N – 2, where N is the number of items. For example, if there are ten items, then each pair will occur against all 10 – 2 = 8 remaining items.

The problem with presenting all possible triples is that there are N(N – 1)(N – 2)/6 of them, which is a quantity that grows with the cube of the number of items. For example, if the domain has thirty items in it, the number of triples is 30 times 29 times 28 divided by 6, which is 4,060. This is too many for an informant to respond to, even over a period of days. The solution is to take a manageable sample of triples. For example, out of the 4,060 triples, we might randomly select two hundred for the respondent to work with. However, a random sample would allow some pairs of items to appear in several triples and allow others not to occur it all. The latter would be a real problem because the purpose of the task is to measure the perceived similarity between every pair of items.

The solution is to use a *balanced incomplete block* or BIB design (Burton and Nerlove 1976). In a BIB design, every *pair* of items occurs a fixed number of times. The number of times the pair occurs is known as lambda (λ). In a complete design (where all possible triples occur), λ obviously equals N – 2, since each pair occurs against every *other* item in the domain. When λ equals 1, we have the smallest possible BIB design, where each pair of items occurs only once. For a domain with thirty items, a $\lambda = 1$ design would have only 435 triads—still a lot, but a considerable savings over 4,060.

In general, however, $\lambda = 1$ designs should be avoided, because the similarity of each pair of items will be completely determined by their relation to whichever item happens to turn up as the third item. For example, if *elephant* and *mouse* occur in this triple below, it is likely that they

MOUSE   ELEPHANT   RAT

will be measured as not similar, since *elephant* is likely to be chosen as most different. But if instead they happen to occur in this triple:

MOUSE   ELEPHANT   OYSTER

it is likely that they will be measured as similar. Thus, it is much better to have at least a $\lambda = 2$ design, where each pair of items occurs against two different third items. The only exception to this rule of thumb is when you give each respondent in a culturally homogeneous sample a completely different triad test, based on the same set of items but containing different triples. For example, respondent #1 might get *mouse* and *elephant* paired with *oyster*, but respondent #2 might get *mouse* and *elephant* paired with *dog*. In a way, this is like taking a complete design and spreading it out across multiple respondents. This can work well, but it means that you cannot compare respondents' answers with each other to assess similarity of views since each person was given a different questionnaire.

A nice feature of the triads task is that, unlike the simple pilesort, it yields degrees of similarity for pairs of items for each respondent. In the simple pilesort, each respondent essentially gives a "yes, they are similar" or "no, they are not similar" vote. In the triads, the range of values obtained for each pair of items goes from zero to λ. Hence, for a $\lambda = 3$ design, each pair of items is assigned an ordinal similarity score of 0, 1, 2, or 3. This means that we can sensibly construct separate multidimensional scaling maps for each respondent.[15]

One problem with triad tasks is that respondents often find them tiring and repetitive. They will swear that a certain triad has already occurred and will suspect that you are trying to see if they are responding consistently, which makes them nervous. Another problem is that respondents tend to become aware of their own thought processes as they proceed and start feeling uncomfortable about using varying criteria (which is unavoidable) to pick the item most different in each triple. This makes them think that they are not doing a good job. In general, triads are only useful for very small domains (twelve items or fewer) or for testing hypotheses (in which it is important that every respondent make an active judgment regarding the similarities among a certain set of items).

Analyzing Triad Data

Perhaps the most interesting use of triads was by Romney and D'Andrade (1964), who used them to test two theories of cognition about American male kinship roles, such as grandfather, father, son, grandson, uncle, brother, nephew, and cousin. One theory, by Wallace and Atkins (1960), held that Americans use two attributes—generation and lineality—to distinguish among the roles, as shown in Table 3.7. In the table, *lineal* refers to kin who are either ancestors or descendants of the speaker, who by convention is labeled *ego*. The term *collineal* refers to non-lineal kin whose set of ancestors include or are included by ego's set of ancestors. The term *ablineal* refers to all other blood relatives.

If the theory is true, in a triads test that included the triple,

GRANDFATHER   GRANDSON   FATHER

Americans should choose *grandson* as the one most different because grandfather and grandson are the least different with respect to the two attributes in the model (all of the terms are lineal, differing only on generation, where *grandfather* and *father* are adjacent, but *grandson* is a step removed).

In contrast, Romney and D'Andrade propose a model with three attributes—generational distance, lineality, and

Table 3.7 Wallace and Atkins Model of American Kinship

Generation	Lineal	Collineal	Ablineal
2 gen. above ego	grandfather		
1 gen. above ego	father	uncle	
same as ego		brother	cousin
1 gen. below ego	son	nephew	
2 gen. below ego	grandson		

Table 3.8   Romney and D'Andrade Model of American Kinship

	Direct		Collateral	
	− Reciprocal	+ Reciprocal	− Reciprocal	+ Reciprocal
Gen ± 2	grandson	grandfather		
Gen ± 1	son	father	uncle	nephew
Gen. 0	brother		cousin	

reciprocal roles—as shown in Table 3.8. In the table, *direct* refers to kin that share the same ancestors as ego, and *collateral* are all others.

According to the Romney and D'Andrade model, when faced with the same triad given here, Americans should choose, with equal probability, either *grandson* or *father* as the item most different, and they should never choose *grandfather*. Given these predictions, it was a simple matter to test the theories by giving the triads to a sample of Americans and seeing which theory best predicted the actual answers on the triads test. Overall, the best theory turned out to be the Romney and D'Andrade model.

Informal Use of Triads

So far, we have only described the formal use of the triads task, which results in the generation of similarities among items. Another way to use triads is as a device to spark discussion of the underlying attributes that people use to distinguish among items in the domain. To do this, we present informants with a small random sample of triples, one at a time. For each triple, the informant is asked to explain in what ways each item is different from the other two. This is an extraordinarily effective way to elicit the attributes that people use to think about the domain. For example, consider this triple:

CANCER   SYPHILIS   MEASLES

This triple can elicit a number of perceived attributes of illnesses, including seriousness ("cancer is fatal"), age of the afflicted ("measles is something that kids get"), morality ("you get syphilis from sleeping around too much"), contagiousness ("you can catch syphilis and measles from other people"), and so on. It is easy to see that it only requires a handful of triples to elicit dozens and dozens of attributes.

Consensus Analysis

In the study of cultural domains, the researcher must be aware of issues of cultural variability among respondents. It is impossible to interpret the results of triads and pilesorts if fundamentally different systems of classification are in use among different respondents. One way to determine whether variability among respondents reflects different systems of classification is the consensus methodology of Romney, Weller, and Batchelder (1986). This method, available in both UCINET and Anthropac, provides a way to (a) discover whether a set of questions has multiple correct answer keys (corresponding to different cultures), (b) uncover what the culturally "correct" answers are for each culture, and (c) assess the extent of cultural domain knowledge possessed by a given member of a culture. Thinking back to the example of dolphins and sharks, consensus analysis would indicate whether our sample includes subgroups of respondents with systematically different answers across all similarity judgments (e.g., because some are sorting on the basis of habitat—where the animal lives—while others are sorting based on phylogeny—the class or family to which an animal belongs biologically) or just on the basis of individual respondent variability, such that some people simply know more about a given domain than others do.

Once consensus analysis has been used to identify culturally homogeneous groups of respondents, it can then be applied within in each group to determine the amount of knowledge regarding the cultural domain possessed by each respondent in that group. In effect, the theory underlying consensus analysis distinguishes between two kinds of variability in people's responses. One kind is systematic difference that we attribute to cultural differences. The other kind is random or piecemeal difference, which we attribute to individual differences in knowledge of the domain. For example, within a culture, people may have similar understandings of types of flowers, but some people simply have more of that cultural knowledge than others. They know more names of flowers, they know more about which are used in what occasions (such as weddings or funerals or romances), and so on. This does not mean they know more in the sense of Truth with a capital *t*, but rather that they know more of their own culture.

Consider the study of crimes discussed earlier in this chapter in which thirty respondents were asked to sort crimes into piles based on how similar the crimes were to each other. As discussed, we can use the pilesort method to uncover various types of crimes (see Figure 3.5 for a MDS plot), and then use consensus analysis to determine whether there was agreement among respondents. Consensus analysis methods of pilesort data using UCINET and Anthropac use individual proximity matrices as input. In this example, the input is an item-by-item matrix for each of the thirty respondents in which $x_{ij} = 1$ if the respondent placed crime i and crime j in the same pile. The program then correlates the thirty item-by-item matrices with each other and runs a factor analysis. The program output includes factor loadings for all respondents. If one factor is predominant, we can conclude that there is a single culture. In this example, the largest eigenvalue = 14.440 and the second largest eigenvalue = 1.653, indicating strong cultural consensus. If the respondents were not culturally homogeneous, we would find multiple factors indicating systematically different response patterns. We are also able to identify respondent 3 as an individual with the greatest amount of cultural knowledge (Table 3.9 shows other competence scores) because he or she has the highest loading on the first factor. We also see that respondent 22 has a significantly lower competence score than all the others—it is possible the respondent did not understand the task.

Visualization of Cultural Domains

Implicit in these data collection and analysis techniques is the idea of the cultural domain as a network of items related by semantic relations, or families of linked meanings. Thus, we can use visualization and analytic techniques drawn from social network analysis to investigate

Table 3.9   Factor Loadings from
Consensus Analysis of Crime Pilesorts

Respondent ID	Competence
3	0.882
2	0.850
16	0.844
25	0.834
26	0.830
15	0.823
29	0.813
21	0.777
5	0.775
12	0.760
19	0.754
27	0.741
28	0.723
11	0.716
8	0.715
14	0.684
23	0.668
6	0.667
17	0.663
10	0.660
7	0.631
4	0.622
13	0.596
20	0.590
9	0.588
1	0.586
30	0.493
18	0.451
24	0.439
22	−0.072

cultural domains. For example, network visualization tools can be used to elucidate the internal structure of a cultural domain and identify how the position of items within this structure distinguishes the items from each other and gives them their unique meanings.

Network visualization is based on graph layout algorithms (GLAs), which locate nodes in space and connect them with lines indicating a close relationship (DeJordy, Borgatti, Roussin, and Halgin 2007). In the case of cultural domain analysis, the lines are determined by the level of similarity among items determined by the researcher (e.g., how often two items appeared in the same pile, the correlation coefficient of two items). Boston College student Heidi Stokes used the pilesort method to collect data on the perceived similarity of twenty-four holidays as part of an undergraduate research methods class. Figure 3.7 is a GLA representation of the holiday data in which an edge is shown connecting holidays deemed similar by at least 50 percent of the respondents. The edges allow the viewer to clearly identify various groupings that exist within the domain of holidays among Boston College undergraduates.

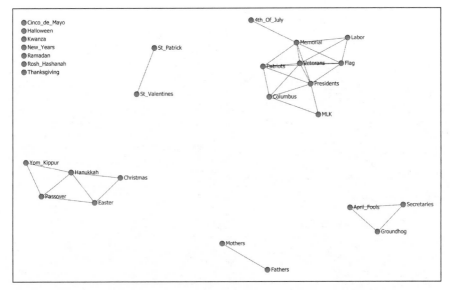

Figure 3.7   Graph layout algorithm representation of holiday data (filtered at 0.50)

We can see that there is a large grouping of religious holidays and a large grouping of patriotic holidays. The GLA also reveals structure within these groupings. The existence of a line from the Fourth of July to Memorial Day but no other holidays in the grouping of patriotic holidays indicates that respondents considered the Fourth of July to be more similar to Memorial Day than to other holidays such as Columbus Day and Martin Luther King Day.

Researchers can use GLAs to investigate the perceived similarity of two items at various strengths to better determine the structure of items within groupings and possible attributes that might give items their unique meanings. For example, we can draw a GLA in which a line is shown connecting holidays deemed similar by at least 70 percent of the respondents (or any other percentage decided by the researcher). Figure 3.8 indicates that respondents in the Catholic school deemed Easter more similar to Christmas than to the Jewish holidays Hanukkah, Yom Kippur, and Passover. We can also see that Christmas is deemed more similar to Hanukkah than to other Jewish holidays, perhaps because both holidays occur at the same time of year.

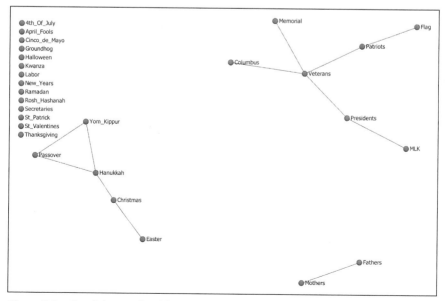

Figure 3.8 Graph layout algorithm representation of holiday data (filtered at 0.70)

CONCLUSION

We have presented basic techniques for eliciting data concerning cultural domains. The free list technique is primarily used to elicit the basic elements of the domain. The pilesort and triad tasks are used both to elicit similarities among the items and to elicit attributes that describe the items. Consensus analysis can be used to uncover the culturally correct items in a cultural domain in the face of certain kinds of intracultural variability, and it enables the researcher to assess the extent of knowledge possessed by an informant about a given cultural domain. In addition, we have touched on the use of multidimensional scaling and graph layout algorithms to graphically illustrate the structure of the domain and locate each item's position in that structure.

NOTES

I am grateful to H. Russell Bernard, Pertti Pelto, A. Kimball Romney, and Gery Ryan for helping shape my views on cultural domain analysis, which is not to say they necessarily agree with anything I have written. I am also grateful to Mark Fleisher and to John Gatewood for giving me permission to use their data to illustrate concepts. Finally, I thank Jean Schensul and Marki LeCompte for their many comments on earlier drafts.

1. Some people use the term *cognitive domain* to refer to domains that are not necessarily shared. For example, a psychologist might make an in-depth study of one person's understanding of nature. Since no other respondents were studied, the psychologist might refer to the person's categories as cognitive domains rather than cultural domains. However, it is important to realize that whether they are shared or not, cognitive domains have all the same properties as cultural domains, including being experienced as outside the individual, as outlined above. In this sense, we can think of cognitive domains as the general category, and cultural domains as a member of that category involving domains that are held in common by a group.

2. Dr. Ryan is a senior behavioral scientist at RAND and an adjunct assistant professor in the department of Psychiatry and Biobehavioral Sciences at UCLA.

3. One such measure, Smith's S, is given in the rightmost column of Table 3.2. The measure is essentially a frequency count that is weighted inversely by the rank of the item in each list. In practice, Smith's S tends to be very highly correlated with simple frequency.

4. Or salience, as captured by Smith's S.

5. While not an artifact, exactly, of the column sums of the matrix (i.e., some items are mentioned more often than others), the core/periphery structure of co-occurrence

matrices is made visible by not controlling for the sums. It is also useful to examine the pattern obtained by controlling for these sums. One way to do this is to simply compute Pearson correlations among the columns. Another way is to count both matches of the ones and the zeros.

6. The number thirty is merely a convention—a rule of thumb. More respondents are always more desirable, but it involves more time and expense.

7. This means that there is a one-to-one correspondence between the rank orders of the data. That is, the pair placed most often in the same pile is the most similar, the pair placed second most often in the same pile is the second most similar, etc.

8. An excellent introduction to multidimensional scaling is provided by Kruskal and Wish (1978). For an introduction to cluster analysis, we recommend Everitt (1980).

9. The data were collected specifically for inclusion in this chapter by Jennifer Teeple, Dan Bakham, Shannon Sendzimmer, and Amanda Norbits. We are grateful for their help.

10. It is best to use a different sample of respondents for this purpose, or wait until they have finished the sort and then ask them to discuss the reasons behind their choices. Otherwise, the discussion will influence their sorts. You can also have them sort the items twice: the first time without interference, the second time discussing the sort as they go. The results of both sorts can be recorded, analyzed, and compared.

11. It is important to remember that the axes of MDS pictures are arbitrary; perceptual dimensions can run along any angle, not just horizontal or vertical.

12. Either as part of the pilesort exercise, or by showing the MDS map to informants and asking them to interpret it.

13. An alternative here is to ask them to divide each pile in two. This is repeated as often as desired.

14. Again, N is the number of items in the domain.

15. The same was true for the successive pilesort techniques described earlier.

RESOURCES

Borgatti, S. P. 1992. *ANTHROPAC 4.0.* Columbia, SC: Analytic Technologies. Anthropac is a menu-driven computer program for cultural domain analysis. The program's capabilities include all the techniques discussed in this chapter. More information is available at www.analytictech.com.

Kruskal, J. B., and M. Wish. 1978. *Multidimensional scaling.* Newbury Park, CA: Sage Publications. This is perhaps the clearest book available on the mathematics and interpretation of multidimensional scaling.

Romney, A. K., S. C. Weller, and W. H. Batchelder. 1986. Culture as consensus: A theory of cultural and informant accuracy. *American Anthropologist* 88(2): 313–38. This is a brilliant paper on the theory of consensus analysis. A seminal article in the field.

Scott, J. 1991. *Social network analysis: A handbook.* Newbury Park: Sage Publications. Scott's book is a popular introduction to the techniques of social network analysis. It discusses everything from data management techniques to advanced analytical methods.

Spradley, J. 1979. *The ethnographic interview.* New York: Holt, Rinehart and Winston. Spradley's book is perhaps the definitive book on interviewing technique in the context of cultural domain analysis. Extremely well written with lots of examples.

REFERENCES

Borgatti, S. P. 1992. *ANTHROPAC 4.0.* Columbia, SC: Analytic Technologies.

Borgatti, S. P., M. G. Everett, and L. C. Freeman. 2002. UCINET for Windows: Software for social network analysis. Harvard, MA: Analytic Technologies.

Boster, J. S. 1994, June. The successive pilesort. *CAM: Cultural Anthropology Methods Journal* 6: 11–12.

Boster, J. S., and J. C. Johnson. 1989. Form or function: A comparison of expert and novice judgments of similarity among fish. *American Anthropologist* 91: 866–89.

Burton, M. L., and S. B. Nerlove. 1976. Balanced designs for triads tests: Two examples from English. *Social Science Research* 5: 247–67.

Casagrande, J. B., and K. L. Hale. 1967. Semantic relations in Papago folk-definitions, in *Studies in southwestern ethnolinguistics*, ed. D. Hymes and W. E. Bittle, 165–96. The Hague: Mouton.

DeJordy, R., S. P. Borgatti, C. Roussin, and D. Halgin. 2007. Visualizing proximity data. *Field Methods* 19: 239–63.

Everitt, B. 1980. *Cluster analysis.* New York: Halsted Press.

Gatewood, J. 1984. Familiarity, vocabulary size, and recognition ability in four semantic domains. *American Ethnologist* 11: 507–27.

Henley, N. M. 1969. A psychological study of the semantics of animal terms. *Journal of Verbal Learning and Verbal Behavior* 8: 176–84.

Kruskal, J. B., and M. Wish, M. 1978. *Multidimensional scaling.* Beverly Hills, CA: Sage.

Lounsbury, F. 1964. The structural analysis of kinship semantics, in *Proceedings of the ninth International Congress of Linguists*, ed. H. G. Lunt, 73–93. The Hague: Mouton.

Romney, A. K., and R. G. D'Andrade. 1964. Cognitive aspects of English kin terms. *American Anthropologist* 66: 146–70.

Romney, A. K., S. C. Weller, and W. H. Batchelder. 1986. Culture as consensus: A theory of cultural and informant accuracy. *American Anthropologist* 88: 313–38.

Scott, J. 1991. *Social network analysis: A handbook.* London: Sage.

Spradley, J. 1979. *The ethnographic interview.* New York: Holt, Rinehart and Winston.

Wallace, A. F. C., and J. R. Atkins. 1960. The meaning of kinship terms. *American Anthropologist* 621: 58–80.

Weller, S. C., and A. K. Romney. 1988. *Systematic data collection.* Newbury Park, CA: Sage.

4 ⬦—•—•—

MAPPING SPATIAL DATA

Ellen K. Cromley

THE SPATIAL PERSPECTIVE

Spatial data analysis and mapping are essential tools in the ethnographer's toolkit. The communities, villages, schools, and other social settings the ethnographer studies do not function in a vacuum. They exist in particular environments that are both natural and human made. The daily activity patterns of individuals are often constrained by the contemporary geography of the community—the culmination of earlier human-environment interactions. From the point of view of the individuals who live in a community, in the short term, the attributes of that community's environment are essentially fixed. In the long term, however, individuals and organizations can be agents of environmental or social change. From the viewpoints of the organizations serving a community, the geographical dimensions of their activities can be a major factor affecting how well the organizations function both in the present and in the future

Most ethnographic research focuses on populations of individuals, although other units of analysis are possible (LeCompte and Preissle 1993; Bernard 2006, 49–52). **Spatial data** are data on the relative locations of units of analysis. Locational data values are collected in addition to other data values describing other attributes of the objects we are studying (Bailey and Gatrell 1995, xi). For most

**Cross
Reference:**
Book 1 discusses
units of analysis

Definition:
Spatial data
are data on the
relative locations of
units of analysis

117

anthropologists, the relevant space is a geographic space, a region on the earth's surface. Spatial analysis of geographic data is concerned with the relationships among individuals or other objects located on the earth's surface, in particular those relationships that vary when the locations of the objects change (Gatrell 1983, 2). As Bailey and Gatrell note, "spatial data analysis is involved when data are spatially located *and* explicit consideration is given to the possible importance of their spatial arrangement in the analysis or interpretation of results" (Bailey and Gatrell 1995, 8).

The importance of graphic and cartographic (mapped) representations of data is clear (Anscombe 1973; Monmonier 1996). The spatial view of data contributes information that cannot be obtained in any other way. Cartographic representation and analysis of spatial data make it possible to go beyond tabular and statistical views of data. We can describe two classrooms of students using information organized in a table. Based on the data viewed in tables, the two classrooms of students are identical (Figure 4.1).

The statistical views of these classrooms would also be the same (same number of observations, same frequency distribution of grades, same median grade, and so on). If, however, we have locational data so that we can map where the students who have earned different grades are sitting in the classrooms, we see that the classrooms are different. In one class, there is no apparent spatial pattern in the grades. In the other class, the students sitting in the front row close to the teacher all earn the highest marks. These are only two of the many ways that the nine students could be arranged.

These displays show the distinction between statistical measures like frequency and geographical patterns like locational arrangement, and they highlight the additional knowledge that can be gained by understanding spatial relationships among the units of analysis. Most statistical methods assume that the observational units "represent independent pieces of evidence about the relationship under study" (Bailey and Gatrell 1995, 4). Spatial analysis enables us to consider the possible importance of neighborhood or environmental or other spatial-contextual influences.

The purpose of this chapter is to define and illustrate the usefulness of spatial concepts and methods for research

The Table View of Data for Two Classes (The Same)

NAME	GRADE
Abdul	B
Bob	B
Carmela	C
Dave	A
Ed	A
Felicia	C
Gordon	A
Hank	B
Inez	C

NAME	GRADE
Abdul	B
Bob	B
Carmela	C
Dave	A
Ed	A
Felicia	C
Gordon	A
Hank	B
Inez	C

The Statistical View of Data for Two Classes (The Same)

GRADE	FREQUENCY
A	3
B	3
C	3

N = 9
Median grade = B
Range = C, A

GRADE	FREQUENCY
A	3
B	3
C	3

N = 9
Median grade = B
Range = C, A

The Spatial View of Data for Two Classes (Different)

Teacher		
B	C	A
C	A	B
A	B	C

Teacher		
A	A	A
B	B	B
C	C	C

Figure 4.1 The spatial view of data provides insights that cannot be drawn from tables and statistics.

in culturally different or culturally complex settings. The underlying theme is that an explicit understanding of the spatial aspects of human-environment relationships in a community can enhance ethnographic research. Maps are an important, although not the only, means for making spatial relationships explicit. Spatial statistical analysis can reveal whether or not there is a spatial pattern in the data and whether or not this pattern could have occurred by chance (Haining 2003; Waller and Gotway 2004).

The first part of the chapter introduces key geographic concepts referring to the spatial dimensions of communities,

individuals, and organizations, and it illustrates the use of
these concepts in ethnographic research. Particular emphasis
is placed on identification of the study area, spatial sampling,
and the identification of community needs through analysis
of spatially referenced data. The second part of the chapter
describes types of maps, critical components of maps, and
techniques for acquiring, analyzing, and mapping spatially
referenced data, including geographic information systems
(GIS) and related technologies and software. Ethical considerations in the collection, representation, and use of spatial
data are discussed in the last part of the chapter.

SPATIAL DIMENSIONS OF COMMUNITY

Study Areas as Regions

Definition:
A community
is a group of
people who interact
in characteristic ways
based on shared values
to meet common
needs

The ethnographic case study focuses on the community, village, school, or other social unit. A **community**
is a group of people who interact in characteristic ways
based on shared values to meet common needs (Johnston,
Gregory, and Smith 1994, 80–81). Because daily human
interaction until very recently has required people to be in
the same place at the same time, there has usually been a
strong spatial dimension to the understanding of community. Most definitions of community include the sharing of
a localized territorial space as a key element. Communities
are thus recognized as both social and spatial-temporal sys-

Definition:
Community
space is where
social interactions
take place

tems. **Community space** is the territory defined by the set
of locations where the interactions of interest take place,
including the homes of participants.

The interactions that typically occur within a community are not equally likely to occur everywhere within the
community space. The time-space of the community has
nested within it personal and group spaces that are defined,
in part, by the rules of behavior associated with them. Most
communities recognize the personal spaces of individuals,
the range of conversation and social interaction space, and
the range of public space beyond (Hall 1966; Jakle, Brunn,
and Roseman 1976). In addition, we can identify socially
sanctioned private places that provide regular inhabitants
with freedom from observation or demands by others and

socially sanctioned public places with freedom of access but a set of behavioral expectations. Private places generally include some part of an individual's home, but may include other places like a social club where the regular inhabitants enjoy a degree of privacy and control. Control over public territory creates jurisdictions or administrative regions.

Introducing the spatial perspective into ethnographic research begins by describing the configuration of the community space and documenting where the interactions of interest occur. An early step in ethnographic research design, after formulation of the theoretical problem, is making decisions about selection of an appropriate method and study site (Bernard 2006, 70). The identification of the study area involves the ethnographer in defining a region. A **region** is an area of earth-space with attributes that differentiate it from surrounding areas (Johnston, Gregory, and Smith 1994, 506–09). In defining a study area, we are differentiating the places where observations will be made from the places where they will not. How the study area boundaries are drawn will affect what the researcher observes.

To understand the issues involved in defining the study area, it is necessary to understand the different ways regions are constructed. The region is one of the most important constructs in geography, and there are a number of different ways to define regions. One type of region, the **formal region**, is defined by the presence or absence of one or more attributes.

In this definition, the regional boundaries are determined based on the researcher's understanding of the underlying spatial distribution of the units of observation with the attributes of interest, and the identified areas are considered homogeneous with respect to the attributes. A soil region is an example of a formal region based on analysis of samples taken at various locations and analyzed for soil type. A residential area of houses built at the same time might also be considered a formal region.

Another type of region is the **functional region**. A functional region is defined by flows or interactions of people, goods, or information (Figure 4.2). In this definition, the region is organized around nodes that are linked to the periphery by flows of people, goods, or information.

Cross Reference:
Books 1, 2, and 3 discuss strategies for making these decisions

Definition:
A region has attributes that differentiate it from surrounding areas

Cross Reference:
Books 1, 2, and 3 also discuss ways to create boundaries around the population to be studied

Definition:
A formal region is defined by its attributes

Definition:
A functional region is defined by flows of people, goods, or information

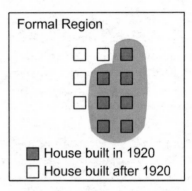

Figure 4.2   Different types of regions

An example of a functional region is a store's market area or a hospital discharge area. The boundaries of functional regions often are fuzzy.

A third type of region, the **administrative region**, is a type of formal region in the sense that it is identified based on nominal data (see Figure 4.2). An area on the surface of the earth is either in an administrative region or not. In Figure 4.2, the region's boundary distinguishes "in the town of West Hartford" from "not in the town of West Hartford."

The boundaries of administrative regions are well defined, usually legally defined and even demarcated. Nevertheless, there is a very important difference between them and other regional boundaries regarding what the boundaries of administrative regions represent.

The boundary of the administrative region is rarely drawn based on an understanding of the underlying geographical distribution of objects or flows. Indeed, it would be difficult to develop a boundary that would respect all of the widely varying distributions of different objects and flows on the earth's surface. Administrative boundaries instead generally are arbitrary. As a consequence, administrative regions are usually not internally homogeneous with respect to an attribute even though they may look like formal regions when mapped. Population, for example, would not be uniformly distributed within a census tract (Figure 4.3).

And, administrative regions often arbitrarily partition the spatial distribution of the object and flow phenomena we wish to study (Figure 4.4).

The development and widespread adoption of the Internet and mobile communication devices like cell phones and notebook computers have contributed to the emergence of new kinds of social networks. Anthropologists have been studying electronic mail, texting, and other

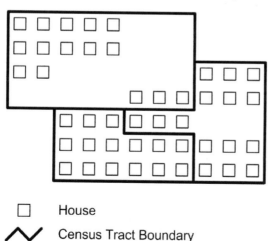

☐　House

〴〵　Census Tract Boundary

Figure 4.3　Uneven distribution of housing units within administrative regions

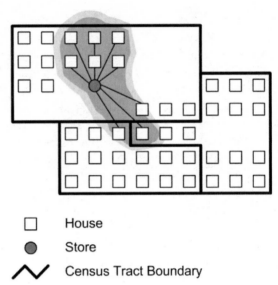

☐ House

● Store

⋀⋁ Census Tract Boundary

Figure 4.4 Arbitrary partitioning of a functional region by administrative boundaries

forms of communication and social media that depend on these technologies and have concluded that people use a wide range of different channels to communicate with a small number of close ties (Broadbent and Bauwens 2008). Although new technologies make it possible for there to be communication between people who are not at the same place at the same time, and they have broadened access to communication technologies among poor and immigrant people worldwide, geography still matters. The Internet and other communication infrastructures operate in real geographic space, and the organization of this space has been studied and mapped (Zook 2005). Some forms of communication in cyberspace challenge the dominance of the state by enabling a range of social groups—from transnational social movements to global criminal networks—to create and maintain social cyberspaces that do not stop at the border (Zook and Graham 2007). Regions are important for describing, analyzing, and administering geographic space. Understanding the nature of regions is key to successful study area delimitation. The goals of defining the study area are the following:

- To maximize internal homogeneity within the study area to assure that as many of the units of analysis as possible are included
- To minimize flows across the study area boundary so that as many of the interactions of interest are included (Foot 1981, 14)

Ideally, the ethnographer would define a study area based on the distribution of the units of analysis and/or the patterns of interactions of interest. Unfortunately, most data collection and reporting units are based on administrative regions where boundaries may not reflect the distributions and flows of interest.

Defining the Study Area

Suppose a researcher is interested in an ethnographic study of the organization of public education in the United States. In the United States, public education is a function of state and local governments. The investigators want to study a town in Hartford County, Connecticut, because the population there is ethnically and socioeconomically diverse.

EXAMPLE 4.1

ORGANIZATION OF PUBLIC EDUCATION IN A U.S. TOWN

For this study, the town of West Hartford was selected (the town is the local unit of government in most New England states) because of an ongoing debate occurring there over the organization of the school system and how it serves different groups within the community (Trotta 1994; de la Torre 2009). Among the issues are crowding, segregation within the schools, differences in academic achievement, and how these problems might be addressed through redistricting. In this case, the administrative region of the town represents a formal region because the services delivered by the town's school system are provided within the town boundaries. All schools—the locations of relevance where public education is provided—that are part of the school system are located within the town (Figure 4.5).

Perhaps, however, the schools are not the units of analysis of interest for this study. Because the issues of interest involve which grades, students, and teachers will be assigned to which schools, it is important to look at the educational system as a functional region where the schools serve as nodes of activity for students and

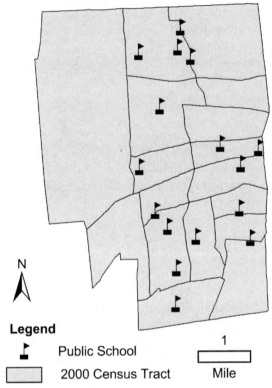

N

Legend

𝄃 Public School

☐ 2000 Census Tract

1

Mile

Figure 4.5 Public school locations in the town of West Hartford

teachers who travel from their home locations. In this case, we would want to talk to individual teachers, students, parents, and administrators.

When systems are viewed this way, the researchers need to have an understanding of the residential locations of teachers, administrators, and students, and how a school reassignment would affect their daily travel and activity patterns. This requires them to check the validity of the assumption that the town boundaries describe the relevant study area. Clearly, in a culture with high levels of personal mobility, it is unlikely that all of the teachers and administrators would live within the town. Researchers might assume that all of the students in the system would live in West Hartford, given the nature of the administrative boundary. Anecdotal evidence, however, suggests that there is significant but unquantified movement of students from neighboring towns into adjacent school systems, including West Hartford (Rocha 1994).

If researchers consider the flows of teachers and students, the functional space of the West Hartford school system extends beyond the borders of the town. The magnitude of these flows of teachers and students and the participants' percep-tions of the school district space are something that the ethnographer will have to

take into account in defining the study area and the units of observation that will be included. The spatial perspective on the interactions that define communities is grounded in an understanding of the daily travel and activity patterns of the community members and how these influence their views of space.

Ethnographers can use maps in many other ways. Table 4.1 displays the role that maps can play in a number of issues that interest ethnographers. Table 4.1 also lists questions that ethnographers must consider when using maps in their research.

SPATIAL DIMENSIONS OF INDIVIDUAL LIFE

Understanding the Activity Space

When the unit of analysis in an ethnographic study is the individual person, introducing the spatial perspective into ethnographic research involves understanding the daily travel and activity patterns of the individuals and how their direct experience of the environment influences their perceptions of geographic space. Studies of how people allocate their time to activities during the day have their origins in nineteenth-century studies of social conditions in cities (Anderson 1971). Research that relies on **time budgets**, or systematic records of an individual's use of time over a given period, has been conducted in a wide range of fields for a wide variety of purposes from market research to urban planning and design to investigation of cultural change (Golledge and Stimson 1987). Time studies, though they use common data collection techniques, "do not constitute a unified research field" (Anderson 1971, 353).

When the locations where activities take place are incorporated into time budgets, they become **space-time budgets**. Although we can choose to view the spatial-temporal pattern of activities as a matter of individual choice, it also is possible to emphasize the spatial and temporal constraints implicit in the patterns the budgets encode. In the short run, the individual faces a fixed-feature space. The attributes of the natural and built environment are given, and the

Key point

Definition: Time budgets are systematic records of an individual's use of time over a specific record

Definition: Space-time budgets are systematic records of an individual's use of time in a specific location over a period of time

Table 4.1   Using Maps in Community-Based Research Projects

Research Task	Questions to Consider	Role of Map	Data Collection and Mapping
Define the study area	What is the community I am studying? Is the study area best defined as a formal, functional, or administrative region for the purposes of my study? Do I need to show multiple views of the study area? Do the members of this community occupy a single contiguous region, or are they dispersed? What scale map is needed to represent the entire study area? What scale map is needed to represent the level of detail required by the study? Do I need more than one map and/ or maps at different scales? What symbols should I use to represent the features of interest?	Provides a basis for study-area delimitation and for reference by showing the distribution of a feature of interest on the earth's surface, by showing flows of interest on the earth's surface, or by showing administrative regions of interest on the earth's surface	Acquire base map or maps at the appropriate scales by purchasing existing paper maps or digital spatial databases or by making your own Be aware of the accuracy and timeliness of the data represented on the paper map or in the digital spatial database Be aware of any restrictions on reproducing or copying and distributing paper maps and digital spatial databases
Describe the geographical distribution of community members	What is the geographical distribution of community members based on home location? Do I need to show the locations of individuals or individual housing units, or are aggregate counts and ratios for geographical areas sufficient?		

Research Task	Questions to Consider	Role of Map	Data Collection and Mapping
	If I map residential locations of individuals, will I be violating confidentiality or putting community members at risk? How could the map be designed to prevent this?	Shows residential distribution of population and/ or housing units by administrative region or researcher-defined formal or functional region Provides a framework for spatially stratified random sampling of community members	Population data tabulated for administrative regions and/or interpolated for researcher-defined regions Housing unit data tabulated for administrative regions and/or interpolated for researcher-defined regions Counts of housing units by region tabulated for administrative regions and/or interpolated for researcher-defined regions Investigate sources such as city directories Address-ranged street network database for geocoding addresses Acquire existing maps/images showing residential locations, including: Cadastral maps showing property boundaries and building footprints; Air photos or satellite images showing locations of individual housing units; Insurance maps Are these data public data? Can they be redistributed?

(continued)

Table 4.1　(*continued*)

Research Task	Questions to Consider	Role of Map	Data Collection and Mapping
Describe the activity spaces of community members by showing the locations of activity sites other than the home	What are the relevant activities (based on the underlying research questions) outside the home, and where do they take place? Are the timing, duration, and sequence of activities occurring at various locations important? Is the route from the home to the activity site and from activity site to activity site important? Do I need to include explicitly travel time and travel mode in data on activity patterns? If I map travel and activity patterns of individuals, will I be violating confidentiality or putting community members at risk? How could the map be designed to prevent this?	Geocode activity sites Plot geographical distributions of activity sites Show travel flows among activity sites Identify individuals who have similar travel and activity patterns by map comparison	Observation, diaries, or surveys of individuals to collect travel and activity data Investigate sources such as city directories and gazetteers for locations of activity sites Address-ranged street network database for geocoding addresses Acquire existing maps/images showing activity locations, including: Cadastral maps showing property boundaries and building footprints; Air photos or satellite images showing locations of individual structures; Insurance maps Maps showing activity sites such as schools
Describe the locations of community organizations of interest	What are the relevant (based on the research questions) community organizations? Where are the facilities of these organizations located?	Show the geographical organization of community institutions, including locations and flows	Key-informant interviews with organization representatives Archival research

Research Task	Questions to Consider	Role of Map	Data Collection and Mapping
	How would I characterize the size, centrality, and level of integration of various facilities? Are there linkages between facilities? How can these be represented?		
Identify locational problems	Does the geographical organization of facilities cover the population? If new facilities are needed, where should they be located? Do people's social obligations make it difficult for them to coordinate their activities in time and space? If facility locations and schedules are changed, who will be positively and negatively affected?	Show the geographical relationships (proximity, accessibility) among community institutions and the people they serve Show geographical constraints on meeting service objectives (for example, four schools cannot be located in such a way that no child is more than two miles from a school) Suggest solutions to geographical problems (for example, locate a new facility, improve transportation, change the scheduling of activities, improve neighborhood quality) Be aware of the values expressed in maps	Measure the spatial relationships described in the data collected and represented on maps Use maps in the description of community problems

individual must adapt his or her activity patterns to them. This issue, "the fate of the individual human being in an increasingly complicated environment," and the outlines of a model for exploring the time-space of the individual, were considered by the geographer Torsten Hagerstrand (1970, 7).

Hagerstrand identified three constraints on human movement in the environment and interaction:

- **Capability constraints**
- **Coupling constraints**
- **Authority constraints**

Definition: Capability constraint is anything that limits the geographic range of an individual

Definition: The time-space prism is the maximum area around home base where the individual can travel before having to return home

The need for people to have a permanent or semipermanent home base where they return periodically to rest and to eat constrains the part of the environment where the individual is capable of being during any given day. The **daily time-space prism** is the island of the individual, the maximum area around the home base where the individual can travel before having to return home (Figure 4.6).

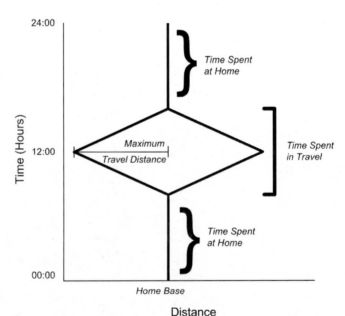

Figure 4.6 Daily time-space prism. Based on concepts discussed by Hagerstrand (1970)

The size and shape of the time-space prism are affected by the mode of transportation available, the amount of time the person is required to spend at home, and the amount of time the person is required to spend at activity sites away from the home. The daily time-space prism will thus vary from culture to culture and from person to person, including those people who share the same home base.

The amount of time spent at particular locations is ruled by **coupling constraints**, which define where, when, and for how long a person has to join with others (Figure 4.7).

Definition: Coupling constraints define limits on where, when, and for how long a person can join with others

The time-budget itself reflects the importance of clock and calendar as key mechanisms for organizing time in industrial and postindustrial societies. Activities requiring face-to-face interaction require colocation in time and space. In order for Mary and Pablo to meet at the playground at the same time, it must be possible for them to be at the same place at the same time. If their other activities make it impossible for them to be at the same place at the same time, coupling constraints cannot be satisfied. Communication innovations like the telephone require only co-"location" in time. The need for colocation in time and space has been viewed negatively, as a set of problems to be overcome, and positively, as a

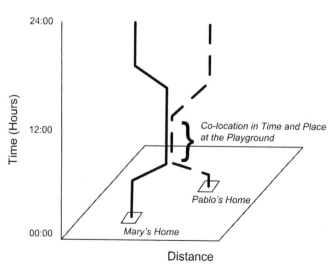

Figure 4.7 Coupling constraints. Based on concepts discussed by Hagerstrand (1970)

mechanism for enabling social activity and the construction of social meaning (Dyck 1990).

The final constraints affecting the environment of the person are **authority constraints**. Personal and public spaces represent a set of spatial domains where the priorities of particular individuals or groups for use of the space are enforced. Authority constraints are based upon which individuals or groups can legitimately expect their priorities to be enforced. Authority constraints limit and define the timing and nature of interactions that can occur within spatial domains. Unlike Mary and Pablo agreeing on their own to meet at the playground at a mutually convenient time, Mary and Pablo are not free to agree when they will meet at school. The school authorities determine where and when instruction will occur (Figure 4.8).

The constraints considered by Hagerstrand mean that access to resources or avoidance of hazards in the environment involve more than simple juxtapositions of features and populations. They involve "a time-space location which really allows the life-path to make the required detours" (Hagerstrand 1970, 19). As Hagerstrand points out, for example, predetermined timetables exist for the school, and the schoolchild does not have the freedom to choreograph the activities of the day (1970, 15). He emphasizes that

> **Definition:** Authority constraints are imposed by those with control over the use of space who limit both the time possible and the kinds of interaction within a particular space

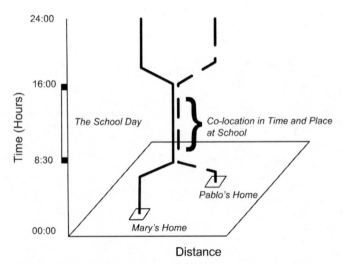

Figure 4.8 Authority constraints. Based on concepts discussed by Hagerstrand (1970)

travel and activity patterns may be particularly complicated for dependent members of households such as children. A study conducted in Australia found clear evidence that adolescents' lives are contingent on adult space and time (Williams, Pocock, and Bridge 2009).

The **activity space** of the individual, the area in which time is spent, is built up out of daily travel and activity patterns and includes the home base, other activity sites, and the pathways connecting these locations (Johnston, Gregory, and Smith 1994, 4). As such, elements in a person's activity space may be separated by areas that the person hardly knows at all because no time has been spent there. Direct personal contact with a place is an important means of acquiring spatial knowledge and a sense of place.

Definition: Activity space is the area in which an individual spends time

The environment of the person has an objective reality in the geographical locations where the person is observed or reported to be. The environment of the person also has a subjective reality in perception and assessment of the lived space. The spatial perspective on community, based on an understanding of the travel and activity patterns of its members, is enriched by the consideration of individuals' geographic perspectives and experiences.

Cognitive maps, as used in geography, are "long term stored information [stored in the heads of individuals] about the relative location of objects and phenomena in the everyday physical environment" (Garling, Book, and Lindberg 1979, 200). The environments that are the basis for the individual's cognitive map may be known to exist or may be imagined, and they often represent a mix of information drawn from different periods of time (Golledge and Stimson 1987, 72). Both cognitive and developmental approaches have been applied to the study of spatial cognition.

Definition: Cognitive maps are bodies of information that people store about the location of things in physical space

Spatial learning involves intellectual development (Piaget and Inhelder 1967) as well as acquiring information over time, largely as a result of direct contact with the environment (Jakle, Brunn, and Roseman 1976, 93). In a developmental sense, spatial perception begins with the awareness of perceived objects, the location of the object in time and space, the recognition of attributes of the object, and the attachment of meaning to it (Golledge and Stimson 1987, 53).

Some of the earliest research on cognitive mapping addressed the "imageability" of the environment. Lynch's work (1960) on the image of the city identified key elements of urban environments: paths, edges, districts, nodes, and landmarks. This work has been extended to the imaging of small local cultural areas or neighborhoods.

Definition: Neighborhood is defined as a physical area with shared social features

The **neighborhood** has a physical area readily identifiable on a map (Lebel, Pampalon, and Villeneuve 2007). Many cues used to identify neighborhoods are physical—housing types, land use, and density. The street network or sets of other paths are the most important single factor used to identify neighborhood boundaries (Golledge and Stimson 1987, 65). While neighborhoods are physically demonstrable, it is not easy to define a neighborhood—in advance of studying it—based on specific area or population size criteria alone. The size and shape of the physical neighborhood varies from place to place and culture to culture, depending on the location and size of settlement where the neighborhood is found, travel modes, household density, and patterns of interaction.

The neighborhood also has a social component. Local social interaction, social class, ethnic and racial origins, life-cycle characteristics of the population, length of residence, and place of work—all have been considered as factors defining neighborhoods. Level of education and social class affect the range of cues used to identify neighborhoods (Golledge and Stimson 1987, 67) and their perceived size and complexity (Orleans and Schmidt 1972).

The "imageability" of the environment is, according to Gulick (1966), more than just the recognition of physical features. It is a function of the individual's perception of the form of physical features in the landscape and the social or behavioral significance which that individual attributes to the feature. **Sense of place** refers to how people evaluate places and decide that they are distinctive based on their unique characteristics (Johnston, Gregory, and Smith 1994, 548–49). "Kilimanjaro" and "Paris" evoke a strong sense of meaning for many people, even those who have not directly experienced these places. Sense of place also develops as a deep attachment through experience and memory to the places where we have lived (Eyles 1985). In both cases,

Definition: Sense of place means assessment of a place as distinctive based on unique characteristics

objective aspects of location are combined with subjective experience, direct or indirect. Most recently, attention has been focused on how sense of place is created by intention in contemporary architecture and planning (Ley 1989). This may be accomplished by preserving the physical features of derelict structures in the rehabilitation process, but assigning a new use to the old space.

Georeferenced data on the built environment that are available in cyberspace through applications like Google Maps are becoming part of people's experience of places in contemporary life. The term *DigiPlace* refers to a hybrid of physical and virtual space (Zook and Graham 2007b). Digi-Place results from the use of data ranked in cyberspace to produce dynamic visualizations of actual locales. DigiPlace is automatically produced based on code that is privately controlled by the corporations offering search services. At the same time, the searches that produce DigiPlace are individualized, actualized by a person's search behavior. In addition to varying from person to person, DigiPlace is highly dynamic temporally, both because the indexes underlying search rankings are updated frequently and new websites and material are frequently being introduced and reconfigured. Zook and Graham note that "perceptions of restaurants in Lexington, Kentucky, or neighborhoods in Santiago, Chile, are no longer based simply on an individual's sensory experiences or cognitive map. They are also based on the geo-referenced information one chooses to look at and, more importantly, have been allowed to look at, in Google Earth" (Zook and Graham 2007a, 1341). Authority constraints affecting access to the Internet or blocking particular sites also exist in emerging technology spaces. By supporting sharing of individuals' flags or spatially referenced annotations, systems like Google allow people who have access to share their perceptions of places with others. In Figure 4.9, one can "visit" a West Hartford high school using these systems, learn more about the school, and understand the neighborhood context of the school.

Cognitive maps and geographical experiences have been explored in many populations, from children (Aitken 1994) to the elderly (Rowles 1986). As a process that develops throughout the lifespan in all humankind (Siegel 1981),

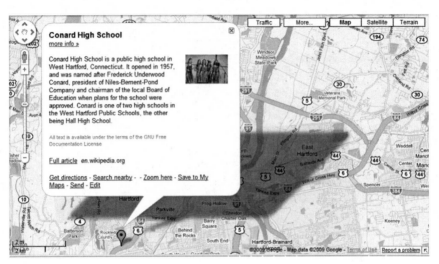

Figure 4.9   Digital experience of place through online mapping applications

cognitive mapping is potentially relevant in a wide range of ethnographic research. A full treatment of research methods for investigating how people learn about the environment, perceive it, and make locational decisions within it is not possible in this chapter. A number of sources cover these themes in greater depth (Golledge and Stimson 1987, 1997; Miller 2007).

Collecting Data on Activity Spaces

WAYS TO RECORD DATA ON ACTIVITY SPACES

- Direct observations
- Remote observations
- Diaries
- Recalled data elicited via interviews
- Games

Several techniques have been used for gathering information on people's travel and activity patterns during a specified period of time (Golledge and Stimson 1987,

155). The main data collection methods for activity analysis are observational (observations in the field conducted by the field researcher or remote observations using the Global Positioning System or GPS), the diary method (kept either by the field researcher or by the participant), or the recall method (in which researchers interview participants). Researchers also have used game-based methods, often postdiary or postinterview, to explore the impact of changes in the contingencies of a decision-making environment (Jones 1979). A researcher might, for example, ask how a person would allocate additional free time if he or she had the choice.

Technological change has affected communication in time and space, coordination of activity in time and space, and perceptions of space. It has also affected our ability to collect data on people's travel and activity patterns using the Global Positioning System, now commonly known as GPS. The **Global Positioning System** supports primary data capture of spatial data designed, built, operated and maintained by the U.S. Department of Defense (Laurini 2001). In 1978, the first operational GPS satellite was launched. By the mid-1990s, the system was fully operational. The system today has several components: twenty-seven satellites orbiting earth at an altitude of 12,500 miles, five monitoring stations, and the receivers that individuals use to determine their locations. The satellites send continuous radio signals and receive correctional data from monitoring stations. Signals are received by GPS units held at different locations on the earth. The receiver measures how long it takes the signal to travel from the satellites. By measuring the distance from three or more satellites, the location of the receiver can be obtained by triangulation.

Definition: The Global Positioning System or GPS is a system that supports primary data capture of spatial data

Until now, GPS has been the only system of its kind. Russia and India, the European Union, and China now are developing their own systems that may be fully deployed within the next decade. It is not clear what the implications for international research using spatial data will be when these alternatives become available.

STRATEGIES FOR COLLECTING ACTIVITY RECORDS

- Continuous direct or remote observation
- Continuous direct or remote observations of sampled activity units
- Direct or remote observation of a sample of subjects and times
- Subject recall
- Subject record keeping
- Personal recall interviews on activities and time spent

Data collected by these methods can be used to construct activity records of five main types (Anderson 1971, 356):

- Time budgets (describing allocation of time to activities)
- Space-time budgets (describing allocation of time to activities engaged in at specific locations)
- Longitude/latitude coordinates acquired from GPS
- Travel records (describing the temporal sequence of trips from origins to destinations, including the purposes of the trips and the modes of transportation but ignoring allocation of time to activities at the destinations)
- Contact records (describing face-to-face and person-to-person communication)

Activity records present some challenging problems for data collection and analysis (Ricci, Jerome, Megally, Galal, Harrison, and Kirksey 1995; Amadeo, Golledge, and Stimson 2009). The most important are the validity and reliability of time-space data and the cost of collecting it. Continuous direct observation (i.e., the field researcher observes and records in a diary how and when people spend their time) can yield accurate and representative information. In these "broad-focus" time use studies (Grossman 1984), all activities are observed over a sufficient time period to capture daily and other periodic variations in activity patterns.

EXAMPLE 4.2

COLLECTING DATA ON DIETARY INTAKE, ENERGY EXPENDITURE, AND PARTICIPANT LOCATION

A study of dietary intake and energy expenditure by Edmundson attempted to observe and record how and where people spent their time. Over a one-year period, four researchers continuously observed and recorded activities of fifty-four Javanese villagers almost to the minute for fourteen hours per day. This represented 324 researcher-days of continuous observation (Edmundson 1976).

If study participants are equipped with GPS devices, the locations and times of activities can be observed continuously by a remote observer, but the nature of the activities would have to be captured using one of the other methods. GPS data could be integrated with information from subject records like activity diaries. For some types of research such as research on physical activity, other devices like accelerometers can collect data on energy expenditure to provide researchers with information on whether the individual is walking, running, or engaging in some other kind of physical activity (Troped, Oliveira, Matthews, Cromley, Melly, and Craig 2008).

These methods of data collection, however, pose ethical and practical problems. The ethical issue of surveillance of individuals is discussed in the last section of this chapter. The practical problems are basically problems of cost in collecting and managing the voluminous databases that result. In the case of the West Hartford school system (see Example 4.1), prekindergarten through grade twelve school enrollment during the 2007 to 2008 school year was reported as 9,990 (Connecticut Department of Education 2008). It would be extremely expensive and impractical to observe directly or remotely all of these students throughout the school year. It probably also would be unnecessary. Valid data on school population activity patterns can be obtained by studying a sample. Spatial sampling techniques for selecting individuals to be included in travel and activity data collection efforts are reviewed in a later section of this chapter dealing with spatial sampling.

Two alternatives to broad-focus, direct, continuous observation are broad-focus time-space studies by direct observation of a sample of subjects and times (Johnson 1975) or direct continuous observation of only selected activities for a limited period during the day (Ruddle 1974; Smith 1981). The first alternative limits the number of observations as illustrated by the following example.

EXAMPLE 4.3

A BROAD-FOCUS TIME-SPACE HOUSEHOLD STUDY BY DIRECT CONTINUOUS OBSERVATION HOUSEHOLD IN PERU

In Johnson's study of time allocation in a Machiguenga community in Peru, thirteen households were selected as a sample. The sample was divided into two groups, each group observed on an alternating basis. A random numbers table was used to select days and hours for group observation in advance. During the designated observation period, the effort was made to locate and observe all individuals within the group and to record the individual's activity at the time of observation. The hours of observation were confined to daylight. Over a ten-month period, observations were made on 134 different days yielding 3,495 records for individuals in the sample households. Percentage-of-time estimates were developed by dividing the number of observations of a particular activity by the total number of observations of all activities (Johnson 1975).

The number of observations that must be made to ensure a representative sample in this type of study can be quite large, depending in part on how frequently activities occur (Bernard and Killworth 1993).

A second alternative limits the number of activities and observations. Studies that focus on specific activities can be valuable, but care must be taken in the use of this approach, particularly for comparative research. Differing viewpoints among field researchers as to which activities count as "work," "school," or "leisure" can have "negative implications for cross-cultural, cross-spatial and cross-temporal comparisons" (Carlstein 1982, 332). In West Hartford, "public elementary education" means tax-supported kindergarten through fifth grade education available to all residents of the town. In other communities in the state, elementary schools may serve a different age range of students. In other countries, public elementary education might mean something still different. In Ghana, for example, children must be six years of age before they can attend public primary school and can attend until age twelve.

In some cases, the field researcher will not be directly observing and recording activity data as the activity takes place. Instead, the subjects themselves keep records with or without the aid of devices like GPS or recall and verbally report on their activities. Adopting data collection techniques that ask individuals to keep their own activity records enables researchers to collect much more data than they could by direct continuous observation. It also avoids, if remote devices like GPS are not used, the ethical issues of surveillance and the practical problems of individuals altering their daily travel and activity patterns because they are being observed by the field researcher. However, disadvantages of the diary kept by the research subject arise when the research subjects are illiterate or otherwise incapable of recording events accurately, when the time-reckoning system used by study subjects does not match the system (hours and minutes, days, months) represented in the diary, and when records must be kept over a long period of time. People also are notoriously careless in recording daily events meticulously. The quality and completeness of the diaries has been observed to decline over time as respondents tire of record keeping—which has probably become a significant new activity in and of itself (Grossman 1984). For these reasons, respondent diaries would probably be very difficult to implement among populations such as young elementary school children in West Hartford.

A final data collection technique for individual daily activity patterns is personal or face-to-face interviewing with a questionnaire that asks respondents to recall activities and the amounts of time spent on them for one or more days prior to the time of the interview. This technique has numerous drawbacks.

- Respondents who do not have or do not usually rely on time-keeping devices have difficulty stating precisely how much time was spent on various activities.

- If the recall period is extended for weeks or months it is difficult to incorporate periodic changes or cycles in activities.
- Respondents may overestimate the amount of time spent on arduous activities while understating the amount of time spent on leisure or discretionary activities (Grossman 1984).

One review of recall studies concluded that half of what respondents report is inaccurate in some way (Bernard, Killworth, Kronfeld, and Sailor 1984).

To enhance the validity and reliability of the activity data, the researcher must understand the local context and have clearly defined research goals. The various data collection strategies can be and have been used individually and in combination to improve data quality.

Focal Sampling as an Alternative to Spot Sampling

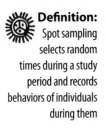

Definition: Spot sampling selects random times during a study period and records behaviors of individuals during them

Key point

Spot sampling is "the basis for time allocation studies in anthropology" (Bernard and Killworth 1993, 207). Spot sampling is most easy to implement when the number of individuals in the sample for observation during any particular time period is kept small and when the activity sites where individuals will be observed are relatively close together in space so that individuals can be located easily. *If researchers must spend time in travel to observe activities directly for a large number of individuals in a large area, it may be impossible to make the required direct observations.* "To locate and observe the activities of numerous villagers from several different households within the same hour, with people scattered over the entire 39 km^2 territory, would require a herculean effort" (Grossman 1984, 452). In highly mobile, automobile-based societies, these problems would be magnified. Although recall can be used to fill in gaps, this may bias the data, particularly those affecting by inclusion of activities that occur at remote locations and the travel effort that the individuals being studied (or researchers) must put into reaching those locations.

Even in less mobile societies, spot sampling requires researchers to understand the relevant footprint of the area within which to observe the sampled activities. Without clear understanding of the extent of daily travel zones, researchers may miss important activities that occur some distances away from the study community.

EXAMPLE 4.4

EXPOSURE TO SCHISTOSOMIASIS MEASURED USING GPS

A study of exposure to schistosomiasis in a village in Sichuan Province in China where the disease is endemic provided GPS receivers worn in vests to a sample of twelve people who gave informed consent to monitoring of their activities. The people wore the vests for eight hours during the day on two separate days. Researchers found, based on review of the spatial data, that people spent much more time than expected outside the study village, given that walking was the mode of transportation, including visiting the township square that was 3.5 kilometers away. Maps of the individuals' activity patterns produced from the GPS data also proved to be an aid in the recall of activities (Seto, Knapp, Zhong, and Yang 2007).

Spot sampling may also understate time devoted to travel as an activity itself. Time spent in travel is a key component of the Hagerstrand model because time spent in travel is time that cannot be allocated to other in-home or out-of-home activities. Studies of time use often neglect time spent in travel altogether or simply incorporate it into the time effort put into other activities (Carlstein 1982). This is a glaring problem, particularly in cross-cultural work or longitudinal research, because personal mobility varies greatly from culture to culture and over time.

EXAMPLE 4.5

MEASURING CHANGING TIME ALLOCATION PATTERNS

A study of changing time allocation patterns from 1968 to 1988 among adults eighteen to sixty-five years old in metropolitan Washington, D.C., found that time spent at home decreased eighty minutes per day during the twenty-year period. Thirty minutes of that time was accounted for by increased time at work, twenty minutes by increased time at other places, and thirty minutes by increased time spent in travel (Levinson and Kumar 1995).

While spot sampling may be valuable when the researcher is interested only in gross allocation of time to different activities and not *where* activities regularly occur, spot sampling creates problems when the researcher is interested in temporal and spatial patterns because spot sampling does not place the observed activity in its temporal and spatial context. In the case of redistricting West Hartford elementary schools, this context is important. Any redistricting that significantly alters travel time to school for children in either direction (increasing it or decreasing it) would obviously affect the amount of time that children could devote to *other* (nonschool) activities during the day and that parents needed to devote to providing care for children when they are not in school (Jones 1979). In this case, it also would be important to obtain data on before- and after-school activities. These activities would be of varying duration and might be missed under different spot sampling scenarios.

As Hagerstrand's model suggests, spot samples basically support analyses of gross allocation of time (*what* people spent time on). Because of the spatial biases that can be introduced when activities occur over large geographical areas, they are less useful than focal samples for creating valid data for activity space (*where* people spend time) analyses. **Focal sampling** involves sampling individuals, not times, and then developing relatively complete travel and activity records for a period of time. Respondents who have similar travel and activity patterns in similar locations can then be grouped.

Definition: Focal sampling samples individuals and follows them over time

The temporal span of observation and data collection is of critical importance. In the case of the West Hartford school system, elementary school students never attend classes on Saturday or Sunday. On the other days of the week, the school day begins at 8:35 a.m. and ends at 3:20 p.m., except on Wednesdays when students are dismissed at 2:00 p.m. so that teachers can engage in staff-development activities. Other exceptions to the regular pattern include holidays, summer vacation, and days when the school schedule changes because of inclement weather. Observations on any single day will obviously not capture this rich temporal variation in the schedule for the school as a

 Key point

whole, let alone variations that might affect individual students and teachers.

When an activity being observed takes place in a particular spatial domain where activity is restricted to certain times, the broad temporal parameters of activity can be determined in advance for many individuals simply by examining the rules for use of space enforced by the individual or organization that controls the domain. In the case of the West Hartford school system, these data can be obtained by purposive sampling and interviewing of school officials. In the chapter section "Defining the Study Area," the geographical problem of defining the school district boundary as representative of where students actually come from (i.e., assuming that no students have home locations outside the school district) was discussed. Analogous to this is the temporal problem of the official school day period (the official time boundary) as representative of when students actually arrive and depart from the school. The schedule rules for the system are perhaps more important for suggesting an appropriate temporal sampling scheme for data collection; they capture temporal variation in activity schedules better than describing actual travel and activity patterns of individual students. For other specific activities that are not "regulated," important aspects of the general timing and periodicity of the activities may not be easy to determine in advance of data collection, and bias may result as a consequence.

Implications of Activity Data Collection for Analysis

Much of the analysis of individual activity data is concerned only with gross allocation of time to different classes of activity. This approach masks other important dimensions of human spatial behavior, including the sequencing and duration of activity episodes in time and space and how these are affected by and affect the spatial arrangement of sites in the individual's activity space. For spatial analysis, these sequencing, duration, and arrangement patterns are key. Whenever activities occurring in sequence do not occur at the same location, some transportation time cost is incurred in switching from one activity to another

(Hensher and Stopher 1979, 12). Two women may each work eight hours per day, but if one has to be away from work and at home from noon to 1:00 p.m. to feed and care for children, she has a very different and less flexible activity pattern in time and space.

EXAMPLE 4.6

PERCEIVED CONSTRAINTS ON BREAST-FEEDING AMONG URBAN MOTHERS

One focal study of breast-feeding in a population of low-income urban mothers concluded that time constraints were not a "real" barrier to exclusive breast-feeding but might be "*perceived* [emphasis added] as time-consuming, not so much because of the *total* amount of time required, but because it is more likely to interrupt the mother's activity and thereby causing her to 'lose' time" if the activity is perceived to be incompatible with breastfeeding (Cohen, Haddix, Hurtado, and Dewey 1995).

"Interruption" is just as real a time barrier to performing certain activities as a total lack of time. In another research context, analysts observed that, while the average duration of time spent on travel increased over a twenty-year study period, the temporal and spatial patterns of travel also became more complex, with an increase in multipurpose trips and a change in the time-of-day distribution of work and nonwork trips, especially those made by car (Levinson and Kumar 1995).

When so much effort will be put into the collection of rich data on the nature, frequency, sequence, duration, and location of activities, reliance solely on analytical techniques like aggregate time allocation seems an unjustifiable, though common, practice. By contrast, time-space path data are a kind of event-history data indicating the timing of moves in a sequence (Tuma and Hannan 1984). If events may occur at any time, the process generating the event data is a continuous-time, discrete-state stochastic process. **Stochastic process models** are built using inferential statistics (Johnston, Gregory, and Smith 1994, 594–95). These models are based on the idea that the same process can produce a very large number of different outcomes. Stochastic models are different from deterministic models that can yield only one outcome for one set of inputs.

Definition: Stochastic process models are statistical models that describe sequences of outcomes in terms of their probability of happening

In an effort to explain why particular individuals engage in activities at particular locations, geographers have developed these kinds of models for spatial search and destination choice. One particular type, the Markov process model, has been used extensively to examine search and learning processes (Golledge and Brown 1967), alternative structures of time use (Kamakura 2009), and travel behavior (Hensher and Stopher 1979; Goulias 2002). These models require the researcher to define a set of possible states or conditions an individual might be in at various points in time. For example, "married," "divorced," and "single" might define a set of states. In geographical analyses, *states* generally refer to locations. Based on a matrix of probabilities of changing from one state to another state, the probability of an individual being in a particular state at a particular time can be defined. Markov models have also been used to address sampling and analysis problems of time budget data (Rugg and Buech 1990).

In studies of human travel and activity patterns, states represent the activity sites people visit during the course of their daily lives. Most households function as organizations from a single activity site—the home base—whose location is permanent or semipermanent. The home is one "state" where a person could be. Community organizations and institutions also function in space. Their operations are based at particular locations and imply flows of staff and clients. As the next section reveals, the spatial organization of their activities is an important component of communities, reflecting and influencing patterns of social interaction.

SPATIAL DIMENSIONS OF COMMUNITY INSTITUTIONS

Dimensions of Service Provision

Community organizations are locations from which people obtain services and satisfy physical, social, or economic needs. Community organizations function in time and space as much as individuals. Some organizations, like schools, operate at one or more fixed locations. These organizations are service centers that represent nodes in the activity spaces of service providers and service users.

Definition: Community organizations are locations from which people obtain services and satisfy physical, social, or economic needs

Other individuals or organizations that provide services
to people move around (the visiting nurse or physician
making a house call, the home-delivered meals service, the
postal delivery service). These services' activity patterns
can be evaluated using time budget approaches like those
described for analyzing individual travel and activity patterns. In addition to the location or set of locations where
services are provided, other dimensions of community
institutions (Alter 1988) have geographical implications.

Definition:
Size of
organization is
defined as the number
of service sites an
organization has

The relationships between total **size** of an organization or system (measured as the number of service sites
that organization has) and capacity or volume of service
are important, but not always straightforward. In the case
of the West Hartford school system, there were ten elementary schools in the academic year from 2008 to 2009 (Figure 4.10) (West Hartford Public Schools 2009). Community
organizations located in communities of similar size can
provide varying volumes of service depending upon eligi-
bility requirements and intake.

When there are threshold requirements before a facility can be opened (for example, no elementary school
should serve fewer than one hundred students) and/or
minimum standards for service delivery (for example, no
child should live more than five miles from an elementary school), the number, location, and capacities of service centers will be strongly influenced by the underlying geographical distribution of the population to be
served. In fact, depending on the distribution of children,
it may be geographically not feasible to meet both the
threshold and the minimum service standard identified
above. This would happen if there were a small residential neighborhood located more than five miles from an
existing elementary school with too few students to meet
the threshold requirement. If state law required the provision of public elementary school services to the children,
one of the requirements would have to be broken. Either
taxpayers would pay a subsidy to run the small school or
students would pay in excessive travel time to school.

Definition:
Centrality
refers to the
number of users
flowing through one
organization relative to
other organizations

Centrality is another dimension of community organizations. It refers to the total number of users flowing
through one organization relative to other organizations.

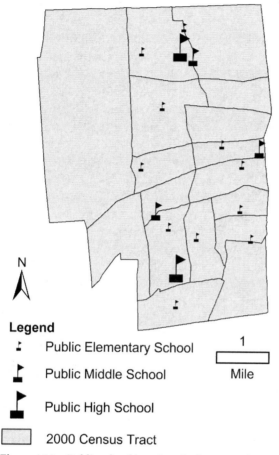

Legend

⚑   Public Elementary School

⚑   Public Middle School

⚑   Public High School

▢   2000 Census Tract

1 Mile

Figure 4.10   Public school locations in the town of West Hartford showing the hierarchy of educational services

When the total volume of users flows through a single organization, that organization has a high degree of centrality. There is a strong relationship between differentiation of activity functions and degree of centrality. The West Hartford public school system as a whole provides several different levels of educational services: elementary school education, middle school education, and secondary or high school education. The middle and high school services are more centralized than the elementary services because a higher proportion of students flow through those schools. There are ten elementary schools but only two middle schools and two high schools in the system (see Figure 4.10).

The geographical relationships among service centers with varying degrees of centrality is the focus of **central place theory** (Christaller 1933) and subsequent research on human settlement systems and public and private service systems (Foot 1981; Ghosh and Rushton 1987). When a population is uniformly distributed, those service centers with smaller threshold requirements will be more common in the landscape and spaced relatively close together, as the elementary schools in West Hartford are. Those activity sites with larger threshold requirements will be less common in the landscape and spaced relatively far apart. The service areas of small activity sites are sometimes nested in the service areas of larger activity sites.

Integration refers to the linkages or interdependencies among units with a system. A **forward linkage** is a linkage to a supplier of a service. In the school system, the linkage from an elementary school to a middle school is a forward linkage. The linkage from a high school to a middle school would be a backward linkage. In the case of a public school system in the United States, alternative pathways through the service hierarchy generally do not exist. Students from a particular neighborhood are assigned to a particular elementary school and will move on to a particular middle school and a particular high school. For other systems of community organizations, alternative pathways may exist.

Definition: Central place theory explains the size and spacing of service centers

Definition: Integration is the interdependency among units in a system

Definition: A forward linkage is a linkage to a supplier of a service

Collecting Data on Community Organizations

The activity sites where people travel to obtain some good or service or to satisfy some physical, social, or economic need can be thought of, loosely, as community organizations. A major difficulty in studying how people relate to these organizations is that there are wide variations from culture to culture and from time to time in how these organizations are governed and function. A human service that might be provided under central government auspices in one place could be provided by a local unit of government in another and may be left to the market in still another. In countries like the United States, there have been important shifts in responsibility between the public and private sectors over time (Fuchs 1996). Numerous typologies of human service and community organizations have been developed within the social work and public administration literature (Gans and Horton 1975; Rabin and Steinhauer 1988).

These distinctions are important because they affect the availability of data on community organizations that are critical to evaluating access or power to use. Penchansky and Thomas (1981) identify five dimensions of access: availability, accessibility, affordability, accommodation, and acceptability.

- *Availability*—the relationship of volume and type of activity to volume and type of community need
- *Accessibility*—the relationship between the location of supply and the location of users taking into account the factors that affect human travel behavior
- *Affordability*—the relationship between the cost of obtaining the service once the user is onsite and the user ability to pay
- *Accommodation*—the relationship between the manner in which the supply resources are organized to accept users (hours of operation, telephone communication, and so on) and the users' perceptions of and abilities to adapt to these patterns
- *Acceptability*—the relationship between users' attitudes about characteristics of providers and providers' attitudes about users

Information to evaluate the accessibility of the locations of community organizations' offices or service centers usually is relatively easy to obtain from published directories or other archival sources, from government agencies if the service is publicly provided, or from direct observation and knowledge of the study area. The nature of the organization more seriously affects availability of data on the capacities of service providers, the nature of the service provided, utilization, and service users within the community. Organizations may not want to collect some forms of information or, if collected, may not allow it to be used.

When the provider is a government agency, there often are legally mandated reporting requirements, and these reports may constitute a useful data archive for the ethnographer. In the case of the West Hartford School System, for example, the school system provides information on its website, and the Connecticut Department of Education publishes online school district profiles and an education directory on an annual basis. These publications give locations of schools, enrollments, names and contact information for school officials, and financial or operating expense data, like the per-pupil expenditure and property tax base in the town.

Researchers working in the United States operate in a country with relatively strong requirements regarding freedom of information access and reporting. Federal government documents are not copyright protected in the United States. There is a federal depository institution program to disseminate data on government organizations to libraries around the United States, and these data are often available in multiple formats (print and digital). In other countries of the world, access to government data is much more likely to be restricted.

When the organizations are private, data availability may be even more restricted. Private organizations release some information in an effort to disseminate information about themselves and to market their services. However, organizations that compete for users will not wish to reveal their data on the fundamental aspects of their organizations (staffing, pricing, and so on). A consortium of private schools might publish a directory of private schools in Connecticut, but participation in these kinds of reporting is usually voluntary.

Even when organizations are willing to make data available about the organization, the locations of its service centers, and its operations, data on the individuals served by the organization may not be accessible. For example, the researcher may be interested in obtaining information on individual students in a school by interviewing them or obtaining information from their school records. This means that the research involves human subjects. Ethical constraints on access to information from human subjects served by various kinds of community organizations are enforced by Institutional Review Boards (IRBs).

Record keeping by organizations has been influenced in many countries by the development of computer-based management information systems. Laws affecting disclosure of information by organizations will, as noted, vary from country to country (Rule 2007). An important concept related to record-keeping law is confidentiality (Rabin and Steinhauer 1988, 396–401). Confidentiality laws are intended to protect relationships between service providers and service users, not to shield wrongdoing by organizations or individual providers.

Cross Reference: The role of IRBs is discussed in detail in Book 1 and in Book 6 of the *Ethnographer's Toolkit*

In the United States, interestingly, common law did not provide a privilege against disclosure of private communications because this privilege would inhibit the court's ability to reveal the whole truth through the adversarial process (Brakel, Parry, and Weiner 1985). Even illness was at one time considered publicly knowable and disclosable. With attorney-client privilege as the precedent, however, legislative bodies began to authorize a confidentiality privilege for other types of relationships, including those affecting medical service providers and patients, balancing judicial access against privacy. In the United States, many social service providers do not enjoy privileged communication with their clients, and certain kinds of information (for example, information on child abuse) are not privileged.

Disclosure laws also take into account affirmative record-keeping requirements. Without records, it is very difficult to document the delivery and review the quality of service provided. Thus, data will almost always be collected for individuals or individual contacts to meet affirmative record-keeping requirements, but it will almost always be reported in aggregates to avoid disclosure of confidential information. This has particular implications for geographic research.

Setting aside the institutional barriers to obtaining data on dimensions of community organization, services are notoriously hard to measure. It is often difficult to describe exactly the unit of service provided by a particular organization. For example, can we best measure educational service by the time the teacher spends with each student or by the tasks in which the teachers and students engage? Do we evaluate services in terms of the money spent on service units, or in terms of what clients actually achieve or gain from receiving the services?

Quality of service is even more difficult to measure. This is usually accomplished by measurement of outcomes. Here, too, it is not always clear what the most valid outcome is for assessing quality. In the case of the school system, is it the number of children who pass state mastery tests? Would it be the number of children who complete the educational program? These issues raise some important implications for the analysis of data collected on community organizations.

Although some archival data on community organizations' locations and operations may be available to the ethnographer, high-quality data on how organizations currently function will almost always need to be collected from or verified by directors and staff of the organizations. Key informant interviews and observations will be an important part of the data collection process (Bernard 2006, 196–200). These ethnographic data collection techniques balance, supplement, and may replace the archival and other forms of data collection mentioned above.

Cross Reference: Books 1 and 3 also discuss key informant interviews

Analysis of Data Collected on Community Organizations

The spatial analysis of community organizations usually relies on modeling the organization as a network (see Figure 4.10), including a set of nodes identifying the headquarters of the organization and the places where services are delivered and a set of links representing the possible pathways connecting or linking the nodes in geographic space. An important motivation for modeling the organization in this way is to explore potential opportunities for improving access to the organization and its operation efficiency.

In geography and regional science, this analysis has generally been accomplished by the application of

normative modeling techniques. These techniques determine the maximum or minimum of a function. Unlike positive models relying on multivariate statistical methods to describe and analyze what is or was, normative models are concerned with what ought to be; they rely on mathematical programming methods. In particular, mathematical programming models are useful in attempts to maximize or minimize some function like total transportation cost of obtaining services given a set of constraints (Foot 1981). For example, instead of describing the actual route a school bus takes to collect and take students to school, normative models determine the optimal route. This would involve specifying an objective function like distance traveled and finding the minimum value of the function subject to a set of constraints, like the constraint that every student on the route must be picked up. If a researcher were evaluating the locational efficiency of a system of ten schools, the *p*-median problem might be used to determine which candidate locations for schools should be selected to minimize the aggregate distance traveled from all households sending children to school. The *p*-median problem is a widely used normative model that minimizes total travel from a set of origins to a set of destinations (Ghosh and Rushton 1987). Although many early models specified single objectives, multiobjective mathematical program models have been developed (Malczewski and Ogryczak 1995, 1996). Mathematical programming models are widely used in operations research. Geographers and regional scientists use these models in locational analysis, but most social scientists receive much less training in mathematical programming as a method of quantitative analysis than in multivariate statistical techniques.

There has been vigorous debate about the role of location theory in planning services, particularly in non-Western countries where the sociospatial circumstances are often very different (Rushton 1984, 1988). Location-allocation models developed for the United States, for example, where there are high levels of personal mobility and a dense street network, might not be appropriate for a country like Ghana where travel is difficult and roads, especially in rural areas, are absent and private transportation is rare (Oppong 1996).

Definition: Normative modeling techniques determine what should be the maximum or minimum of an organization's function

The occurrence of a rainy season, which makes some road segments impassable during certain times of the year, means that any modeling effort based on the functioning of the transportation system during the dry season might produce disastrous results. Despite the limitations of single-objective mathematical programming models, normative modeling can provide some quantitative benchmarks for evaluating service delivery systems and exploring temporal and spatial constraints in service delivery.

Increasingly, the "solution space" for location problems like siting, districting, and routing is being explored through **spatial decision support systems (SDSS)**. These computer-based systems provide decision makers with a tool for solving poorly or semistructured problems. Very often members of a community will express a variety of desires for service availability, including minimizing the cost of providing services while guaranteeing that everyone has a reasonable travel time to the service site. Through SDSS, it is possible to explore the trade-offs among various desires.

Definition: Spatial decision support systems are computer-based systems that provide a tool for solving loosely defined problems

In a study of educational service districts in Iowa, for example, the planning group learned through modeling the problem with an SDSS that it was not feasible to attain a threshold of forty thousand students within a service distance of one hundred kilometers for each service center because of the underlying geographical distribution of student population in the state (Honey, Rushton, Lolonis, Dalziel, Armstrong, De, and Densham 1991). The SDSS in this case produced maps of various service arrangements in addition to tables and other types of output.

One important implication of data collection issues for this type of geographical analysis of community organizations is that data must often be collected from numerous sources, even for a study in a relatively small target area involving few organizations (Foot 1981, 17–19). This increases the probability that the data will refer to different time periods, be reported for different aggregate spatial units, and be based on different operational definitions of variables. These inconsistencies in data are problematic. If data on the number of teachers were reported for the year 2000 but data on the numbers of students were reported for 2005, we could not develop an accurate teacher/student ratio for 2005. However, several techniques are available for converting a set of data from one system of spatial units to another and for protecting confidentiality in dealing with spatially referenced data.

Areal interpolation refers to a set of techniques to estimate the distribution of a phenomenon across one set of spatial units (the source units) in terms of a second set of spatial units (the target units). A common approach to areal interpolation is the area-weighting method, relying on the concept of map overlay (Lam 1983). In this approach, a variable like "total population for a census tract" is weighted by the proportion of the census tract's area that lies in the target unit. The resulting number of people is then assigned to the target unit as part of that unit's population (Figure 4.11).

Definition: Areal interpolation involves using techniques to estimate the distribution of a variable across one set of spatial units in terms of a second set

The areal interpolation can be enhanced by incorporating ancillary data (Flowerdew and Green 1989). For example, if we know that no one actually lives in a certain part of the census tract based on the distribution of streets or houses, we can derive a better estimate of the population residing in the area of overlap between the two sets of spatial units (Figure 4.12).

Mapping data poses particular confidentiality problems. For example, revealing that a particular individual was a female between the ages of twenty and twenty-four would probably not be sufficient information to reveal the identity of that person within a community. However, mapping the home location of a person will almost always be sufficient to identify a small group of individuals or, in some cases, a single individual.

Research has demonstrated that, even when there is little detail and the resolution of the published map image is low, the point locations can be reengineered or reverse geocoded to reveal the address (Brownstein, Cassa, and Mandl 2006; Curtis, Mills, and Leitner 2006). In addition, software utilities available for free download from the Internet make it easy for people who do not have computer mapping software to convert a table of addresses to lon/lat (longitude/latitude) coordinates and to map these online, or to take a digital database in shapefile format

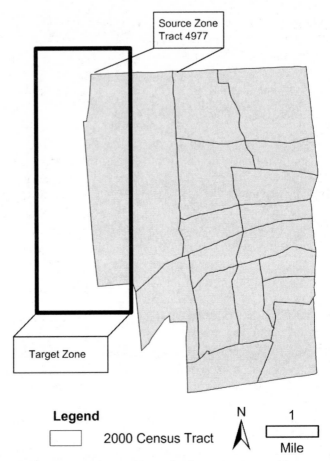

Figure 4.11   Without additional information, we would estimate that about half of the total population of Census Tract 4977 lives in the target zone because about half of Tract 4977's area lies within the target zone.

and convert it to Keyhole Markup Language, the language used to map features in applications like Google Maps.

The spatial analysis generally can be conducted based on locations of individuals encoded in a database without actually mapping those locations. There are a number of strategies that researchers can use to prevent the disclosure of confidential data by mapping it. Data can be aggregated to larger spatial units before mapping. Research using data from the 2001 Canadian census studied the relationship between geographic area population size and uniqueness

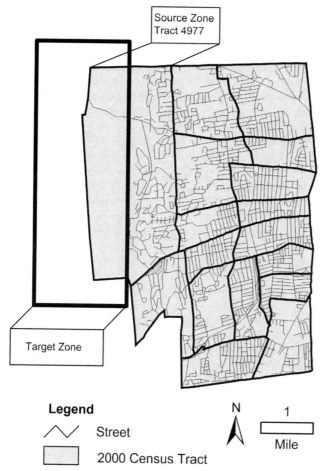

Figure 4.12   Ancillary street network data show that not many people live in the target zone, and the area-weighting method of areal interpolation would probably overestimate the number of people in the target zone.

for common demographic variables (Khaled, Brown, and AbdelMalik 2009). Analysts were able to estimate the minimum population size at which a geographic area's population is sufficiently large so that no further data aggregation is necessary to present the data without suppressing values reported for areas.

It is possible to develop "geographical masks" that preserve the security of individual data points while retaining enough location information to make it possible to answer questions that can only be answered with some knowledge of the disaggregated geography. Both the validity of these masks and their relative security have been examined (Zimmerman and Pavlik 2008; Cassa, Wieland, and Mandl 2008). *To describe and report locational patterns to protect confidentiality, point locations like the locations of individual houses can be randomly offset before they are mapped or data can be aggregated to a set of areas (census blocks, towns) that are relevant to the research question.*

Key point

When researchers are obtaining informed consent from study participants for research involving collection of individual spatial data, it is important that the risks of disclosure from mapping these data be described. The specific procedures for protecting participants from these risks should also be explained.

SPATIAL SAMPLING

Community research that requires collecting data on how individuals and organizations function in a particular environment or how they perceive a particular environment usually entails sampling because it is too difficult and costly to observe an entire population. In geographic terms, there are two main types of sampling: sampling *of* space and sampling *in* space (Goodchild 1984). **Sampling of space** draws samples from all possible places in the study area (Goodchild 1984, 47). It is most appropriate when the variable being studied is continuous or observable everywhere over the earth's surface. Variables like elevation or land cover or precipitation that can be measured at any point on the land surface are usually measured by sampling in this way, at a set of designated control points, because the set of all places where these variables could be measured is infinite. When the control points are laid out in a regular grid, the sampling is systematic rather than random and the sample will be unbiased unless the variable being measured has marked periodic properties.

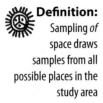 **Definition:** Sampling *of* space draws samples from all possible places in the study area

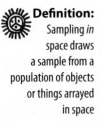 **Definition:** Sampling *in* space draws a sample from a population of objects or things arrayed in space

Sampling in space draws a sample from a population of discrete objects of things arrayed in space. It involves drawing a sample from a population of discrete objects (like people, housing units, or neighborhoods) that are themselves distributed across the earth's surface. Sampling in space is a variant of the general sampling problem involved in selecting a sample from a population of discrete objects without regard to location. The concepts of random, systematic, and stratified sampling can be evaluated for the case of sampling in space. A random sample of villagers will not be a random sample of all villagers in a settlement (the location in which they live) unless the villagers happen to be uniformly distributed within it. Placing a grid over a map and obtaining one case from each grid will yield a random sample of the set of all *places* but it will probably not yield a random sample of the set of all *villagers*. Instead, we would want to take a spatially stratified, random, or systematic sample of all villagers. Unfortunately for most community-based research, while the sampling frame for all places in the community is easy to determine from a map, the sampling frame of all villagers or households is more difficult to develop, and some type of cluster sampling strategy is often necessary.

Cross Reference: Books 1 and 3 discuss sampling

⬤━⬤━⬤ **EXAMPLE 4.7**

USING CLUSTER SAMPLING TO STUDY SCHOOL CHILDREN

In the case of the West Hartford school district, it would be difficult to obtain a list of all school-aged children in the town of West Hartford (some of whom would not attend public school anyway), but it would be possible to perform cluster sampling by obtaining a list of all enrolled students from each school. A random or systematic sample could then be taken of the list provided by each school. If a neighborhood sent only a few children to school, however, it is likely that children from that neighborhood would not be adequately represented in the sample. In this instance, where the redistricting impacts would be variable by neighborhood yet of equal concern for every child regardless of the neighborhood where the child resided, we would need to take a spatially stratified random or systematic sample of each neighborhood in the town to ensure a representative sample.

Because human beings are not uniformly distributed across the surface of the earth and because they organize themselves into households and communities with different social and economic characteristics, a sample of individu-

Key point als from a population is implicitly a spatial sample. ***Despite the elaborate sampling schemes developed to produce representative samples, too little attention is explicitly paid to spatial sampling.*** Given the high degree of residential segregation by class and race in many communities in the United States, any population sample by race is a spatial sample as well because some racial groups live only in certain neighborhoods. If we see a correlation between race and low birth weight, for example, how can we be certain that race is not simply a surrogate measure for living in a particular part of town and being subjected to all of the environmental contaminants present there? Spatial methods can help us to understand these configurations.

Key point *Meaningful community-based research requires us to have an understanding of where individuals are located in the community and what parts of the community environment they use so that we can develop appropriate sampling schemes even when the ultimate object of the research is not spatial analysis* **per se.** A map can be a most useful tool for modeling the locations of individuals and organizations within a community.

MAPPING SPATIAL DATA

Maps as Models

Maps are models of the earth's surface. As models, maps are generalized representations of reality. Sophisticated map users realize that maps distort reality by simplifying the phenomena occurring on the complex, three-dimensional surface of the earth for representation on a flat sheet of paper or video screen. The "cartographic paradox" is that "to present a useful and truthful picture, an accurate map must tell white lies" (Monmonier 1996, 1). Scale, projection, and symbols are the three basic attributes of maps, and each is a source of distortion.

Definition: **Map scale** is the ratio of the map model to reality. Map scale is It tells the user how much smaller the model is than the the ratio of the reality it represents. Map scale can be stated as a ratio, as a map model to reality phrase, or as a simple bar graph. Ratio scales are particularly useful for map comparison (Figure 4.13). A 1:5,000

Ratio   1:24,000

Phrase   1 inch = 2,000 feet   **Figure 4.13**   Different methods
                                                        for representing map scale

Bar Graph

map is a large-scale map (a map of a relatively small area showing high detail); a 1:1,000,000 is a small-scale map (a map of a large area showing limited detail). Graphic scales are particularly useful ways of representing scales on paper and digital maps because the scale will remain useful even if the map is enlarged or reduced during reproduction.

Scale is an important component of maps because scale affects the detail that can be represented. At the map scale in Figure 4.10, for example, the locations of the schools in West Hartford can be represented. If the map had been drawn at a smaller scale, for example, a scale sufficient to depict the state of Connecticut on the page, the schools' locations could not be shown clearly. Most ethnographic research would involve the use of relatively large-scale maps of communities or settlements.

Projection, a second basic component of maps, is the mathematical function that transforms locations from the curved, three-dimensional surface of the earth to a flat, two-dimensional representation (Pearson 1990). This process can distort map scale significantly. Although scale can be constant at all points and in all directions on a globe as a true scale model of the earth, scale varies from point to point and with direction from a point on a paper map because flat maps stretch some distances and shrink others. Choice of map projection affects other spatial relationships represented in a map, including direction and sizes and shapes of areas (Figure 4.14).

Definition: Projection transforms the curved earth surface into flat representation

Map projection is probably a more serious issue for users of small-scale maps and projected digital spatial databases. Paper maps of small areas, the kinds of maps many ethnographers would likely use, would not be as seriously affected by choice of map projection as maps of the world or continental land masses prepared using different map projections. Nevertheless, map projections have certainly

Geographic Coordinates (Lon/Lat)

Projected Data
(Connecticut State Plane Coordinate System NAD83)

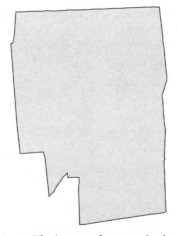

Figure 4.14   The impact of map projection is demonstrated by displaying the view of the unprojected boundary of West Hartford in geographic coordinates (longitude/latitude) and the view of the projected boundary of the town using the Connecticut State Plane Coordinate System NAD83.

influenced cultural perceptions of size, shape, and orientation of land surfaces (Monmonier 1996, 97–99).

Symbols are used to represent objects on the earth's surface as points, lines, and areas. Topographic maps are used to depict the surface configuration. They indicate changes in elevation and the locations of objects like surface water features, roads, and structures. These maps are

Definition: Symbols are used to represent objects on the earth's surface as points, lines, and areas

useful for wayfinding and locating places. Topographic map coverage is available for most countries of the world at scales generally ranging from 1:24,000 to 1:100,000. Maps of this type often rely on standardized symbologies.

Another common type of map developed over the last two centuries is the statistical map. These maps are a kind of statistical graphic intended to show the distribution of a variable in geographical space (Tufte 1983). Most statistical maps rely on a single type of symbol like a dot to represent population (Figure 4.15).

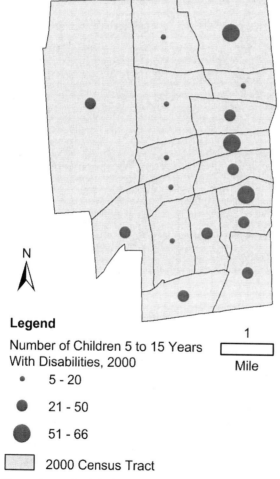

Figure 4.15 Statistical map using graduated circles to depict the distribution of students requiring special education services by census tract

Monmonier (1996, 20) identifies six dimensions of visual variability of map symbols: size, shape, value, texture, orientation, and hue. These aspects of symbolization can be and are manipulated to achieve certain objectives in cartographic communication. Standard cartography texts provide useful guidelines for map compilation and design (Slocum, McMaster, Kessler, and Howard 2009), and one body of cartographic research evaluates the impact of different symbolizations on the perceptions of map users (MacEachern 1994).

Geographic Information Systems

Cartography and spatial database management have been profoundly influenced by the development of computers (Dobson 1983). Computer-assisted cartography enables a separation of the data storage and data display functions that are completely integrated in the paper map. This makes it possible to produce many different kinds of displays from the same databases relatively quickly. Computer cartography also made it possible to separate the geographic data (the locations of points, lines, and areas) from the thematic data (the attributes of the points, lines, and areas). If we have a database of census tract areas, for example, stored separately from a database of census tract populations, we can change the population without having to reproduce the entire map by hand. Computer cartography has also made it possible to produce displays like three-dimensional maps that are often extremely difficult to produce by hand.

Over the last several decades, advances in computer hardware, graphics software, and database management systems have come together in geographic information systems. **Geographic information systems (GIS)** (Longley, Goodchild, Maguire, and Rhind 2001; Chang 2010) use computer software that supports three main functions: spatial database management, visualization and mapping, and spatial analysis. As a result, GIS software systems are more powerful than computer graphics or mapping software. GIS can provide the multiple views of data—tabular, graphic, and statistical—described in Figure 4.1.

Definition: Geographic information systems (GIS) are computer-based systems for analyzing and integrating geographic data

In response to this technology, the government agencies traditionally responsible for map production in the United States and other countries have created digital spatial databases containing the same kinds of information found on topographic maps. Many of these databases are available via the Internet, and commercial vendors have entered the market to upgrade and customize databases to meet particular user needs. In fact, GIS technology is now being used to produce and manage most of the spatial data compiled by government agencies at all levels in the United States and internationally.

"Map" information is increasingly being delivered in the form of a digital database rather than a paper map, through a variety of means including online and mobile applications (Peng and Tsou 2003). This enables a high level of mapmaking both in the research laboratory and in the field.

Maps and spatial databases can be incorporated into many phases of ethnographic research. Prior to fieldwork, maps may be used for examining a study area or selection of a sample. During research, maps may be used for wayfinding and data collection. Finally, maps can provide a method for analysis in addition to spatial statistical analysis and are useful for reporting the results of community-based research. The primary requirement for mapping or spatial database development is that objects of interest can be located on the earth's surface.

Operationalizing Location

Spatial analysis requires us to describe the locations of the people and organizations we are studying. Location means position in space. When we think about the earth's surface as a geographic space, there are two fundamental approaches to modeling it. On the one hand, we can subdivide the surface into a set of conformal equal-area units, units of the same size and shape, called a regular tesselation. We can then assign attributes to these locations (land cover, soil type, and so on) (Figure 4.16). This model of space, the **field model**, helps us to represent "what is everywhere" (Worboys and Duckham 2004, 138). Very often, the kinds

Definition: 🌀
The field model identifies units of space and assigns attributes to them

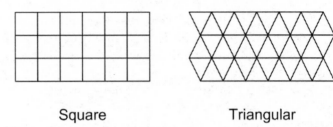

Square   Triangular

Figure 4.16   Regular tessellations associated with the field model of space

Definition:
The object model identifies objects of interest and assigns them to a space

Key point

Definition:
Geocoding involves giving an entity of the earth's surface a spatial designation or label

of features modeled in this way represent features that are continuously distributed across the earth's surface. On the other hand, we can identify objects of interest (people, farms, schools) and position these objects in an otherwise empty space (Figure 4.17). This model of space, the **object model**, helps us to represent "where everything is." This model is useful when the features modeled are discrete. *The units of analysis in most ethnographic research will be discrete from a geographic point of view.*

Geocoding is "the process by which an entity on the earth's surface, a household, for example, is given a label identifying its location with respect to some common point or frame of reference" (Goodchild 1984, 33). There are two main approaches to describing the position of an object in space. *Absolute location* describes the position of an object with respect to an arbitrary grid system like latitude/longitude, *state plane coordinates,* or a coordinate system devised by the researcher. The state plane coordinate system in

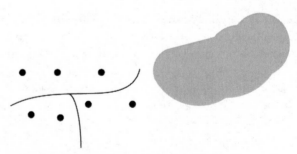

Figure 4.17   Points (cabins), lines (trails), and areas (surface of a lake) associated with the object model of space

the United States is a coordinate system based on zones drawn state by state on transverse Mercator or Lambert conformal projections (Pearson 1990). The absolute location states the position of a point in such terms that the point's unique position with respect to all other points on the earth is clear. "West Hartford town center is 41.45 north and 72.45 west" is a statement of absolute location. *Relative location* describes the position of an object with respect to other objects in the geographic space. "West Hartford is the town immediately west of Hartford" and "West Hartford is a sixty-minute drive from New York City" are statements of relative location.

In conducting research on travel and activity patterns, the ethnographer can make lists of places where respondents live and engage in other activities (Tom's house, 20 Beverly Road, Whiting Lane School). As noted, these lists or tables do not generally preserve or reveal the spatial arrangements of activity sites. In order to map the activity sites, there must be some way to convert "Tom's house" to its location on the earth's surface.

Absolute location can be measured directly from the earth's surface by surveying (Moffitt and Bossler 1998). With the development of satellite technology, we can now use global positioning systems (GPS) to ascertain absolute locations on the earth's surface (Van Sickle 2001). Latitude/ longitude geocodes that have been determined for particular places are also sometimes published in gazetteers or other archival sources (see, for example, Abate 1991).

More commonly, absolute location is estimated from an existing model of space that has been created at a particular scale. For example, we could estimate the latitude/ longitude location of a school by taking it off an appropriately annotated topographic map. We could also estimate the latitude/longitude of a school by using a GIS to address-match geocode to an address against a digital, address-ranged street network (Rushton et al. 2008).

Digital images are also available to aid location. Digital orthophotos are photos of portions of the earth's surface taken from satellite images. These images are available at scales that enable identification of landscape features such as buildings and roads (Figure 4.18).

Figure 4.18 Portion of a digital orthophotoquad featuring a residential neighborhood in West Hartford

Because GIS enables integration of spatial databases from different sources compiled at different scales, intelligent users of spatial data need to be sensitive to the issue of error in spatial databases (Goodchild and Gopal 1989). As the discussion on maps indicates, spatial data are inherently inaccurate. Even a location estimated using GPS may be accurate within several meters at best. The error issue is complicated by digital processing of spatial data. The precision with which computer mapping and GIS software can calculate distances, areas, and other spatial attributes is much greater than the underlying accuracy of the location measurement. As spatial databases are combined within GIS to create new databases, error propagates through the stages of the analysis.

Depending upon the research application, absolute map accuracy may not be paramount. Instead, it may be important to capture only accurate *relative* locations of activity sites within the study area. Regardless, researchers should be aware of the level of error present within the spatial databases used in the research project and select analytical procedures that are tolerant of that level of error.

Most ethnographic research brings the researcher into the community. As a consequence, there will be an opportunity for direct observation of the environment and assessment of error in available spatial databases. Large-scale map and digital database coverage varies widely from place to place, and few large-scale maps may be available for the study area of interest. An appendix provides a brief summary of sources of maps and digital spatial data. For those communities for which no appropriate cartographic base is available, researchers can develop their own cartographic representations.

Mapping Home Locations and Activity Sites

In the same way that anthropologists and other social scientists have examined gross time allocation, geographers have mapped the allocation of individuals to space. We are familiar with many of these maps yet rarely think of them in terms of the time-space patterns of individuals that underlay them. It is relatively easy to map the activity space (show the locations) for a single individual, even over a long period of time. However, displaying the activity spaces (showing the multiple locations) (Figure 4.19) of many individuals often results in a map that is illegible (Figure 4.20).

A common response to this problem is to limit the number of activity sites that are represented for each individual and to aggregate the sites spatially. The most obvious example is the map of population distribution based on residential location, the home location having been selected by virtue of its importance as a node in the individual's activity space. Although time and space can both be measured continuously, time allocation studies often convert a continuous variable such as time into discrete units of a variable by observing activities at particular time intervals. A number of approaches have been taken to mapping aggregated population data: the dot density map, the graduated circle map, and the **choropleth map** (Figure 4.21).

Definition: A choropleth map displays numerical data for areas by shading the areas to represent classes of the numerical data

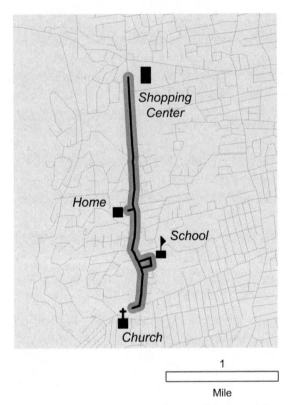

Figure 4.19 GIS network analysis models the activity space for a single child showing the home base; other activity sites, including school, church, and a shopping center; and travel routes.

Location can also be measured continuously, as when analysts assign a longitude/latitude geocode to an individual engaged in a particular activity. Until the introduction of computer-assisted cartography, it was very difficult to compile a map that stored and displayed the locations of many individuals in continuous space at a reasonable scale. The two main analytical approaches to representing this complexity have been grid cell techniques (often used with associated travel vectors) and centrographic techniques like the mean center, standard distance, and standard deviational ellipse (Ebdon 1977; O'Sullivan and Unwin 2003).

Taking a different approach, some activity maps simplify by examining the relationships between home loca-

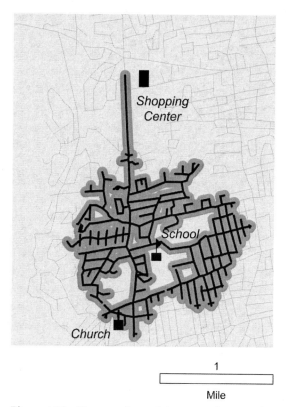

Figure 4.20 Representing activity spaces for several children produces a map that is difficult to interpret for individual children.

tion and other destinations where only one kind of activity (work, school, shopping, receiving medical care) takes place (Figure 4.22). Beyond this, representation of the activity space becomes more difficult. Some analysts have identified a set of locations or divided space into a set of geographic "intervals" or areas (by superimposing a grid) and then measured the number of times individuals are found at those points or in those intervals. This approach is useful when the analyst wishes to evaluate how many people will be affected by changes in the local environment, not because the place that is being changed is where they live, but because the place is a place they visit regularly in their travel and activity patterns (Stutz 1976).

Dot Density Map

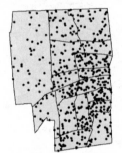

Number of Children 5 – 18 Years

1 Dot = 20 Children

Graduated Symbol Map

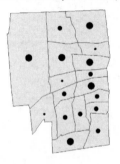

Number of Children 5 – 18 Years

·   291 - 385

•   386 - 657

⬤   658 - 903

Choropleth Map

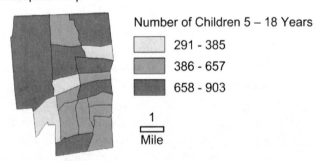

Number of Children 5 – 18 Years

291 - 385

386 - 657

658 - 903

1
☐
Mile

Figure 4.21   Representing the same population data using dot density, graduate symbol, and choropleth maps

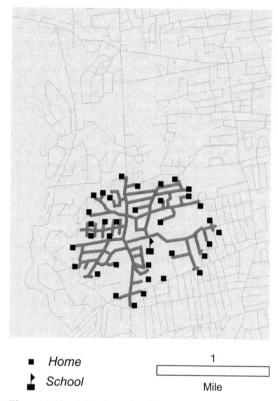

■ Home

‖ School

1

Mile

Figure 4.22 Mapping trips from many origins to a single activity site—the journey to school

Map Comparison

Travel and activity patterns are often analyzed for groups of individuals defined beforehand by one or more characteristics like age and sex or neighborhood of residence. For example, time allocation patterns for women and men are often compared. An alternative approach to analyzing individual travel and activity patterns enables researchers to group individuals based on similarity of travel and activity patterns.

One approach to this problem would be to prepare maps of individual activity spaces and attempt an assessment of similarity by visual comparison. Visual map comparison, a basic and often effective research method, is facilitated by a GIS, which makes cartographic overlay of maps very easy—provided that the maps can be depicted at the same scale using the same projection and the same origin. The most important drawback to this approach is that not everyone will perceive the same degree of areal association among the distributions being compared.

Some numerical measures are available for evaluating similarities of geographical distributions. In its earliest application, one similarity measure that can be modified for this purpose was used to track the behavior of individual animals in migrating herds (Cole 1949; Lehner 1979). The similarity measure was later adapted to analyze activity spaces of elderly residents of Flint, Michigan, who recalled destinations regularly visited for work, shopping, recreation, medical care, and other activities (Cromley and Shannon 1986). This similarity measure compared the total number of times two individuals were observed in the same place to the total number of times both individuals were observed. It is possible to extend this model to compare the total number of times two individuals are observed at the same place, at the same time, engaging in the same activity to the total number of times both individuals are observed.

$$I_{ab} = 2ab/(a + b)$$

where I_{ab} = index of similarity value for individuals A and B.

ab = total number of observations for which individuals A and B are in the same place at the same time engaged in the same activity.

a = total number of observations of person A.

b = total number of observations of person B.

The value of the index varies linearly from 0.0 (no correspondence in activity patterns) to 1.0 (perfect correspondence of activity patterns in time and space) when a and b are constant as the number of matching activities increases. High index values identify respondent pairs with similar activity patterns; low index values identify respondent pairs with different activity patterns. If home location is included as an activity site, perfect correspondence can only be achieved for the activities spaces of individuals who share a home location. It is possible to adapt the similarity measure for different research purposes by dropping home location as an observation point, for example, to identify people whose activity spaces are the same when they are not at home.

This measure can be used based on place alone, without involving maps. That is, we can develop similarity measures based on reported names of places or street addresses even if the latitude/longitude locations of those places were not known. We could not, however, develop cartographic representations of the individual and shared activity spaces without being able to locate the activity sites on a model of the earth's surface.

When we have mapped the locations where people spend time, either as points or areas, numerical measures of map correspondence can be applied. Minnick's (1964) coefficient of areal correspondence (or C_a) is similar to the measure described above and is calculated using the formula below:

$$C_a = \frac{\text{places or areas over which phenomena are located together}}{\text{total places or area covered by both phenomena}}$$

Once groups of respondents who have similar travel and activity patterns have been identified, it is relatively easy to map the set of locations they visit in common. It is also possible to analyze other attributes of groups of individuals who share common activity spaces. The researcher can identify, for example, activity patterns only associated with particular age, sex, ethnic, or residential neighborhood groups and activity patterns not associated with other characteristics of group members.

These geographical dimensions of activity space similarity/dissimilarity can be meaningfully explored by multidimensional scaling. ***Multidimensional scaling is a procedure that assigns numbers to various quantities of attributes of the phenomena being scaled such that the numbers directly reflect variations in the quantities of the attributes among the phenomena being scaled*** (Golledge and Rushton 1972). Objects (in this case the activity spaces being scaled) are likely to vary with respect to the number of activity locations, dispersion of activity locations, and

Key point

other attributes. These attributes form a multidimensional series, and the scaling procedure is designed to identify a number of relevant dimensions of the activity spaces. The quantity of each attribute associated with a given object can then be interpreted as a coordinate that, when used in conjunction with the coordinates of other attributes, determines the location of each object in the multidimensional attribute space. Greater degrees of similarity in the original data result in smaller distances in the attribute space, and lesser degrees of similarity are associated with greater distances in the attribute space.

The chief input required for multidimensional scaling is a set of proximity measures such as measures of similarity or dissimilarity that may be metric or nonmetric (Kruskal, Young, and Seery 1976). A proximity matrix is created by listing every unit of observation as a row and as a column of the matrix and then recording the similarity of every observation with every other observation in the cells of the matrix. The aim of multidimensional scaling is to take the proximity matrix and convert the measured dissimilarities into explicit distances along a set of dimensions identified by the scaling procedure. *In effect, multidimensional scaling enables a remapping of space.* In using multidimensional scaling to explore similarities and differences in individuals' activity spaces, we can group individuals into new "neighborhoods" based not solely on residential location but on their total use of the environment. Multidimensional scaling has also been used to evaluate dimensions in individuals' mental maps of their living environments (Golledge, Rivizzigno, and Spector 1976).

The various data collection and analytical approaches described in the preceding sections involve spatially referenced data. As such, the data and output of the analyses can be mapped in most cases, although the data *need not* be mapped. As shown in Figure 4.23, mapping and numerical analysis provide alternative but complementary views of the data, and multiple views of data are necessary to provide a complete picture of the community at hand. The use of maps to describe data is constrained by confidentiality issues in a way that reporting summary statistics may not be. Regardless, the aim of mapping and numerical analyses

Cross Reference: Chapter 3 in this book for more information on multidimensional scaling

Key point

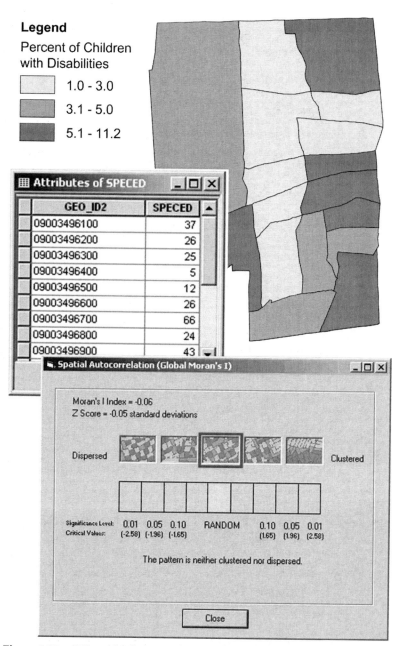

Legend
Percent of Children
with Disabilities

	1.0 - 3.0
	3.1 - 5.0
	5.1 - 11.2

Figure 4.23 GIS enables the researcher to access multiple views of data—
a table, a map, and a spatial statistical analysis of spatial autocorrelation in
data on the percent of school-aged children with disabilities by census tract in
West Hartford.

is to provide a richer understanding of how communities work in real and imagined geographic space, perhaps as an aid to solving problems within communities.

The Power of Maps

Maps are recognized as one of the main categories of cultural materials available for ethnographic research (Murdock 1971), and geographic information systems are also contributing to ethnographic research (Matthews, Detwiler, and Burton 2005). Maps are tremendous stores of data. Consider how long it would take to describe verbally all of the information on even a simple statistical map. Maps also provide alternative views or visualizations of data from the views offered by tabular presentation or statistical analysis. As such, maps can be an important component of ethnographic research.

Effective map interpretation and map making requires skill, however. Although often viewed as precise portrayals of the earth's surface, maps are necessarily distorted models of the reality they represent. An understanding of how maps work is perhaps more important than ever given the explosion of spatial databases and computer-based systems for analyzing them.

That map making is no longer solely in the hands of expert cartographers (if it ever was) is not necessarily a cause for concern (Wood 1992). Maps are not neutral. They promote specific interests, and there is no reason why the interests and viewpoints of ethnographers should not be explored through maps.

Key point *Nevertheless, care must taken to consider the extent to which maps produced as an aid to ethnographic research might harm community members.* One potential source of harm is revealing confidential information. Another potential source of harm is alerting individuals to problems that they cannot address. For example, producing a map of environmental contamination within a community can have serious psychological and health implications for residents who live within a contaminated zone but do not have the means to leave or eliminate the contamination.

An important ethical standard for research involving human subjects is that people participating in research projects should enjoy the benefits of the research and that the results of the research should not be withheld. Given that map-making and spatial data compilation and analysis are increasingly accomplished through computer-assisted means, researchers using these methods need to think about how they can and should share the research with community members. Some spatial databases sold by vendors cannot be freely distributed. GIS software, like other software, may be subject to licensing requirements that prevent copying. Communities may not have access to the hardware, software, and databases necessary to use the spatial data or analytical procedures the ethnographer has used. Concerns about GIS as a means of surveillance and control merit serious consideration (Pickles 1995). There have also been efforts to develop community-based geographic information systems so that maps reflecting the interests of community groups can be developed as counterpoints to the maps offered by government agencies, corporations, and planners (Figure 4.24) (Kyem and Saku 2009).

A more subtle issue in the use of maps for ethnographic research is their contribution to a spatial fallacy. Everything that occurs on the surface of the earth can be mapped. That is, we can map almost anything, but mapping does not necessarily create meaning. Maps, because of their visual power, often become metaphors for the social relationships and problems that are contained in geographic space. This makes it tempting to look for spatial solutions to problems. Although many social problems have a spatial dimension and some issues in society can be addressed by changing locational relationships like drawing new school district boundaries, mapping may not be an aid to analysis for other problems. Even for problems that have a strong spatial dimension, changes in spatial organization often contribute to the emergence of new locational conflicts.

With these caveats, the role of maps in ethnographic research is potentially great. Maps are important for describing study areas, collecting and analyzing data, and reporting results. As computer technology continues to

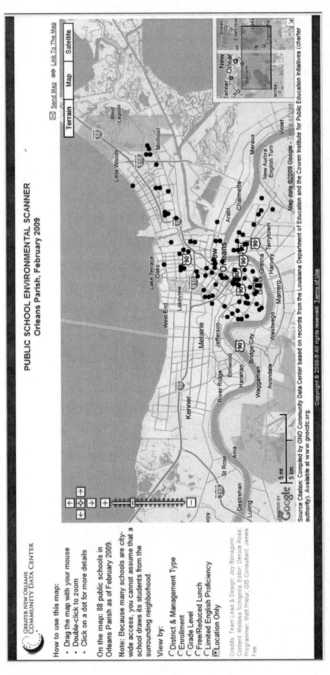

Figure 4.24 The Greater New Orleans Community Data Center provides up-to-date, reliable data for the community. Bonaguro, Joy, Melissa Schigoda, Denice Ross, Matt Priour, and James Fee. February 2009. Public School Environmental Scanner Orleans Parish (map). Greater New Orleans Community Data Center. Retrieved from http://www.gnocdc.org/schools/index.html.

transform our spatial data handling and mapping capabilities, new roles for mapping in ethnographic research may emerge. The tools for exploring the spatial dimensions of community life will continue to be an essential part of the ethnographer's toolkit.

SUGGESTED ADDITIONAL RESOURCES

The growth of the Internet has had a significant impact on access to digital spatial data. A number of sources provide points of contact for acquiring maps and spatial databases that might be of use in ethnographic research.

Alexandria Digital Library
alexandria.ucsb.edu
> The Alexandria Digital Library (ADL) is a distributed digital library that links users to collections of georeferenced materials. In addition to the library, which provides HTML clients with access to various nodes and their collections and to its gazetteer, ADL includes a research program.

Library of Congress, Geography and Map Division
memory.loc.gov/ammem/gmdhtml/gmdhome.html
> The Map Collections site offers access to items in the Geography and Map Division collection that have been converted to digital form, a fraction of the more than four million items in the collection.

U.S. Census Bureau, Census Bureau Geography
www.census.gov/geo/www
> The Geography Division of the U.S. Census Bureau provides downloadable maps and digital spatial databases of Census data for the United States and its territories.

U.S. Geological Survey
www.usgs.gov/pubprod/
> The U.S. Geological Survey provides access to topographic maps, digital earth sciences databases, and aerial photographs and satellite imagery.

Numerical Cartography Laboratory, The Ohio State
University
ncl.sbs.ohio-state.edu/home.html
At the state and local levels in the United States, and in
other nations, various agencies have taken the lead to
develop and publish digital spatial databases. Links to
many of these sites have been provided by the Numerical Cartography Laboratory at Ohio State. These sites
can also be found by online searches for digital spatial
databases for particular states or localities.

East View Cartographic
www.cartographic.com
East View Cartographic is an international company
selling authoritative maps and spatial data from around
the world.

REFERENCES

Abate, Frank R. 1991. *Omni gazetteer of the United States of America*. Detroit: Omni-graphics.

Aitken, Stewart C. 1994. *Putting children in their place*. Resource Publications in Geogra-phy, Washington, DC: Association of American Geographers.

Alter, Catherine Foster. 1988. The changing structure of elderly service delivery systems. *Gerontologist* 28: 91–98.

Amadeo, Douglas, Reginald G. Golledge, and Robert J. Stimson. 2009. *Person-environment-behavior research: Investigating activities and experiences in spaces and environments*. New York: The Guilford Press.

Anderson, J. 1971. Space-time budgets and activity studies in urban geography and plan-ning. *Environment and Planning* 3: 353–68.

Anscombe, F. J. 1973. Graphs in statistical analysis. *American Statistician* 27: 17–21.

Bailey, Trevor C., and Anthony C. Gatrell. 1995. *Interactive spatial data analysis*. Essex, England: Longman Scientific and Technical.

Bernard, H. Russell. 2006. *Research methods in anthropology, fourth edition*. Lanham, MD: Altamira Press.

Bernard, H. Russell, and Peter D. Killworth. 1993. Sampling in time allocation research. *Ethnology* 32: 207–15.

Bernard, H. Russell, Peter Killworth, David Kronfeld, and Lee Sailor. 1984. The problem of informant accuracy: The validity of retrospective data. *Annual Review of Anthro-pology* 13: 495–517.

Brakel, S., J. Parry, and B. Weiner. 1985. *The mentally disabled and the law*. Chicago: American Bar Association.

Broadbent, Stefana, and Valerie Bauwens. 2008. Understanding convergence. *Interactions* 15: 23–27.

Brownstein, J. S., C. A. Cassa, and K. D. Mandl. 2006. No place to hide—Reverse identification of patients from published maps. *New England Journal of Medicine* 355: 1741–42.

Carlstein, T. 1982. *Time resources, society and ecology.* London: Allen and Unwin.

Cassa, Cristopher A., Shannon C. Wieland, and Kenneth D. Mandl. 2008. Re-identification of home addresses from spatial locations anonymized by Gaussian skew. *International Journal of Health Geographics* 7: 45.

Chang, Kang-tsung. 2010. *Introduction to geographic information systems, fifth edition.* Boston: McGraw Hill Higher Education.

Christaller, Walter. 1933 [1966]. *Die zentralen Orte in Söddentschland.* Jena: Gustav Fischer, translated (in part), by Charlisle W. Baskin, as *Central Places in Southern Germany.* Prentice Hall, 1966.

Cohen, Roberta J., Kimber Haddix, Elena Hurtado, and Kathryn G. Dewey. 1995. Maternal activity budgets: Feasibility of exclusive breastfeeding for six months among urban women in Honduras. *Social Science and Medicine* 41: 527–36.

Cole, L. C. 1949. The measurement of interspecific association. *Ecology* 30: 411–24.

Connecticut Department of Education, State of Connecticut. 2008. *Strategic school profiles by district, 2007–2008.* Retrieved October 29, 2008, from www.csde.state.ct.us/public/der/ssp/dist0708/district.htm#W.

Cromley, Ellen K. 2009. West Hartford, Hartford, Connecticut, Conard high school. Retrieved October 29, 2009, from maps.google.com.

Cromley, Ellen K., and Gary W. Shannon. 1986. Locating ambulatory medical care facilities for the elderly. *Health Services Research* 21: 499–514.

Curtis, Andrew J., Jacqueline W. Mills, and Michael Leitner. 2006. Spatial confidentiality and GIS: Reengineering mortality locations from published maps about Hurricane Katrina. *International Journal of Health Geographics* 5: 44.

de la Torre, Vanessa. 2009. Redistricting a contentious issue for board candidates. *Hartford Courant*, October 27, 2009, 5E West Hartford, B2.

Dobson, Jerome E. 1983. Automated geography. *Professional Geographer* 35: 135–43.

Dyck, I. 1990. Space, time and renegotiating motherhood: An exploration of the domestic workplace. *Environment and Planning D* 8: 459–83.

Ebdon, David. 1977. *Statistics in geography: A practical approach.* Oxford: Basil Blackwell.

Edmundson, Wade C. 1976. *Land, food and work in east Java.* Armidale, Australia: Department of Geography, University of New England.

Eyles, J. 1985. *Sense of place.* Warrington, UK: Silverbrook Press.

Flowerdew, R., and M. Green. 1989. Statistical methods for inference between incompatible zonal systems, in *Accuracy of spatial databases*, ed. M. F. Goodchild and S. Gopal, 239–48. London: Taylor and Francis.

Foot, David. 1981. *Operational urban models.* London: Methuen.

Fuchs, Victor R., ed. 1996. *Individual and social responsibility: Child care, education, medical care, and long-term care in America.* Chicago: University of Chicago Press.

Gans, Sheldon P., and Gerald T. Horton. 1975. *Integration of human services: The state and municipal levels.* New York: Praeger.

Garling, T., A. Book, and E. Lindberg. 1979. The acquisition and use of an internal representation of the spatial layout of the environment during locomotion. *Man-Environment Systems* 9: 200–08.

Gatrell, Anthony. 1983. *Distance and space.* Oxford: Clarendon Press.

Ghosh, Avijit, and Gerard Rushton, eds. 1987. *Spatial analysis and location-allocation models.* New York: Van Nostrand Reinhold Company.

Golledge, Reginald G., and Lawrence A. Brown. 1967. Search, learning and the market decision process. *Geografiska Annaler* 49B: 116–24.

Golledge, Reginald G., Victoria L. Rivizzigno, and Aaron Spector. 1976. Learning about a city: Analysis by multidimensional scaling in *Spatial choice and spatial behavior,* ed. Reginald G. Golledge and Gerard Rushton, 95–116. Columbus: Ohio State University Press.

Golledge, Reginald G., and Gerard Rushton. 1972. *Multidimensional scaling: Review and geographical applications.* Commission on College Geography Technical Paper No. 10, Washington, DC: Association of American Geographers.

Golledge, Reginald G., and Robert J. Stimson. 1987. *Analytical behavioural geography.* London: England: Croom Helm.

Golledge, Reginald G., and Robert J. Stimson. 1997. *Spatial behavior: A geographic perspective.* New York: The Guilford Press.

Goodchild, Michael F. 1984. Geocoding and geosampling, in *Spatial statistics and models,* ed. Gary L. Gaile and Cort J. Willmott, 33–53. Dordrecht, Netherlands: D. Reidel Publishing Company.

Goodchild, Michael F., and S. Gopal, ed. 1989. *Accuracy of spatial databases.* London: Taylor and Francis.

Goulias, K. G. 2002. Multilevel analysis of daily time use and time allocation to activity types accounting for complex covariance structures using correlated random effects. *Transportation* 29: 31–48.

Greater New Orleans Community Data Center. 2009. *Public school environmental scanner, Orleans Parish, February 2009.* Retrieved October 29, 2009, from www.gnocdc. org/schools/.

Grossman, Lawrence S. 1984. Collecting time-use data in third world rural communities. *Professional Geographer* 36: 444–54.

Gulick, J. 1966. Images of an Arab city. *Journal of the American Institute of Planners* 29: 179–97.

Hagerstrand, Torsten. 1970. What about people in regional science? *Papers and Proceedings of the Regional Science Association* 25: 7–21.

Haining, Robert. 2003. *Spatial data analysis: Theory and practice.* Cambridge: Cambridge University Press.

Hall, Edward T. 1996. *The hidden dimension.* Garden City, NY: Doubleday.

Hensher, D., and P. Stopher. 1979. *Behavioural travel demand modelling.* London: Croom Helm.

Honey, R., G. Rushton, P. Lolonis, B. T. Dalziel, M. P. Armstrong, S. De, and P. J. Densham. 1991. Stages in the adoption of a spatial decision support system for reorganizing service delivery regions. *Environment and Planning C: Government and Policy* 9: 51–63.

Jakle, John A., Stanley Brunn, and Curtis C. Roseman. 1976. *Human spatial behavior: A social geography.* North Scituate, MA: Duxbury Press.

Johnson, Allen. 1975. Time allocation in a machiguenga community. *Ethnology* 14: 301–10.

Johnston, R. J., Derek Gregory, and David M. Smith, ed. 1994. *The dictionary of human geography, third edition.* Oxford: Basil Blackwell.

Jones, P. M. 1979. HATS: A technique for investigating household decisions. *Environment and Planning A* 11: 59–70.

Kamakura, Wagner A. 2009. American time-styles: A finite-mixture allocation model for time-use analysis. *Multivariate Behavioral Research* 44: 332–61.

Khaled, El Eman, Ann Brown, and Philip AbdelMalik. 2009. Evaluating predictors of geographic area population size cut-offs to manage re-identification risk. *Journal of the American Medical Informatics Association* 16: 256–66.

Kruskal, J. B., F. W. Young, and J. B. Seery. 1976. *How to use KYST-2, a very flexible program to do multidimensional scaling and unfolding.* Murray Hill, NJ: Bell Labs, 1976.

Kyem, Peter A. K., and James C. Saku. 2009. GIS and the future of participatory GIS applications within local and indigenous communities. *Electronic Journal on Information Systems in Developing Countries* 38: 1–16.

Lam, Nina S-N. 1983. Spatial interpolation methods: A review. *American Cartographer* 10: 129–49.

Laurini, Robert. 2001. *Information systems for urban planning: A hypermedia co-operative approach.* London: Taylor and Francis.

Lebel, Alexandre, Robert Pampalon, and Paul Y. Villeneuve. 2007. A multi-perspective approach for defining neighbourhood units in the context of a study on health inequalities in the Quebec city region. *International Journal of Health Geographics* 6: 27.

LeCompte, M. D., and J. Preissle. 1993. *Ethnography and qualitative design in educational research.* San Diego, CA: Academic Press.

Lehner, P. N. 1979. *Handbook of ethological methods.* New York: Garland STPM Press.

Levinson, David, and Ajay Kumar. 1995. Activity, travel, and the allocation of time. *Journal of the American Planning Association* 61: 458–70.

Ley, David. 1989. Modernism, post-modernism and the struggle for place, in *The power of place: Bringing together the geographical and sociological imaginations,* ed. J. Agnew and J. Duncan, 44–65. London: Unwin Hyman.

Longley, Paul A., Michael F. Goodchild, David J. Maguire, and David W. Rhind. 2001. *Geographic information systems and science.* Chichester, England: John Wiley and Sons.

Lynch, Kevin. 1960. *The image of the city.* Cambridge, MA: MIT Press.

MacEachren, Alan M. 1994. *Some truth with maps: A primer on symbolization and design.* Washington, DC: Association of American Geographers.

Malczewski, J., and W. Orgyczak. 1995. The multiple criteria location problem: 1. A generalized network model and the set of efficient solutions. *Environment and Planning A* 27: 1931–60.

———. 1996. The multiple criteria location problem: 2. Preference-based techniques and interactive decision support. *Environment and Planning A* 28: 69–98.

Matthews, Stephen A., James E. Detwiler, and Linda M. Burton. 2005. Geo-ethnography: Coupling geographic information analysis techniques with ethnographic methods in urban research. *Cartographica* 40: 75–90.

Miller, Harvey J., ed. 2007. *Societies and cities in the age of instant access*. Dordrecht: The Netherlands, Springer.

Minnick, R. F. 1964. A method for the measurement of areal correspondence. *Papers of the Michigan Academy of Science, Arts and Letters* 49: 333–44.

Moffitt, Francis H., and John D. Bossler. 1998. *Surveying, tenth edition*. Menlo Park, CA: Addison-Wesley.

Monmonier, Mark. 1996. *How to lie with maps, second edition*. Chicago: University of Chicago Press.

Murdock, G. P. 1971. *Outline of cultural materials, fourth revised edition*. New Haven, CT: Human Relations Area Files.

Oppong, Joseph R. 1996. Accommodating the rainy season in third world location-allocation applications. *Socio-Economic Planning Sciences* 30: 121–37.

Orleans, P., and S. Schmidt. 1972. Mapping the city: Environmental cognition of urban residents, in *Environmental design: Research and practice*, ed. W. J. Mitchel, 1.4.1–1.4.9. Proceedings of the ERDA 3/AR8 Conference, Los Angeles, California, University of California, Los Angeles.

O'Sullivan, David, and David J. Unwin. 2003. *Geographic information analysis*. Hoboken, NJ: John Wiley and Sons, Inc.

Pearson, Frederick II. 1990. *Map projections: Theory and applications*. Boca Raton, FL: CRC Press.

Penchansky, Roy, and William J. Thomas. 1981. The concept of access: Definition and relationships to consumer satisfaction. *Medical Care* 19: 127–40.

Peng, Zhong-Ren, and Ming-Hsiang Tsou. 2003. Internet GIS: Distributed information services for the Internet and wireless networks. Hoboken, NJ: John Wiley and Sons.

Piaget, J., and B. Inhelder. 1967. *The child's conception of space*. New York: Norton.

Pickles, John. 1995. *Ground truth: The social implications of geographic information systems*. New York: The Guilford Press.

Rabin, Jack, and Marcia B. Steinhauer, ed. 1988. *Handbook on human services administration*. New York: Marcel Dekker.

Ricci, Judith A., Norge W. Jerome, Nadia Megally, Osmal Galal, Gail G. Harrison, and Avanelle Kirksey. 1995. Assessing the validity of informant recall: Results of a time use pilot study in peri-urban Egypt. *Human Organization* 54: 304–08.

Rocha, Joseph. 1994. School districts track gate-crashers; Nonresident students are targeted. *Hartford Courant*, October 10, 6 Hartford South Final, B1.

Rowles, Graham D. 1986. The geography of ageing and the aged: Towards an integrated perspective. *Progress in Human Geography* 10: 511–40.

Ruddle, Kenneth. 1974. *The Yukpa cultivation system: A study of shifting cultivation in Colombia and Venezuela*. Berkeley: University of California Press.

Rugg, David J., and Richard R. Buech. 1990. Analyzing time budgets with Markov chains. *Biometrics* 46: 1123–31.

Rule, James B. 2007. *Privacy in peril*. Oxford: Oxford University Press.

Rushton, Gerard. 1984. Use of location-allocation models for improving geographical accessibility of rural services in developing countries. *International Regional Science Review* 9: 217–40.

———. 1988. Location theory, location-allocation models and service development planning in the third world. *Economic Geography* 64: 97–120.

Rushton, Gerard et al., ed. 2008. *Geocoding health data: The use of geographic codes in cancer prevention and control, research, and practice*. Boca Raton, FL: CRC Press.

Seto, Edmund Y. W., Freyja Knapp, Bo Zhong, and Changhong Yang. 2007. The use of a vest equipped with a global positioning system to assess water-contact patterns associated with schistosomiasis. *Geospatial Health* 1: 233–41.

Siegel, A. W. 1981. The externalization of cognitive maps by children and adults: In search of better ways to ask better questions, in *Spatial representation and behavior across the life span*, ed. L. S. Liben, A. Patterson, and N. Newcombe, 167–94. New York: Academic Press.

Slocum, Terry A., Robert B. McMaster, Fritz C. Kessler, and Hugh H. Howard. 2009. *Thematic cartography and geovisualization, third edition*. Upper Saddle River, NJ: Pearson Prentice Hall.

Smith, Nigel J. H. 1981. *Man, fishers, and the Amazon*. New York: Columbia University Press.

Stutz, Frederick P. 1976. Adjustment and mobility of elderly poor and downtown renewal. *Geographical Review* 66: 391–400.

Troped, Philip J., Marcelo S. Oliveria, Charles E. Matthews, Ellen K. Cromley, Steven J. Melly, and Bruce A. Craig. 2008. Prediction of activity mode with global positioning system and accelerometer data. *Medicine and Science in Sports and Exercise* 40: 972–78.

Trotta, Brian M. 1994. Board sets deadline for reorganizing elementary schools. *Hartford Courant*, July 6, 5E, West Hartford Farmington Valley, D3.

Tufte, Edward J. 1983. *The visual display of quantitative information*. Cheshire, CT: Graphics Press.

Tuma, Nancy B., and Michael T. Hannan. 1984. *Social dynamics: Models and methods*. Orlando, FL: Academic Press.

Van Sickle, Jan. 2001. *GPS for land surveyors, third edition*. New York: Taylor and Francis.

Waller, Lance A., and Carol A. Gotway. 2004. *Applied spatial statistics for public health data*. Hoboken, NJ: John Wiley and Sons.

West Hartford Public Schools. 2009. Schools. Retrieved October 29, 2009, from www .whps.org/whps/primary-schools.

Williams, Phillipa, Barbara Pocock, and Kennedy Bridge. 2009. Kids' lives in adult space and time: How home, community, school and adult work affect opportunity for teenagers in suburban Australia. *Health Sociology Review* 18: 79–93.

Wood, Denis. 1992. *The power of maps.* New York: The Guilford Press.

Worboys, Michael, and Matt Duckham. 2004. *GIS: A computing perspective, second edition.* Boca Raton, FL: CRC Press.

Zimmerman, Dale L., and Claire Pavlik. 2008. Quantifying the effects of mask metadata disclosure and multiple releases on the confidentiality of geographically masked health data. *Geographical Analysis* 40: 52–76.

Zook, Matthew A. 2005. *The geography of the Internet industry: Venture capital, dot-coms, and local knowledge.* Oxford: Blackwell.

———. 2007. Your urgent assistance is requested: The intersection of 419 spam and new networks of imagination. *Ethics, Place and Environment* 10: 65–87.

Zook, Matthew A., and Mark Graham. 2007a. The creative reconstruction of the internet: Google and the privatization of cyberspace and Digiplace. *GeoForum* 38: 1322–43.

———. 2007b. Mapping Digiplace: Geo-coded Internet data and the perception of place. *Environment and Planning B* 34: 466–82.

5 ━━◆━●━◆━━

CONDUCTING ETHNOGRAPHIC NETWORK STUDIES: FRIENDS, RELATIVES, AND RELEVANT OTHERS

Robert T. Trotter II, Jean J. Schensul, and Margaret Weeks

INTRODUCTION TO NETWORK RESEARCH

There is a Spanish proverb that states, *Di me con quien andan, y dire quien eres*, which generally translates as "tell me who you walk with, and I will tell (you) who you are." We all reflect our values and beliefs, as well as our hopes and accomplishments, through the people with whom we choose to associate and those whom we avoid. Our social world is made up primarily of our family and friends, work partners, acquaintances, and the organizations and communities in which we participate. Anthropologists have studied the composition of these relationships or **social networks** in villages, towns, and urban centers all over the

Definition: ☼
A social network is a specific type of relation linking a defined set of persons, organizations or communities

193

world. Social scientists have used studies of social networks for several primary purposes:

- To identify the members of and patterns of inter-action among groups and organizations of vari-ous kinds, including friendship, work, and kinship groups, work sites/businesses, and power brokers
- To understand how network membership influences beliefs and behaviors
- To understand how cultural and behavioral innova-tions are transmitted through networks
- To learn how resources, information, and behavioral risks flow through networks
- To use our understanding of social networks to introduce innovations that result in normative and behavioral change in individuals, groups, and the wider community

Today, however, the social network approach has been put to use for more sophisticated purposes. Once ethnog-raphers noticed how group structures differ within and between cultures, and began to question how these differ-ences might influence what people think and do, network research has gained importance in understanding and pre-dicting individual knowledge, behavior, and beliefs. Dif-ferences in the structure and organization of relationships among people, as well as their positions within social orga-nizations and communities, affect information flow, influ-encing and constraining both the amount and content of information that people receive. Studies of social networks allow social scientists to explore cultural differences in the ways that humans organize themselves into groups, com-municate within groups, and work out the problems they encounter in everyday life. They also help us to understand how organizations relate to each other through their staffs, trustees, or board members or other influential people and how this affects resource and information exchanges. This information can be used to very good effect in studies as widely varying as explorations of drug use patterns, analy-ses of why parents choose particular schools for their chil-dren, investigations into the reasons why people do or do not welcome agricultural innovations, explorations of the social networks surrounding opinion leaders or political figures, and obstacles to innovation uptake.

Typical applications of social network research might include studies of implementation of educational innovations, shifts in voting behavior or diffusion of health care information in a community, and reorganization or restructuring of bureaucratic institutions. Such studies are particularly useful for intervention programs, whose purpose is to induce change in how a particular group of people behave. In this chapter, we use an extended case study along with brief additional illustrative examples to describe the uses of ethnographically based network analysis. In our case study, network analysis was instrumental in identifying various kinds of drug user networks. It also illuminated how different patterns of behavior among the drug users within specific networks are affected by the different bases, or purposes, upon which the networks are based. In the pages that follow, we demonstrate how the social network approach can be used across fields and disciplines.

Historical Evolution of Network Research

Two early and different approaches to understanding cultural networks are important in the history of network research in ethnography. Pasternak summarized the first systematic exploration of kinship groups (Pasternak 1976). He described methods for collecting comparative data on the ways that different cultural groups identified genealogical relationships. Bott (1971) outlined how a more ethnographic exploration of social networks evolved during studies she conducted in England. She provided both an in-depth exploration of the intimate or personal support networks that most people use to survive in their culture and a model for exploring these relationships across cultures. These two seminal works represent anchor points for ethnographically framed social network analysis.

Since then anthropologists and sociologists have crafted increasingly fine-tuned network-based examinations of both informal and formal human groups and associations (Wasserman and Faust 1993, Galaskiewicz and

Wasserman 1993, Johnson 1994, White and Johansen 2004). These works have allowed us to expand our knowledge of the dynamics and effects of both kinship and nonkin organizational and interpersonal networks in all aspects of human cultures.

There are now a number of ways to approach social network research in ethnographic studies ranging from the purely qualitative descriptions of groups and associations to highly technical quantitative models derived from graph theory and matrix algebra. These approaches are compatible with each other, and each provides valuable and complementary insights into human cultural relationships and social interactions. In combination, they provide powerful explanations for the ways that humans think, act, and organize their daily lives within their personal cultural and social contexts. The same approaches detailed in this chapter for describing and analyzing social networks made up of individuals can be applied to networks consisting of organizations such as service agencies, towns, cities, and larger social entities.

Four primary contemporary approaches to networks are:

- The ethnographic exploration of social networks—ethnographic network mapping
- The investigation of ego-centered (single-person-focused) networks
- The collection of data on full relational networks, in which each person describes his or her relationships with each other person in the network
- The identification and construction of interconnected networks in dynamic open systems

Definition: Ethnographic network mapping uses ethnographic field research methods to describe the most common groups found in a culture

Ethnographic Network Mapping

We first describe **ethnographic network mapping**, a type of network research that can be used to describe family groups, friendship networks, work groups, voluntary associations, problem-solving groups, and any other types of social groups that are found in different communities and cultural settings. Ethnographic network mapping is accomplished through extensive qualitative interviewing at the community level, combined with observations of people's behavior. An example of this approach currently in use in medical anthropology is the study of drug-using networks (Trotter, Bowen, and Potter 1995; Friedman 1995, Latkin 1995; Bourgois 1996; Weeks et al. 2002; Weeks et al. 2009). These drug networks are groups of individuals who may or may not be related through kinship, and whose primary activities are purchasing, distributing, and/or using illegal drugs. The ethnographic description of these networks includes:

- The identity of the people in them
- How people define or self-define themselves as group members
- The rules they use for including and excluding members
- Familial, trust, resource exchange, and sexual relationships within the groups
- Information about how group members avoid the police and prosecution

These are, of course, only a few of the interactions that occur within such groups and between these groups and others such as the police and other drug traffickers.

While one primary purpose of this type of approach to network mapping is to understand how and why members relate to one another, many such studies also concentrate on descriptions of the contexts in which drugs are sold and used (for example, crack houses, local manufacturing and distribution systems, or police approaches to drug busts), and they create typologies or classifications of different types of drug use networks. These studies are very useful for understanding group-based differences in drug use and for creating targeted intervention and education activities for the highest risk groups (Trotter, Bowen, and Potter 1995). Classic gang studies also use the concept of ethnographic networks, considering differences in group organization and functions and changes in groups in space and over generations (cf. Moore, 1991; Vigil 1988). Other examples of ethnographically mapped network studies may involve families, clans, or other extended networks followed over time (cf. Allen et al. 2000). Similarly, anthropologists White and Johansen embedded network questions in a ten-year longitudinal field study of a Turkish nomadic clan (White and Johansen 2004).

Definition:
Ego-centered networks are the personal networks of individuals, also called "egos" or "focal individuals"

Definition:
Alters are those people whom individuals identify as members of their personal networks

Ego-Centered or Personal-Network Research

The second approach to network research focuses on **ego-centered (personal) networks**. Studies based on this approach describe index or focal individuals (often called egos) and all of the people (sometimes called "**alters**") whom these index individuals identify as being associated with them. The data collected on personal networks usually includes information about the size of the network as well as the gender and ethnic composition, age, and socioeconomic attributes of all the people that "ego" names as being close to themselves. This allows the researcher to describe "typical" network profiles. These profiles can be related to an infinite variety of other characteristics (level of social support in a specific cultural area, success in personal relationships, risks for infection, quality of life, educational attainment, types of help-seeking behavior members use regarding their health, ideas about success in the future, etc.) that are associated with people's lives. Ego-centered network research gives ethnographers the ability to describe the context of people's social lives beyond their individual social and psychological characteristics. Ego-centered network data, for example, can include the number of people in an individual's personal network, friendship network, drug-using network or work-related network. It can identify the proportion of a personal network from which emotional, social, and economic resources can be accessed and the balance of resource accessing to resource provision in an individual's life. It can also determine the degree of risk to which an individual might be exposed through relationships with network members. These social contextual elements can be treated as variables and then summed to describe "ego's" network characteristics, much as demographic variables such as sex, age, political affiliation, and ethnicity describe individual "egos."

Full Relational Social Networks

The third approach to network research is the study of **full relational networks**, which requires different analysis procedures (Knoke and Kuklinski 1982). This approach requires the researcher to identify a **naturally occurring social network** (a network of people already established and interacting in an existing setting, such as a building, classroom, shooting gallery, sexual service establishment, after-school program or summer camp) and to explore key relationships among and between *all* of the members of the network. This is accomplished through prior identification, observations, or interviewing, or all three. The questions or the observations are designed to allow the ethnographer to explore reciprocal actions that potentially take place between each member of the network and every other member. All of the questions asked and the observations conducted focus on dimensions of relationships described in terms of what respondents are doing with one another, such as "Who attends social events together?" "Who trusts whom and how much?" and "Who shares food, space or ideas with whom?" and discovering through additional inquiry more about the question. For example, a researcher might ask first about "Which social events occur in this community?" "What meaning or purposes do these events have?" and "What do people do together there?" These questions usually can be qualitative—that is, they are phrased as open-ended or semi-structured questions. If the social network is small enough, the researcher can conduct in-depth interviews with all its members. Network research with larger networks (e.g., ten people or more) calls for quantitative interviews with very specific questions, such as "Did you ever share a needle with X?" (answer "yes" or "no"); "How many times in the last thirty days did you share a needle with X?" (Answer in absolute numbers); "How much do you trust X?" (response is a Likert scale from 1 = low to 5 = highest); "Have you ever borrowed money from X?" (answer "yes" or "no").

These relationship questions allow researchers to:

- Explore both the actual and potential connections between people in the network

Definition: A full relational social network is a socially bounded group in which the relationships of all members to each other can be defined

Definition: A naturally occurring social network is a network that can be spatially/geographically bounded and that exists and interacts in a specific setting independent of researcher intervention

Cross Reference: Book 3, chapters 4 and 6, on open-ended and semistructured interviewing

Definition:
Cliques are subunits within a larger network that are distinctive because the people or units in them are more strongly interconnected with each other compared with other parts of the network

Definition:
Bridges are people or organizations that connect two networks

Definition:
A macro network in an open dynamic system is a socially unbounded group of multiple linked individuals in which the various relationships of some members to each other can be identified and specified

Cross Reference:
Book 4, chapter 6, on research within hidden populations

- Describe the primary sources of power, influence, and communication in a network
- Find subgroups (**cliques**) within the network
- Identify common or unusual social roles and positions in the networks
- Find **bridges** or connectors between networks and portions of networks
- Identify how information and other resources flow from one member or group to another in a network
- Identify and compare the overall structure of one social network with others

Macro Networks in Dynamic Open Systems

The fourth approach to network research is the study of **macro networks in open systems**. These also are naturally occurring social networks of linked individuals often involved in multiple and overlapping or concurrent types of relationships. The difference between a macronetwork approach in a closed network and a macronetwork approach in an open dynamic network is that the social boundaries of the closed network can be socially and spatially defined, but open system boundaries cannot. For example, residents of a building or town, students in a classroom, and members of an industrial work unit can be considered geosocially bounded networks in which each and every member can be identified and interviewed in relation to all other members. This is not the case in an open system, where there is no logical way of establishing the boundaries of the network, the network members may vary, and any boundary definition is arbitrary and not grounded in a known social/spatial universe with an identifiable membership. The membership of these networks can expand or contract to include individuals who enter into or terminate relationships with others.

The questions researchers ask in order to study open macronetworks are similar to those used to define and characterize closed full relational networks, such as with whom each person has ties and what is the nature of the relationships. However, it does not require (or may not allow) the collection of the same information from all network members, many of whom might not be known or reachable.

The data can be generated through a combination of qualitative (observation, interview) and quantitative (survey) methods used to gather as much information as possible about members of the network and their relationships. The approach also makes possible the exploration of reciprocal actions and special dynamics (e.g., feedback systems) that take place between network members or groups of members within pockets, sectors, or cliques within the larger network, as well as chain reactions that pass from one or a few individuals through the larger network system, including information flow, innovation diffusion, risk behavior, or disease transmission.

The study of macronetworks allows the testing of **network structural characteristics**, density of ties among members and location of central individuals, cliques, and bridge individuals in order to understand how characteristics of members' relationships with each other in the broader system of linkages create dynamics that affect the whole group or some portion of it.

A challenge with the study of open macronetworks is that it is never possible to study all members or to know the full extent of relationships and their characteristics among network members. Nor is it possible to put boundaries around the network or any sectors within it because of the open and continuously changing nature of the system. Further, as with any open system, the influx and departure of members over time results in continuously changing relationship patterns and potentially new structural features of the overall macronetwork. Thus, measures of density, centrality, and other network structural characteristics are inevitably limited, leaving open the possibility of unknown but significant ties or dynamic forces that might change the nature of the whole group or system. Nevertheless, looking at unbounded macro networks even within these limits allows a broader understanding of social forces and dynamics, as well as the identification of key individuals or core groups, that shape the whole and the individual members within it.

Definition: Network structural characteristics include the density of known ties among all members of a particular relationship, location of central individuals, and the existence and location of cliques and bridge individuals

The social network approach allows ethnographers to move beyond the level of the individual and the analysis of individual behavior into the social context, where most people spend the vast majority of their lives living and interacting with the small groups that make up the world around them. The results of these studies can be used in a number of practical solutions to human problems by identifying people or organizations who can influence the behavior of the remainder of the network in some desired fashion, or by making use of the social network itself to set group goals and change group norms in relation to behaviors that are to be modified.

KEY CONCEPTS IN ETHNOGRAPHIC APPROACHES TO SOCIAL NETWORKS

 Key point *Ethnographic studies of sociocultural networks are needed in almost all areas of life.* Some of the most common activities associated with these studies include:

- Defining the boundaries and core participants of social groups
- Creating network typologies that explain the variation in people's life experiences
- Studying embedded behaviors (the things that go on in specific groups)
- Exploring cross-group differences in the cultural behavior of networks

Cross Reference:
Book 1, chapter 1, for a discussion of culture

Boundaries and Bridges

Definition:
Boundaries constitute the edges of networks and are defined by rules for entry and exit from groups as well as by other cultural patterns that differentiate one group from another

The ability to understand and identify **boundaries**—the "edges of networks"—and **bridges**—people who connect networks and act as intermediaries among them—is central to any understanding of both small and large groups. Ethnographic techniques, including direct long-term observation of behavior and relationships, provide important clues to the formation, maintenance, change, and dissolution of network boundaries and the identity and functions of people or groups of people who serve as bridges between networks.

The mechanisms that allow members of a group to get together, identify themselves as a group, maintain an identity even when the group changes its membership over time, and eventually loosen their boundaries and disappear can all be explored descriptively, through observation and open-ended interviewing. Ethnographic documentation shows that these conditions change according to key environmental and cultural conditions, such as population density, gender differences, and cultural values and beliefs. **Bounded groups** are networks with clearly defined membership. Once bounded groups have been identified, it is possible to determine how interpersonal connections are created between different persons and groups of persons and to understand the strength of the links between network members.

The ethnographic study of bridges and boundaries helps social scientists understand both the cognitive models of roles held by network members and indigenous understandings of the conditions that produce and maintain boundaries at the edges of networks. For example, detailed qualitative description of the behavior and function of boundaries and bridges between networks can be used to create a model of how vulnerable different types of networks are to infectious disease risk. This type of description also can show how a teenage fad is transmitted throughout a high school, or be used to trace a technological innovation through a culture.

Definition: Bridges are people, components of networks (subnetworks), or organizations that connect two networks. Bridges act as intermediaries between networks and are connected with all networks but are strongly affiliated with none

Definition: Bounded groups are networks with clearly defined membership

Cross Reference:
Book 3, chapters 4, 5, and 6

Network Typologies

Ethnographers can use typologies of networks or descriptions of different kinds of networks as useful tools for understanding some of the cultural variations that exist within any group. Different types of networks may be focused on a particular problem, a resource, an idea, or a social condition. For example, lifestyle groupings such as the following can typically be found among teenagers in most high schools in the United States; they clearly reflect different behaviors and interests:

- Skaters
- Jocks and cheerleaders

- Drug users
- Preppies
- Goths
- Dweebs and nerds

Ethnographers generate typologies by looking for the terms people in the setting use to define such natural groupings. At the same time they identify common behaviors that cut across groups, and they describe relationships within and between groups. These comparative activities help to define and differentiate one group from another. The groupings listed above represent only one kind of typology of peer groups in high school settings; there may be many more defined by club or organizational membership, preferred sports activities, income and class, and other characteristics.

An example of how a typological study can be carried out comes from the Flagstaff Multicultural AIDS Prevention Program (FMAPP). The purpose of the FMAPP project was to find new ways to reduce the transmission of HIV among active drug users. In this study we asked a series of questions guided by structural characteristics of networks. Some of the questions the researchers asked elicited information on:

- How long people had been using drugs
- What drugs they used
- Why they were using drugs
- What kinds of risks they were taking (especially those risks that might lead to HIV infection)
- What the characteristics of their own drug-using networks were

The purpose of these questions was to provide an overview of local drug use and drug-using groups.

One of the first uses of our ethnographic network mapping was to develop a drug networks classification or typology to see if risks varied across different kinds of networks. Our ethnographic interviews indicated there were three major structural conditions that differed among the various drug networks. These were:

- The **openness versus the closed condition** of networks
- The **types of social bonds** present in the groups
- The different kinds of **social interactions** that existed between network participants.

An **open network** is one that has a high percentage of newly or recently recruited members; a **closed network** is one that does not allow the recruitment of new members to any significant degree over time. We measured the **openness** of the networks by the number of new members recruited over time, combined with the length of time it took for someone to join a network from the outside. The types and the number of **social bonds** we identified across different groups include kinship relations, long-term friendships, shorter-term acquaintanceships, and weak or close-to-anonymous relationships. A single drug-using group may include all or only some of these relationships.

The third variable we used to construct our classification was the type and amount of **social interactions** (or activities) that exist within networks, such as group drug use, joint recreational activities, or work-related associations. Joint drug use, in particular, is a key social activity for these groups. We defined this variable along a continuum from absence of joint activities among group members to a high level of social interaction among most or all group members. Moving from no to low joint activity levels, we encountered face-to-face activities limited to dyads or triads within the larger group, which we considered to be a midpoint on the continuum. The far end of the activity continuum included a high level of social interaction, including parties, participation in softball leagues, and other recreational activities involving the entire group.

Our ethnographic network data combined these three structural domains to produce a typology with four distinct, internally consistent, and externally divergent kinds of drug networks. These were:

- Long-term injector networks
- Family-based drug networks
- Friendship-based networks
- Convenience networks

Definition: Network openness/closedness refers to the number of new members recruited during a designated period of time

Definition: Social bond refers to the type of relationship between "ego" and other members of the network. Social bonds may be multiple and weak versus limited and strong

Definition: Social interactions refer to activities network members participate in together

We found that *long-term injector networks* often included individuals from a variety of social, economic, and ethnic backgrounds. The primary purpose of such a group was to pool resources for the acquisition of drugs. Joint drug use activities did not extend very much beyond "scoring" (acquiring drugs). The group had social bonds based on kinship and very long-term friendships that helped to maintain the group, but they almost never got together socially. One of our ethnographic respondents described the group's primary activity, "scoring," as follows:

> Somebody in the group will get ahold of the others when they want to score or when they are going to score. Whoever wants some will put their money together and someone will go to . . . [major city] . . ., usually and get the stuff and call the others. The others will come and get their part and go home and use.

These drug users tended to be very secretive. Most of them were married or in monogamous relationships. They were employed at various economic levels. They might use drugs on a maintenance level during the week and get "loaded" on weekends or special occasions. The major area of risk for HIV transmission was contact with persons outside their own group, with whom they had **weak ties** and in this example, whose HIV status would be unknown.

Definition: Weak ties are links between people characterized by lack of intimacy and infrequent contact

These networks are quite different from *family-based networks* that were predominately kinship groups (parents, children, siblings, in-laws, or fictive kinship or godparenthood or *compadrazgo* relationships among Latinos). One particular drug network we studied consisted of a three-generation family of more than ten injection drug users. Members of this network were either born into, had married into, or had a steady sexual partner in the group. The participants had gone to school together, and many were raised together. The groups tended to be homogeneous in terms of socioeconomic status and ethnic identification. Drug use with this group could be considered a family tradition; a special case of peer pressure. Within such groups, individuals faced very strong pressure to conform to group norms. Nonusers were viewed as critical or condemning of the group's behavior. An example of this was reported by a group member who was attempting to abstain from drug use.

> They called me names, they said I was too good for them . . . I fought with them. . . . I beat two of them up but I still had to go to the hospital.

HIV risk in this group primarily stemmed from the sharing of injection equipment between family and friends. For the most part, the membership of family networks consisted of individuals in long-standing monogamous partnerships; thus within them there was little exchange of sex for drugs, although there was the occasional co-occurrence of sex with drug use among otherwise monogamous couples. The most common drugs of choice in this group were cocaine, crack, rock, crystal meth, marijuana, and alcohol.

Long-term friendship networks (friendship-based networks) were semiopen systems whose members scored together and were socially bonded through drug use and through duration of relationship, including kinship. The majority of these networks, like family-based networks, were relatively homogeneous in terms of socioeconomic status and ethnicity. Individuals in these networks involved each other in both drug use as well as other types of social activities. Further, members often were connected through work. These groups were somewhat open to recruitment of new members, although the process took time. "Good friends" could be invited to "party" (use drugs) with the group, but becoming a full-scale member could take from twelve to eighteen months. Drugs used in this type of group included injected heroin, cocaine, crack, speed, and alcohol, and members were both injectors and noninjectors. A respondent described a night of mixed drug use as follows: "People will be drinking or doing coke and those who want to shoot up go in the other room."

Risk in this group centered on the sharing of works (drug paraphernalia, needles) "among friends." Group members had multiple sex partners that changed over time. Sex was sometimes exchanged for drugs, although these exchanges generally were part of an ongoing social relationship, rather than commercial in nature.

Convenience (acquaintance) networks were the most open of the four drug network types. These networks were characterized by people who used many kinds of drugs and who "bridged" or skipped from group to group. The most commonly used drug was crack cocaine; crack dealers tended to operate more openly than did most of the other suppliers. Known buyers were more rapidly introduced to and accepted in the group. Group members with little knowledge of a buyer generally made the introduction to the dealer, saying, "He's okay, he's buying." This indicated that the group member performing the introduction had observed the new person scoring or buying drugs. Buyers had money, and having money was an important credential for entry into these networks and expedited acceptance. Individuals in these groups regularly exchanged sex for drugs, and there were far more "impersonal" exchanges than in the other groups. A long-time drug user derogatorily referred to members of this type of group as "trash can addicts" because of their use of any kind of drug. These networks tended to consist of users new in the area, those who were unpopular with other groups because of the frequency and intensity of their drug use, those in transition between groups, and young drug users who had not been recruited to a stable network.

The convenience or acquaintance groups appeared to be at highest risk for HIV infection because they engaged in a full range of activities involving the exchange of sex for drugs (commercial and noncommercial), sex with multiple partners, and needle sharing with strangers. They also included a large proportion of individuals who were highly mobile and who were likely to move back and forth to nearby urban areas during the year. Their contact with higher HIV prevalence sites and their random interaction with local drug and sex partners increased the local risk of HIV exposure and infection.

Understanding these different types of networks and their associated HIV risk was valuable for our AIDS prevention project. It allowed us to relate drug users' social contexts to other types of behavior. We used statistical procedures to test the usefulness of the classification system and found that network membership was an important predictor of the likelihood of getting tested for HIV (an important element in preventing the disease). The networks also differed in the frequency of overall drug use among members, the context of drug use (family versus friends versus strangers), the frequency of injection (from not using injectable drugs to frequent injection and sharing needles), the frequency and type of sexual encounters within the networks, and the frequency of self-protection by using condoms. These data were very useful for targeting HIV intervention and education activities.

This example illustrates how typologies can advance our understanding of the important social relationships that exist within and between networks. They allow us to classify differences among social networks based on conditions such as the amount of time people spend with relatives, the types of economic exchanges that people engage in, the risks people are willing to take, or any other set of social conditions that are important for understanding a culture. Finally, they can be used to generate hypotheses about social groups that can be tested in other studies.

Classification exercises such as the one described above that characterize different groupings within social settings can be applied to most domains of social interaction, including friendship groups, student playgroups, political activists, and others.

Interaction and "Embedded Behaviors"

Much research in the social sciences has concentrated on individual behavior, motivations, and other personal conditions that influence behavior. However, most human behaviors are not conducted alone. They are set in the midst of, and may be the result of, interactions with other people. Network research is first and foremost the study of these interactions. Social network research is extremely important for examining specific kinds of behavior in the context of interaction, particularly in cases where researchers want to study if, how, and under what circumstances people learn new behaviors or change their behavior. Such research takes place directly within the context where behavioral learning and change takes place; for example, in personal and social networks. It is thus "embedded" in these settings, contexts, and interactions.

One example of the importance of studying embedded behaviors comes from research on adolescents (Domínguez and Watkins 2003; Moreno et al. 2009). While individual teenagers can differ in their motivation, their intention to behave or misbehave, and their own values or norms, it is clear that the actual behavior of most teenagers, regardless of their ethnic/racial affiliation, often matches with that of their peers more so than with any other group. Peer pressure occurs within a natural network, and studying how the structure and elements of a network shape and influence individual behavior can tell us a great deal about how cultural systems, including those of teenagers, really work. For example, young people often start using drugs like alcohol and marijuana because some of their friends offer such drugs to them and exert pressure either directly or indirectly to use them. Using them (and exerting social pressure to use them) demonstrates that they "belong" to the group. By contrast, other friends may protect teens against such risks by modeling resistance or avoidance behavior and by supporting each other to avoid harmful behavior. These conditions can be studied through an ethnographic description of the behaviors associated with specific networks and the processes through which such behaviors are transferred and supported or encouraged. The advantage of ethnographic description is that it can discover behavioral details and patterns of communication and influence specific to the group, which can then be quantified when the ethnographer wishes to measure them in other networks.

Cross-Group Differences

Ethnographic network research also is useful for comparing and contrasting structural and social differences among groups as well as differences in group dynamics across cultural, social, age, and gender configurations. It can be used to consider how the characteristics of networks influence behaviors (both positively and negatively) and meet or fail to meet social needs. For example, different kinds of kinship groups can be examined for the ways in which they support group members during periods of economic stress or place demands on group members because of emotional or economic needs or familial responsibilities.

Voluntary associations are composed of and reinforce existing social networks, or can even replace them when they are disrupted or destroyed by war or environmental disasters in various cultures. They function to integrate migrants or immigrants to urban areas, solve social problems, and provide various forms of voluntary and professional social services (Tomeh 1973). Such organizations provide another example of the economic, social, and spiritual impact of social networks on individuals' survival and success across cultures.

Definition: Voluntary organizations are those that people join voluntarily to meet a variety of their personal, economic, and social needs

The above examples suggest a number of logical steps that can be taken to initialize and conduct network ethnography.

STEPS IN THE CONDUCT OF NETWORK ETHNOGRAPHY

- Identify "neighborhoods" or geographic areas where research will take place.
- Obtain lists of "groups" by name or local jargon/terminology from local experts in the research domain.
- Identify individuals who are members of these groups.
- Develop "rapport"—a close and trusting relationship with these individuals—by spending time with them in the field.
- Use interviewing and participant observation techniques to gather information about them, their group, their activities, and the relationships of group members.
- Interview as many other members of the group as possible to find out whether their views of the group, their activities, and their relationships are similar to each other.
- Define inclusion/exclusion rules (the boundaries of the group), bridges, bonds, activities, and relationships with other groups.

- Continue this work with other named or otherwise identified groups.
- Systematically compare and contrast groups on an ongoing basis (using continuous comparison) to identify dimensions or characteristics of difference in structures, boundaries, and behaviors among groups.
- Use either qualitative or quantitative (survey) methods to associate network (group) characteristics with other behaviors of group members (drug or sex risk, educational achievement, social mobility).

EGO-CENTERED APPROACHES TO UNDERSTANDING NETWORKS

Definition: Ego-centered networks are defined in relationship to a single individual. An ego-centered network consists of all the people that that individual—or "ego"—defines as important in some specific way

People resemble and are influenced in their behavior and belief by those with whom they associate. The most immediate way to understand these associations is through the establishment and description of personal or **ego-centered networks**. Ego-centered networks are a primary cultural anchor point. Information about ego-centered personal networks allows ethnographers to identify and describe some of the important traits of "average" or typical networks in a given cultural setting as well as their variations. They also can help to describe and analyze individuals' perceptions of the social influence of personal networks on their own beliefs and behaviors. These traits, such as the size of networks, the closeness and duration of relationships between "ego" and personal network members, and the impact of peer norms on "ego" can be collected from every person in a community or other setting, or from a selected sample of people in a community or an ethnic/cultural group.

Personal network data in a moderate to large sample normally are collected through the use of a survey in which everyone is asked the same questions. The survey includes a variety of questions of interest to the study (demographic, health, economic, leisure-time activity, risk behaviors, etc.), and a network component consisting of specific questions about the respondent's personal network. The survey may be administered as a questionnaire that people fill out themselves, or as an interview in which people are asked questions either face to face or via a computer-assisted program or both.

Most people's personal networks include relatively large numbers. But most studies are not interested in ALL the people the respondent knows or with whom he/she has a relationship. They ARE interested in the specific set of relationships that has to do with the topic of the study. For this reason the leading question that elicits members of the personal network is critically important. Leading questions for a drug use study might include: tell me the names or nicknames of all the people with whom you inject drugs and all the people who you know who use any kind of drug. Leading questions for a study of youth party culture might include: tell me the names or nicknames of all the people you go to clubs or bars with and all the people you go to parties with.

In a standard ego-centered network survey, it is not necessary to retain network members' names, since they will not be contacted in any way and the data for the entire personal network are summarized as frequencies and percentages, or means. The researcher records names and nicknames but then assigns a code to each "alter" or individual in a respondent's network. Alters are identified by nicknames, or numbers. Figure 5.1 provides examples of questions asked to interviewees (egos) about their networks. Figure 5.2 is an example of a form that can be used to fill in basic information about alters. Figure 5.3 lists questions asked to egos about the demographic characteristics and drug and sex risk behavior of each alter. Data such as these can be recorded in a data collection matrix such as the one in Figure 5.4, and then used in conjunction with questions such as those listed in Figure 5.1.

To use the social networks matrix, each "alter" is given a number from 1 to 25 (or however many the researcher thinks makes sense based on knowledge of the study population). Each number refers to an alter (someone identified in accordance with the leading question as a member of

(Interviewer: <u>Do not</u> record client responses on these sheets or attach them to Client Network Questionnaire Packet. These pages are <u>Interviewer prompts only</u>. They are to be kept separated from Questionnaire packets and reused at each interview session.)

[RECORD ALL RESPONSES TO Q43-Q90 ON SOCIAL NETWORKS MATRICES 1 AND 2]

[INTERVIEWER READ:]
Now I would like to get an idea of the people who are important to you in a number of different ways. In order to do this, I will be asking you a lot of personal questions about yourself and the people who you have close, personal contact with. However, all of the information that you give us will be kept strictly confidential. I will ask that you list the people who you have contact with by their full names and nicknames so we can keep track of who we are referring to in this and future interviews. The people you list here are covered by the same protections in this project as you are. We will not share any of the information with them that you give us at any time during the project without your permission.

Q43. I'd like you to think about people you have contact with, who are involved in your life in a significant way during the <u>past 6 months</u>. *[give respondent a specific date, a benchmark, to go back to]* Start with current people and work your way back. Some of these people may hassle you or argue with you, making your life difficult at times. But, if they are important in your life, then you should include them in your list.

Q43a. First, please tell me the first and last names and any nicknames of all the different people who you have <u>used **any kind of drugs**</u> with in the last <u>6 months</u>. Please keep in mind that all this information will be kept strictly confidential. *[Get a full list of these before going on to Q43b. **Place a 1 in column 43a after each person's name.**]*

Q43b. Next, please tell me the first and last names and any nicknames of all the different people who you have **injected drugs** with in the last 6 months. *[Get a complete list of names; write down new names only. **Place a 1 in column 43b after each person's name who was mentioned here.**]*

Q43c. Next, please tell me the first and last names and any nicknames of all the different people who you have **had sex** with in the last 6 months. *[Get a complete list of names; write down new names only. **Place a 1 in column 43c after each person's name who was mentioned here.**]*

Q43d. Next, please tell me the first and last names and any nicknames of all the different people who you <u>are **close to**</u> *[Get a complete list of names; write down new names only. **Place a 1 in column 43d after each person's name who was mentioned here.**]*

Q43e. Next, please tell me the first and last names and any nicknames of all the different people who you <u>have a **serious conflict with**</u>. *[Get a complete list of names; write down new names only. **Place a 1 in column 43e after each person's name who was mentioned here.**]*

Figure 5.1 Interviewer guide social networks

For Identification of "Alters"

DATE: _____

PARTICIPANT ID#: _____ MASTER #:

#	Full and Nick Name(s)	Relationship	Sex m/f	Eth. aa/l/w/o	Age
1					
2					
3					
4					
5					
6					
7					
8					
9					
10					
11					
12					
13					
14					
15					
16					
17					
18					
19					
20					

Note: This instrument is an adaptation of a data collection matrix used by the Institute for Community Research and the Hispanic Health Council in Hartford, Connecticut, to record basic background data from "ego" about the members of his or her social network ("alters").

Figure 5.2 Basic data entry form for identification of "alters"

You have listed _____ people that you identify as being important to you, or being significantly
                    (num.)
involved in your life in some way. For each one of these individuals I would like you to answer the following
questions <u>to the best of your ability</u>.

Q44.   Is _____ male or female ?

                   Male   1
                   Female   2

Q45.   Is _____ **(Interviewer: read list and circle <u>only</u> one):**

                   Black (not Hispanic)   1
                   White (not Hispanic)   2
                   Hispanic/Latino   (ASK Q45a BELOW)   3
                   Other **(Specify):** _____   4
                   DK/Unsure   77
                   Refused   88

NOTE TO INTERVIEWER: FOR OTHER THAN HISPANIC, GO TO Q62 BELOW

        Q45a.   (If Hispanic, ASK) Is _____ **(Interviewer: read list and circle <u>only</u> one):**

                   Puerto Rican   1
                   Cuban   2
                   Mexican Am./Chicano   3
                   Mexican   4
                   Dominican Republican   5
                   Central or South American   6
                            Specify country
                   Other _____   7
                   DK/Unsure   77
                   Refused   88

Q46.   How old is _____ ?

                   AGE _____   DK/UNSURE - 77   REFUSED - 88

Q47.   What is _____'s relationship to you ?

01 Mother/Father   07 Niece/Nephew   13 Lover, girl-/boyfriend 19 Dealer
02 Sister/Brother   08 Grandchild   14 Ex-lover/Ex-spouse   20 Houseman
03 Child   09 Spouse   15 Friend   21 Doctor
04 Grandparent   10 Mo./Fa. In-law   16 Roommate   22 Counselor
05 Aunt/Uncle   11 Si./Br. In-law   17 Neighbor   23 Priest/Pastor/etc.
06 Cousin   12 Compadres/   18 Running Buddy/   24 Other

Q48.   How long have you known _____ ? Q48a. Months ____Q64b. Years

Q49.   On a scale of 1 (not at all) to 5 (extremely), how strong is your relationship with _____?

            (Score) _____   DK/UNSURE   7   REFUSED   8

Figure 5.3   Demographics and drug use of alters

Q50.   On a scale of 1 (not at all) to 5 (extremely), how important is _____ to you?

     (Score) _____   DK/UNSURE   7   REFUSED   8

Q51.   On a scale of 1 (not at all) to 5 (completely), how much can you trust _____?

     (Score) _____   DK/UNSURE   7   REFUSED   8

Q52.   If you were HIV positive, or had AIDS, would you be willing to tell _____?

     No   0   Yes   1   DK/UNSURE   7   REFUSED   8

Q53.   How many days in the past 30 days have you been in contact (in person, phone, etc.) with this person ?

     Number of days _____

HIV RISK BEHAVIORS: NETWORK MEMBERS

		No	Yes	DK/Unsure	Refused
Q54.	Does _____ know that you use drugs ?	No	Yes	DK/Unsure	Refused
		0	1	7	8
Q55.	Does _____ provide you with drugs of any kind ?	No	Yes	DK/Unsure	Refused
		0	1	7	8
Q56.	Do you provide _____ with drugs of any kind ?	No	Yes	DK/Unsure	Refused
		0	1	7	8
Q57.	Does _____ inject drugs ?	No	Yes	DK/Unsure	Refused
		0	1	7	8
Q58.	Does _____ inject drugs in a shooting gallery ?	No	Yes	DK/Unsure	Refused
		0	1	7	8
Q59.	Does _____ inject drugs, using needles that he/she knows had been used by someone else ?	No	Yes	DK/Unsure	Refused
		0	1	7	8
Q60.	Does _____ share needles in a shooting gallery ?	No	Yes	DK/Unsure	Refused
		0	1	7	8
Q61.	Does _____ inject drugs using needles that had previously been used by you ?	No	Yes	DK/Unsure	Refused
		0	1	7	8

Figure 5.3   (*Continued*)

Q62.	Do you inject drugs using needles that had previously been used by _____?	**No**	**Yes**	**DK/Unsure**	**Refused**
		0	1	7	8

Q63.	Does _____ share cookers or cotton with other people?	**No**	**Yes**	**DK/Unsure**	**Refused**
		0	1	7	8

Q64.	Do you and _____ share cookers or cotton ?	**No**	**Yes**	**DK/Unsure**	**Refused**
		0	1	7	8

Figure 5.3   (*Continued*)

the ego's personal network). Question numbers head each column of the matrix, and the questionnaire is physically placed beside the matrix during the interview. As the questions are asked, the matrix is filled in with codes corresponding to the participant's answers.

To assess the connectedness of the network, from "ego's" perspective, respondents may be asked how each member of the personal network interacts with every other member—based on their own knowledge (Figure 5.5). This question provides information on the ego's perception of how his or her network members relate, and from it a personal "macronetwork" can be created and described using concepts applied to macronetwork or full relational network analysis. Later on in this chapter, we will discuss how a full relational network analysis proceeds from this point.

Information such as that above, which is used to describe typical personal networks, is normally reported in the form of tables, such as Table 5.1, which comes from the Flagstaff Multicultural AIDS Prevention Project (FMAPP). Table 5.1 compares the people who provided the information (respondents or egos) with the people whom they named as being part of their personal network (alters). In this case, we asked about the demographic characteristics of people who had been part of their network for the past thirty days, and people who were present the last time they used drugs with other people.

When we analyzed all of the personal network questions in our questionnaire, we found that the number of people each respondent or ego reported spending time with ranged from zero (they were isolates) to more than twenty-five people, with the majority responding that they spent time with from one to ten other people. Thus the typical

DATE:

MASTER #: _____

[INTERVIEWER: Refer to Social Network Interview Guide for questions to fill out matrix. Copy list of network members by full and nick names and general characteristics on Network Matrix Pull Out List.]

#	Initials	43a	43b	43c	43d	43e	44	45	45a	46	47	48a	48b	49	50	51	52	53	54	55	56	57	58	59	60	61	62	63	64
		Drugs with	Inj. with	Sex with	Close with	Confl. with	M/F	Ethn.	Hisp. Eth.	Age	Relat. Code	Months know	Yrs. know	Strength relat.	Import. relat.	Trust relat.	Tell HIV+	Days contact	Know use dr.	Provide you dr.	You prov. dr.	Injs. drugs	Injs. in gallery	Use used needles	Share ned. gall.	Use your used ndl.	U use X's used ndl.	X shares cookers	U & X share ckr.
1																													
2																													
3																													
4																													
5																													
6																													
7																													
8																													
9																													
10																													
11																													
12																													
13																													
14																													
15																													
16																													

Figure 5.4 Social networks matrix. This instrument is an adaptation of a data collection matrix used by the Institute for Community Research and the Hispanic Health Council in Hartford, Connecticut, to record basic demographic and drug-risk-related data from "ego" about the members of his or her social network ("alters").

Total network members:

MASTER #: _____   DATE:

Interviewer: For each person in the network, place an X over the appropriate letter in relation to that contact's interactions with every other contact. Insert contacts' initials in the numbered boxes at the top and left using the Pull-Out Matrix to translate numbers into names.] For each contact, ASK: 1) Do (2) and (1) know each other [if yes, CROSS out K]...; 2) In the past 4 months, have (2) and (1) done drugs together [CROSS out D]; 3) In the past 4 months, have (2) and (1) had sex together [CROSS out S]; and 4) In the past 4 months, have (2) and (1) gotten into a serious physical fight with each other | CROSS out V]: ETC.

Initials ↓ →	1		2		3		4		5		6		7		8		9		10
2	K	D																	
	S	V																	
3	K	D	K	D															
	S	V	S	V															
4	K	D	K	D	K	D													
	S	V	S	V	S	V													
5	K	D	K	D	K	D	K	D											
	S	V	S	V	S	V	S	V											
6	K	D	K	D	K	D	K	D	K	D									
	S	V	S	V	S	V	S	V	S	V									
7	K	D	K	D	K	D	K	D	K	D	K	D							
	S	V	S	V	S	V	S	V	S	V	S	V							
8	K	D	K	D	K	D	K	D	K	D	K	D	K	D					
	S	V	S	V	S	V	S	V	S	V	S	V	S	V					
9	K	D	K	D	K	D	K	D	K	D	K	D	K	D	K	D			
	S	V	S	V	S*	V	S	V	S	V	S	V	S	V	S	V			
10	K	D	K	D	K	D	K	D	K	D	K	D	K	D	K	D	K	D	
	S	V	S	V	S	V	S	V	S	V	S	V	S	V	S	V	S	V	

Figure 5.5   Data recording matrix for collection of data on interaction of all members of the network. *This instrument is an adaptation of a data collection matrix used by the Institute for Community Research and the Hispanic Health Council in Hartford, Connecticut, to record basic demographic and drug-risk-related data from "ego" about the risk-related interactions among the members of his or her social network ("alters").

Table 5.1 Gender, Age, and Ethnic Distribution of Respondents, and Respondent's Thirty-Day and Recent-Use Networks

	Respondent (Ego) N = 52	People in Respondent's Thirty-Day Network N = 127	Alters Present in Most Recent Use N = 90
Gender			
Male	34(67)[a]	81(63)	62(68)
Female	18(33)	46(37)	28(31)
Age			
10–19[b]	12(23)	36(28)	28(31)
20–29	14(26)	38(29)	25(27)
30–39	23(44)	43(33)	30(33)
40–49	3(5)	9(7)	7(7)
50–59	0(0)	1(1)	0(0)
Ethnicity			
African American	10(19)	22(17)	16(17)
Hispanic	19(36)	64(50)	42(46)
Anglo	18(34)	35(27)	27(30)
Native American	5(9)	6(4)	5(5)

[a]Number in brackets is the percentage figure.
[b]In order to participate, individuals had to be eighteen years of age or older, could not have been in treatment in the past twelve months, and had to have a positive urine screen for cocaine or heroin or needle marks (tracks) and a positive urine screen for some other injectable illicit drug. Therefore, this category includes only eighteen- and nineteen-year-olds.

personal network included up to ten family members and all but sixteen of the respondents fell into this range. These relatively small networks commonly include both drug users and nonusers, some kin relations, and close friends. Only 25 percent responded that all of the people they spent time with use drugs. Of those alters who used drugs, 25 percent injected drugs, 69 percent smoked crack, and the rest used some other drug.

By combining and examining all of the ego-centered network data, we determined that the majority of drug networks are small (two to ten individuals), are based on close friendships or kinship ties, and are relatively stable in their composition. The data also indicated that the majority of risky encounters, such as needle-sharing activities or sexual relationships, occur with the first three people named by ego as members of their network. A smaller proportion of the needle sharing and sexual encounters occur with people beyond ego's closest or most salient personal network members. It is exactly these encounters, called **weak ties**, that are the most risky kinds of contacts for the majority of drug users. Weak ties are defined by less intimacy and infrequent association. Weak ties bring new "information" or risk and fewer interpersonal responsibilities and obligations into an existing closely connected network. Based on this data, part of our HIV prevention and education effort has been directed at making recommendations that would help these individuals break, reduce, or decrease the risks associated with their "weak tie" relationships.

In the same project we also explored how useful other ego-centered measures of network structure were in identifying conditions that linked individual social networks to the individual's risk of spending time in jail or becoming infected with HIV through drug use. This process allowed us to use relatively simple and nonthreatening questions that could be asked about an individual's social relationships, and at the same time, could tell us important information about their probable health status and risk-taking behavior.

Definition: Ties are links between people. They are measured by perceived intimacy and frequency of association. Indicators of tie strength are "How close are you to X?" and "How often do you see X?"

EXAMPLE 5.1

THE NATURE OF PERSONAL NETWORK RELATIONSHIPS AND RISK FOR HIV, DRUGS, AND INCARCERATION

In our study of drug use and its relationship to HIV/AIDS risk, we were able to collect data from a total of 496 active drug users. We hypothesized that the nature of personal relationships (close to distant, dense to dispersed, few to multiple connections among members) had an impact on the average level of risk that a person incurs over time. Measuring different elements of personal network structure should be significantly related to individuals' HIV, drug, and incarceration risks. This is possible because differences in personal networks may result in differences in the amount of information that is transmitted to a particular individual; the length of time it takes information to reach a person in the network; differences among people who are gate keepers for the information flow; measures of differential influence in the group; and measures of the probability that someone can or cannot receive information sent through the network (cf. Doreian 1974; Ford and Fulkerson 1956; Gomory and Hu 1964; Katz 1953; Taylor 1969).

We assumed that for individuals, risk taking is a generalized, rather than specific, activity. If they take risks in one area of their life, they are much more likely to take risks in other areas. Therefore, the individuals who were most likely to accept early recruitment into our program were more likely to be higher risk takers than the individuals recruited from the same network later in the process. Since they did not know us or our project well, it was as much a risk for them to participate (and possibly be caught up in a drug sting) as it was for them to interact with other strangers. We hypothesized that entering a project as one of the first members of a network to be recruited (engaging in a bridging activity) might be a proxy measure for individual influence or centrality in the network. We based our analysis on the assumption that the individuals most willing to try out a new program were also those most likely to take the lead in other social undertakings, or risky behavior.

We were able to show that the program recruitment order data (the rank order in which each individual in a network was recruited into the project) was associated with network structure measures (how they were connected, what subgroup they belonged to, etc.), and with increased risk taking (Trotter, Baldwin, and Bowen 1995; Trotter, Bowen, and Potter 1995; Trotter et al. 1996). Early arrivals in each network were more likely to have tried a drug treatment program than the later recruits in the same network, while later arrivals were more likely to have no sex partners who used injection drugs. Those recruited earlier in networks were very likely to have sex partners who were also injection drug users—that is, they participated in double risk relationships.

Some 321 individuals in our study participated in only one drug network (66.5 percent), and 162 individuals (33.5 percent) were members of two or more drug networks. We also hypothesized that membership in two or more networks involved more potential risk and risk taking than membership in a single network. Analysis confirmed this hypothesis. We were thus able to conclude that simply asking individuals to self-identify as having either single or multiple network membership was sufficient to provide a direct indication of both their type and level of risk taking in their personal drug-using networks.

These results showed us that this type of personal or ego-centered network data collection could be very useful for finding out important facts about the most common personal networks of individuals in our projects. The same type of information could be easily collected on personal networks associated with participation in educational or economic development programs, social integration into community life, exposure to violence, gang affiliation, or any other cultural domain.

STEPS IN THE COLLECTION AND ANALYSIS OF EGO-CENTERED NETWORK DATA

■ Develop an instrument on your topic that includes collection of information on the research topic (for example drug use) in five ways:

1. from the individual;
2. about each individual (alter) mentioned by the individual;
3. about the interaction of the individual with each alter;
4. whether alters know each other;
5. what known risk behaviors occur between each alter and all others.

■ Identify a representative sample of individuals from whom to survey—or include these questions in your regular survey.
■ Interview the sample of individuals.

Below we describe the steps used to analyze ego-centered network data in a study of drug use. In this study, the network characteristics of "ego" with regard to risky drug- and sex-related behavior can be analyzed in association with other behaviors or conditions, such as whether ego and his or her alters are infected with the HIV virus. Demographic and other known risk-related differences in the characteristic of ego-centered networks can be identified and the origins and impact of those differences explored. In the example these network differences include size of network, gender ratio, and drug risk indices. Ethnographers can use the procedures similar to those listed below for network studies addressing any other topic in the social sciences.

SOME STEPS IN ANALYZING EGOCENTRIC NETWORK DATA

1. Describe the networks of individuals in terms of the following:

   - Network size (number of network members named)
   - Gender ratio
   - Sexual preference
   - Ethnicity ratio (the relative proportions of people from various ethnic groups)
   - Age (in terms of the mean and modal age of members, the range of ages in the network, and their standard deviation)
   - The ratio of kin to nonkin sexual partners among members
   - Intensity of the relationships between ego and all other members of the network

2. Establish levels of risk for ego as an individual by creating two indices: a drug risk index and a sex risk index.

   - Sum up all of ego's risky drug behaviors.
   - Sum up all of ego's risky sex behaviors.
   - Add together the sum of ego's risky drug behaviors and the sum of ego's risky sex behaviors. This sum total is an overall index of risk behavior for an individual.

3. Establish risk indices for drugs and sex (as in #2) for every network contact, based on what ego reports for the contact or alter.

4. Obtain ego's total risk exposure score using the following steps:

   - Add ego's combined drug and sex risk index to the combined drug and sex risk indices for all network members (obtained in #3).

- Divide this total score by the number of people in ego's network to create an average risk index.

5. Obtain the total risk exposure score of ego's network:

- Count and add together risky behaviors of all alters with one another.

The variables obtained in this way measure variations in ego-centered networks that differ from variation created by demographic characteristics. They can be correlated with demographic variables and used as "predictors" or correlates of other behavior or conditions (such as health or mental health status).

CONSTRUCTING COMMUNITYWIDE MACRONETWORKS FROM EGO NETWORK DATA

It is possible to use the data collected on ego networks to construct and map a macro network of connected individuals in an open system and to identify the structural characteristics of that macro network, including the location of key individuals and the types of relationships **Key point** among members. *This requires significant knowledge of the network through prior observation and the ability to confirm ties among individuals using ethnographic data and personal field experience.* It can be begun through quantitative means, using the methods described above in the collection of data on ego network members and their characteristics and types of relationships with ego. However, ensuring the utility of ego-network data in the construction of macro networks requires seeking the most complete naming information possible (e.g., full names, all formal first and last names, all nicknames, etc.) when generating the list of ego network members. This list will be the initial source of information needed to identify members of the group who are named on one or more name lists of other network members.

Information collected from respondents about named individuals in their personal network involves potential risk of loss of confidentiality with respect to respondents' peers and contacts. Institutional Review Boards (IRBs) that monitor the ethical treatment of human subjects in research usually deem reports about the behavior of others in the context of a health study as involving more potential benefit than risk, but they and the researchers must always be concerned about the possibility of confidentiality violations. It is important to note here that using personal identification information (e.g., names, addresses, or other personal identifiers) in research must be done with great caution and with attention to ethical considerations of informed consent; protection of "study participants" from research related risks, including breaches of confidentiality and inadvertent disclosure of sensitive information; and the rights of individuals to autonomy and voluntary participation in research. Thus, all procedures for constructing networks should be fully reviewed by an Institutional Review Board and thorough protections put into place to protect network name data. It is also good practice to include in the mapped macronetwork only those individuals who have agreed through informed consent to participate in the study and were interviewed in the study, not those who may have been named but not interviewed (in other words, who did not give their consent to be included in the research), though this may result in a reduction of information that can be included in the network map.

Cross Reference: 🐰 Book 6 for a discussion of IRBs and ethnographic research

In order to encourage naming of all network members who are important to a particular question (e.g., individuals who potentially share the risk of disease transmission, members of a grassroots organization, teenagers participating in shoplifting, organic gardeners wanting to share information about seed cultures), the process of name generating should begin with a request for full information from the participant and heuristics to assist him or her to remember important people who might not otherwise be named. This could be phrased as in the following introduction we used in a study of drug using network members in Hartford.

EXAMPLE 5.2

INTRODUCTION FOR A DRUG USE NETWORK STUDY

"Now I would like to get an idea of the people who are important to you in a number of different ways. In order to do this, I will be asking you a lot of personal questions about yourself and the people who you have close, personal contact with. However, all of the information that you give us will be kept strictly confidential. I will ask that you list the people who you have contact with by their *full names and nicknames* so we can keep track of who we are referring to in this and future interviews. The people you list here are covered by the same protections in this project as you are. We will not share any of the information with them that you give us at any time without your permission. Now I'd like you to think about people you have contact with, who have been involved in your life in a significant way during the *past 6 months. [Give respondent a specific date, a benchmark, to go back to.]* Start with current people and work your way back. Some of these people may hassle you or argue with you, making your life difficult at times. But, if they are important in your life, then you should include them in your list." (Weeks, Clair, Borgatti, Radda, and Schensul 2002).

After this introduction, the researcher follows with a series of questions to generate names of people with whom the participant has particular relationships or interactions (e.g., does drugs with, has sexual relations with, attends meetings with, receives support/resources from, etc.). After generating the full name list, questions about characteristics of each named individual (attributes) and about the types and characteristics of relationships (trusting, long/short term, friend/family/instrumental, shared risk, etc.) can also be collected for use in defining individuals within the total group and various ties in the network.

With the name lists of a set of members of a particular open network, mapping the macronetwork can proceed by constructing a matrix of all individuals by all other individuals in the group for whom data are available and who have consented to be interviewed. Researchers then begin a painstaking procedure of indicating the presence or absence of a link between each of those network members and each of the other members. Links can be indicated as unidirectional (A named B, but B did not name A), bidirectional

(A and B named each other), or nondirectional (neither A nor B name each other but they are known to have a relationship, based on ethnographic observation). Matched same or similar names (i.e., the name of a member of the interviewed network matches a name on someone else's ego network name list) generally need to be verified as the same person, either by looking at other demographic information about the individual (e.g., sex, ethnicity, age) or through direct observations of interactions between the two individuals, and even with other network members they both name. Thus, the process is enhanced by deep ethnographic knowledge of and experience in the community from which the network members are drawn and the ethnographers' or outreach workers' familiarity with respondents and their networks through interaction with them in the field/recruitment site.

Upon completing the identification of as many linked members of the total network as possible, the constructed macronetwork matrix can be brought into UCINET (Borgatti, Everett, and Freeman 1999) or Pajek V.1.28 (cf. Batagelj and Mrvar 2010) with data on individual attributes and types and characteristics of relationship ties. This allows analysis of the entire network structure and components, such as density of ties, various centrality measures of network members, and other analyses of associations between network structural factors and attributes of individuals (nodes) or relationship types (ties). These data can also be displayed in various network maps using NetDraw (Borgatti 2002), which provide illustrations of linkages among network members who have the same or multiple relationship ties.

FULL NETWORK RELATIONSHIPS: RECIPROCAL NETWORK INFORMATION

Data collected about the reciprocal relationships within social networks can be very useful in helping ethnographers understand complex conditions in everyday life. Ethnographic research on entire relational networks and open macro networks includes information about the **connectedness**; the **power and influence** that individual actors

Definition: Connectedness is the extent of reciprocal relationships among individuals in a network

Definition:
Power/
influence is
the degree to which
a person in a network
gives and receives
information or other
resources

Definition:
Role
relationships
are those associated
with a particular place
or position in a social
network

Definition:
Cliques/
components
are subunits within
a larger network
designed by the
greater strength of
their inconnectedness
compared with other
parts of the network

Definition:
Density is the
actual number
of relationships found
in a network compared
with the total
number of possible
relationships

exhibit in a network; the **role relationships** that are demonstrated in a network; the impact of that particular social network position (such as a bridge, or a particular configuration of network connections) on people; the subdivision of the network into **cliques and components**; and the overall **density** of a given network, compared with other networks. The following sections identify some of the most common ways that these aspects of networks are analyzed and understood.

Communication Flow

Communication (speaking, visiting, sending messages) in networks can be assessed by measuring the presence or absence of changes in the level of information flow within the network (Hubbell 1965; Taylor 1969). Network data can be collected to identify the presence or absence of particular topics of communication between individuals and between sets of individuals. The patterns of information flow within networks, sometimes called connectivity (Doreian 1974), can be characterized by several measures, including the amount of information that passes through a network; identification of the people who are gatekeepers to the information flow; measures of differential influence in the group; and measures of the probability that someone can or cannot receive information that is introduced into the network (Ford and Fulkerson 1956; Gomory and Hu 1964; Katz 1953; Taylor 1969). A social network research project that focused on communication would describe most or all of these conditions for each of the relationships or behaviors that were studied.

Distance and Segmentation

Network researchers have created two primary methods for identifying key structural elements of groups. One is based on the idea of social cohesion, where cliques or circles of social actors are identified by the bonds that link them together (Bron and Kerbosch 1973; Mokken 1979). The other is based on the idea of structural equivalence, where people who are similarly connected (have the same types of links to others) are thought to be more similar to each other than to people in the same network who have different types of links to others (Killworth and Bernard 1974, Burt 1976). These different measures all provide information on the ways that networks work.

Some of the configurations of relationships and the changes in relationships between individuals in a network also can be identified. Changes may be caused by some kind of intervention or event, or may be attributable to natural changes in people's lives. These changes can be assessed by the number of reduced connections among all network members or among some portions of the network (Doreian 1974; Burt 1976) or by looking at changes in the composition or location of subgroups or cliques and the reasons for them. For example, in some drug-using networks, people who go into drug treatment programs decide to not interact with their drug-using friends in order to stay away from drugs. This avoidance causes significant changes in the social networks of both the drug users and the nonusers.

Positions and Roles of Network Members

The roles people play and the positions they hold in a network also affect how communication flows in a network, since people who are more central to a network tend to have control over information. Looking at the centralization of a network provides a way to measure the degree to which information is controlled by specific individuals within a network (Stephenson and Zelen 1991). For some networks, a reduction of centralization should correlate with the creation of more communication linkages between noncentral individuals. Careful ethnographic observation should be able to detect changes in influence, as is the case when individuals take on new roles within the group (Bonacich 1987). Ethnographic studies should also be able to detect changes in influence, both for drug taking and sexual issues, as individuals take on new roles within the group to reinforce protective behaviors and reduce risks. These issues are explored below with examples from Flagstaff projects to illustrate how data can be collected on these characteristics.

EXAMPLE 5.3

CONSTRUCTING A FULL RELATIONAL NETWORK IN A SUBSTANCE ABUSE STUDY

One of our substance abuse projects provided full network relationship data on a total of ten active drug using networks. The size of these groups varied from five to forty-two people. During the full network data collection process we brought each group together and asked them to rate their interactions with each member of their network, based on a structured set of questions about their social relationships, their drug using patterns, and communication about intimate subjects such as sex. Analysis of this relational network data allowed us to describe each of these groups according to the conventional types of analysis that can be run on network relational data (cf. Killworth and Bernard 1974; Burt 1976; Panning 1982; Knoke and Kuklinski 1982; Glover 1989; Scott 1991). A description of one of these networks illustrates the types of information we were able to gather by this method (Trotter, Baldwin, and Bowen 1995; Trotter, Baldwin, and Potter 1995; Trotter et al. 1996). This network is a multigeneration, family-based drug-using network. It contains members from two kinship groups. The group includes both males and females who are drug users. The drugs of choice for the group are cocaine and crystal meth (methamphetamine), and the group includes both injection drug users and noninjection drug users. The socioeconomic status of the group is low, as denoted by the fact that they live in local public housing projects and receive welfare, or government-provided financial assistance. Three individuals from Mexico who do not have legal residency documents for the United States are members of the group. The core group has been using drugs together since high school, with some of the members now in their forties. The network is relatively closed; membership is restricted to kin and sexual partners of kin.

The relationships in this network can be thought of as:

Definition:
Actors are individuals in a social network

- The different types of connections between **actors**—the common network term used for identifying different individuals in the network
- The centrality or influence of individual actors, or of subgroups within the larger group
- Roles or "positions" actors hold within the network (cf. Knoke and Kuklinski 1982)

Relational network information is commonly presented in the form of diagrams, charts, tables, data matrices, cluster diagrams, and verbal descriptions.[1] One of the most common ways of displaying the data is to construct a sociogram that indicates actors by circles, and connections or interactions among them by lines. Figure 5.6 is a model of the social relationships in the drug using network.

The connecting lines between individuals (identified by a number) indicate the existence of a strong connection between those two people. All individuals in this group have some weak interactions with each other, but the influence or communication between some is minimal; Figure 5.6 concentrates on the strong ties. Females are represented by a number in a circle, and males by a number in a square. An arrowhead indicates a one-way connection between two people, while a solid line indicates a two-way connection. The width of the line indicates the strength of the connection. For example, the larger, lighter circle around Anita, #13, indicates that she is the central person in terms of influence measures. She is also the most central communication node in the network. The core of the network is composed of Anita (#13), Lydia (#6), Adelita (#4), Marcos (#5), Jaime (#9), and Josepha (#3). All of these individuals

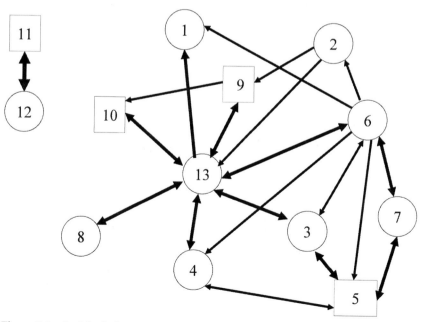

Figure 5.6 Social relations network diagram

have close kinship ties, and communication between them is strong (i.e., frequent and intimate). Miguel (#11) and Dolores (#12) are married, and Miguel is the first cousin of Maria (#1) and Lydia (#6). Aida (#7) is Lydia's (#6) niece and Josepha's (#3) first cousin.

The *drug network* characteristics, which we derived from analysis of the drug questions on our network matrix, are an interesting contrast to the *social* relationships described above. In the drug-related networks, several people changed position from peripheral to more strongly connected, or vice versa, as can be seen in Figure 5.7.

Drug issues create a change in the information flow and influence patterns of the network. Aida (#7) is a non-user, which is clearly represented in her lack of connections on the drug questions. Anita (#13) shares the influence in the drug networks with her son, Marcos (#5), and with Jaime (#9), who is a central member because he is a bilingual communication bridge between the Spanish (only) and the English (only) portions of the network. Marcos (#5) scores drugs for this network, keeps track of drug-related conditions, and influences the network through his

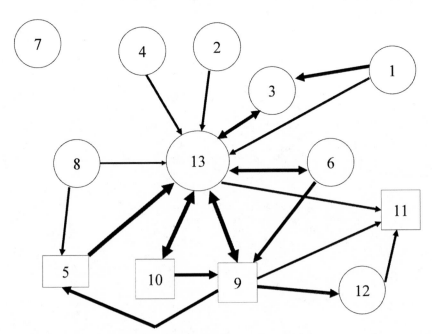

Figure 5.7   Drug relations network diagram

mother's close connections with everyone else. Some of the individuals who were strongly connected by social relationships are connected by weak ties, or no longer directly connected in terms of their drug relations. For example, #4 and #5, who are married to each other, are strongly tied in the diagram on social relationships, but #4 does not communicate much about drugs with her husband, only with her mother-in-law (#13). The kinship ties between #9 and #2 (living as married) are not visible in the drug relationship diagram, nor is the aunt-niece connection between #6 and #7. This indicates that some people who can be reached for *drug-related* HIV risk reduction information through the drug relationships network must be accessed via different people and lines of communication if they are to receive *social* risk reduction information, such as, for example, information about the need to reduce the number of sexual risks they encounter or how to negotiate condom use.

We have also analyzed several other classic measures of network connections and network structure for this group of drug users. An analysis of the network structures termed **factions** and **cliques** associated with the drug use network (cf. Bron and Kerbosch 1973; Seidman and Foster 1978; Borgatti, Everett, and Shirey 1990) indicates that when social relations alone are considered, most members are closely connected to central members; only a small number of people are marginal to the core of the group (Figure 5.7). However, the configuration within the group changes significantly when the drug relation questions are analyzed. In this second analysis, the core drug group is divided into two subsystems: a predominantly English-speaking clique, and a predominantly Spanish-speaking clique. This division was discovered in initial ethnographic research and confirmed in this second, quantitative analysis.

This information on cliques and factions can be used to identify boundaries where information needed for the successful implementation of an intervention may be blocked—unless at least one individual from each subgroup is involved in the intervention. Information provided to centralized networks like this one, which has only a few marginal individuals, passes through fewer contacts and through a smaller number of individuals than it does

Definition: ☀ Factions and cliques are small groups formed by their close and special connections to one another within a larger network

in diffuse, less tightly constructed networks. Moreover, if a network is badly fissured or fragmented, information must be provided to multiple individuals.

As a final note on the relationships displayed by these two representations, the shape of the drug relations network diagram (Figure 5.7) is very similar to a classic problem-solving configuration displayed by networks. It is called a star pattern, in which one person acts as a center, in direct communication with the rest of the network through dyadic relationships and with relatively few interconnections among other members of the network. This configuration allows rapid input from the central person to all members on any issue, thus facilitating problem solving for the group as a whole. The social network diagram (Figure 5.6) is a classic communication configuration where there are **multiplex ties** within the group. Multiplex ties are based on each individual's having several different kinds of relationships with the other people in their group at the same time. This structure ensures that loss of a network member will not cause communication to break down, since everyone in the core group is tied to a number of other people and connected to each other through many different relationships.

Definition: Multiplex ties in a group means that each group member has many different relationships with most or all other members in a group

These findings parallel those from other networks we have investigated. The majority of drug-using networks are small and relatively tight. They depend on kinship and long-term friendship for entry, and they show a strong tendency for tight communication and reinforcement of the group's norms. These norms can support the elimination of risks through the elimination of ties that produce HIV risks, such as needle sharing with strangers, or unprotected sex with casual partners. In addition, the existing boundaries can be reinforced, and some assessment of HIV risk can be added to the trust issues that already affect new recruitment in the group. New recruits could be sought only from among people who engage in low-risk categories of drug abuse or sexual behavior. All of this information allows us to go far beyond an understanding of individual network members into the social organization and culture of drug use and relevant associated social action.

Network Reliability and Stability and the Measurement of Change

In the late 1990s, network researchers who were involved in longitudinal studies of HIV risk and transmission began to raise questions about several areas of concern. One concern was related to the reliability of network measures; in other words, would responses to questions about network membership and characteristics network measurement be similar if asked in the same way at two time periods spaced from one to two weeks apart? Most quantitative measures are evaluated for reliability. A second concern relates to the speed at which networks change, and how they change. Finally, a third relates to the measurement of network characteristics over time. Here we comment briefly on each of these concerns.

With respect to the reliability of responses to network questions, surprisingly there is only a limited literature. One example that sheds light on the dynamics of stability and change in networks that would be expected to be highly volatile comes from a study of youth culture and polydrug use in Hartford.

EXAMPLE 5.4

MEASURING NETWORK RELIABILITY AND STABILITY AMONG URBAN YOUTH

A study, conducted by Jean Schensul and colleagues, collected network reliability data on the ego-centered networks of approximately forty youth between the ages of sixteen and twenty-four living in Hartford, Connecticut, and recruited through standard street recruitment methods. In a face-to-face interview process, survey questions were asked on demographic characteristics, trust, residence, and drug use and drug selling on up to twenty people identified as close to ego. Youth were asked to return in a week for a second, repeat interview, and thirty-five completed repeat interviews. Results showed comparability on several key questions, including overall level of trust, size of network, demographic characteristics, and patterns of drug use and drug dealing. These overall results gave the study team confidence that youth were responding consistently to the same questions within a two-week time span. One interesting finding was that there were changes in some individuals, but these did not constitute changes in roles or relationship to ego; in other words, a cousin was replaced with another cousin, a drug user with another drug user, and so on. The analysis concluded that though individuals were replaced, the structure of the personal network and the roles and responsibilities of individuals in it were stable (Clair et al. 2003).

More such studies are required to understand better the balance between stability/reliability and change in networks over time, especially in the case of longitudinal research.

Measuring changes in networks over time is very important in any research involved in disease spread or "social contagion." Social contagion, a term that links social influence with network transmission, first appeared in the late 1980s (Crandall 1988). It refers to the transmission of undesirable behaviors from one individual to another in a social network configuration (Aral et al. 2009; Burke and Heiland 2007; Scherer and Cho 2003; Valente and Fujimoto et al. 2009). Social contagion studies are generally cross-sectional, but many network studies of HIV and sexually transmitted infection are longitudinal, with measures taken using network surveys every six months to a year for up to three or even four years.

One of the earlier such longitudinal studies was conducted by Rothenberg and colleagues (1998) on a low-risk network of drug users in Colorado Springs.

EXAMPLE 5.5

A PROSPECTIVE STUDY OF DRUG USE NETWORKS IN A LOW-PREVALENCE COMMUNITY

This study was conducted with injection drug users who, because of their shared injection behaviors, were believed to be at high risk of HIV in a community in Colorado that had a low prevalence of HIV. The study examined the social networks of a subsample of ninety-six people drawn from a total cohort of 595 people, including commercial sex workers, injection drug users, and sexual partners of drug users. The subsample was interviewed once a year for three years. The analyses assessed network configuration, network stability, and examined changes in risk behavior using a combination of epidemiologic and social network analysis. The study used a stability index to evaluate change in networks over a three-year period, considering changes in all relationships and specifically in risk-related behaviors, including sex, drug use, and needle sharing (Klovdahl et al. 1994). The researchers identified two cohorts who were interviewed three times: one group interviewed for the first time in the first year of the study, and the second in the second year. They considered the following network connections from one time point to another: sexual, social, drug using, needle sharing, and other types of contacts. With data on egos and contacts who cross-referred, they identified structural characteristics (degree and information centrality) of subgroups as measures of interconnectedness, which could be assessed as changing over time.

Stability ratios varied by relationship and were higher (nearly 40 percent) for sex relationships and low (6 percent) for drug use relationships. Social and sexual relationships were stable from time two to time three, but drug use and needle-sharing relationships remained low at both time points. The larger the social and network relationships were over time, the less stable. Interconnected components were not stable over time and tended to shrink in size. This was a major study finding. The study found that people with HIV infection were peripheral to the central networks and of low centrality. Their potential influence within networks diminished over time as networks disconnected. Thus, in this low HIV prevalence environment, risk can be said to diminish over time as networks shrink and become disconnected (Rothenberg et al. 1998).

Studies of changes in bounded classroom or building interaction pose new challenges to network researchers different from those that arise in efforts to understand macronetworks in unbounded community settings. These studies, generally using mixed methods analyses, offer rich promise for understanding social influence, social contagion, and information and influence diffusion in bounded systems. The methodology for such studies at baseline is fairly well articulated (cf. Martínez et al. 2003), but problems arise in attempting to understand changes over time. For example, these studies require that each person in the setting refer to every other person at each time point. Generally, baseline data are available, but macronetwork analysis programs such as UCINET and Pajek do not have the capacity to handle missing data. Thus it is unclear as to how to address missing data at future time points.

NETWORK SAMPLING STRATEGIES

Ego-centered network sampling is based on random, representative, or any other form of quota sampling. Full relational network sampling begins with the identification of

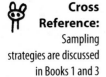

Cross Reference: Sampling strategies are discussed in Books 1 and 3

individuals who act as entry points to the network. Entry to a full relational network can begin with any specific individual in the network. Usually, however, there are multiple entry points, and the bounded nature of the network is critical to define in advance.

Once the ethnographer has identified people who can grant entry to the network, the next step in relational network sampling requires creating a sample using one of the following four different strategies:

- A complete sample of all individuals in the full network, or the entire population of the network
- A randomized sample of index individuals' alters
- Individuals screened and selected as index persons because of their specific characteristics
- Individuals selected because they are the alters of a specific index person

Creating a Sample of all Individuals in the Full Network

This type of sampling is time consuming and costly if the network is large and widely distributed—as it often is in an urban community. It is most useful when conducting research in smaller bounded communities, such as classrooms, very small villages, girls' basketball teams, or circles of artisans and craftworkers.

Creating a Sample by Selecting a Randomized Sample of Index Individuals' Alters

To use this type of sample, the ethnographer first selects a number of index individuals for interviewing. If ten index persons are selected, they may, for example, identify up to twenty-five contacts or alters. From these twenty-five contacts, any number of individuals is then randomly selected for the second step of the interviewing process. For example, the ethnographer might randomly choose six people from the twenty-five identified alters for the second stage of the interview process. The ethnographer bases his or her decision regarding how many alters to interview on how many people are needed for the entire interview project and the resources available for the study.

During the second stage of interviews, each of the six alters is, in turn, asked to identify his or her own alters. The ethnographer then randomly selects six more alters of each of these six individuals for the third step of the interviewing process. Usually only from two to four "nodes" or interview steps—and consequent identification of persons to interview—are feasible in a relational network study. More steps or nodes render the sample size too large and are not cost effective.

Creating a Sample by Screening and Selecting Individuals Because of their Special Characteristics

Often, social scientists seek to study individuals because they display the characteristics important for the study. For example, drug use studies might seek to find injection drug users; studies of campus politics would look for school "leaders"; health care studies would try to identify users of spiritual healers, or pregnant older women; ecological studies would seek environmental activists. These individuals are asked to list alters, and among alters, only those who fulfill specific criteria (such as those criteria used for identifying the specific individuals sought for the first step of interviews) are included in the sampling frame for the network sample. Thus, instead of selecting six alters randomly from among the total of twenty-five, six alters are selected on a randomized basis from among *only those* who possess or display the characteristics that are key to the study. Interviewing of index individuals continues on the same basis as above, organizing from two to four steps or nodes out to complete the desired sample size for the study.

Creating a Sample by Choosing an Index Person, Identifying All Alters, and Randomizing Selection of Their Network Members

This type of sampling is called a "random walk design." It involves first selecting an index person and asking him or her to identify all of his or her alters. The next step involves randomly selecting one or more of these alters for interviewing. These alters, in turn, list *their* own alters. From these lists, the ethnographer randomly chooses one or more individuals to interview. In this way, the ethnographer can "walk" from linkage to linkage in a connected chain of individuals who are part of a much larger social network. The result is a randomized sample of the larger network structure. Other sampling approaches are discussed in Book 3, chapter 10.

SUMMARY AND CONCLUSIONS

Social network analysis is a rapidly evolving field of study that can be significantly enhanced by both basic and advanced ethnographic methods and ethnographic theory. There has been an exponential explosion of social networking sites on the web that are allowing people to populate and expand their natural social connections or to construct artificial (virtual) connections through the use of web-based technologies. Websites have been constructed to allow people to present their identify and share it with others (Facebook, YouTube), create communication and gossip networks that are constantly available (Twitter), engage in professional or work connections (LinkedIn), engage in dating and mate attraction activities (eHarmony, JDate), or pursue sales activities that include a social network element, including networking algorithms that suggest new products based on former purchases (Amazon.com). The web is also populated by multiple self-help or social support websites for everything from addictions to obesity, and beyond, and it is increasingly populated by "closed" networks that are only accessible to small, homogenous groups. Outside the web, social network paradigms and theory are being used by governments to track and attempt to disrupt terrorist organizations, by businesses to design better organizational connections and functioning, by community-based organizations to create more effective social assistance networks, and by social movements (including terrorist organizations and political movements) to connect their memberships, organize activities, and maintain the functional elements of the organization directed at achieving their political, polemical, or power goals. Each of these issues is a legitimate and interesting focus for anthropological research and ethnographic inquiry.

All of the current attention to the formal and informal organization of human groups (the structural elements of communication, the creation of appropriate roles and statuses, the support of cultural structures such as families, voluntary associations, institutional functioning, etc.) presents both a need and an opportunity for theoretical contributions from anthropology and ethnography to the understanding of social networks and culturally based structures in general.

Targets for Ethnographic Theory and the Exploration of Key Social Network Issues

A quick review of the leading social network research blogs or listserves allowed us to identify five very interesting research and methodological issues that have a significant need for further exploration and understanding based on an ethnographic and/or anthropological theoretical approach. Historically, much of the original social network analysis was an ethnographic exploration of the small critical social groups that make up the organizational structure of cultures. These include family and kinship structures, roles and functions, as well as the organization of cultural associations such as age grades, social strata, and voluntary originations. In some cases it has evolved into anthropological theories of different types of organizations of whole cultures, including tribal organizations and clan-based systems that are relevant to many of the economic development efforts, as well as war and global conflict issues that face global society presently. Following this solid qualitative, exploratory foundation, social network analysts found that the structure and characteristics of networks could also be described using mathematical formulas from graph theory and matrix algebra, combined with multivariate statistical approaches. At the present time, the explosion in the mathematically driven models of networks has produced a parallel need for qualitative/ethnographic explorations of the meanings of those numbers and models; a need to tie the mathematics into cultural realities. The current focus of this new movement for increased ethnographic engagement in network analysis is on:

- New advances in the qualitative theory of social network formation, maintenance, and evolution
- Advances in systematic qualitative methodologies that allow researchers to explore and test new ethnographic network theories (as well as confirming existing theory)
- Development of new, technologically enhanced (computer, web, etc.) processes for the collection and management (computer programs, etc.) of qualitative network data
- Advances in models and methods that allow the integration of qualitative and quantitative theory and approaches to social network research (mixed methods models and paradigms)
- Empirical and descriptive explorations of the evolution of social networks in an increasingly global and technologically dependent world

Some of the interesting areas for the ethnographic exploration of social networks can be found by addressing crucial or troubling questions that quantitative social network researchers are asking, such as the questions that follow:

1. How do you identify and define the important boundaries that define a social network?
Social networks are composed of a finite number of people who are linked together by some form of social relationship. The relationship has to be defined carefully in order to identify and refine the membership of the group: the fuzzier the definition of the relationship, the fuzzier the definition of the boundaries of the group. In addition, multiplex (rather than single or simplex) relationships create numerous difficulties in defining network membership. Small, closed, single relationship networks are fairly easy to define and study. Open networks with malleable membership are much more difficult to study

(Gregg 2008, Erickson and Kellogg 2000). There is a lot of room for a significant contribution from ethnographic theory and methods to help define boundaries, boarders, and membership characteristics of both open and closed networks from family types, to friendship networks, to complex organizations and social movements (Hewitt and Forte 2006, Chin and Chignell 2008).

2. How does culture shape or have an impact on the characteristics of social networks, and how do social networks shape or have an impact on society and culture?
There is a significant, ongoing need for comparative studies of social networks both within and across sociocultural boundaries. We know that the organizational structure of families, kinship groups, voluntary associations, and other culturally embedded organizations differ across language, cultural, and social boundaries. However, there gaps in our knowledge that could be addressed by focused ethnographic studies of social networks in a comparative context, especially on the question of "what difference does it make on people's lives?" when their social networks are bound or "unbound" by cultural differences in values, gender rules, social class issues, or even technology. There are numerous network studies that are exploring these issues, including ones focused on gender theory (Cohen and Shade 2008, Driscoll 2008), cultural values and intimacy (Livingstone 2008), or risky behaviors (Mitchell and Ybarra 2009, Moreno et al. 2009).

3. How do changes in the structure and functions of social networks (especially technologically based networks) have an impact on core cultural values?
Many of the current network studies of web-based social networking sites and the networking capabilities of the web are attempting to see if technology, and changing values about communication, privacy, and access to knowledge about other people, is having temporary or permanent impacts of core social values. For example, there is a great deal of concern over the impact of social network sites and the general values for privacy in U.S. culture (Barnes 2006, Boyd 2008, Cohen and Shade 2008, Fogel and Nehmad 2008, Hodge 2006).

4. What is the cultural "meaning" of social networks as culturally constructed groups, and how does that meaning (and the groups) change through time?

Anthropologists spend a considerable amount of effort exploring the cultural definitions of meaningful groups (family, kinship networks, voluntary organizations, businesses, and cultural institutions like schools, or the military). As social network research moves rapidly from small to large groups, there is a need for determining ways of identifying key social groups, such as a quantitative network definition of community on the basis of networks as community (Baym 2007, Goodings et al. 2007, Komito and Bates 2009). There is also the need to maintain a focus on smaller groups, especially those in difficult or hard-to-reach environmental conditions (Johnson et al. 2003), including the need to observe and understand change over time (Trotter et al. 2008).

5. What do we need to know about social networks in order to manage important relationships and processes in business, government, or everyday life?

A large number of social network research efforts are focused on the network effects of knowledge acquisition (Allen et al. 2007), on organizational management (Wittek et al. 2003), and on improvement of partnerships and organizational success for both nonprofits and proprietary organizations (Cross et al. 2008, Uzzi and Dunlap 2005, Kleinbaum and Tushman 2008).

An Ethnographic Model: Multiple Methods in Approaching Social Network Investigations

The preceding sections clearly suggest that a multiple method network approach has numerous advantages for most ethnographic research projects. Ethnographic network mapping is fully compatible with other forms of ethnographic research. It can be accomplished best by a combination of observation and interviewing, and either of those approaches can be combined with other forms (or foci) of ethnographic data collection. It is possible to collect network data using a life history perspective, a cultural modeling approach, or by using reflexive and systematic cognitive methods. Since ego-centered networks represent components and entry points into larger network configurations, ego-centered data collection can form an interesting bridge to full reciprocal network data collection.

Cross Reference: See Books 2, 3, and 4 for elicitation methods in ethnographic research

Once the basic norms, beliefs, and values of specific social groups have been discovered through the ethnographic approach, many anthropologists find they need to turn to survey types of data collection. These efforts include household surveys, population-based (probabilistic) surveys, and special group questionnaires. It is easy, and usually highly productive, to include ego-centered network questions along with the other questions embedded in this type of questionnaire. Of course, one must keep in mind that the addition of network questions takes quite a lot of extra time, so the purposes for including these questions must be clearly defined in your study.

Finally, full relational network data collection on reciprocal relationships in the network provides a level of detail about human groups that cannot be collected in any other manner. The overall measures of network structure and network connections that can be computed from network relational data are clearly associated with cultural differences in individual behavior. This approach shows a great deal of promise for both research and intervention work. Wherever data on the overall structures of full networks can be collected, these data can provide important guidelines for targeting both general (to everybody through social diffusion) and specific (to individuals) messages, and for developing community intervention programs, behavioral change training, and group assessment strategies.

Ethnographic network approaches have some additional advantages that work in parallel with general ethnographic research approaches and enhance the success of those approaches. First, many research projects in the United States require making contacts with hard-to-reach or hidden populations. This is a difficult process, and one of the hardest parts of ethnographic outreach is orchestrating the initial entry into a new group. Network-based contact can make that recruitment easier because it follows existing social relationships, and once the initial contact is made, members of the network can recruit other members rather than each new recruit requiring a cold contact from an outsider. The normal network gatekeepers can then act as go-betweens who reduce barriers to participation by endorsing the project to others in the network, rather than creating barriers to participation. Second, following natural social network connections makes keeping track of people and recontacting them easier. Keeping track of network members is something the members of a network do naturally. This fact can assist in the long-term follow-up phase of any project, from ethnography to longitudinal survey research. If the core or most influential members of the network are identified and tracked, they can act as primary links between outreach workers and other members of the group. Because those core members—or gatekeepers—generally know the whereabouts of network members, they can make it easier for outreach workers—who usually have little time to track down and locate network members—to conduct individually based follow-up. Third, using a social network approach allows the researcher to concentrate on the structure of relationships, not just the content or meaning of relationships. At the simplest level, network data identifies the patterns of communication between individuals, and between sets of individuals, on particular topics. At the next level network information data can identify the central person or persons who exert the most influence on the group, the nodes (or central persons) in the network that act as gatekeepers for interaction, or the subsets of individuals who interact more among themselves than they do with others in the larger network. Information on each of these factors can suggest plans for direct and indirect action and provide outcome measures of the efficacy of programs that are trying to change people's lives. Network data can also provide in-depth information on the social context of change.

The three network approaches described in this chapter provide analytical tools that allow ethnographers to design and measure both the individual and the cumulative group effects of economic-, agricultural-, educational-, ecological-, political-, and policy-oriented programs. Our ethnographic findings demonstrate that we can use qualitative descriptions of network conditions as a direct adjunct to applied programs. The ethnographic data act as an important theory-generating bridge to quantitative measures of the impact of social networks on cultural dynamics.

ADVANTAGES OF ETHNOGRAPHIC NETWORK APPROACHES

- Identifying and assessing hidden populations
- Recruiting, retaining, and following up of intervention populations
- Understanding personal social influences on the lives, decisions, and behaviors of individuals
- Enhancing the efficacy of interventions by working with groups that have maximum impact on the lives of the individuals in them
- Understanding and intervening to change barriers and facilitators to information flow in order to reach individuals and groups more effectively

We have found that an individual's potential for social, marital, economic, educational, or any other kind of success can be directly related to network variables. We should be able to measure the impact on individuals of such network characteristics, including such factors as divisions or conflicts in the group. We also should be able to assess differences in how groups within the networks address risk taking and how these differences affect the likelihood that both individuals and the groups will encounter risks. We may be able to detect changes in influence patterns when individuals assume new roles within the group that involve taking responsibility for encouraging group members to engage in protective behaviors and to reduce risks. In sum, network analysis in its various forms appears to be a highly desirable and productive tool for a wide variety of ethnographic research projects.

NOTES

Funding for much of the research reported in this chapter was provided by two grants from the National Institute on Drug Abuse (NIDA). These were Grant #U01-DA07295, the Flagstaff Multicultural AIDS Prevention Project, and Grant #R01 DA09965, Small Town Drug Networks and HIV: Transmission Dynamics.

1. Full relational network data can be readily analyzed and displayed in a variety of diagram formats using computerized programs developed by Borgatti and colleagues, UCINET and Pajek. These program resources are described as additional resources at the end of this chapter.

All of the names in this description are pseudonyms, to protect the identity of the individuals in the network. The networks we investigated included African Americans, Native Americans, Hispanics, and Anglo Americans. In this case, the example is a predominantly Hispanic network, but it easily could have been from either of the other cultural groups.

All of the calculations were conducted using the program UCINET 4.0.

REFERENCES

Allen, J., A. D. James, and P. Gamlen. 2007. Formal verses informal knowledge networks in R&D: A case study using social network analysis. *R&D Management* 37(3): 179–96.

Allen, K. R., R. Blieszner et al. 2000. Families in the middle and later years: A review and critique of research in the 1990s. *Journal of Marriage and Family* 62(4): 911–26.

Aral, S., L. Muchnik et al. 2009. Distinguishing influence-based contagion from homophily-driven diffusion in dynamic networks. *Proceedings of the National Academy of Sciences* 106(51): 21544–549.

Barnes, S. 2006. A privacy paradox: Social networking in the United States. *First Monday* 11(9).

Batagelj, V., and A. Mrvar. 2010. Pajek: Program for large network analysis, version 1.28.

Baym, N. 2007. The new shape of online community: The example of Swedish independent music fandom. *First Monday* 12(8).

Bonacich, P. 1987. Power and centrality: A family of measures. *American Journal of Sociology* 92: 1170–82.

Borgatti, S. P. 2002. *NetDraw: Graph visualization software.* Boston, MA: Analytic Technologies.

Borgatti, S. P., M. Everett, and L. Freeman. 1999. UCINET 5 for Windows, software for social network analysis. Natick, MA: Analytic Technologies.

Borgatti, S. P., M. G. Everett, and P. R. Shirey. 1990. LS sets, lambda sets, and other cohesive subsets. *Social Networks* 12, 337–57.

Bott, E. 1971. *Family and social network: Roles, norms, and external relationships in ordinary urban families.* London: Tavistock.

Bourgois, P. 1996. In search of respect: Selling crack in El Barrio. New York: Cambridge University Press.

Boyd, Danah. 2008. Facebook's privacy trainwreck: Exposure, invasion, and social convergence. *Convergence* 14(1).

Bron, C., and J. Kerbosch. 1973. Finding all cliques of an undirected graph. *Communications of the ACM* 16: 575–77.

Burke, M. A., and F. Heiland. 2007. Social dynamics of obesity. *Economic Inquiry* 45(3): 571–91.

Burt, R. 1976. Positions in networks. *Social Forces* 55: 93–122.

Chin, A., and M. Chignell. 2008 Automatic detection of cohesive subgroups within social hypertext: A heuristic approach. *New Review of Hypermedia and Multimedia* 14(1): 121–43.

Clair, S., J. Schensul, M. Raju, E. Stanek, and R. Pino. 2003. Will you remember me in the morning? Test-retest reliability of a social network analysis examining HIV-related risky behavior in urban adolescents and young adults. *Connections* 25(2): 88–97.

Cohen, Nicole S., and Leslie Regan Shade. 2008. Gendering Facebook: Privacy and commodification. *Feminist Media Studies* 8(2): 210–14.

Crandall, C. S. 1988. Social contagion of binge eating. *Journal of Personality and Social Psychology* 55(4): 588–98.

Cross, R. L., K. Ehrlich, R. Dawson, and J. Helferich. 2008. Managing collaboration: Improving team effectiveness through a network perspective. *California Management Review* 50/4, 74–98.

Domínguez, S., and C. Watkins. 2003. Creating networks for survival and mobility: Social capital among African-American and Latin-American low-income mothers. *Social Problems* 50(1): 111–35.

Doreian, P. 1974. On the connectivity of social networks. *Journal of Mathematical Sociology* 3: 245–58.

Driscoll, Catherine. 2008. This is not a blog: Gender, intimacy and community. *Feminist Media Studies* 8(2): 198–202.

Erickson, T., and W. A. Kellogg. 2000. Social translucence: An approach to designing systems that support social processes. *ACM Trans. Computer-Human Interaction* 7(1): 59–83.

Fogel, J., and E. Nehmad. 2008. Internet social network communities: Risk taking, trust, and privacy concerns. *Computers in Human Behavior* 25: 153–60.

Ford, L. R., and D. R. Fulkerson. 1956. Maximum flow through a network. *Canadian Journal of Mathematics* 8: 399–404.

Friedman, S. R. 1995. Promising social network research results and suggestions. In *Social network analysis, HIV prevention and drug abuse*, ed. R. H. Needle, S. L. Coyle, S. Genser, and R. T. Trotter II, 196–215. NIDA Monograph 151. Bethesda, MD: National Institute on Drug Abuse.

Galaskiewicz, J., and S. Wasserman. 1993. Social network analysis: Concepts, methodology, and directions for the 1990s. *Sociological Methods and Research* 22: 3–22.

Glover, F. 1989. Tabu search—Part I. *ORSA Journal on Computing* 1: 190–206.

Gomory, R. E., and T. C. Hu. 1964. Synthesis of a communication network. *Journal of SIAM (Appl Math)* 12: 348.

Goodings, L., A. Locke, and S. D. Brown. 2007. Social networking technology: Place and identity in mediated communities. *Journal of Community and Applied Social Psychology* 17(6): 463–76.

Gregg, Melissa. 2008. Testing the friendship: Feminism and the limits of online social networks. *Feminist Media Studies* 8(2): 206–09.

Hewitt, Anne, and Andrea Forte. 2006. Crossing boundaries: Identity management and student/faculty relationships on the Facebook. Poster presented at CSCW, Banff, Alberta.

Hodge, Matthew J. 2006. The Fourth Amendment and privacy issues on the "new" Internet: Facebook.com and MySpace.com. *Southern Illinois University Law Journal* 31.

Hubbell, C. H. 1965. An input-output approach to clique identification. *Sociometry* 28: 377–99.

Johnson, Jeffrey C. 1994. Anthropological contributions to the study of social networks: A review. In *Advances in social network analysis*, ed. S. Wasserman and J. Galaskiewicz. Thousand Oaks, CA: Sage.

Johnson, Jeffrey C., James S. Boster, and Lawrence A. Palinkas. 2003. Social roles and the evolution of networks in extreme and isolated environments. *Journal of Mathematical Sociology* 27: 89–121.

Katz, L. 1953. A new status index derived from sociometric data analysis. *Psychometrika* 18: 34–43.

Killworth, P., and H. R. Bernard. 1974. CATIJ: A new sociometric and its application to a prison living unit. *Human Organization* 33: 335–50.

Kleinbaum, A. M., and M. L. Tushman. 2008. Managing corporate social networks. *Harvard Business Review* 86/7: 26–27.

Klovdahl A. S., J. J. Potterat, D. E. Woodhouse, J. B. Muth, S. Q. Muth, and W. W. Darrow. 1994. Social Networks and Infectious Disease: The Colorado Springs Study. *Social Science and Medicine* 38(1):79–88.

Knoke, D., and J. H. Kuklinski. 1982. *Network analysis*. Beverly Hills, CA: Sage.

Komito, Lee, and Jessica Bates. 2009. Virtually local: Social media and community amongst Polish nationals in Dublin. *ASLIB Proceedings* 61(3): 232–44.

Latkin, C. A. 1995. A personal network approach to AIDS prevention. In *Social network analysis, HIV prevention and drug abuse*, ed. R. H. Needle, S. L. Coyle, S. Genser, and R. T. Trotter II, 181–95 (NIDA Monograph 151). Bethesda, MD: National Institute on Drug Abuse.

Livingstone, Sonia. 2008. Taking risky opportunities in youthful content creation: Teenagers' use of social networking sites for intimacy, privacy and self-expression. *New Media and Society* 10(3).

Martínez, A., Y. Dimitriadis et al. 2003. Combining qualitative evaluation and social network analysis for the study of classroom social interactions. *Computers and Education* 41(4): 353–68.

Mitchell, K. J., and M. Ybarra. 2009. Social networking sites: Finding a balance between their risks and benefits. *Archives of Pediatrics Adolescent Medicine* 163(1): 87–89.

Mokken, R. 1979. Cliques, clubs and clans. *Quality and Quantity* 13: 161–73.

Moore, J. 1991. *Going down to the barrio: Homeboys and homegirls in change*. Philadelphia, PA: Temple University Press.

Moore, J., D. Vigil, and R. Garcia. 1983. Residence and territoriality in Chicano gangs. *Social Problems* 31(2) (December 1983): 182–94.

Moreno, M. A., A. VanderStoep, M. R. Parks, F. J. Zimmerman, A. Kurth, and D. A. Christakis. 2009. Reducing at-risk adolescents' display of risk behavior on a social networking web site: A randomized controlled pilot intervention trial. *Archives of Pediatrics Adolescent Medicine* 35–41.

Panning, W. 1982. Fitting blockmodels to data. *Social Networks* 4: 81–101.

Pasternak, B. 1976. *Introduction to kinship and social organization*. Englewood Cliffs, NJ: Prentice Hall.

Rothenberg, R. B., J. J. Potterat et al. 1998. Social network dynamics and HIV transmission. *AIDS* 12(12): 1529–36.

Scherer, C. W., and H. Cho. 2003. A social network contagion theory of risk perception. *Risk Analysis: An International Journal* 23(2): 261–67.

Scott, J. 1991. *Social network analysis: A handbook*. Newbury Park, CA: Sage.

Seidman, S., and B. Foster. 1978. A graph theoretic generalization of the clique concept. *Journal of Mathematical Sociology* 6: 139–54.

Stephenson, K., and M. Zelen. 1991. Rethinking centrality. *Social Networks* 13: 81–101.

Taylor, M. 1969. Influence structures. *Sociometry* 32: 490–502.

Tomeh, A. K. 1973. Formal voluntary organizations: Participation, correlates, and interrelationships. *Sociological Inquiry* 43(3–4): 89–122.

Trotter, Robert T. II, Julie A. Baldwin, and Anne M. Bowen. 1995. Network structure and proxy network measures of HIV, drug and incarceration risks for active drug users. *Connections* 18(1): 89–104.

Trotter, Robert T. II, Anne M. Bowen, Julie A. Baldwin, and Laurie J. Price. 1996. The efficacy of network based HIV/AIDS risk reduction programs in midsized towns in the United States. *Journal of Drug Issues* 26(3): 591–606.

Trotter, Robert T. II, Anne M. Bowen, and James M. Potter. 1995. Network models for HIV outreach and prevention programs of drug users. In *Social networks, drug abuse, and HIV transmission*, eds. R. H. Needle, S. L. Coyle, S. G. Genser, and R. T. Trotter II, 144–80. NIDA Research Monograph 151. USDHHS. Rockville, MD: National Institute on Drug Abuse.

Trotter, Robert T. II, E. K. Briody, G. H. Sengir, and T. L. Meerwarth. 2008. The life cycle of collaborative partnerships: Evolutionary structure in industry-university research networks. *Connections* 28(1): 40–58.

Uzzi, B., and S. Dunlap. 2005. How to build your network. *Harvard Business Review* 83/12, 53–60.

Valente, T. W., K. Fujimoto et al. 2009. Adolescent affiliations and adiposity: A social network analysis of friendships and obesity. *Journal of Adolescent Health* 45(2): 202–04.

Vigil, J. D. 1988. Group processes and street identity: Adolescent Chicano gang members. *Ethos* 16(4): 421–45.

Wasserman, S., and K. Faust. 1993. *Social network analysis: Methods and applications*. New York: Cambridge University Press.

Weeks, M. R., S. Clair, S. P. Borgatti, K. Radda, and J. J. Schensul. 2002. Social networks of drug users in high-risk sites: Finding the connections. *AIDS and Behavior* 6(2): 193–206.

Weeks, M. R., J. Li et al. 2009. Outcomes of a peer HIV prevention program with injection drug and crack users: The risk avoidance partnership. *Substance Use and Misuse* 44(2): 253–81.

White, D., and U. C. Johansen. 2004. *Network analysis and ethnographic problems: Process models of a Turkish nomad clan.* Lanham, MD: Lexington Books.

Wittek, Rafael, Marijtje A. J. van Duijn, and Tom A. B. Snijders. 2003. Frame decay, informal power, and the escalation of social control in a management team: A relational signaling perspective. In *The Governance of Relations in Markets and Organizations: Research in the Sociology of Organizations, Volume 20*, ed. Vincent Buskens, Werner Raub, and Chris Snijders, 355–80. Amsterdam: Elsevier Science.

6

STUDYING HIDDEN AND HARD-TO-REACH POPULATIONS

Merrill Singer

WHAT ARE HIDDEN AND HARD-TO-REACH POPULATIONS?

The reemergence of infectious disease as a major health issue in developed countries brings into bold relief the fundamental importance of learning about populations that are hard-to-find, hard-to-retain in intervention, and hard-to-relocate for follow-up assessment. In an epidemic, what have come to be called "hidden populations," groups who reside outside of institutional and clinical settings, and whose "activities are clandestine and therefore concealed from the view of mainstream society and agencies of social control" (Watters and Biernacki 1989, 417) as well as from local community-based organizations and various other public or private service providers, may be at special risk for infection and for transmitting infection to other populations.

This chapter focuses on approaches for studying disadvantaged and disenfranchised hidden and hard-to-research populations because these are groups that are in need and at risk and that may significantly benefit from improved applied social science research, including tested services

and other forms of intervention. Overcoming limitations in our existing knowledge about these groups by examining their special features and thereby avoiding stereotyped or misplaced generalizations about them, is the first objective of this chapter. The second objective is to call attention to the significant role of hidden and hard-to-reach groups in a wide range of contemporary health and social problems, underscoring thereby the importance of refining our techniques for studying these populations.

Populations vary in terms of whether they or specific behaviors they participate in are hidden. In some cases, it is the population itself that is "hard to reach" (by social interventions or monitoring programs like the census) because group members actively avoid contact with representatives of mainstream or even community institutions (e.g., individuals involved in drug smuggling). In other cases, groups are hard to reach because there are no readily available venues or other means through which they can easily be identified and contacted (e.g., sex partners of injection drug users). In either case, lack of knowledge about these groups hampers intervention strategies, while intentional or inadvertent concealment makes it difficult to reach them with targeted services. An example is seen in the following case (Singer and Marxuach-Rodriquez 1996).

EXAMPLE 6.1

RESEARCH TO LOCATE A HIDDEN POPULATION OF LATINO MSM

In 1991, the Hispanic Health Council, a community-based health research and service organization in Hartford, Connecticut, was funded through the Northeast Hispanic AIDS Consortium to implement an AIDS prevention project targeted to Latino men who have sex with men (MSM). This initiative was launched because it was recognized that despite higher rates of HIV infection among minority MSM compared with their straight counterparts, many Latino MSM are not widely involved in existing AIDS prevention programs targeted to gay men in the city. In fact, many Latino MSM do not identify themselves as "gay" even if all of their sex partners are male because they think that this label would diminish their ethnic heritage. Consequently, Latino MSM were less well known than their white counterparts, and their specific risk patterns and needs for AIDS prevention were unclear. Also unclear was the extent of diversity among Latino MSM in terms of sexual identity, sexual practices, lifestyle patterns, drug use, and involvement with mainstream institutions. Some Latino MSM could be identified at established gay bars, but it was not evident whether bars were a good recruitment site for reaching the full target population. Despite a commitment to developing a project that was sensitive to and appropriate for the target population, problems were encountered in implementing the project that stemmed from limitations in the Hispanic Health Council's familiarity with intragroup diversity among Latino MSM and with the values and concerns emphasized in different sectors of this population. Activities and approaches that proved to be effective in recruiting or retaining some individuals were inappropriate and uncomfortable for others. Thus, while a transvestite outreach worker was able to recruit other transvestites, he was unable to recruit many nontransvestite MSM. His replacement, an acculturated middle-class Latino MSM, was not effective with individuals who were unemployed, high school dropouts, or from rural Puerto Rican backgrounds. Only as the project gained deeper familiarity with the diverse social and cultural worlds of Latino MSM through ongoing applied ethnography was it possible to become fully effective in reaching and serving the target population with AIDS prevention services.

As this example suggests, hidden populations are not necessarily unified, but they may consist of an amorphous set of subgroups, each of which may require different strategies to contract or a unique set of recruiters if they are to be reached. Moreover, the issues raised in this example are not limited to the implementation of public health efforts. Beyond health programs, particular hidden populations may be of keen research interest in evaluations of the impact of social policies (e.g., welfare reform), examinations of so-called deviance behaviors (e.g., criminal offenders), and in social needs assessments (e.g., in establishing programs to address social problems). They also may be of interest in monitoring programs like the census. Indeed, failure by the census programs in a number of countries has led to the development of alternative census initiatives. Garcia and Martinez (2002, 2005), for example, argue that Latino farmers and farm workers in the United States— especially the segment of that population that is mobile— have low English language competence and are unfamiliar with the census, so they are significantly undercounted. As a result, the statistics used by the U.S. Department of Agriculture and other federal or state agencies to set priorities, establish policies, and develop service programs may be skewed. Unless alternative approaches are used to more accurately find members of this hard-to-reach population, Garcia and Marinez (2005) maintain that providers may not be aware of their existence.

In all of the types of research and monitoring noted, social scientists commonly target specific "populations." A population—defined as a group of individuals that share at least one nontrivial characteristic—is the largest group (or other unit) of research interest (see http://www.investorwords.com/3738/population.html for a definition of the term *population*). For example, researchers may study runaway youth (a hidden population of growing research interest) with the intention of understanding the health risks, such as street violence, exposure to the elements, poor nutrition, disease, and drug use, that they face and to use this information to design interventions that effectively address their health needs. As Greene et al. (2003, 1), point out, however, there is little empirical evidence about the prevalence or incidence of homelessness or of becoming a runaway or a throwaway, largely because of the challenges inherent in studying this population: contradictory definitions of what constitutes homeless, runaway, and throwaway experiences; an absence of standardized methodology for sampling this population; and an overreliance on data from shelters and agencies. Such challenges likely lead to inaccurate conclusions about the size and characteristics of the population.

One way to go about answering questions about the health risks of runaways would be to interview and to conduct medical examinations of runaways who are staying in homeless shelters. Because they are connected with an institution, these youth would be easy to reach and studies of them would be less costly than of youth who are still on the streets. However, it may be that only some types of runaways seek out shelters for youth; others may avoid them completely. Moreover, it may be the case that shelter avoiders have different or more severe health problems than those who seek shelter residence. In other words, it may be inappropriate to infer the features of an entire population from a study of only one part of the population. Consequently, it may be necessary to go beyond subgroups of a population that are easier to find and easier to recruit. In short, it may be necessary to identify ways to conduct effective research with population segments that are to some degree concealed from the view of the census (or even the alternative census), social programs, and existing data health or other databases. As this example suggests, hidden and hard-to-reach populations present significant challenges to the conduct of useful research, challenges that have led to the development of special sampling, recruitment, and retention strategies, all of which are addressed in this chapter.

There are many different types of hidden and hard-to-reach populations. Notable examples include illicit drug users, such as injection drug users and crack cocaine users, as well as skid row alcoholics, commercial sex workers, recent inmates, school dropouts, unwed pregnant teens, nongay identified men who have sex with men, transgendered individuals, street youth, gang members, criminal offenders, runaways, abused children and women subjected to domestic violence, carriers of genetic abnormalities or asymptomatic sufferers of infectious diseases (e.g., sexually transmitted diseases, tuberculosis), undocumented people (illegal aliens), members of stigmatized groups who are "passing" as members of the majority population, sexual abusers and pedophiles, and the homeless. These are all groups the existence of which is known but about whom we do not know a great deal. They may have significant rates of health, mental health, nutritional, social, or other needs but are not easy to find using institutionally based and more cost-effective means of identification and recruitment.

Even within these hidden and hard-to-reach populations, there may be particularly invisible subgroups. Among drug users, for example, some women may be especially hard to find. As Gross and Brown (1993, 447) note, "Women are less visible in semipublic settings because of the widespread pattern of men copping [buying] drugs for use in private" with their partners. Similarly, Hunt et al. (1993, 465), in discussing AIDS risk, observe, "There is . . . another perhaps even more hidden population at risk for HIV infection [than injection drug users]: their sex partners.

Partners of those injection drug users who are not injection drug users themselves are often not connected with traditional sources of contact with drug users [e.g., drug treatment providers]; nor are they always part of the injection drug user world in which some information is shared about human immunodeficiency virus (HIV). They are the wives and lovers of injection drug users who may or may not be fully aware of their partner's intravenous drug use." Indeed, artificial groups like sex partners of drug users or school dropouts may be especially hard to find because they are composed of "individuals who happen to share a particular kind of experience," but this experience is not necessarily temporally or spatially shared with other member of the "group" (Kane and Mason 1992, 212). There are, for example, no natural settings in which sex partners of injection drug users gather, institutions that they visit, or public records that monitor their characteristics or distribution.

From a research perspective, hidden and hard-to-reach populations are methodologically the opposite of "captive populations," such as prison inmates, clinical and hospital patients, students, and employees. Hidden population generally are "neither well defined nor available for enumeration" (Braunstein 1993, 132). With captive populations, by contrast, the universe is relatively well known, group boundaries are identifiable, and institutional records exist on the individuals who are members of the group. Moreover, captive populations are, by comparison, easy to reach.

Cross Reference: See Books 1 and 6 for a discussion of legal and ethical requirements governing research on "vulnerable populations"

Midway between hidden and captive populations are what might be called specialized "patron or membership populations," such as customers at a bar, theatergoers, or members of a church or club. Like captive populations, these individuals generally are easily reached, in that by definition they must congregate at a particular site to be members of the group; however, like hidden populations there may not exist any records to define the features of group members *a priori*. Of course, some types of patron and member populations may be more hidden than others, such as customers at a "biker bar" (a bar patronized by members of motorcycle gangs), bettors at an illegal gambling site (e.g., clandestine dog fighting or cock fighting arenas), or members of a secret society (e.g., the Ku Klux Klan) or a street gang.

As this discussion suggests, it is reasonable to think of target research populations in terms of a continuum that ranges from: (1) those who are well known and highly accessible; to (2) those who are semihidden and hard to find; to (3) those who are hidden and harder to find; to (4) those who are quite invisible and (intentionally or unintentionally) resist being drawn in to research initiatives. Each of these types of target groups presents its own challenges to the development of good sampling designs.

Within each of the four types of hidden or hard-to-reach population types listed above, there may be considerable variability. In criminality studies, for example, it would be far easier to recruit a sample of petty street hustlers than it would of "made men" (those who have undergone formal induction into the Mafia), even though both would be considered hidden populations. In either case, recruiting a *representative sample*, one that well reflects the range of characteristics of the wider target population, is very difficult.

As the examples presented above reveal, the concept of hidden or hard-to-reach populations incorporates two somewhat different (yet intertwined) notions: on the one hand it refers to populations that are *comparatively difficult to find and to recruit* into a research project, and on the other it designates *populations whose boundaries, characteristics, and distribution are not known*. Hence it is difficult to be sure that a sample recruited for research is a reasonable reflection of the target population as a whole. Often hidden populations have both of these features. In some cases, however, the general characteristics of the group may be known, at least to some degree (e.g., because institutional records exist on the population), even though they are hard to find (e.g., school dropouts or runaway youth). In other cases, many members of the group are relatively easy to find but their representativeness is unclear (e.g., the homeless) because the target population is dispersed and includes an unknown number of subgroups with different coping and survival strategies. In this chapter, we will be concerned with both hidden and hard-to-reach populations.

Social concealment is a reflection of two social factors: *intentionality* and *capacity*. Some groups intentionally conceal their activities because they are illegal or

Definition: Social concealment refers to the distinctive feature of hidden populations, the fact that their behaviors and presence are hidden from public view and awareness

otherwise subject to outside interference. Concealment in these cases is a consequence of active efforts to disguise or hide behavior. In their study of injection drug users, for example, Kane and Mason (1992) found that some individuals go to considerable lengths to camouflage their drug involvement in order to avoid arrest. They describe the case of Mike, a forty-two-year-old man who had been an injection drug user for twenty-five years at the time he was interviewed:

> Mike says he has always wanted to avoid looking like a *dope fiend*. That means he tries to be clean and well shaved, he dresses nicely, and he is careful to avoid scarring his body with tracks (darkened scar lines produced by collapsed veins). His maneuvering around the stigmatized image of the addict is an important survival strategy, for, as elsewhere, image counts for a lot in the streets. It has taken on an even greater significance in his efforts to avoid arrest as he gets older. (Kane and Mason 1992, 205)

Stigmatization is another factor that propels concealment. Groups that are subject to social condemnation (on moral, religious, or other grounds) or even vigilante-style aggression commonly seek to hide their identities and activities. One such group is composed of transgendered individuals.

> A cultural category or niche . . . among gay and bisexual men [and women] is . . . represented by transgendered individuals—those who are either transvestites or pre- or postoperative transexuals. Transgendered males typically dress like females or at least androgynously. . . . Transgendered persons represent a particularly challenging population in that they are not well understood, experience considerable discrimination, and often have difficulty obtaining appropriate services. As with other marginalized populations, they tend to migrate to major metropolitan areas . . . Although this subgroup's population is at extremely high risk . . ., there is a

dearth of information available about their lifestyle. (Gorman, Morgan, and Lambert 1995, 172)

Similarly, particular ethnic groups may be harder to reach than others because of the way they have been treated in the larger society. As Marín and Marín (1991, 42) point out,

> Hispanics could be expected to be more wary of researchers than are other ethnic or racial groups for a variety of reasons. Primary among these reasons is the concern that providing personal information may place some Hispanics at risk—for example, when income or immigration information could be used against an individual. In addition, some community members perceive social science research as a form of exploitation in which nonminority individuals reap the benefits of the data collection effort . . . Concerns about participating in research are particularly salient when prospective participants are first contacted in person or over the phone. It is not uncommon for unscrupulous commercial firms to prey on the newly arrived and convince them to purchase unnecessary or expensive goods at high interest rates.

Other groups may be hidden, but not as a result of intentional concealment. Like sex partners of drug users, these populations, though of special interest to particular research initiatives, may not recognize their "membership" in a particular population or be readily available for identification by researchers. Parish et al. (2003), for example, discuss the hidden epidemic of chlamydia in China. Because this sexually transmitted infection can remain asymptomatic, sufferers may not know they are infected and in need of health intervention. Investigation by these researchers affirmed that rates of infection were significant. They recommended the development of targeted campaigns to reach those at especially high risk, including a sexually linked network of commercial sex workers, their high-income male customers, and the wives and other regular sex partners of these men.

Finally, there are populations that are hidden simply because they have not been identified as being of interest to researchers. Sex partners of drug users, for example, only became of interest because of the AIDS epidemic and the recognition that HIV could be transmitted both through the multiperson of injection equipment and through sexual contact. Consequently, for a number of years, years during which HIV was being sexually transmitted to women, AIDS researchers and public health officials in the Western world conceptualized the disease as an affliction of gay men and failed to recognize and define similar and related symptoms among women as AIDS. In this sense, while reachable, women were a hidden population in the epidemic.

Definition: Capacity refers to the ability to conceal behavior that may be socially frowned upon or illegal because of special knowledge, social connections, or financial resources

Second there is the issue of **capacity**. Some groups have greater power to conceal their behavior than others. Drug addicts, for example, include a wide range of individuals, from so-called street drug users, individuals who hang out on city street corners and "cop" (buy, borrow, or beg) drugs from street dealers, to physicians who practice in major hospitals and secure drugs through their own prescriptions. As this statement suggests, hidden populations are especially common at both ends of the socioeconomic pyramid. The rich, and especially the "super-rich" (the wealthiest 1 percent of the population), generally are quite hidden because they have the power and resources to conceal their lives and behaviors from social science researchers. Consequently, far more is known about the lives of hidden populations among the poor than among the well-to-do (Domhoff 1970). Even behaviors of the wealthy that have important effects on the lives of those who are not wealthy are hidden from view and general awareness. For example, wealthy philanthropists who choose anonymity often are able to achieve it despite the public impact of their contributions. Similarly, the wealthy frequently are able to hide embarrassing or even criminal behavior from public awareness. As a result, many social problems (e.g., child abuse, domestic violence, illicit drug abuse, alcoholism, teen pregnancy) popularly are conceived as characteristics of the poor and working classes rather than as being widely distributed across all social strata. Strategies for studying the upper classes, often from a distance, may involve analyzing lists or other public or semipublic notifications used by the wealthy both to communicate their place among the elite and to enhance opportunities for interaction (and their children's interaction) with other "worthy" individuals. These strategies, including examinations of social registries of particular cities, enrollment in exclusive private schools, membership in wealthy businessmen's clubs, activities of exclusive resorts, and reviews of published marriage notices, have been developed but are infrequently used by social scientists.

EVOLUTION OF HIDDEN AND HARD-TO-REACH POPULATION RESEARCH

It is only in recent years that the study of hidden and hard-to-reach populations has emerged as a distinct field of social science research. Examinations of groups that fall within this domain of research, however, are not new. Although it is difficult to determine the earliest study of hidden and hard-to-reach populations, several candidate studies dating from the nineteenth century are noteworthy. In 1822, Thomas De Quincey published a book titled *Confessions of an English Opium-Eater*. De Quincey studied opium users at both the top and bottom of the socioeconomic pyramid during an era when the use of the drug was not outlawed. Using a rough-hewn ethnographic approach, De Quincey sought to describe opium use among the working poor in London in the context of the impact of the oppressive social conditions in which poor people lived. In 1845, Friedrich Engels published his book *The Condition of the Working Class in England*, in which he described the hidden lives of members of the working class of Manchester. His account was the product of his extensive ethnographic wanderings through the unmaintained and filthy streets of Manchester's working-class residential districts.

Both of these studies stand out as very early efforts to acquire firsthand understanding of the day-to-day lives and experiences of populations that were socially discounted and largely unknown (because their lives were not granted much importance among policy makers and scholars of the day). The researchers in question were not completely systematic in their approaches to data collection, and their methods would be subject to some degree of criticism in the contemporary social sciences. Their findings about hidden populations, nonetheless, were powerful, insightful, and historically significant. Beginning in the 1930s, there was increasing interest in the study of hidden populations, especially by researchers affiliated with the Chicago School of social research. Bingham Dai's *Opium Addiction in Chicago* (1937) and Alfred Lindesmith's *Opium Addiction* (1947) are important studies from this period.

Concern with hidden populations has expanded significantly since the 1960s, as have the number of social scientific studies of diverse populations that fall within this rubric and methods for research. Procedures for finding and sampling hidden and hard-to-reach populations have evolved rapidly since the early studies noted, especially in recent years. Researchers at a number of sites have contributed to this process. Those involved in drug use and AIDS risk studies have been especially active in seeking to overcome the challenges of effectively sampling elusive populations. Some researchers have selected readily available samples, like people in drug treatment, but then added on additional individuals recruited through other means such as advertising, as a way to broaden the sampling frame. In Portland, Oregon, researchers ensured variability in their sample of injection drug users by recruiting from multiple sources, including a corrections facility, county health clinics, private welfare organizations, and street outreach. In Baltimore, researchers added sexually transmitted disease clinics and emergency rooms to the list of potential recruitment sites that would add diversity to the sample construction process. Another approach has been to begin with convenience and snowball sampling techniques, participant recruitment strategies that involve sampling in nonrandom ways among individuals that are readily available from the target population, and moving out along their social networks to recruit additional and potentially more hidden participants. All of these efforts have produced increasingly improved sampling approaches that attempt to draw on an ever-broadening cross-section and to be more representative of the invariably heterogeneous target population.

In recent years, especially with drug users but with other populations as well, researchers have adopted some version of the network-based approach know as respondent-driven sampling (Salganik and Heckathorn 2004). Research participants are selected from the reported social networks of a small initial set of participants called "seeds." Seeds recruit other participants from members of their social networks, who, in turn, recruit additional participants from their own social networks. This process continues until the desired sample size is reached. While there has been considerable debate on this issue, adherents argue that with sufficient waves of recruitment a representative sample is achieved. Other newer approaches for the study of hidden populations include use of a privileged access interviewer team (Griffiths et al. 2006), use of the worldwide web (Duncan et al. 2003), and venue-based sampling (Muhir et al. 2001).

Cross Reference: Book 3, chapter 10, on sampling in mixed methods research, and chapter 5 in this book on network research

Over time, as described below and in Table 6.1, these approaches have been combined and refined to establish increasingly widely used procedures for studying hidden and hard-to-reach populations, and variants of the new approaches have developed in a number of research sites. The sharing of information among researchers across sites, a process that has been facilitated through forums created by the National Institute on Drug Abuse (NIDA) and other federal public health institutions in the United States, have allowed a mixing and merging of potential strategies like those described below for learning about, gaining access to, and recruiting hidden and hard-to-reach populations into research. These models all share important features (e.g., use of outreach). While they were first developed in the study of drug users, they are highly relevant to the study of all hidden and hard-to-reach populations.

The Chicago Model

Developed by drug researchers at the University of Illinois at Chicago in the late 1970s, this early approach combined **epidemiologic** survey techniques, **street ethnography** focused on congregation sites of the target population, and the use of secondary data from institutional sources

Definition: Epidemiologic refers to the study of the distribution, frequency, and determinants of disease and injury in human populations

Table 6.1 Models for Hidden and Hard-to-Reach Population Sampling
and Recruitment

Model	Distinctive Features
Chicago	Early effort to mix qualitative and quantitative data sources to gain a broader understanding of noninstitutionalized target populations, including the ethnography of congregation sites of noninstitutionalized members of the target group.
San Francisco	Adopted the multimethod approach to develop a target sampling plan as an advance over convenience sampling.
Dayton	Intensified the use of ethnography to allow the development of proportional sampling quotas for high-, medium-, and low-density areas for recruitment of the target population.
Philadelphia	Used a targeted sampling plan approach that emphasized rapport building with relevant gatekeepers in the community to aid participant recruitment.
Hartford	Implemented a targeted sampling plan based on ongoing community-based organization service delivery to the target population and coalition building among research and service organizations.

 Definition: Street ethnography refers to the study of inner-city urban populations based on the immersion of an observant researcher in the day-to-day life of the target group

Cross Reference: See Books 1, 2, 3, and 5 for ways that these approaches can be combined

(e.g., drug treatment admissions) to identify and target heroin use social networks. The goal of this approach was to develop an understanding of a heroin epidemic in the city. Later the method was adapted for use in studying the AIDS epidemic among drug users. The Chicago Model typifies the movement in hidden population studies toward mixed quantitative/qualitative methodological approaches, a feature that characterizes much of the work done in recent years with hidden populations. The orientation of this work is to combine as many sources of and kinds of data as possible to gain both depth (a more detailed comprehension of the target population) and breadth (insight concerning the range and distribution of target population characteristics) in research understanding.

The San Francisco Model

The MidCity Consortium to Combat AIDS was one of the first research-driven HIV prevention projects in the United States to target street drug injection populations. Recognizing that drug injectors form a dispersed hidden population, in 1985 the Consortium united street ethnography, key informant interviewing, theoretical sampling techniques, and **chain referral sampling** to develop categories of drug injectors within specified and mapped sampling areas within the city of San Francisco. Participants were then recruited from identified sections of the city. This approach evolved into the *targeted sampling strategy*, discussed further below, that has become central to the study of drug use populations during the AIDS epidemic. A strength of this approach borrowed from the inductive orientation of ethnography is flexibility. The project was designed to be interactive, allowing for modifications in the sampling strategy as new data were collected. The ultimate objective was to improve researcher confidence in the generalizability of findings from participants in the study to the wider, more hidden sectors of the injection drug user population.

Definition:
Chain referral sampling involves using existing study participants to refer other members of their group for participation in a study

The Dayton Model

Building on the efforts of the MidCity Consortium in San Francisco, in the early 1990s researchers at Wright State University developed a sampling approach for studying hidden populations of drug users that combines various sources of data, especially ethnography, to estimate the density of the target group residing in zip code–defined areas of Dayton, Ohio. Through this approach, researchers were able to generate and use proportional sampling quotas for high-, medium-, and low-density zones of the city (based on the estimated number of target group members in each zone). This approach allowed researchers to shape recruitment to reflect the estimated characteristics of the target population. This model advances the targeted sampling approach toward greater confidence in the outcome of studies in which, as is always the case with hidden populations, it is difficult to know the full range of features and their distribution in the target population.

The Philadelphia Model

In 1987, the Philadelphia Health Management Corporation developed an approach to studying hidden populations that emphasized rapport building with relevant gatekeepers in the community. Designed to recruit out-of-treatment drug users, the model emphasized developing working relations with local drug dealers and shooting gallery operators, as well as local residents and merchants. Contact was also made with the police department. These efforts helped project staff to gain access to individuals and to avoid opposition to this access that might not otherwise have been possible. This approach revealed the importance of building a solid community foundation for studying hidden populations in minority communities.

The Hartford Model

A somewhat similar approach to the study of hidden populations was developed by researchers in Hartford, Connecticut (Singer and Weeks 2005). It built on the data triangulation features of the San Francisco Model but added a strong emphasis on enduring community-based efforts that unite research with direct service provision, advocacy, and the building of community research capacity (Singer 1993, Singer et al. 2006). Uniting the efforts of a consortium of community-based organizations, including minority community organizations, drug treatment providers, and community-based researchers, the Hartford Model emphasizes collaborative research methods, anthropological field techniques, and the inclusion of community service providers in research efforts. This approach enabled researchers to move rapidly into diverse urban zones and to work effectively and comprehensively in ethnically diverse populations, a strategy that protected against antiresearch backlash that sometimes develops in communities in the wake of university-directed research.

 Cross Reference: See Book 1 for a more detailed explanation of the use of ethnography in this context

Through efforts like these, researchers have been able to refine methods for studying hidden populations. The specific features of current approaches in hidden and hard-to-reach population research are described in more detail below.

REACHING THE HARD-TO-REACH:
METHODS FOR STUDYING HIDDEN POPULATIONS

MARKING THE TERRITORY: DEFINING TARGET
POPULATION BOUNDARIES

- Targeted Sampling: Mixing Qualitative and Quantitative Methods
- Mapping Preparation
- Secondary Data Sources: Exposed Features of Hidden Populations
- Ethnography
- Ethnographic Mapping
- Finalization of the Targeted Sampling Design

Marking the Territory: Defining Target
Population Boundaries

A significant challenge for the study of hidden and hard-to-reach populations is the establishment of target group boundaries, including setting inclusion and exclusion criteria for determining group membership. Decisions of this sort are necessary in research even though boundaries between groups often are fuzzy, membership can be transitory and situational, and insider definitions of essential in-group characteristics may be conflicted. Researchers recognize (or should recognize) that human social life does not unfold in discrete packages with well-defined and clearly demarcated boundaries. Nevertheless, some standards must be used to guide the selection of study participants.

Populations, it should be stressed, are social constructs. Their existence *as a distinct group* is not so much given in nature as it is constructed by researchers (although not arbitrarily and always for a specific research purpose). Consider, for example, the population called *injection drug users*, a term that is widely used in the AIDS literature as labeling a hidden population of considerable public health interest. In fact, this term only achieved generalized usage with the advent of the AIDS epidemic. Before this time individuals who consumed illicit drugs through hypodermic injection were referred to as intravenous drug users. Recognition that some individuals "skin pop" (inject a drug under the surface of the skin rather than in a vein) led to a terminological shift, but, more importantly, to a broadening of the boundaries of the population of interest since "skin popping" was a behavior with the potential to expose practitioners to HIV and STI infections. Moreover, the drugs that people inject vary considerably. For example, some individuals have been found to be alcohol injectors. This practice, though apparently limited, is legal, although, if syringe transfer between individuals occurs, it is no less risky in terms of HIV transmission than illicit drug injection. Additionally, research has shown considerable variation in injection frequency among drug users. To what degree is it likely that individuals who "shoot up" (inject drugs) one or twice a month are living the same lifestyle as those who shoot up eight times a day? Does a single behavior, in other words, one that exists in considerable variation (across class, racial/ethnic, geographic, sexual identity, and gender lines), create a distinct population? In many recent studies of injection drug users, in fact, researchers have had to specify the timing of the individual's last injection as a criterion for recruitment (e.g., injection sometime within the thirty-day period before being interviewed). It is far from evident where to draw cultural boundaries around drug injectors when studying an inner-city population in which drug use of various kinds is extensive and changing, while lifestyles among drug users and nonusers have much in common because of the impress of harsh social conditions. Additionally, it is important to remember that the category *injection drug user* may have little correspondence with the active social identities of those who inject drugs.

Similar problems are encountered in bounding other populations as well. People who engage in commercial sex work, for example, also are hard to delineate. For the most part, "street walkers" (usually down-and-out individuals who solicit customers by standing or walking along busy streets) form the popular stereotype of commercial sex workers. Nonetheless, highly paid "call girls" and escorts (who may live in exclusive apartments, attend college, and dress in the latest fashions) are also part of the population of commercial sex workers. Similarly, while commercial sex workers commonly are thought of as females, there are many male sex workers too, primarily, but not solely, catering to men who have sex with men. Additionally, while the label *prostitute* implies a longer-term illicit career, many individuals engage in commercial sex work for very limited periods of time or to raise funds for very specific purposes. In our studies with inner-city impoverished populations in Hartford, for example, we have interviewed mothers who occasionally engage in commercial sex with specific known individuals (i.e., men they know in the neighborhood) in order to obtain enough money to be able to feed their children until their next welfare payment arrives. Similarly, some women may be "taken care of" by a "sugar daddy" but would deny that their sexual relations with that person provider constitute prostitution—the sexual exchange is only one albeit significant component of certain types of intimate relationships.

In sum, the fixing of group boundaries—for the purposes of research—is a necessary if difficult task. In light of the discussion above considerable caution must be exercised in avoiding unduly wide or narrow boundaries. Rather, researchers must strive to draw boundaries that are grounded in knowledge of the target group. Unavoidably, this means that boundaries may need to shift as researchers become more aware of the target population. This is precisely what occurred, as noted below, during the development of the San Francisco targeted sampling model.

Key point

Targeted Sampling: Mixing Qualitative and Quantitative Methods

Targeted sampling has emerged as a methodologically reasonable solution to the difficult problem of sampling hidden populations. Despite known limitations, many researchers who study hidden and hard-to-research populations have adopted targeted sampling as a method for participant selection. The purpose of a targeted sampling plan is to allow researchers systematically to develop "controlled lists of specified populations within geographic districts" along with "detailed plans . . . to recruit adequate numbers of cases with in each of the targets" (Watters and Biernacki 1989, 430). Targeted sampling relies on multimethod research (Bluthenthal and Watters 1995), and it is noted for mixing qualitative methods (to identify hidden arenas of behavior and social life) and quantitative methods of data collection (to insure the generalizability of results). Although targeted samples are not random, neither are they convenience samples. Rather, they are a middle ground for achieving a sample that reflects available knowledge about the target group when truly random sampling is not possible and when a higher degree of research rigor is needed than can be conferred through convenience sampling. For example, a multimethod approach with target sampling for specific methods was adopted by the Office of HIV/AIDS Policy of the Department of Health and Human Services to help communities across the United States to identify hidden populations and behaviors that were not being addressed by existing HIV/AIDS programs for prevention (Bowser et al. 2007). A similar approach was adopted by the Human Resources Service Administration to identify hidden groups of HIV/AIDS-positive individuals who were not getting into treatment (Convisor et al. 2007).

Key components of targeted sampling are described below using experience gained in Hartford, Connecticut, in developing and using a targeted sampling plan for a study of AIDS risk prevention among injection drug and crack cocaine users through the NIDA Cooperative Agreement for AIDS Community-Based Outreach/Intervention Research. The steps in the development of a targeted sampling plan included the following:

- Preparation for the mapping of indicator data on the target population

- Identification of available secondary data sources on the target population
- Ethnographic clarification of target group characteristics, behaviors, and distribution
- Finalization of the sampling plan

Mapping Preparation

The first step in the development of a targeted sampling plan involves geographically bounding the research area and establishing zones for data mapping. In San Francisco, during the development of target sampling as a recruitment method, this entailed an identification of those neighborhoods with the highest concentration of injection drug users and drug-related activity. In Dayton, Ohio, researchers used zip code boundaries to examine the distribution of concentration densities of drug users (Carlson et al. 1994). In Hartford, our research team divided the city in terms of the existing configuration of identified, bounded, and named neighborhoods. There are seventeen such neighborhoods in the city. The city government has developed readily available maps of these neighborhoods, with streets drawn in, which proved to be very helpful in conceptualizing a citywide sampling plan. We knew various things about many of the neighborhoods from previous research as well as from general familiarity with the city. We knew a considerable amount about the history of the neighborhoods, for example, and some of the ethnic transitions that had occurred within them over time. In addition, we knew which were high- and low-density residence zones and which were business or undeveloped zones (e.g., two neighborhoods had negligible populations). Also, we knew, at least roughly, about the general ethnic composition and the relative income levels in the different neighborhoods. In completing this first phase of the development of a targeted sampling plan, we ruled out neighborhoods with limited residential populations as potential target areas. For other neighborhoods, we pooled existing data from various sources, as described below, to get a better understanding of the distribution and composition of the target population across neighborhoods.

*Secondary Data Sources: Exposed Features
of Hidden Populations*

To help in the sampling frame selection process, researchers have, in part, turned to available institutional data sources. In different locations, different kinds of secondary data may be available and accessible. Unfortunately, researchers often have learned the hard way that data that have been collected by governmental, educational, or other institutions may not be easily accessible because of turf issues, bureaucratic barriers, lack of staffing, outdated record-keeping systems, or disorganization. Sorting through which data exist and which are accessible, researchers have attempted to use multiple secondary data sets because of the inherent biases of any individual set. For example, relying only on arrest data would skew sampling frame selection to parts of the city where the police are most active or most successful in arresting members of the target population. Similarly, relying only on treatment or social service admission data could skew selection to those sections of the target area that have more treatment or service programs or more resources that assist people to get into interventions.

In studies of drug users, for example, a broad range of secondary indicator data sources have been identified (Braunstein 1993, Wiebel 1990):

- Law-enforcement data on the location of arrests, seizures, and laboratory analyses of controlled substances
- Urinalysis results of new arrestees by home residence (e.g., performed by the Drug Use Forecasting System of the National Institute on Justice)
- Substance abuse-related emergency room admissions, including data from the Drug Abuse Warning Network
- Medical examiner (coroner) reports on the residences of individuals who died of drug-related causes
- Residence data on individuals admitted to drug treatment programs

- Prescription tracking systems for psychoactive pharmaceuticals
- Surveillance reports on identified AIDS cases by residence
- Admissions data on individuals treated for STDs, TB, or related diseases that tend to be prevalent among drug users

These indicator data sources are most helpful if they are linked with locations (e.g., residence) so that the information can be mapped (the location of each case identified and marked on a map of the targeted area) to assist in the location of high- and low-density areas (based on the frequencies of mapped behaviors or cases) for the target population. All of these sources of data are subject to some types of bias. The use of multiple sources collected by diverse organizations for differing purposes helps to limit systematic bias.

EXAMPLE 6.2

USING MULTIPLE SOURCES TO LIMIT BIAS IN TARGETED SAMPLING

In Hartford, while all of the data sources noted above were not available, researchers did have access to a variety of secondary data sources. In addition, data from a completed prior study of injection drug users and their sex partners were available. Data sources used were:

- Existing research data on the residences of injection drug users and sex partners recruited through convenience street outreach
- Existing data on the residences of HIV-positive injection drug users and sex partners
- City of Hartford data on the residences of sexually transmitted disease cases
- City of Hartford Police Department data on the location of drug arrests for two years
- City of Hartford Police Department data on the residences of individuals arrested for drug-related offenses
- Drug treatment admission data on the residences of opiate users
- Census data on the sociodemographic characteristics of city neighborhoods

Potential sources of bias in these data sets are noteworthy. For data from prior research, sources of potential bias include over/under sampling of particular neighborhoods based on outreach worker preference, misidentification of individuals as drug injectors (which was based solely on self-report), participant provision of false residences, and changes in residence since the period of data collection. HIV testing data may have been skewed by a lack of representativeness of the sample recruited for testing and differential self-selection for testing. Potential sources of bias in arrest data lay in police attitudes about potential violators that shape arrest patterns and in geographic variation in law enforcement (e.g., disproportionately targeting ethnic minority neighborhoods for drug surveillance). Potential sources of bias in drug and STD treatment data include geographic, ethnic, and gender differences in access to treatment. Despite all of these possible sources of bias, the data listed above were collected by different institutions and groups with differing agendas and missions, and hence by relying on multiple data sources it is possible to restrict skewing in any particular direction. For example, while drug arrests may "oversample" minority drug users because of prejudicial arrest patterns, drug treatment enrollment has been found to "oversample" white drug users.

Data from all of the sources noted above were computer entered by neighborhood or street address into a geographic information system (GIS) desktop software package to enable us to develop summary risk profiles for each of the major identified neighborhoods of Hartford. Comparisons show that findings from our prior studies, police arrest records, and STD and drug treatment records tended to fit together, with some neighborhoods having notably higher rates across all indicators and others having comparatively lower rates across most or all measures. GIS profiles on each of the neighborhoods were added to ethnographic information to complete our starting image of the distribution of the target group across city neighborhoods.

Ethnography

The key features of ethnography for understanding hidden and hard-to-reach populations are:

- Its capacity for *discovery* of unknown social beliefs and behaviors
- Its emphasis on *"experience-near,"* on-the-ground research (Geertz 1984)
- Its emphasis on a *holistic approach*

Cross Reference: Book 1, chapter 1, and Book 2, chapter 1 and 2, for a discussion of the critical features of ethnography

First, while there is considerable opportunity for new discovery in most social science research, some research approaches are more open to encountering the unexpected than are others. Ethnography, as a form of naturalistic inquiry, is a highly porous approach that imposes little in the way of researcher control over the field of study and hence is quite open to serendipity, including unearthing of patterns or relationships that are outside the awareness of and hence are not self-reported by research subjects. Ethnographers commonly enter the field with a set of issues of primary concern. Experiences in the field, however, have been known to send ethnographers home with research and results that are very different from those they anticipated on entry to the field, and more locally salient. This emergent feature of ethnographic research makes it an especially important tool in the study of elusive populations and their potentially well-concealed behaviors. Second, as a context-sensitive approach, ethnography takes the researcher out of the academic or institute suite and into the street or other settings, where members of the target population live out their lives. Through rapport building, concern with the subject's point of view, and long-term presence in the field, ethnographers often are able to gain access to places, events, and information that might be hard for other methods to achieve. Using level of participation in the lives of the target group as a criterion, ethnographic strategies can be said to form a continuum, with unobtrusive measurement lying at the least involved end of the continuum, participant observation techniques forming a middle ground, and intrusive strategies, those that take the researcher deeply into the lives and activities of the target group, forming the other end of the continuum. The relevance of each of these approaches for the study of hidden and hard-to-research populations is examined below. Finally, ethnographers are able to use this access to move about, visiting and mapping the social scenes of target group life, ensuring thereby a holistic understanding of diverse and often dispersed group features, behaviors, and subgroups. All of these traits, which find expression through the data collection strategies discussed below, make ethnography an appealing approach in the study of hidden populations.

Key Informant Interviewing

This is a term ethnographers use to refer to ongoing conversations with knowledgeable insiders (individuals from the target group) who are able and willing to work with them to produce an accurate, insider-guided picture of the target population. Although immersed in the target group, its lifestyle, culture, and social settings, key informants are individuals who are capable of stepping back from their involvement and offer objective accounts of group behavior, beliefs, experiences, and related matters. Good key informants not only answer ethnographers' questions—to varying degrees, they anticipate them. In other words, they grasp the ethnographer's objective, what s/he is trying to get at (a full account of group life), and to provide or help to acquire the needed information.

As the following two examples suggest, key informants are sources of two items that are critical to the successful study of hidden populations: information and access. Information provided by key informants can be used to evaluate the meaning of social indicator data, assess the validity and biases of such data, and check preliminary understandings that have been gained by reviewing institutional sources of information. By providing access to the target population, key informants help the ethnographer to determine the existence of as-yet-unidentified layers of target population members that should be represented in the study sample (Whyte 1955).

Cross Reference: Book 3, chapters 3, 4, and 5, for a broader discussion of in-depth and key informant interviewing

EXAMPLE 6.3

THE ROLE OF KEY INFORMANTS IN PROVIDING ACCESS TO HIDDEN POPULATIONS

In *Street Corner Society*, a classic study of a hidden population (impoverished, inner-city Italian immigrants and their children), William F. Whyte described the important role Doc, a street gang leader, played in his research. Whyte was an outsider;

he did not know his way around, he did not know the local customs, and he was suspect to those inside the gang and the local Italian community. Doc taught Whyte how to avoid problems in the field (e.g., by not asking questions of people before his presence was fully accepted), and he took him places and introduced him to people. He taught Whyte that by being patient and unassertive in his research, in time the information he needed would come to him. As a result, Whyte gained rapport with many members of the community and was able to develop a seminal account of a population that was otherwise resistant to examination by outsiders.

   **EXAMPLE 6.4**

THE ROLE OF KEY INFORMANTS IN IDENTIFYING POLYGAMISTS ENGAGED IN BANNED MARITAL PRACTICES IN UTAH

A study of polygamists in Utah, individuals involved in illegal behavior who have been excommunicated because they continue to practice banned marital customs of the early Mormon church, would have been impossible without the help of a key informant. Because of laws against bigamy and opprobrium from mainstream members of the Mormon Church, fundamentalists (as they call themselves) often lead quite secretive lives. Historically, police raids have not been uncommon and hence fear of undercover agents is widespread. This concern has increased in recent years with the police raid and arrest of fundamentalists at Yearning for Zion Ranch in Texas in 2008. Through the friends and contacts of the researcher's initial key informant (an individual who sought the researcher out when he heard about her desire to study the fundamentalists), she was able to attend group meetings, interview many group members (male and female), and to gain insight into life as an underground polygamist. This work led to an ever-growing awareness of previously unknown segments of the target group, including individuals who were still participating in the Mormon Church because their involvement in polygamy was so well hidden.

Participant Observation

This is the core research strategy of ethnography, and it is vital to the development of a targeted sampling plan. It entails spending a considerable amount of time with research subjects in their natural settings as they perform day-to-day activities, observing these behaviors and listening to the comments and conversations of subjects, and recording this information as field notes for latter analysis. In participant observation research, ethnographers approach members of hidden populations from a "one-down" position. This means that ethnographers recognize that insiders are the experts on their group. It is the ethnographer's responsibility to gain the trust and cooperation of target group members rather than the other way around. Accepting and validating the knowledge and experience of the target population within their realm of specialization (e.g., among the homeless, in finding shelter and food on the street) is a means of laying the groundwork for the development of rapport. However, being "one-down" can contribute to feelings of uncertainty and caution on the ethnographer's part. Knowing that scheming or conning are common practices of economic survival among hidden populations, ethnographers attempt to approach their work with alertness, recognizing that study populations themselves appreciate the value of "street smart" behavior.

The objectives of participant observation in targeted sampling are described by Clatts, Davis, and Atillasoy (1995, 122–23), based on a sampling design for the study of homeless youth in New York.

EXAMPLE 6.5

THE USE OF PARTICIPANT OBSERVATION IN IDENTIFYING STREET YOUTH IN NEW YORK

"One of the initial tasks given to the ethnographers was that of mapping the geography of the street youth population, that is, locations where youth were involved in prostitution, drug dealing, hanging out, eating, and sleeping. . . . A second goal was to identify differences within the street youth population that could be mapped by reference to time or location. . . . Ethnographers began research in areas where street youth were known to congregate . . . and moved into other areas as they learned more about the movement of the street youth population." This approach led to the realization that homeless youth are a diverse population and that different kinds of street youth tend to congregate in different locations. For example, those found in the Port Authority Bus Terminal comprised the youngest group identified in the study; they were newer to street life, and they were more likely to engage in prostitution than drug dealing. These youth contrasted on all of these dimensions with those found hanging out in Times Square. This finding revealed the importance of including multiple sampling frames. Had the researchers assumed that the youth found at the bus terminal were typical of all street youth, they would have misunderstood the population, and they would have recruited from only one segment of a far more diverse group. Interestingly, in this case, life history interviews revealed that youth found hanging out at the bus terminal were not a distinct group but rather represented an early phase in the adolescent "street career." Learning about the lives of youth in Times Square in detail, for example, revealed that previously they, too, had hung out at the bus terminal and engaged in prostitution.

These findings are typical of the kind of discoveries made in ethnographic research. As this example affirms, social boundaries in the field are complex. Consequently, targeted sampling must by necessity remain flexible as new information about the target population is collected.

Unobtrusive Approaches

In addition to participant observation, ethnographers may use various unobtrusive measures to assess density levels and behaviors for the target population (Webb et al. 1966).

 **EXAMPLE 6.6**

USING UNOBTRUSIVE MEASURES TO ASSESS BEHAVIOR OF HIDDEN POPULATIONS

In Hartford researchers developed an assessment based on the discard of drug use paraphernalia such as syringes, cookers (containers used to mix drugs with water), bottles of syringe rinse water, and crack pipes. Research team members systematically visited abandoned buildings, parks, alleyways, and open fields and, using survey methods (walking through areas—eyes to the ground—to spot surface deposits of discarded drug use "works"), identified places of drug user congregation and drug use (usually during times when no drug users were actually present). This information, including counts of identified items and descriptions of the site, was recorded. Syringes recovered at these sites were later tested for HIV antibodies to allow the mapping of infection patterns in the targeted areas. We also systematically visited pharmacies to interview pharmacists about the frequency of drug user purchases of over-the-counter syringes. Approaches like these allow ethnographers to add further information to their mapping of sampling areas without imposing on individuals who may wish to maintain their seclusion. Researchers in other cities have used similar techniques to identify commercial sex locations based on the discard of condoms.

Intrusive Approaches: Going Somewhat Native

Definition:
Going native refers to situations in which ethnographers give up any semblance of scientific objectivity and become thoroughly enmeshed in the life and culture of the target group

Cross Reference:
Book 6 includes further discussion of issues involved in the use of "undercover" research strategies

Some ethnographers have used approaches that are quite intrusive in the lives of the target population. At the intrusive end of the continuum, to gain participatory access to the target population, researchers may use techniques characterized by a degree of subterfuge. The classic and still controversial example is Laud Humphrys's (1970) study, published under the title *Tearoom Trade*, of a hidden population of men who have sex with men in public bathrooms. As part of his research on this population, Humphrys hung out in a public bathroom that was a frequent site for sexual encounters among men. He gained a role at the site as a look out, warning men if someone was coming. However, he also recorded the license plate numbers of the men who participated in sexual liaisons in the bathroom, acquired their home addresses from the department of motor vehicles, and visited their home posing as a researcher conducting a door-to-door community survey of various kinds of behavior, including sexual practices.

A method that incorporated an even greater level of participation and artifice was developed by Ralph Bolton in his study of sex practices among gay men in Belgium. His report follows.

EXAMPLE 6.7

USING OBTRUSIVE MEASURES TO IDENTIFY SPECIFIC BEHAVIORS IN HIDDEN POPULATIONS: SELF-IDENTIFICATION AS A MEMBER OF THE GROUP

"I spent most of my time, at all hours of day and night . . . , in settings where gay men in Brussels hang out: bars, saunas, restaurants, parks, tearooms, streets, and private homes. . . . My presentation of self was simple and straightforward: I was a gay man doing research as a medical anthropologist on AIDS and sex. . . . In my casual sexual encounters with men I picked up in gay cruising situations, my approach during sex was to allow my partner to take the lead in determining which sexual practices to engage in. Low-risk activities posed no problem, of course, but to discover which moderate and high risk behaviors they practiced, I assented to the former (oral sex, for example) while declining the latter (unprotected sexual intercourse)" (Bolton 1992, 133–35).

Through this strategy, Bolton was able to determine that high-risk sexual behavior was quite common and quite accepted in the privacy of the bedroom among gay men in Brussels. This finding was of importance because health officials in Belgium had come to the conclusion, based on several surveys, that gay men had significantly curtailed risky sexual behavior and that it was no longer necessary, therefore, to focus prevention efforts on the gay community. However, because he did not formally tell his sex partners that *their* behavior was being studied, until they advanced to unprotected sex, Bolton's approach, like Humphrys's, has been subject to criticism by some research ethicists.

Another approach for going beyond self-reported sexual practices in the study of a hidden population was developed by Terri Leonard in her research on male clients of street sex workers in Camden, New Jersey. Leonard conducted her research by hanging out at an inner-city "stroll" area (a street where sex workers seek business among the drivers of passing cars).

EXAMPLE 6.8

USING OBTRUSIVE MEASURES TO IDENTIFY BEHAVIORS IN HIDDEN POPULATIONS: APPEARING TO BE A COMMERCIAL SEX WORKER TO ATTRACT CLIENTS FOR A SURVEY

"All men who attempted to solicit my services, assuming I was a sex worker, were invited to participate in a 'sex survey.' Men initiated contact using several approaches. Some pulled up alongside the curb or onto a side street and, with engines idling, engaged me in conversation. Some men parked alongside the street and got out to make a phone call or have a drink in a nearby bar, initiating conversation en route. Some men 'cruised' by several times per day, several days per week, or once every few weeks before approaching" (Leonard 1990, 43).

Leonard found that twenty men out of the forty-nine she was able to interview reported that they used condoms during commercial sex. However, despite this self-report, only five of the men actually had condoms with them at the time they solicited sex with Leonard. Like Bolton's work, Leonard's shows that more intrusive ethnographic approaches can produce data on hidden target populations that reflect actual rather than idealized behaviors.

Ethnographic Mapping

Cross Reference: See Book 3, chapters 3 and 5, for a broader discussion of types of ethnographic mapping

One of the common start-up tasks of ethnography is to draw a map of the geographic disbursement of the target group, their activities, and specialized activity areas. In part, this is done to help the ethnographer learn his/her way around, but it is also a strategy for ensuring the completeness, to the degree possible, of the researcher's gaze. Map making allows ethnographers to systematically visit and holistically gather information about all spheres of target group life. In the study of hidden and hard-to-reach populations, this approach is adapted for use in sampling frame construction. As Bluthenthal and Watters (1995) indicate, the goals of ethnographic mapping in this kind of research are to:

- Gather information to compare and rank candidate zones or sections of the larger research area for possible selection as research sampling areas (in which to recruit study participants)
- Refine district boundaries
- Clarify in which zones contacts and key informants exist and where they must be cultivated
- Help establish sampling quotas for study participants located in identified zones

In the development of the targeted sampling plan for the study of drug injectors in Dayton, for example, ethnographers mapped the presence of five different types of sites in all of the thirty-two zip code areas of the city: crack houses, crack copping areas, drug shooting galleries (places drug injectors pay for the right to come in and inject drugs), dope houses (places were drug injectors buy drugs, and possibly inject them), injection drug copping areas, and drug injector residences (dwellings where injection drug users gather to inject drugs). Later, this information was used to calculate the relative density of drug sites in the zip code areas. A similar strategy was used in Hartford, with a focus on the mapping of all crack houses and shooting galleries/drug injector residences. This information was then compared with the rates found for the various social indicators to establish a continuum of drug use density across geographic units.

Finalization of the Target Sampling Design

In the final step, data from various sources, like those described above, are triangulated to establish project sampling units, including, as in the case of Dayton, setting proportional sampling quotas (specific percentages of individuals to be recruited from each sampling unit based on the relative density of target population members present). By combining diverse data sets, developing them as indicators of target population density, comparing outcomes across the range of indicators used, and verifying suggested overall distribution patterns and distribution by subgroup types based on ethnography, researchers are able to achieve a reasonably high level of confidence that they will be able to construct a sampling design that, unlike opportunistic selection, is reflective of the hidden population of interest. In one sense, of course, targeted sampling plans can never be finalized, in that each research project produces new insights that lead to revisions in researcher conceptualization of the target group, its behaviors, and its distribution across the landscape.

This recognition has led to efforts to maintain ongoing monitoring of emergent behavioral trends and patterns in hidden and hard-to-reach population of high interest. In this approach, research is not episodic (i.e., it is not organized into three-to-four-year grant-defined discrete projects); it is continuous. The objective is to identify rapidly and monitor changes in the target population, as well as attempting to understand the forces driving the changes. Ongoing monitoring has the advantage of allowing very rapid recognition of new developments in the target population (recognition that may occur in advance even of many members of the target group who are not yet caught up in the new developments). Ongoing monitoring can be conducted through the deployment of field-based ethnographers, the use of mobile vans, or through the establishment of field stations.

RECRUITING STUDY PARTICIPANTS

A range of methods, described below, are available for the recruitment of participants from hidden and hard-to-reach populations into applied research projects. Although these approaches are effective, researchers have accepted the fact that recruitment of many types of hidden populations requires the use of monetary or other incentives (e.g., facilitated access into treatment). In out-of-treatment drug users studies, for example, the use of incentives is a standard practice. Methodologies that have been developed for recruiting hidden populations include the following.

Street Outreach Methods

The practice of community outreach and the use of indigenous outreach workers became increasingly common in public health with the advent of the community mental health movement and other community-based health promotion efforts, beginning in the 1960s. Outreach is seen as a bridge that spans the social distance separating service providers and those in need of service, including hard-to-reach populations. It is intended as a mechanism that allows access to arenas of human life that normally are beyond the influence of mainstream social institutions. When tied to a targeted sampling plan, outreach becomes a tool for the selective recruitment of participants from designated zones and by specific subgroups (e.g., specified numbers of females). Outreach occurs "on the street, in public places, or by storefronts at the point of initial contact with the potential client for intervention services" (Hunt et al. 1993, 466). There are three criteria for evaluating outreach:

- Does it reach the target population?
- Does it successfully recruit appropriate study participants?
- Can it re-recruit participants for follow-up assessment?

There has been much discussion in recent years about the use of *indigenous outreach workers*. For example, some have raised questions about the ethical implications of the common practice of sending former drug users back into a drug-using setting to recruit study participants. Risk for relapse is always great for individuals who are in recovery from an addiction, and consequently common practice in treatment is to help people to avoid temptation by teaching and assisting them to avoid social settings and groups in which drug use occurs. Because of our concerns about this issue, some outreach programs targeted to drug users do not make prior drug use a criterion for the hiring of outreach workers.

Definition: Indigenous outreach workers are those who come from and share characteristics of the target population

The methods used by street outreach works to find and recruit participants are illustrated in the following example drawn from our work in Hartford.

EXAMPLE 6.9

USING STREET OUTREACH TO FIND AND RECRUIT PARTICIPANTS

Stowe Village is a large, low-income housing project on the north side of Hartford, Connecticut. During the summer of 1989, two outreach workers from our research team, Lucy and Angel, began visiting Stowe together as part of their daily effort to identify and recruit drug injectors for participation in a research project. On their first outreach visit to Stowe, these outreach workers encountered a group of young men hanging out on a street corner. They parked their car nearby and walked to the group. Several thoughts raced through the minds of the two outreach workers. On the one hand, they attempted to spot visual clues that might suggest the men were injection drug users. They observed the men, searching for signs of nervousness and intranquility, indicators that they might be getting anxious for a "fix." On the other hand, they attempted to calculate the potential risk of walking up to the men; would they be offended by the outreach workers' approach; would they see the outreach workers as an exploitable source of cash or valuables convertible into cash; would Lucy be subject, as she occasionally was while doing her job, to verbal abuse or sexual harassment? As they got close to the group, the outreach workers greeted the men in Spanish and told them they were HIV outreach workers. Reaching into their shoulder bags, the outreach workers pulled out the safety kits containing one-ounce bottles of bleach, several condoms, and AIDS prevention literature being distributed by the project.

Lucy told the men, "I have some bleach and condoms in case you are interested." One man responded, "What do we want bleach for, we ain't got anything to use it with." When Lucy told the men they could always use it to wash their clothes, they laughed and the first step toward establishing rapport was made. The outreach workers launched into an explanation of the project, including mentioning that it offered HIV testing and counseling, referral for health care social services, and AIDS education and counseling. Additionally, they were told that they could earn $24 for participating in a one-hour interview. One of the men, noticeable because he looked so tired and desperate, expressed interest. After further explanation, one of the outreach workers issued him an appointment card indicating a date and time that he could go to the project's Intake and Assessment Center for enrollment in the project. Because he lacked transportation and did not appear to know the location of the Assessment Center, the outreach workers provided him with a bus token and directions.

As this account indicates, outreach, by necessity, requires that the worker *enter the target population's home turf*, places like street corners, housing projects, shelters, and surplus food distribution sites of inner-city neighborhoods. The outreach worker *enters this field with an understanding of target population behavior,* an understanding born either from previous personal involvement in the group of interest or because the outreach worker was raised in the same community in which the target population is found. This knowledge is supplemented through *training* and prior outreach or similar *experience.* Training is geared toward developing a realistic understanding of the difficulties of working with hidden populations as well as an emphasis on treating program participants as individuals who have generously volunteered to assist the project achieve its goals. Further, training must prepare the outreach workers to be sensitive to ethical issues in studying hidden populations, as discussed below. As Ronald Valdiserri notes in his book *Preventing AIDS,* the outreach worker who is an indigenous community member provides a *positive role model* and *credible information source.* Such a person may be more effective than other health workers in persuading at-risk individuals to participate in prevention research programs. The role modeling exhibited by outreach workers is expressed in their willingness to risk both potential arrest and bodily harm by inserting themselves into social settings in which danger is commonplace. Sim-

ply put, community outreach workers daily put themselves
at risk to help others avoid risk.

Effective outreach hinges on *personal involvement with
members of the target population.* Outreach workers get to
know project participants, build rapport with them, and
attempt to establish a trusting relationship based on gen-
uine interest and concern. Developing good rapport with
members of hidden and hard-to-reach populations can be
particularly difficult, but studies show that demonstrating
concern about a participant's well-being and providing
useful and *nonjudgmental* information about how to get
needed services are significant aids in the development and
maintenance of good relations with study participants.

EXAMPLE 6.10

DEVELOPING POSITIVE RELATIONSHIPS WITH HARD-TO-REACH PREGNANT TEENS

The Comadrona (the Spanish term referring to the traditional midwife) Program at
the Hispanic Health Council in Hartford, Connecticut, includes a component that is
specially targeted to pregnant teenagers. Often, pregnant teens are unwed, and may
be living with a boyfriend or with their family of origin. Because of pregnancy denial,
conflict with parents and/or boyfriends, and embarrassment, pregnant teens constitute an important hidden population. Commonly, pregnant teens are late to enter prenatal care, and the Comadrona Program was developed to facilitate this process and
to provide case management designed to help educate the expectant mother about
reproductive and maternal health, facilitate attendance at prenatal care appointments,
and provide prepartum and postpartum support and well-baby education. Clients
enter the program through referral, walk-in, and outreach. Outreach in the Comadrona Program includes several components, including going door-to-door to ask
about pregnant teens in the neighborhood, following up on the pregnant friends of
existing clients, and walking through targeted neighborhoods attempting to spot teen
girls that appear to be pregnant. When pregnant teens are identified on the street,
outreach workers initially engage them in friendly, nonjudgmental conversation, telling them "what a beautiful belly you have" and asking when they are expecting to
deliver. When the outreach worker perceives that the girl is ready, she will ask if she is
enrolled in a prenatal care program. If the girl provides a negative response, the outreach worker will proceed to stress the importance of prenatal care and to introduce
the idea of enrollment in the Comadrona Program. As this account suggests, outreach
workers attempt a seamless and natural progression that moves from a friendly conversation among women about women's issues into more directed client recruitment.

Effective outreach requires maintaining a positive attitude, both toward the work being done (public health research) and toward the people being reached. The starting point is *empathy*. Empathy begins with recognizing that someone else's subjective reality may be different from one's own; their life experiences are different, their values are different, and the day-to-day world they live in may be different. Empathy involves identifying emotionally with the other person. Empathy does not mean condoning all behavior; rather, it means understanding the behavior and the other person in the context of their life (i.e., to the degree that such a thing is possible, seeing the world through their eyes). A key part of the outreach worker's job is *active, sympathetic listening*. This means staying very conscious of what the other person has to say, staying attuned to both verbal and nonverbal communication, and taking the time to hear the speaker's core concerns. It may involve asking questions (e.g., "How did you feel about that?") or expressing confirmatory remarks. Finally, it involves refraining from expressing judgments about the other person's behavior (while acknowledging to oneself the experience of negative reactions). In the end, good outreach means caring about the participants and respecting them as people. These approaches have proven to be effective in making hard-to-reach populations reachable and hidden populations findable.

Because outreach workers spend many hours on the street, often in inner-city neighborhoods with comparative high crime rates, they must be on guard against sexual or other harassment or physical threat in the field. These concerns are handled to a large degree by remaining alert to risk and danger and through constant evaluation of risk during interactions with participants on the street. Training should emphasize that when outreach workers feel uncomfortable in a particular setting, they should leave as soon as possible.

Network Recruitment Strategies

Since the mid-1980s, a growing number of researchers have incorporated network concepts into the study of hidden populations. This work emerged from recognition that focus on the individual as the primary driving force in behavior is restrictive and fails to consider that most individuals do not live their lives independently of family members, friends, and acquaintances. Understanding people in their natural social contexts often requires an examination of social network structures and patterns that may channel behaviors of research interest, including effective intervention service delivery (Weeks et al. 2006). For example, the emergence of a new risk behavior in a drug-using population probably tends to spread along preexistent lines of social relationship. Understanding how these changes take place requires a shift in research focus and conceptualization from the individual to the social network level.

Cross Reference: See Trotter, Schensul, and Weeks's discussion of social network research in this volume

Network approaches also constitute an alternative approach to participant recruitment.

EXAMPLE 6.11

RECRUITING DRUG USERS THROUGH PERSONAL NETWORKS IN HARTFORD'S PUERTO RICAN COMMUNITY

In Hartford, we have begun to apply network approaches for studying the patterning of violence among drug users in the Puerto Rican community. In this study, we are using an ego-centered network approach. Outreach workers recruit out-of-treatment drug users who are interviewed about their past and present experience of and involvement in violence. These individuals are designated as Index Participants. As part of the interview process, these individuals identify members of their social networks, including members of their risk networks (those with whom they use drugs and have sex). Index Participants are then asked to recruit three members of their risk social networks to participate as Network Participants in the study. For each member of their network that Index Participants bring in, they are paid a small "finder's fee." If they are unable to recruit at least two network members, then they are dropped as study participants.

Cross Reference: See chapter 5 on social network research in this volume

As this example shows, in network studies, in addition to outreach workers, *members of the target population play a key role in the recruitment of study participants.* This approach opens access to individuals who may not have

been successfully contacted or recruited by outreach workers (e.g., individuals who do not spend much time on the streets or in drug copping and do not use areas visited by outreach workers). Network approaches may be especially effective in reaching women, who are harder to reach than men through outreach. Reaching all sectors of an at-risk population may also be aided by network designs. Weeks et al. (2006), for example, used a peer-driven chain-referral recruitment method to find and enroll street drug users in HIV prevention education.

In some hidden and hard-to-reach populations, of course, it may turn out that network approaches to research are especially difficult because of the fragile, shifting, and shallow nature of connections among individuals. At the same time, as the earlier discussion of sex partners of drug users suggested, there may not be network linkages among members of the target population. Still, methodologically, focus on networks is an important step in the study of hidden populations.

Mobile Van Approaches

Another approach for the recruitment of hidden populations into research is through the use of vans or other vehicles that travel to identified locations or neighborhoods that have been identified as likely target population contact sites. Vans or even RVs have been used in this way as temporary field stations in designated areas. These sites then become bases of operation for outreach workers and ethnographers who engage potential study participants in the vicinity of the vehicle. Individuals who meet study inclusion criteria and agree to participate can then undergo intake procedures in the van or sit down (perhaps over a cup of coffee) with an ethnographer for more in-depth interviewing. By regularly visiting the same sites over time, van-based outreach workers and ethnographers can begin to get known in various locations and develop rapport with individuals who live or congregate in the area. Use of the van allows outreach workers and ethnographers to have a "safe haven" and rest station in a new area of research penetration, limits the quantity of supplies (e.g., condoms, intervention, and referral literature) that outreach workers and ethnographers need to carry with them, and facilitates the rapid intake of participants without requiring them to travel to a research center. Additionally, vans allow the easy transport and use of computers in the field.

A related approach involves the use of a service delivery van for recruitment and research. Several types of van-based health care delivery or public health promotion projects targeted to hidden populations are now in operation. Syringe exchange programs often are operated from vans that stop in or park close to drug copping and use areas. Outreach workers and ethnographers ride with the van to its designated exchange sites and engage members of the target population on or in the vicinity of the parked van. This approach has been used in the evaluation of syringe exchange but also in other types of studies of drug-using populations. Primary health care and health screening vans that serve the needs of hard-to-reach clients or those in remote locations are another base of operations for researchers studying hidden populations.

Linking participant recruitment to mobile service or clinic vans entails certain limitations. Use of a needle-exchange van as the sole source of recruitment for injection drug user participants, for example, limits the sample population to those who use such programs. Studies show, however, that many injection drug users do not make use of needle exchange (e.g., because they have alternative sources of sterile syringes). Similarly, limiting recruitment of the homeless to a mobile clinic would restrict participant selection to program users. As these examples suggest, multiple recruitment strategies expand the diversity of a study sample.

The Field Station

A related approach to the use of mobile vans is the fixed research field station. Field stations are research "outposts" located in the community of interest to the researchers. Like vans, field stations serve as bases of operation for outreach workers and ethnographers, but they can also house structured survey studies or even computer-based interview studies. Because they are located in fixed sites,

often storefront spaces that are visible to the community, field stations can evolve into drop-in locations where members of the target population always know they can find a cup of coffee, snacks, prevention materials (e.g. condoms), referrals for service, or just other individuals for conversation. In other words, field stations have the potential to become established parts of local neighborhoods, and hence excellent places from which to conduct ongoing monitoring as discussed below.

A significant variant of the field station approach is the development of research capacity in community-based organizations, as described earlier for the Hartford Model. In this case, the field station can be a full or partial service center that immediately links research to the provision of services.

EXAMPLE 6.12

BASING RESEARCH IN COMMUNITY-BASED SERVICE ORGANIZATIONS

The Hispanic Health Council, for example, is located in the center of the Puerto Rican community of Hartford. Shooting galleries situated in abandoned buildings, homeless shelters, drug copping areas, and a public park that is a regular site for drug purchase and use are all located in the area immediately surrounding the Council's Main Street building. Oftentimes the lobby of the Council is filled with individuals who are awaiting appointments with their case managers sitting next to study participants awaiting appointments with interviewers. Ethnographers and outreach workers based at the Council have easy access to and a recognized base for work in the surrounding community. Nearby, across the street from a housing project that has long been the site of drug distribution and use, is the Institute for Community Research, which collaborates with the Hispanic Health Council in the study of hidden populations.

METHODOLOGICAL CONSIDERATIONS

Sampling Bias

Methodologically, the field of hidden and hard-to-reach population studies is driven by the issue of appropriate sampling. There are two issues here: knowing the population of interest well enough to construct a representative sample and being able to recruit such a sample into the study. Sampling is a necessary feature of social science research because it would be impossible, due to limited research funds and lack of time, to study every member (i.e., what researchers call "the universe") of all but the most narrowly defined populations (e.g., members of a specific household). Since researchers are forced to sample from the larger population of interest, they are especially concerned that their research sample effectively *represents* the wider target population, allowing them to have confidence that inferences drawn about the sample apply to the whole population of interest. For example, if a researcher is studying pedophiles and it is known that 10 percent of pedophiles are women, then the sample should reflect this proportion. Of course, the very reason the field of hidden and hard-to-reach population studies emerged was, in part, because it is concerned with groups like pedophiles whose number, distribution, characteristics, and behaviors are concealed and hence it is difficult, *a priori*, to construct a representative sample. Failure to construct a representative sample can lead to biased results. Sampling bias is a major problem of all social science research, but it is of special significance in the study of unknown or poorly known groups.

Watters and Biernacki (1989) have identified a number of ways in which sampling bias can distort research findings. Their specific focus is on bias in sampling injection drug users, but their arguments have relevance for the study of all hidden populations. They note (Watters and Biernacki 1989, 417) that while the largest portion of injection drug users in drug treatment are enrolled in methadone programs, the "bias introduced by sampling research subjects only in methadone treatment clinics . . . could lead to the erroneous conclusion that all injecting drug users are heroin addicts whose primary drug use involves daily heroin injection." A comparison of treatment-seeking and untreated opiate addicts, for example, found important differences in the severity of addiction, risk-taking behavior, and level of social and psychological functioning. ***Basing interventions solely on the characteristics of those already in treatment could limit their appeal to and effectiveness with the wider population of concern.*** The same point holds for all generalizations from institutionalized to noninstitutionalized populations. This

Key point

issue is significant because of various studies indicating the necessity of matching patients to appropriate intervention modalities if treatment is to be effective.

Convenience samples that are drawn in whole or primarily from institutionalized populations may be inappropriate for generalization to populations that are not connected to institutions because the behaviors of concern—for example, behaviors that transmit diseases—tend to occur outside of clinical settings. Studies have shown that risk behaviors are significantly more frequent among non-institutionalized populations than among those who are in treatment. At the same time, some behaviors of interest in hidden population research, such as domestic violence, may *only* occur outside of treatment settings.

The ethnic and gender composition of institutionally connected populations may be quite skewed relative to the population that is hidden from institution intervention. In drug treatment, for example, women, and especially pregnant women, may be significantly underrepresented. Similarly programs targeted to youth that are based on students may be inappropriate for and unappealing to school dropouts.

Behaviors of concern among hidden and hard-to-reach populations may be relatively rare in the general population. Attempting to understand injection drug use, for example, through general population surveys or even door-to-door community surveys reveal that this is an infrequent practice in the population as a whole. Gathering an adequate sample of drug injectors or pregnant teens through a general survey would be very costly. Understanding drug injection or many other behaviors of interest among hidden and hard-to-reach populations, therefore, requires a targeted study designed to find and recruit individuals who engage in this behavior. This type of targeting tends to produce nonprobabilistic convenience samples. As discussed below, however, researchers who study hidden populations have developed methods for increasing confidence in the generalizability of their research findings.

Studies of hidden and hard-to-reach populations must confront four issues as they attempt to assemble representative, nonbiased samples: the precision with which a target group has been defined for purposes of research, the

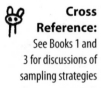
Cross Reference: See Books 1 and 3 for discussions of sampling strategies

adequacy of the size of the sample, the internal diversity of the target group, and the level of concealment or embeddedness of the target group. By definition, it is difficult to precisely define hidden and hard-to-reach populations. Oftentimes, insufficient knowledge about the target group encumbers definitional precision. Consequently, it is necessary to define geographic boundaries (e.g., members of the target group who live or are found within specified borders) and inclusion/exclusion criteria (i.e., specific traits, behaviors, or other qualifying or disqualifying features of group membership). As this implies, definitions of the target group are artificial (i.e., they are imposed by the researcher), but their use removes ambiguity about how the sample was constructed. Ethnography is such a useful tool in hidden and hard-to-reach population research precisely because it has the potential of limiting the artificiality of group definitions by grounding research parameters within the context of actually observed behaviors, the insider understandings (e.g., cultural meanings, beliefs, values, expectations) and self-reported identities of the target group, and the specific social scenes (i.e., locations, settings, socially defined occasions and events) that mark group activities. In this sense, the design of hidden and hard-to-reach population research is a carefully controlled balance between the research needed to impose controls and the capacity of research techniques to avoid imposing false categories and boundaries on the target group (Kane and Mason 1992). Targeted sampling, by imposing geographic or other boundaries for purposes of recruitment yet retaining the flexibility to adjust recruitment in light of newly learned information about the target group, reflects this tension between researcher control and social reality. Another approach for addressing these issues is known as "adaptive sampling" (Thompson and Collins 2002). While conventional quantitative sampling involves setting sampling targets prior to the beginning of data collection, in adaptive sampling newly learned information about the target group at each stage of data collection is used to adjust the sampling design to more accurately reflect the distribution and features of the target group. Various adaptive sampling strategies are in use, depending on the nature of the population of interest. As Thompson and Collins (2002, 66) note, "For rare and clustered populations adaptive designs can give substantial gains in efficiency over conventional designs, and for hidden populations link-tracing and other adaptive procedures may provide the only practical way to obtain a sample large enough for the study objectives."

When the size of a target population is unknown, it is always difficult to know the size of an adequate sample. For example, how many abused women would you have to interview to adequately represent the population of women subjected to domestic violence? Since it is believed that thousands of women each year are victims of domestic abuse (although the exposed features of this population are limited to actually reported cases), it is unlikely that interviews with five such women could very effectively capture the experience, social features, or health implications of spousal abuse. Researchers must grapple with the issue of sample size based on awareness of the target group and the need to perform statistical tests on associations between variables of concern.

The issue of sampling adequacy is directly linked to the degree of heterogeneity of the target population. A more diverse target group will, by necessity, require a larger sample if all of its diversity is to be effectively represented by the study sample. Oftentimes, researchers use measures of statistical power to calculate sampling adequacy (i.e., procedures for measuring how large a sample is needed to test the strength of relationships that are found among research variables).

As we have seen, level of active concealment or passive embeddedness (e.g., such as sex partners of drug users or those lacking distinct group identity, congregation sites, or activities) is a major stumbling block in the construction of study samples of hidden and hard-to-reach populations. These factors make it difficult to construct random samples because the size and dimensions of the pool from which participants would be randomly drawn is unclear. Consequently, hidden population studies limit sampling bias by using strategies designed to approximate structured random sampling (i.e., identifying population segments and selecting the sample proportionate to segment size).

Limiting Attrition in Longitudinal Studies

Just as they do for initial recruitment, hidden and hard-to-reach populations present significant challenges for retention in intervention or experimental studies as well as for follow-up data collection in longitudinal studies. Unfortunately, the impact of attrition—the term that is used to describe the loss of participants from a study—on intervention evaluation research is a significantly understudied topic. Many intervention studies with hidden populations fail to report attrition rates, and few analyze the impact of resultant selection bias on the validity of project findings. However, from a scientific perspective, the potential impact of attrition is severe—no less so than recruiting skewed samples that do not accurately reflect the target population—and hence identifying strategies for limiting attrition in studies with hidden populations is of utmost importance.

There are many reasons why individuals may be lost to a research project. They may move away, become ill, be arrested, or even die. In studies with drug users all of these factors contribute to both loss to intervention and loss to follow-up. Additionally, individuals may have bad experiences in research (e.g., feel that an interviewer was disrespectful or asked intrusive questions) that lead them to decide to end their participation. Also, they may find work, enter into a treatment program, begin school or a training program, or grow fearful that their confidentiality will be breached. With hidden populations, all of these potential reasons for attrition are multiplied because such populations often are attempting to avoid the police or other government institutions, keep their activities secret, handle numerous health risks, cope with the consequences of poverty and unstable housing, and avoid street violence.

Tracking techniques and incentives have been suggested as a means of limiting attrition in hidden and hard-to-reach populations. Still, reducing attrition from data collection in studies of these populations remains a difficult task. Consequently, approaches have been suggested for using statistical techniques to compensate for missing data caused by participant attrition. However, questions have been raised as to whether such techniques are adequate to estimate the true effects of an intervention with a high loss of participants before follow-up. Without understanding the effect of attrition in a specific type of program, it is unlikely that appropriate adjustments can be implemented.

Consequently, special efforts are needed to retain participants in longitudinal studies of hidden and hard-to-reach populations. A review of effective methods to track these populations has been developed by Desmond et al. (1995). They identify ten strategies: collecting complete locator information (e.g., in addition to common items like address and phone number, information on a participant's social security number, relatives' addresses and phone numbers, common hang-out areas, and the location where the participant's mail is delivered) at the start of the intake interview, fully informing participants about follow-up interview requirements, providing adequate monetary incentives (participant fees), hiring ethnically and experientially appropriate staff, documenting all follow-up work, making exhaustive use of institutional information about participants (e.g., welfare files), streamlining the follow-up data collection to make the procedure as rapid as possible, conducting follow-up interviews in a mutually acceptable location, providing travel support for participants to the interview site, and building in adequate time for follow-up data collection with the entire project sample.

Additional strategies have been suggested by Cottler et al. (1996), including expanding locator data collection to include the maximum number of items possible, updating locator information at each subsequent follow-up interview, attaching incentives to intervention sessions, and implementing a three-stage tracking methodology that incorporates phone tracking (regular phone calls to participants), systems tracking (using available health, social service, or criminal justice computer-tracking programs on the target population), and field tracking (home visits and street ethnography).

Other strategies that have been used by hidden population researchers include: using street-aware outreach/ interviewers; picture taking of all participants at intake (for use in follow-up recruitment); conducting brief, paid, postintervention session evaluation interviews and offering an incentive bonus to individuals who complete all intervention sessions; conducting brief contact interviews at periodic intervals to ensure regular interaction with participants during the follow-up period; sending postcard reminders to participants; identifying and regularly visiting all congregation points; maintaining positive relations with community agencies and other providers to allow participant tracking; community newspaper checks to identify arrests of study participants; fully informing participants about the benefits of applied research; ensuring that project staff build sensitive, supportive, and trusting relations with participants; using a wide variety of posters, radio announcements, and flyers to publicize follow-up interviewing; and maintaining contacts with researchers in other cities where participants may migrate.

In studies of drug users in Hartford, a city with high attrition rates due to particularly high rates of HIV infection among injection drug and crack cocaine users, comparatively high participant arrest rates, high frequencies of drug injection, and a notably mobile population, researchers have tested a number of additional approaches, including:

- House-to-house visits to "abandoned" apartment buildings (where numerous homeless people, in fact, reside in Hartford)
- Rapport-building with the "house men" (owners or managers) at local drug shooting galleries and crack houses to allow drop-in visits for the purposes of participant contact
- Utilization of the inmate computer-tracking system maintained by the state Department of Corrections
- Provision of AIDS education sessions to allow regular contact with homeless shelter residents
- Identification of homeless encampments hidden under densely wooded highway overpasses and along the Connecticut River
- Nighttime emergency room checks at the three local hospitals

Each of these strategies allowed the researchers to find missing participants for follow-up interviewing. Follow-up with hidden and hard-to-reach populations remains a difficult assignment. Using relocation strategies like those noted above have enabled the inclusion of these populations in successful longitudinal studies.

Reliability and Validity

In all studies, researchers must confront issues of *reliability* and *validity*. The former term addresses issues of consistency (e.g., does a homeless individual report the same life history information each time he/she is interviewed?), while the latter is concerned with issues of accuracy (e.g., does a research instrument designed to study risk behaviors of people with sexually transmitted infection actually measure the issue of concern?). Given the special problems of studying hidden and hard-to-reach populations, the health, residential, and other difficulties individuals in such populations commonly face in their lives, and the dearth of baseline information available when studies of these populations are being designed, it is not surprising that reliability and validity are especially thorny problems in this arena of social science research. Consequently, it is particularly important to incorporate reliability and validity checks (research procedures for routinely examining the quality and dependability of the data being collected) in studies of hidden and hard-to-reach populations.

The **reliability of data** is established when measures taken by two different researchers or the same researcher at two or more points in time are the same. For example, researchers may wish to rate the level of health risk faced by homeless individuals (e.g., to assess whether those who stay at shelters experience greater or lesser risk than those who do not). During interviews, homeless individuals can be asked a series of questions about risk behavior and experiences. A set of judges (e.g., other researchers not involved in the study) can then be asked to establish, based on the number, kind, and frequency of risk, to rank an individual as being at high, medium, or minimal health risk. Having two or more judges independently rank the same indi-

Cross Reference: See Book 3, chapter 11 discussions of reliability and validity in ethnographic research

Definition: The reliability of data is established when measures taken by two different researchers or the same researcher at two different points in time are the same

viduals can be used as a check on **interrater reliability**. Alternately, some researchers have compared findings on face-to-face interviews with those from computer-driven interviews to test the reliability of research findings. In longitudinal studies in which members of hidden populations are interviewed two or more times over the course of a period of study, the data produced can be considered reliable if an individual's answers are consistent for items that are not expected (in most instances) to change over time (e.g., ethnicity, gender, place of birth, date of first using drugs, etc.). Assessment of congruence on *stable features* (traits, like gender, that are constant over time for most individuals) and *established features* (attributes that once established cannot be undone, such as "ever slept in a homeless shelter") can serve researchers as a reliability check in longitudinal research.

Definition: Interrater reliability refers to the degree of correspondence among researchers in ratings, rankings, or coding decisions

As noted, **validity** refers to the accuracy of data. For example, in a study of access to drug treatment among out-of-treatment drug users, researchers must establish that study participants are, in fact, drug users (and not just individuals seeking to be paid for conducting an interview). Urine toxicology (a chemical check for the presence of substances in a urine sample) often is used to validate self-reported drug use.

Definition: Validity refers to the accuracy of data

There are various threats to the validity of a study (Campbell and Stanley 1963). Some factors may jeopardize a study's *internal validity* while others threaten *external validity*. The first of these refers to the validity of inference on the targeted study population. In addition to threats posed by errors in information collection or unrecognized baseline differences between comparison groups (e.g., in a study contrasting the efficacy of two alternative intervention models designed to lower risk in a target population), selection biases may distort estimates of the intervention effect in the targeted study group. If comparison groups (e.g., those assigned to the experimental group versus those assigned to the intervention group) experience differential dropout rates in an intervention resulting in altered baseline risk in the experimental and comparison groups, measures of outcome differences may be invalid.

External validity refers to the degree to which outcomes are peculiar to the special conditions of the study or can be generalized to conditions beyond those of the study. For example, can the findings on a study of "bottle gang" behavior (i.e., collectively acquiring and sharing drinks from a common bottle) among skid row alcoholics in downtown Los Angeles be generalized to all skid row alcoholics in the country, only to skid row alcoholics in the West, only to those in Los Angeles, or only to those who actually participated in the study? Can the findings be generalized only to specific times of the year (e.g., because people may be forced to behave differently as the weather changes), only to big-city social settings, or only to members of specific ethnic groups? The answer to these questions lies in the representativeness of the sample population and the research setting to the population universe and wider set of contexts in which the target population is found. Limitations on representativeness restrict the generalizability of findings. In the study of hidden and hard-to-reach populations, researchers are constantly struggling with the issue of representativeness and hence with the generalizability of their research results.

Experimental studies with hidden and hard-to-reach populations face important threats to validity because of the difficulty of retaining these populations in interventions or relocating them for follow-up. For example, attrition threatens external validity to the degree that subjects who remain in a study are systematically different from those who drop out. Existing attrition research shows that attrition can have consequential effects on intervention effectiveness. For example, in a study of an adolescent smoking prevention program the heaviest smokers were the most likely to drop out of the treatment group but not the control group. Dropouts generally were heavier alcohol and drug users, were more likely to associate with other smokers, and had lower educational goals than program completers. Because of the greater loss before follow-up of heavy smokers in the treatment group, findings interpreted without factoring in the probable effect of selection bias would suggest that the intervention was more effective than was warranted. This finding is supported by research showing external validity problems that result from the tendency of the heaviest substance users to drop out of intervention.

Various other factors can weaken the external validity of a study. The recruitment interaction or instruments used to measure the target population at baseline may influence the reaction of study participants to an intervention. For example, outreach workers in recruiting participants into a study inadvertently may influence participant behavior (e.g., by sharing prevention information about risky behavior). Additionally, the setting of an intervention may threaten external validity. Will the findings of an intervention conducted in a hospital setting with homeless individuals be the same if the intervention is conducted in a homeless shelter? If the setting of the intervention influences the behaviors of concern then generalizability to other conditions is not possible. Finally, because various interventions are targeted to hidden and hard-to-reach populations, involvement in prior intervention may impact outcomes on the intervention being tested. If participants from the target population have experienced a prior intervention in their locale, findings may not be generalizable to individuals in another city that did not implement the prior intervention. For example, an intensive public health mass media campaign on condom use previously implemented in the target city may make it difficult to generalize the findings of a condom skills-building intervention for commercial sex workers to other cities that lacked the public health campaign.

All of these threats to external validity must be considered in designing studies with hidden and hard-to-reach populations and with the reporting of research findings.

ETHICAL ISSUES IN STUDYING HIDDEN POPULATIONS

All research with human populations must confront a range of ethical issues. Since World War II (and in light of Nazi experimentation with human subjects), standards of ethical conduct in research have developed. These standards include:

- Respecting study participants as autonomous individuals (in part by ensuring that their involvement in research is completely voluntary and based on fully informed personal consent)

- Treating study participants with beneficence and avoiding maleficence (in part by limiting their exposure to risk)
- Seeking to be fair to study participants (in part by avoiding discrimination or a recreation of historical patterns of social inequality in the distribution of all benefits and risks of research participation)

In some cases, Institutional Review Boards have concluded that particular hidden populations, such as homeless adolescents under the age of sixteen, are not yet able to provide fully informed personal consent to participate in a research project. Consequently, they have refused to give approval for the study of these populations, making them, in effect, not just hidden but unstudiable populations. In other cases, questions have been raised about the capacity of various groups (e.g., long-term skid row alcoholics) to give fully informed consent because of mental health impairments. For the most part, however, review boards have not blocked the study of hidden and hard-to-reach populations, even those with youth under the age of eighteen. Nonetheless, there are a number of special ethical issues that arise in the study of these populations that merit specific attention.

These issues stem from several sources, including the involvement of study participants in illegal or dangerous activities, the collection of highly sensitive information on participant activities, the recruitment of individuals with significant health and social service needs, and the potential exposure of project staff to risky settings. Given the serious (even life-and-death) nature of the ethical issues confronted in the study of hidden and hard-to-reach populations, careful review of ethical issues that may be confronted and thorough training in how to avoid or, if necessary, respond to ethical dilemmas is a critical component of project implementation. There has been growing recognition that hidden populations present various ethical challenges for researchers and that special protections and approaches are needed in research with such populations (Buchanan et al. 2009).

Maintaining Confidentiality
with Highly Sensitive Data

Hidden populations often want to stay hidden or at least to conceal certain behaviors, such as drug use or involvement in other illegal activities (drug dealing, prostitution, gambling, theft, physical violence, etc.). Moreover, some research on hidden populations (e.g., AIDS research) focuses on very private behaviors such as sexual activity. As a result, studies of hidden populations often produce highly confidential information. Fully protecting the confidentiality of research participants (from the police, the courts, insurance companies, creditors, employers, other research participants, etc.) is a fundamental responsibility of researchers. In federally funded research, an array of procedures (e.g., subject consent to research protocols) must be followed to protect confidentiality. Universities and research institutes commonly have committees to review risks to human subjects in research projects and to ensure the enforcement of protections. Additionally, procedures have been established at the federal level to protect research records from seizure by the police.

Cross Reference: See Book 1, chapter 11 and Book 6 for further discussion of this issue

In spite of these protections, there is always a potential risk that participant confidentiality might be breached. For example, drug researchers may inadvertently schedule interviews with two individuals who are involved in a relationship but conceal their drug use from their partner, and they encounter each other unexpectedly at the research site. More commonly, confidentiality is breached because, over the course of a research project, adherence to human subject protocols slackens. Good training procedures for project staff, with regular updates and refresher courses, are critical. Keeping participants' names or other identifying materials (e.g. photographs, locator forms) separate from interview data (so that linkage by those outside the project would be difficult) is of equal importance. Consistent use of locked filing cabinets and password-controlled computer files is another important requirement of research with hidden populations. Most importantly, researchers must give careful thought to all potential avenues through which confidentiality might be violated and regularly monitor to insure that protections are in place and are being followed.

Working with Populations at High Risk: Educational and Intervention Responsibilities

Another ethical issue confronted in the study of hidden populations concerns the responsibilities of the researcher relative to the health needs of research subjects. If researchers see study participants engaging in highly risky behavior (e.g., directly sharing syringes during drug injection), are they obligated to intervene in some way? Is it ethical to study such behavior and to record field notes without offering intervention or prevention information? If a research participant is known to a research project to be HIV positive and then shares information about unprotected sexual behavior, what are the responsibilities of researchers to notify the individual's sex partner(s)? If participants share information about illegal activities, are researchers obligated to report this information to the police? If participants report their role in ongoing acts of physical or emotional violence, should researchers take some action to stop the behavior? These are just a few of the ethical questions that confront researchers studying hidden populations. Unfortunately, there is no uniformity of opinion about the appropriate response to many of these questions. Some university review boards have taken the position that researchers must report all illegal behavior described by participants to the police. This type of requirement would effectively terminate many studies of hidden populations. Most ethicists, however, have sought to identify a middle ground that will allow research on hidden populations to proceed while standards are put in place to ensure that researchers do not shirk responsibility to intervene where appropriate and possible.

Studying Populations with Significant Health and Social Needs

A related ethical question concerns the responsibilities of researchers to mobilize available resources to address the often considerable economic, emotional, health, and human service needs of participants. If researchers encounter pressing health or social problems in the populations they study, are they responsible to have mechanisms in place for intervention or at least for referral? Should researchers offer referral (called active referral), or only make referrals if participants issue a request for assistance (called passive referral)? These are important questions that must be confronted in studying many hidden populations. Moreover, researchers who have worked with such populations have found that they tend to have complex, intertwined, and pressing needs, as well as complex entanglements with significant others, the courts, landlords, drug dealers, and others that make it difficult to know where to start and how best to intervene.

There are no simple approaches to this issue. Most researchers arrange at least passive referral linkages with health care, mental health, drug treatment and social service providers, while others offer more active assistance in helping to ensure that participants are able to keep their referral appointments and actually receive services. Whichever approach is adopted, it should be thought through prior to the initiation of research and linkages and referral procedures with local providers put in place before the start of data collection. It is also important to consider the stress placed on project staff who are involved in working with hidden and hard-to-reach populations. Constant exposure to suffering and feelings of inadequacy in responding to the problems faced by study participants can lead to staff "burnout." Consequently, staff support and stress reduction mechanisms (e.g., staff debriefings, support groups, training sessions) may be needed, including, if available, the use of professional employee assistance programs.

Protecting Field Staff

In the study of hidden and hard-to-reach populations, researchers have a special responsibility to address the potential risks faced by project staff. These risks include exposure to theft, violence, and disease. Hidden populations among oppressed social classes have disproportionately high rates

for all of these threats to emotional and physical well-being that can, in various ways, impact the lives of researchers. Discussing the use of field stations, Goldstein et al. (1990, 90) comment as follows.

EXAMPLE 6.13

DEALING WITH THEFT

Theft and violence are two issues that must be dealt with when trying to operate an ethnographic field station. Tape recorders, jackets, cash, tools, coffeemakers, and a clock have been stolen from field sites. Thefts are typically difficult for staff members to accept and are often perceived as a violation of the trust between subjects and field researchers. Sometimes staff members interpret a theft as meaning that they have personally failed as researchers, that they are outsiders and "marks," and their feelings of being accepted by subjects were just illusions. Victimized staff members may need informal therapy lest feelings of resentment and suspicion color their interactions with subjects and render them less effective.

Although not very common, incidents of violence or threats made to researchers also have been reported. Sometimes violence has occurred as part of a theft, such as a mugging; at other times it is the result of subjects blaming researchers for some misfortune (e.g., an arrest) that they have suffered. Occasionally, violence is not specifically directed at the researchers but is a consequence of being at the wrong place at the wrong time. Preparation for handling these issues, staff training to minimize exposure to risk (e.g., arming fieldworkers with cell phones, training staff to recognize their own role in theft by leaving valuable items exposed, and to understand the street survival strategies of target populations), clear-cut protocols about appropriate and inappropriate behaviors in the field (e.g., not carry money or other unnecessary valuables, leaving situations that seem threatening, establishing rapport and gaining approved access to sites where illegal activity occurs, building relationships among residents in target neighborhoods), and useful ways to handle threatening situations (e.g., conflict reduction strategies) generally are a prerequisite of field studies of hidden and hard-to-reach populations.

Exposure to disease is another potential risk faced by project staff. Air-borne infectious diseases like tuberculosis are especially problematic because they do not require staff to actually participate in overt risk behaviors. Similarly, easily spread diseases like hepatitis must be considered as potential risks to staff. Other diseases that may be disproportionately common in some target populations, such as sexually transmitted infections and AIDS, generally are not threats to staff unless they engage in specific risk behaviors, many of which may be violations of accepted ethical standards for the researcher/subject relationship. Training in risk avoidance (often available from the Red Cross, city health departments, or local community organizations), periodic testing for exposure, and clear-cut protocols for appropriate staff behavior are all important strategies for preventing the spread of infectious diseases among project staff.

CONCLUSIONS

The concept of the hidden population emerged in the social sciences as researchers concerned primarily with substance abuse and other public health issues confronted the fact that populations that were most accessible, such as those in treatment programs, prisons, and hospitals were not necessarily a fair representation of the broader population of interest. Other segments of the target population were not "in" or connected to (or served by) health and social institutions. These individuals were significantly harder to reach and harder to enumerate. This meant that even if segments of the population of interest were reachable it would still be hard to ensure representativeness in research samples unless all segments and their relative distribution and frequency were known. At this point, researchers started referring to these populations as "hidden" and began to tackle the problem of how to study them. The methodologies that have been developed for gaining access to, sampling, and recruiting hidden and hard-to-reach populations have been described and illustrated in this chapter. This review affirms that it is possible to study various kinds of hidden and hard-to-reach populations, but that researchers must give careful thought to:

- Sampling procedures and threats to reliability and validity
- Sources of secondary data that may be available
- The commitment of resources to the development of a locally grounded target sampling plan
- The recruitment and development of a trained cadre of indigenous outreach workers
- The selection of ethnographers capable of and willing to focus their research efforts on the target population of interest and the social settings in which they are found
- The resources needed for motivating target group participation in research
- The development of a common mission, language, and an esprit de corps in a multidisciplinary team of ethnographers, outreach workers, and others
- The establishment of linkages with service providers for recruitment and referral for services
- The ethical dilemmas confronted in the study of elusive populations
- The patience needed to work with individuals whose lives often are seen (by outsiders and, to varying degrees, by insiders as well) as chaotic, self-destructive, and, at times, filled with suffering

These challenges are considerable but surmountable, especially in light of the significant potential contributions of good applied research with these populations.

KEY RESOURCES

The study of hidden and hard-to-reach populations as a distinct field of research is an emergent field. Consequently, methodological literature in this arena is limited. The National Institute on Drug Abuse has issued a number of edited volumes in its Research Monograph Series that are especially germaine, including *The Collection and Interpretation of Data from Hidden Populations* (#98) and *Quali-*

tative Methods in Drug Abuse and HIV Research (#157). Similarly, the *Handbook on Risk of AIDS* includes a set of chapters on outreach approaches targeted to specific hidden and hard-to-reach populations. Articles by Watters and Biernacki (1989), Braunstein (1993), Clatts et al. (1995), and Carlson et al. 1994 each present thorough descriptions of the construction of targeted sampling plans in specific research settings. All of these references are listed below.

REFERENCES

Bluthenthal, R., and J. Watters. 1995. Multimethod research from targeted sampling to HIV risk environments. In *Qualitative methods in drug abuse and HIV research*, ed. E. Lambert, R. Ashery, and R. Needle, 212–30. (NIDA Research Monograph 157). Rockville, MD: National Institute on Drug Abuse.

Bolton, R. 1992. Mapping terra incognita: Sex research for AIDs prevention—An urgent agenda for the 1990s. In *The time of AIDS*, ed. G. Herdt and S. Lindenbaum, 124–58. Newbury Park, CA: Sage.

Bowser, Benjamin, Ernest Quimby, and Merrill Singer, ed. 2007. *Communities assessing their AIDS epidemics: Results of the rapid assessment of HIV/AIDS in eleven U.S. cities.* Lanham, MD: Lexington Books.

Braunstein, M. 1993. Sampling a hidden population: Noninstitutionalized drug users. *AIDS Education and Prevention* 5: 131–39.

Buchanan, David, Delia Fisher, and Lance Gable, ed. 2009. *Research with high-risk populations: Balance science, ethics, and law.* Washington, DC: American Psychological Association.

Campbell, D., and J. Stanley. 1963. *Experimental and quasi-experimental designs for research.* Boston: Houghton Mifflin.

Carlson, R. G., J. Wang, H. Siegal, R. Falck, and J. Guo. 1994. An ethnographic approach to targeted sampling: Problems and solutions in AIDS prevention research among injection drug and crack-cocaine users. *Human Organization* 53: 279–86.

Clatts, M., W. R. Davis, and A. Atillasoy. 1995. Hitting a moving target: The use of ethnographic methods in the development of sampling strategies for the evaluation of AIDS outreach programs for homeless youth in New York City. In *Qualitative methods in drug abuse and HIV research*, ed. E. Lambert, R. Ashery, and R. Needle, 117–35 (NIDA Research Monograph 157). Rockville, MD: National Institute on Drug Abuse.

Conviser, R., M. Singer, and M. Pounds. 2007. Adapting RARE to assess barriers to service receipt among people out of care. *Journal of Health Care for the Poor and Underserved* 18(3 Supplement): 52–68.

Cottler, L., W. Compton, A. Ben Abdallah, M. Horne, and D. Claverie. 1996. Achieving a 96.6 percent follow-up rate in a longitudinal study of drug abusers. *Drug and Alcohol Dependence* 41: 209–17.

Dai, B. 1937. *Opium addiction in Chicago.* Shanghai: Commercial Press.

Desmond, D., J. Maddux, T. Johnson, and B. Confer. 1995. Obtaining follow-up interviews for treatment evaluation. *Journal of Substance Abuse Treatment* 12: 95–102.

Domhoff, W. 1970. *The higher circles.* New York: Vintage.

Duncan, D., J. White, and T. Nicholson. 2003. Using Internet-based surveys to reach hidden populations: Case of nonabusive illicit drug users. *American Journal of Health Behavior* 27(3): 208–18.

Garcia, V., and J. Marinez. 2002. *Farmworkers transition to farm ownership: Lessons from Mexican origin farmers in southwestern Michigan.* Final Report, Office of Outreach. Washington, DC: U.S. Department of Agriculture.

———. 2005. Exploring agricultural census undercounts among immigrant Hispanic/ Latino farmers with an alternative enumeration project. *Journal of Extension* 43(5). Retrieved online June 18, 2009, from http://www.joe.org/joe/2005october/a2.php.

Geertz, C. 1984. "From the native's point of view": On the nature of anthropological understanding. In *Culture theory: Essays on mind, self and emotion*, ed. R. Shweder and R. LeVine, 123–36. Cambridge: Cambridge University Press.

Goldstein, P., B. Spunt, T. Miller, and P. Bellucci. 1990. Ethnographic field stations. In *The collection and interpretation of data from hidden populations*, ed. E. Lambert, 80–95 (National Institute on Drug Abuse Research Monograph Series #98). Rockville, MD: National Institute on Drug Abuse.

Gorman, E. M., P. Morgan, and E. Lambert. 1995. Qualitative research considerations and other issues in the study of methamphetamine use among men who have sex with other men. In *Qualitative methods in drug abuse and HIV research*, ed. E. Lambert, R. Ashery, and R. Needle, 156–81 (NIDA Research Monograph 157). Rockville, MD: National Institute on Drug Abuse.

Greene, J., R. Sanchez, J. Harris, C. Cignetti, D. Akin, and S. Wheeless. 2003. Incidence and prevalence of homeless and runaway youth. Washington, DC: Office of Planning, Research and Evaluation Administration for Children and Families.

Griffiths, M., M. Gossop, B. Powis, and J. Stang. 2006. Reaching hidden populations of drug users by privileged access interviewers: Methodological and practical issues. *Addiction* 88(12): 1617–26.

Gross, M., and V. Brown. 1993. Outreach to injection drug-using women. In *Handbook on risk of AIDS*, ed. B. Brown and G. Beschner, 445–63. Westport, CT: Greenwood Press.

Humphreys, L. 1970. *Tearoom trade: Impersonal sex in public places.* Chicago: Aldine.

Hunt, D., T. Hammet, C. Smith, W. Rhodes, and J. Pares-Avila. 1993. Outreach to sex partners. In *Handbook on risk of AIDS*, ed. B. Brown and G. Beschner, 464–82. Westport, CT: Greenwood Press.

Kane, S., and T. Mason. 1992. "IV drug users" and "sex partners": The limits of epidemiological categories and the ethnography of risk. In *The time of AIDS*, ed. G. Herdt and S. Lindenbaum, 199–224. Newbury Park, CA: Sage.

Leonard, T. 1990. Male clients of female street prostitutes: Unseen partners in sexual disease transmission. *Medical Anthropology Quarterly* 4: 41–55.

Lindesmith, A. 1947. *Opiate addiction.* Bloomfield, IN: Principia.

Marín, G., and B. V. Marín. 1991. *Research with Hispanic populations.* Newbury Park, CA: Sage.

Muhib, F., L. Lin, A. Stueve, R. Miller, W. Ford, W. Johnson, and P. Smith. 2001. A venue-based method for sampling hard-to-reach populations. *Public Health Reports* 116(1): 216–22.

Parish, W., E. Laumann, M. Cohen, S. Pan, H. Zheng, I. Hoffman, T. Wang, and K. Ng. 2003. Population-based study of chlamydial infection in China: A hidden epidemic. *Journal of the American Medical Association* 289(10): 1265–73.

Salganik, M., and D. Heckathorn. 2004. Sampling and estimation in hidden populations using respondent-driven sampling. *Sociological Methodology* 34: 193–239.

Singer, M. 1993. Knowledge for use: Anthropology and community-centered substance abuse research. *Social Science and Medicine* 37: 15–26.

Singer, M., P. Erickson, L. Badiane, R. Diaz, D. Ortiz, T. Abraham and A. M. Nicolaysen. 2006. Syndemics, sex and the city: Understanding sexually transmitted disease in social and cultural context. *Social Science and Medicine* 63(8): 2010–21.

Singer, M., and L. Marxuach-Rodriquez. 1996. Applying anthropology to the prevention of AIDS: The Latino gay men's health project. *Human Organization* 55: 141–48.

Singer, M., and M. Weeks. 2005. The Hartford model of AIDS practice/research. In *Community interventions and AIDS*, ed. Edison Trickett and Willo Pequegnat, 153–75. Oxford, UK: Oxford University Press.

Thompson, S., and L. Collins. 2002. Adaptive sampling in research on risk-related behaviors. *Drug and Alcohol Dependence* 68(1): S57–S67.

Watters, J., and P. Biernacki. 1989. Target sampling: Options for the study of hidden populations. *Social Problems* 36: 416–30.

Webb, E., T. Campbell, B. Schwartz, and J. Sechrest. 1966. *Unobtrusive measures*. Chicago: Rand McNally.

Weeks, M., J. Dickson-Gomez, K. Mosack, and M. Convey. 2006. The risk avoidance partnership: Training active drug users and peer health advocates. *Journal of Drug Issues* (Summer): 541–70.

Whyte, W. 1955. *Street corner society*. Chicago: University of Chicago Press.

Wiebel, W. 1990. Identifying and gaining access to hidden populations. In *The collection and interpretation of data from hidden populations*, ed. E. Lambert, 4–11 (National Institute on Drug Abuse Research Monograph Series, #98). Rockville, MD: National Institute on Drug Abuse.

7 ❖❖❖❖

USING MULTIMEDIA TECHNIQUES IN ETHNOGRAPHIC RESEARCH

Bonnie K. Natasi

INTRODUCTION

Traditionally, ethnographers have relied on the written record to capture informants' responses or to note their observations in natural contexts. However, multimedia techniques that include both text and visuals or video provide an alternative or complement to the extensive written record that is the hallmark of traditional ethnography.

Researchers now use video technology for documenting observations in natural settings, or interviews with informants face-to-face or via Internet (online interviewing or webcam-facilitated interviewing) and with participants for video-assisted recall (i.e., tape events and interview informants about the experiences), video-cued narrative reflection (using video to facilitate reflection by the practitioner), and video diaries (as alternative to written diaries). Digitized media also facilitate the recording of electronic researcher journals and field notes and documentation of "artifacts" in the field. Furthermore, digital technology facilitates multimedia data storage, management, analysis, interpretation, representation, and dissemination. Thus, multimedia, particularly in digitized format, has the potential to change the way in which ethnographic researchers engage in all forms of data collection and to influence the entire research process. (See Brown 2002, for an excellent discussion of digital technology and qualitative research.)

The primary focus of this chapter is the use of videotaping technology for collection of observational data and how it is handled with regard to data analysis, interpretation, and representation. Of particular interest is the use of videorecording[1] to study human development or behavior in natural settings such as classrooms or communities, in contrast to its traditional application in controlled clinical or laboratory research settings. Such technology is particularly advantageous for collecting certain types of observational data, such as those involving human interaction or ongoing activities (e.g., community events, medical practice) or recordings of in-depth interviewing or focus group interviews. In addition, videorecording provides an alternative to written diaries kept by research participants. One primary advantage of videorecording is that it creates a permanent and complete record "in real-time" that can be used for analysis and interpretation of data. Although not completely free of researcher bias, video recording provides a record of events that can be subjected readily to interpretation by different researchers and from multiple perspectives. In addition, videos can be viewed repeatedly for more in-depth or follow-up analyses. Furthermore, video records provide a mechanism for follow-up interviews or reflexive interviewing with participants.

The chapter also explores several critical issues related to the use of multimedia technology in ethnographic research. These include (a) conceptual considerations that guide the research; (b) methodological considerations for data collection, analysis, and interpretation and data representation and dissemination; and (c) technical and logistical considerations of using multimedia technology as they relate to different aspects of methodology. It concludes with a discussion of potential applications of multimedia technology, with examples drawn from research literature across multiple disciplines including psychology, education, medicine, public health, anthropology, and sociology.

CONCEPTUAL CONSIDERATIONS

The first consideration in any research project involves conceptual issues related to the focus of the research (i.e., the research questions) and the philosophical or theoretical basis of the research questions. As described later in the chapter, the research questions and the researcher's underlying perspectives influence how the processes of data collection, transcribing, coding, interpretation, and representation are approached. For example, a key consideration is whether or not research is conducted in an *inductive* manner, allowing theory to evolve from the data; a *deductive* manner, beginning with specific research questions derived from existing theory, research, and/or the researcher's own applied experiences; or an *abductive* manner, attempting to integrate inductive and deductive approaches in a more iterative manner. Such considerations are critical to decision making about the entire research process and are especially important in data transcription, analysis, and interpretation phases.

Before researchers begin to record anything, they must answer several questions about the focus of the research. The answers to these questions are informed by the purpose of the research and the overall conceptual or theoretical framework.

Cross Reference: See Book 1, chapter 5, Book 2 and Book 5, chapters 5 through 7, for more information on different approaches to research using inductive, deductive, and abductive approaches

- *What is the subject matter* (e.g., students' interactions during cooperative learning in an elementary classroom, community education activities, medical team decision making in emergency rooms, client-counselor communication patterns)?
- *Where can it be found* (classroom, hospital surgery unit, therapy setting, or community context)?
- *What behaviors or interactions should be recorded* (student-student, or teacher-student interactions, therapist-client communication, medical staff team process, group activities involving community members)?

- *Is the researcher interested in process* (e.g., ongoing styles of interaction) or *content* (what individuals communicate), or both?
- *To what extent are verbal and nonverbal behaviors important* (i.e., is it necessary to analyze both verbal and nonverbal behaviors and their synchronicity)?
- *How important is physical and social-cultural contexts for answering the research questions* (Should the physical context and social-cultural milieu be documented? Might specific cultural practices or taboos obviate the use of videotaping under certain conditions with specific members of the population)?
- *When should recording be done* (e.g., only when students are interacting in groups or for the entire class period; during surgery as well as subsequent staffing)?
- *What period of time is sufficient? That is, how frequently should recording be carried out* (daily or weekly; for one month or six months), *and how long should each session last* (thirty minutes, a full class period, or several days)?
- *Should recording be continuous* (for the duration of the fifty-five-minute class session) *or intermittent* (at random ten-minute intervals)?
- *Whom should you record* (all students within the classroom or selected pairs or groups of students, one classroom or several, one grade level or several; similarly, one surgery team or multiple teams, in a single hospital or several hospital settings; therapist with one client or multiple clients)?
- *How do these considerations interact* (e.g., should researchers follow a single therapist or multiple therapists, across multiple clients for duration of their therapy [e.g., over one year]; should every session be recorded, or should a purposive or random sample of sessions be used)?
- *Will multimedia techniques be used for multiple types of data collection* (e.g., videotaping interviews, video-assisted interviewing, making photographs or video-tapes of artifacts, using graphs and maps)?

- *Finally, will videotaped observation sessions constitute the entire data set, or will it be part of a multimethod approach* (e.g., videotape, written narrative observations, in-depth interviews, examination of permanent products)?

Once conceptual questions are answered, then technical and methodological considerations become important. For example, is funding sufficient to support multimedia technology? Is the research staff properly trained? How acceptable is the technology within the cultural context of the research? What resources (time, equipment, and staff) are necessary to accomplish analysis of multimedia data? What resources are needed for data management and analysis as well as data collection? What are the implications of videotaping for data analysis and interpretation? How can technology facilitate the dissemination and use of data? Some of these decisions apply to the collection and analysis of ethnographic data in general (e.g., coding), but others (e.g., taping) are specific to the use of multimedia techniques.

In summary, research questions and logistical considerations (e.g., the number of cameras or tape recorders, the number of data collectors, the available resources for transcribing and coding of records) influence decisions about procedures for data collection. As a general rule, more extensive recording provides the greatest flexibility for data analysis and interpretation; that is, researchers have the luxury of reviewing and reanalyzing archival records. An extensive sample of recorded observations permits subsequent return to the original data to explore other interpretations and, most importantly, to understand the phenomena under study within the captured "real-life" context.

A final important caveat is that researchers must recognize that videotaping is not a substitute for field notes about one's impressions, informal interactions, and global features of the environment, although digital technology can facilitate the recording of much of the process (Brown 2002). Moreover, it is desirable to document decisions as to what to record and also to determine which activities are going to be recorded using video and observational notes; in other words, the types of activities and events in which

Cross Reference: See Books 1 and 2 for a discussion of logistical issues relevant to the choice of research design, sampling issues, and methods

Cross Reference: Book 3, chapters 3 through 6, for discussions of field note recording, observations, and interviews

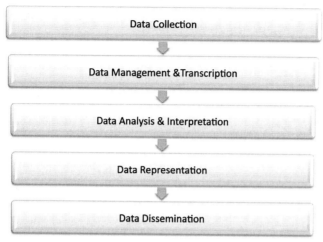

Figure 7.1   Methodological process

multiple forms of data collection and triangulation are desirable. The discussion that follows refers to technical and logistical considerations in the stages in the methodological process, as depicted in Figure 7.1.

METHODOLOGICAL CONSIDERATIONS

The decision to use multimedia techniques has implications for all stages of research methodology (see Figure 7.1). This section explores the specific issues related to the collection, management (including transcription), analysis and interpretation, and finally representation and dissemination of multimedia data. Some issues are unique to multimedia data (e.g., logistics of video recording), whereas others are common to all forms of qualitative data (e.g., balancing induction and deduction in the coding of data). The sections that follow provide an introduction to the application of multimedia techniques across stages of the ethnographic process, from data collection to dissemination; review issues related to each stage; and provide references to resources for further inquiry into specific techniques.

Data Collection

Early ethnographers needed to be equipped with little more than a notebook in which to record field notes, observations, and dialogue. Now, however, the basic tools for ethnographic data collection are far more varied; especially when considering the effective use of multimedia techniques, researchers are confronted with a number of decisions. What type of media should be used—audiotaping, videotaping, photography, visual mapping, and/or tangible artifacts—and for which purposes? Should the researcher collect field notes in addition to videotaping observations? What are the staff requirements for using multiple media? What costs are involved in the purchasing and use of equipment? How should equipment be maintained, stored, and managed? Using video recording technology in natural settings also requires certain considerations not relevant to contrived or laboratory settings where these techniques have traditionally been used. For example, to what extent does the recording equipment (video cameras) alter the natural setting and the behavior of individuals within it? Are there special considerations with regard to the set up of equipment in a natural context (e.g., portability, mobility)? Who will do the recording? To what extent and how can confidentiality or anonymity be preserved when using recording devices? How does one effectively capture specific interactions in uncontrolled settings such as, for example, where background noise is a potential problem (e.g., how do you record a conversation between two individuals in a room full of people)? How will natural conditions affect the maintenance and storage of equipment and recordings (e.g., if climate cannot be controlled, security is difficult, or staff are unfamiliar with the technology)? What happens when the data format is no longer accessible (e.g., as digital technology advances and formats or machinery becomes obsolete)? We address these and other questions as we explore the major technical and logistical issues related to data collection to data representation and dissemination.

Types of Multimedia

One critical decision concerns the types of multimedia to be used in the study. The term *media* subsumes audiotaping and videotaping as well as other forms of visual data such as photography, maps, or graphs. When one has a choice and sufficient resources, and particularly for collecting observational data, videotaping is preferable because it provides a broader array of behavioral data (e.g., verbal, nonverbal, dynamic interaction). Specifically, videos permit the consideration of nonverbal behaviors as well as verbal behaviors in interpretation of individual or interactive responses. Nonverbal behaviors can facilitate the interpretation of the interview as well as observational data. For example, in individual interviews, the addition of nonverbal cues permits one to better interpret the respondents' responses (e.g., through facial cues, or eye contact with the interviewer). In dyadic (pairs) or group interviews, videotapes can facilitate the identification of individual speakers and the examination of group dynamics. Videotapes also provide data on physical contextual variables such as spatial arrangement, lighting, objects, and artifacts. Finally, the continuous videotaped record can foster understanding of the complexity of a situation or the sequence of actions or events.

Videorecording, however, does have serious disadvantages. It requires additional resources with regard to staffing and equipment. For example, staffing is necessary to monitor the recording equipment (e.g., to ensure that the camera stays in focus). The equipment is more visible and thus can be more intrusive than an observer alone. However, the currently available digital cameras are small enough to be minimally intrusive. Additionally, maintaining confidentiality of respondents is more difficult with videotapes because they are visually identifiable. This is particularly important when informants are minors; physically, mentally, or culturally vulnerable; in some type of custody arrangement; or providing sensitive information. These situations do not preclude the use of videotapes, but researchers must take extra precautions to protect access to the tapes, and they may want to use software that permits the protection of the identity of specific individuals. Perhaps the most important constraint on the use of videos is the complex and time-consuming process of transcribing videotapes. Particularly if one is interested in analyzing nonverbal behaviors and physical environment features, video transcription is much more complex and time consuming than that required for textual data. It can take many more hours to transcribe the videotape than it did for the event recorded to occur.

Notetaking

Another consideration is whether some form of notetaking is necessary in addition to video recording. As a general rule, videotaping does not replace field notes as a method of recording the ethnographer's impressions and capturing more global aspects of the context. It is possible to record notes and impressions on videotape at the beginning and end of a recording session, but it also is necessary to take written notes during a session. The need to accompany videotapes with field notes also depends on the context. For example, the researcher may find the tapes sufficient when the entire context is easily captured on videotape, the session is of relatively short duration, and comments and impressions can be recorded easily on tape at the end of the session. There are, of course, situations when notetaking during a session is not feasible; for example, when the researcher must conduct an interview or focus group (in such cases, additional staff might be necessary to gather written notes) or when the observer is a participant in the activities being recorded.

The complexity of natural contexts such as classrooms or community settings present challenges for researchers using video recording. Without multiple cameras, it is impossible to capture permanent records of the multiple activities and events occurring simultaneously. Certainly multiple cameras could be used, but they add to the researcher's logistical burden in terms of resources needed for data collection, transcription, and analysis. In such situations, field notes are essential to documenting contextual factors. The ethnographers' field notes, of course, also provide invaluable data about their own impressions during observations.

Video technology also can be used to supplement written records or field notes. That is, videorecording can be conducted to provide a backup for or archival record of the ethnographer's written records. For example, videorecording a focus group permits clarification or verification of written notes. Furthermore, video documentation permits reviewing nonverbal behaviors, group dynamics, and other contextual variables that may be more difficult to capture in writing. Using videos in interview situations also permits returning to the actual record or film with informants to query further their experiences or responses.

Research Staff

Given the multiple tasks required in conducting video recording, another critical consideration involves staff. Who will perform the multiple tasks necessary for recording? As noted in the previous section, it may not be feasible for one person simultaneously to conduct a session (e.g., as a participant observer or interviewer), monitor the recording equipment, and take written notes. Researchers may want to consider hiring a "research team," especially for video recording, consisting of one or more participant observers or interviewers, technicians to handle the equipment, and notetakers. These decisions are influenced by considerations such as available resources, feasibility, and intrusiveness posed by multiple staff and equipment. Another consideration is the extent of training necessary for staff depending on responsibilities and expertise. Training is discussed in a subsequent section.

Acquiring and Using Equipment

A critical set of decisions involve the selection, purchase, and use of video equipment. The checklist in Table 7.1 is intended to facilitate the acquisition and use of equipment. Given that the database *is* the video record, needless economies should be avoided in the selection and use of the best equipment possible. Ensuring quality equipment will prevent the costly loss of critical information. In this section, each of the recommendations is discussed.

Table 7.1 Checklist for Selecting, Purchasing, and Using Multimedia Equipment

Data Collection
✓ Acquire high-quality (digital) videorecording equipment that meets specific needs.
✓ Purchase good-quality external microphones that meet specific needs.
✓ Purchase a good tripod for positioning the camera (as needed).
✓ Test and monitor your equipment regularly.
✓ Clean and maintain equipment to ensure optimal working condition.
✓ Use appropriately trained personnel for recording.

Data Management and Transcription
✓ Store digital media in secure and climate-controlled setting.
✓ Review the recording as soon as possible to check the quality.
✓ Download files immediately to a computer and make back-up copies.
✓ Secure digital files (e.g., using password access) and back-up copies.
✓ Investigate and purchase transcription equipment and software.

Data Analysis, Interpretation, and Representation
✓ Acquire high-quality Computer-Assisted Qualitative Data Analysis Software (CAQDAS) that meets specific research needs.

Acquire High-Quality Digital Videorecording Equipment

The array of high-quality programs for data collection and analysis provide options for researchers. The specific needs of the research project, from data collection to dissemination of results, should guide the choice of equipment. Over the past several years, digital technology has changed the availability, affordability, feasibility, and quality of multimedia data collection for research purposes. The new technology provides high-quality audio and video, thus helping to ensure usable data. Both video cameras (set on tripods or handheld) and camcorders (portable video camera recorder, i.e., combining video camera and video recorder) are currently available and affordable. Digital camcorders provide smaller, less intrusive, and more portable alternatives to previous video camera technology, thus facilitating multiple uses within research. Current versions of camcorders are typically digital and use flash memory, microdrives, or reduced DVDs with MPEG formats for recording. Or, alternatively they record in DV or HDV format designed for downloading directly to the computer via IEEE 1394 connection (FireWire). Although analog-to-digital transfer is possible, digital technology is preferable, given current technology for data collection, management, and analysis.

Researchers should purchase the best equipment possible, within the limits of the research budget. Although professional production quality might be of interest, even equipment intended for personal use can meet adequately most of a researcher's needs—needs that should be considered with regard to research purposes, context, and logistics. In selecting equipment, portability is likely to be an issue. For example, can the camera remain stationary in the research site, or is it necessary to have a camera that can be moved about easily? How many cameras are needed to capture interactions and activities in a natural setting? How is it possible to balance the ideal and the feasible? For example, in one study of emergency medical teams, researchers proposed the use of three cameras, one focused on the doctor, one on the nurse, and one to capture the broader context. However, only two cameras were possible logistically (Santiano et al. 2008). An alternative to having a camera specifically focused on context might be to have the researcher take field notes on the context, perhaps coupled with a periodic scan of the context with one of the two cameras they did have.

Purchase Good-Quality Microphones That Meet Your Specific Needs

There are a variety of microphones from which to choose. These vary in utility, convenience, and price. It is important to know whether the microphones built into cameras are sufficient for your purposes. The built-in microphones are frequently inadequate for capturing vocalizations of specific individuals in group settings (e.g., focus groups or group intervention) or for recording target conversations in settings with background noise (e.g., recording a student-teacher conversation in a classroom) or when target individuals are moving about (e.g., teacher in a classroom, doctor in an emergency room). In these situations, alternatives are necessary that permit focused recording and minimize recording of background noise. For example, PZM (Pressure Zone Microphones), which can be placed on a flat surface (e.g., table around which a group is seated), are ideal for capturing target conversations while

minimizing background noise. Lavelier (lapel) microphones are ideal for capturing vocalizations of target individuals (e.g., the teacher in the classroom or individuals
within a group). Wireless clip-on microphones are particularly useful in situations in which the target individual is
moving about (e.g., a teacher who moves about the classroom). Shotgun microphones (mounted on a boom) that
can be attached to the camera facilitate both mobility and
close proximity. Investigating the acceptability of any kind
of technology to participants is, of course, critical. Santiano
and colleagues (2008) discuss the critical negotiation process with medical staff and patients that accompanied their
use of cameras in a medical setting; in their study, doctors
and nurses in emergency medical settings opposed the
use of lapel microphones but accepted the use of shotgun
microphones even when that meant close proximity to the
camera. Thus, it is important to balance needs, costs, and
acceptability in the selection of cameras as well as microphones. Researchers are advised to negotiate the type, positioning, intrusiveness, and other considerations when using
cameras and microphones in a natural setting.

Purchase a Good Tripod and Position
the Camera Securely

If the camera must be placed in a stationary position
for video recording, it is important to purchase a good
tripod. Particularly in high-activity situations, the camera
must be secure. In all situations, it is critical to designate
someone to be responsible for monitoring the recording
equipment to ensure that the camera is focused accurately
and that it records continually.

Test and Monitor Your Equipment Regularly

Before every session, make sure both video and
audio functions work. Make sure batteries are still opera-
tive. Always carry additional batteries. Between sessions,
recharge batteries if applicable. Monitor taping throughout the session. Although it may seem more convenient
to let the recorder or camera run unattended, doing so is

risky. Valuable data can be lost when the equipment fails, the memory cards are full, or the target activity or persons move out of video or audio range.

Use Appropriately Trained Personnel for Recording

This is particularly critical when doing videotaping. Make sure camera personnel know how to operate the equipment. If the camera will not remain in a stationary position, make sure the person responsible for the camera can record effectively while moving about. Limit the number of people who are responsible for taping. When multiple recorders must be used, make sure the guidelines for taping are clearly articulated and consistently implemented. Otherwise, the quality of recordings may vary widely, and critical data may be lost.

Review the Recordings Immediately to Check Quality, and Download to the Computer as Soon as Possible to Avoid Loss of Data

Within the constraints required to preserve confidentiality for participants, label data files clearly (date, context, participants, etc.). Critical identifying information about participants or context can be recorded directly on the video at the beginning or end of the sessions. Trying to discern the context of an unmarked session file can be frustrating and result in loss of data, particularly as time passes.

Secure Digital Files and Back-up Copies

Secure the digital files with password protection. Make back-up copies of files and store in a safe and secure place (e.g., locked cabinet in the researcher's office). Make sure back-up files are properly labeled. Use appropriate precautions for protecting the confidentiality of taped respondents. Because researchers cannot ensure anonymity in taped records, efforts to protect the privacy of participants are paramount. There are a number of measures researchers could use: (a) secure storage of tapes; (b) limiting access of tapes to members of the research team responsible for data transcription and analysis; (c) removing individual identifiers from transcriptions; (d) limiting data analysis to deidentified transcriptions when possible; and (e) mechanically blocking the identity of participants on videotapes (e.g., blurring the face). Researchers will need to get IRB approval for audio or videotaping and secure specific informed consent for taping (in addition to consent for participation) from research participants. Participants also can be given the option to block their faces electronically on tapes. In a study of therapist-client interactions, for example, Raingruber (2003) provided that option to clients who all chose to have their identities blocked.

Data Management and Transcription

One of the critical decisions researchers must make about data management and analysis involves the selection of software for Computer-Assisted Qualitative Data Analysis (CAQDAS) (see table 7.2). While the specific choice is dependent on the specific needs and preferences of the researcher, other important considerations include the

Table 7.2   Computer-Assisted Qualitative Data Analysis Software (CAQDAS)

Atlas.ti6
ATLAS.ti Scientific Software Development GmbH
http://www.atlasti.com/

HyperRESEARCH2.8
HyperTRANSCRIBE1.5
Researchware, Inc.
http://www.researchware.com/

MAXqda10
VERBI GmH
www.maxqda.com

QSR NVivo8
Qualitative Solutions Research International
http://www.qsrinternational.com/

Qualrus: The Intelligent Qualitative Analysis Program
Ideaworks, Inc.
www.ideaworks.com/qualrus

Transana 2.4
University of Wisconsin-Madison
http://www.transana.org/

---

types of data to be analyzed, the degree to which research-ers want to assure interactive capabilities across multiple data sources, the number of users who will need access to a single database, the complexity of the anticipated analysis, and data presentation needs. As discussed in a later section, software helps the researcher to *manage* the data analysis and interpretation. Ultimately, however, what gets coded in the process of analysis and how the data are interpreted is dependent on the expertise of the researcher and the pur-poses of the research. Researchers should not be deceived by the automation of CAQDAS. The software does not do the researcher's data analysis! CAQDAS can facilitate the storage, management, analysis, and interpretation of data, but the researcher is still the primary instrument in qualitative research. Only the researcher can create codes that link meaningfully to the conceptual framework and research questions and make the comparisons that result in good analysis and interpretation. Brown (2002), in fact, suggests that under certain circumstances, including the use of small samples, computerized analysis may have to be forgone completely:

> A manual analysis of digital data is currently the only way to get close to the participants as human beings, and [such a] primary analysis is also required to retain the socio-cultural contours of the data. Unde-niably, a manual process takes longer than an auto-mated or semi-automated processing of data—but if closeness is important then it remains a powerful alternative strategy and perhaps the *only* strategy in some cases. (Brown 2002, 7)

Brown's views on the necessity of manual analy-sis, however, are not shared by all qualitative researchers. Lewins and Silver (2007), for example, claim that "whatever [CAQDAS] tools are used, 'live' contact with source data is always easy, increasing the researcher's 'closeness' to the data" (10). Especially given the increasing flexibility and sophistication of analysis software, closeness to data is likely to be less of a problem, despite automation. Nevertheless, the responsibility for analysis and interpretation still lies with the researcher, and the software can serve as a useful tool to facilitate that process (see also Saldaña 2009).

Software to facilitate data management and transcription is available commercially and through academic websites. Table 7.2 lists some of the currently available software programs that can handle multimedia data (e.g., video and text). Earlier versions of these and other CAQDAS are reviewed by Lewins and Silver (2007), and readers are referred to the respective websites for updated information. Commercially available professional transcription equipment and software (e.g., Dragon Naturally Speaking; www. nuance.com) are designed to accommodate audio (though not necessarily video) media and include voice recognition capabilities. Currently available academic products are designed to accommodate both audio and video data, but they require manual transcription (i.e., they do not include voice recognition capabilities). Two academic products developed specifically for qualitative multimedia (audio and video) data transcription and analysis are Transana (University of Wisconsin-Madison, www.transana.org) and Tatoo (www.sonartdesign.se/tattoo). Mavrou, Douglas, and Lewis (2007) and Rostvall and West (2005) discuss and illustrate the application of Transana and Tatoo, respectively, for analysis of videotaped observations in educational contexts. Given the rapid development of technology for multimedia data collection and analysis, researchers are advised to investigate currently available products as they plan studies. For example, the most recent version of HyperRESEARCH has a transcription companion tool.

 Key point *Transcription—or transforming information from visual or audio formats to text—is critical in accessing data for analysis because much analysis is conducted on textual data. However, coding or analysis can be conducted directly from the audio record.* Particularly with currently available multimedia analysis programs, analysis using multiple data forms (text, visuals, graphics) is now possible. Although this section is focused on approaches to transcribing data into textual format, we address the issue of direct coding from videos as well.

Key point *Transcription can be approached in a number of ways. It varies along a continuum from full transcrip-*

tion of all verbal and nonverbal behaviors and contextual factors to a summary limited to critical incidents. The approach chosen depends on the nature of the data needed as well as the feasibility of complete transcription in terms of time and cost. For example, full transcription provides a thorough description of all verbalizations and, in the case of videotapes, nonverbal behaviors and physical context. Sociolinguistic studies that include proxemics and kinesics will require complete transcription, even though it is time consuming and tedious. In this section, we compare the use of full transcription with the transcribing of selected segments. We conclude with the consideration of alternatives to transcribing, such as coding directly from tapes.

Given the complexity of transcribing video data and the inherent interpretative activities, transcribers should be considered part of the research team. Researchers are well advised to select transcribers as carefully as they select "coders" or data analyzers and to interact with transcribers as key members of the research team. Some researchers (Schnettler and Raab 2008) argue that transcription of multimedia data, particularly visual data, actually is part of analysis in that researchers (transcribers) are engaged in interpretative activity as they transcribe. This raises critical questions about the expertise and role of transcribers of video data, as well as the need for training transcribers, a topic also addressed in this section.

Full Transcription

Transcribing entire videotapes is a labor-intensive and time-intensive endeavor, but it yields a level of detail that permits close and repeated analysis of the data. In using this approach, it is necessary to review sections of the tape repeatedly in order to capture both the verbal and nonverbal behaviors as well as physical contextual features. Assuming the "full transcription" is thorough in documenting all aspects of the video data, the researcher can code directly from the transcripts and use the transcripts repeatedly to address alternative questions. This assumption, however, does not obviate responsibility for documenting the interpretative process that accompanies transcription. To ensure accuracy and thoroughness, it is important to have a second transcriber review the tapes, fill in gaps, and raise questions about interpretation inherent in the transcription. Even though transcribing seems straightforward, it does involve some level of interpretation and likely influences the resulting database. Thus, a second transcriber can also provide a reliability check. Alternatively, the coder could serve as a second transcriber, filling in the gaps or raising questions about differences in interpretation of actions or vocalizations. It is much more difficult to do a full transcription of videotapes than of audiotapes. Whereas full transcription of audiotapes requires only detailed recording of all verbalizations, full transcription of videotapes requires description of both verbal and nonverbal behaviors (e.g., vocalizations, body language, interactions, facial expressions and even background/contextual events and processes).

The following examples of full transcription come from a study by Nastasi and Clements (Nastasi 1999) and depict the interaction between two third-grade girls working collaboratively to create a computer graphics program. Both verbal and nonverbal behavior (in parentheses) are depicted. (Note that Student 1 is typing and Student 2 is seated beside her. The command *FD20* moves the pointer on the screen "forward twenty spaces." The protractor is used to help in creating angles.) The first segment shows one student's behavior.

EXAMPLE 7.1

TRANSCRIBING A VIDEOTAPE OF COLLABORATIVE STUDENT WORK

Student 1: (types, looks at the screen) Okay. (typing) FD20. (looking at the screen) Wait a minute. (taking the protractor and measuring the design on the screen) Oh deary me, deary me, deary me. (types, looks at the screen, types, looks at the screen) Oh god, this is difficult. (types, looks at the screen, types, looks at the screen) Now what do I do? (clapping her hands and leaning back in her chair) I know what, no I don't. (looking at the screen, then at Student 2) What are you writing? (Nastasi 1999, 18).

The next segment depicts the interaction between the two students during the same work session.

 **EXAMPLE 7.2**

TRANSCRIBING INTERACTION BETWEEN TWO STUDENTS

Student 1: (pointing to the folder) Write FD20 down.

Student 2: How come you make me do all the work. (reaching for the pencil)

Student 1: Yeah, cause I have to do this. (typing) 10. Where's the protractor? (looking at Student 2)

Student 2: You have your own. (getting out of her seat)

Student 1: No I don't, I only have my folder. (looks toward the camera, then looks toward the door, holding on to the cabinet with her left hand, balancing the chair on the two left legs) Au-uh-uh! (looks at Student 2, takes the protractor from Student 2 and puts in on the screen, making noises with her mouth)

Student 2 (out of view) There, now I'm erasing.

Student 1: (types, looks at the screen, types, looks at the screen) Yes! Ooh! (sitting back, then forward, types, looks at the screen, types, then looks at the screen, then reaches for the protractor, making noises with her mouth while measuring the design on the screen, types, looks at the screen) Ooh ma-ma, ooh ma-ma. (dancing in her seat, making silly noise, then looking at Student 2) [Name], what are you doing?

Student 2: I'm writing a procedure.

Student 1: Oh, okay, while I do this? (looks at the screen, then types)

Student 2: That way I'll have the procedure done.

Student 1: (types, looks at the screen, types, looks at the screen) I got the "M" done. (jumping back, looks at Student 2) (Hands on keyboard, positioned to type) Wait a minute. Go ask [the teacher] if I want to do an "E," how do I get to an "E"? (looking at Student 2, tapping her feet on the floor) (Nastasi 1999, 19).

Transcription software for multimedia data is still in the early stages of development, and the available programs (Transana, Tatoo) combine transcription and analysis and still require manual transcription. Moreover, the flexibility of current versions of CAQDAS for multimedia data (e.g., to insert visual clips, create links across files) makes possible a seamless transcription-analysis-interpretative process.

Transcribing Selected Segments

In lieu of transcribing entire tapes, researchers may choose to transcribe segments of the videotapes. There are three possible approaches to selecting segments.

Sample the Tapes

The first approach is to purposefully or randomly select segments of the tapes to yield a sample of data across time, contexts, and participants. Thus, critical variables might be identified (e.g., level of expertise in problem solving) and then purposefully selected within those constraints (e.g., choose a novice and an expert problem solver). Or, in order to obtain a representative sample of variations across key variables (e.g., problem solvers with different skill levels), segments might be randomly selected segments across all videotaped sessions.

Select Relevant Segments

The second approach is to transcribe only segments of the tape that are relevant to the research question. For example, if the study involves cooperative learning and the researcher primarily is interested in the quality of exchanges between students as they work together, transcription could be restricted to cooperative interactions between students. The remainder of the tapes could be summarized to provide an indication of the larger context; for example, the transcriber could summarize other activities of the class session (e.g., whole class instruction, individual seatwork) during which the cooperative student interactions (e.g., students working in small groups) occur. This second approach requires that the concepts of interest must be operationalized with sufficient clarity for transcribers to recognize phenomena relevant to the research question, and also that the transcriber must be knowledgeable enough about the focus of the research to identify tape segments that need full transcription versus summarizing.

Identify Critical Incidents

The third approach is to identify critical incidents that exemplify the codes and transcribe fully the critical incidents, while summarizing the context. That is, the "transcriber" must first identify the incident (e.g., disagreement between individuals) that exemplifies the code (e.g., idea conflict) and then transcribe it fully. The selection of segments, of course, is guided by the research purpose. When using a deductive approach, this process might be straightforward, as the researcher has already identified key constructs and can with more certainty select representative segments. Using a more inductive or abductive approach requires performing some level of analysis before key segments (e.g., a critical incident) can be identified. Given the general concerns about the interpretative nature of transcribing and difficulty in separating transcription from analysis, researchers are well advised to make decisions about "transcription" as part of the more general approach to analysis and interpretation.

An example of transcription of selected segments, in this case a *critical incident,* comes from research that examined conflict resolution strategies within dyadic (pairwise) interactions in a fifth grade mathematics classroom (Young, Nastasi, and Braunhardt 1996). The critical incident is occurrence of **cognitive/idea conflict** (partners disagree about how to solve a problem) and depicts two different types of conflict resolution, **resolution by teacher** (teacher intervenes and resolves the conflict) and **resolution by negotiation** (two students discuss discrepant ideas and come to a mutually agreeable solution either by compromise or acceptance of one person's idea). The guidelines for transcribing required sufficient detail to justify the "code" (e.g., idea conflict with resolution) and to distinguish it from possible alternative codes (e.g., from other levels of resolution).

EXAMPLE 7.3

IDEA CONFLICT WITH VARYING KINDS OF RESOLUTION

Resolution by the teacher: (Both girls then continue reading or repeating numbers from the [computer] monitor.)

Student 1: (reading from the monitor) Number of the line you wish to save . . . 1.

Student 2: No, you want to save 2.

Student 1: What?

Student 2: You want to save 2.

Student 1: (turns to the teacher) Do we want to save 2?

Teacher: No, you want to save that line you're on right there.

(Student 2 appears confused about which one, asks which line the teacher means, and the teacher says it should be line 2.)

Students 1 and 2: (simultaneously) Oh!

Resolution by negotiation:

(Both girls then read the next question, "How long are the barges?")

Student 1: Uh oh.

Student 2: 200.

Student 1: Okay, 200 feet each . . .

Student 2: No, 200 feet altogether.

Student 1: No, but . . . there was 3 barges, and they were 200 feet each, remember?

Student 2: Oh yeah!

Student 1: Let's put 200 feet (Nastasi 1999, 23).

Alternatives to Transcribing

Transcription is not always necessary, particularly when the researcher uses a deductive approach. For example, when using event recording (e.g., how frequently did the event occur) or time sampling procedures (e.g., for what time period did the behaviors occur), coding can be done directly from video recordings without first transcribing. Thus, one views the tape and records either the occurrence or time engaged in target behaviors or events. This technique is useful if the researcher is interested only in representing the data in terms of frequency or time and is unconcerned with the degree to which incidents of the behavior or activity vary qualitatively. Additionally, the target constructs must be easily defined as discrete, observable verbal or nonverbal behaviors. Such "coding" is typically precluded when approaching data inductively or abductively, at least until clear guidelines can be developed for application of a standardized coding scheme. This issue is discussed further in the next section.

Data Analysis and Interpretation

As noted in the section on transcription, the process of data analysis and interpretation might best be considered an ongoing and perhaps iterative process that starts long before the actual "coding" of data. Furthermore, although there is a tendency to think about analysis and interpretation as separate steps, the analysis of multimedia data, as is the case with much of ethnographic data, involves an interpretive process, even in its beginning stages; it also is important to keep in mind that analysis and interpretation also occur during transcription. Thus, in this section, analysis and interpretation are treated together to reflect more accurately its relatively seamless process. Indeed, Lewins and Silver (2007) depict the analysis process inherent in CAQDAS packages as composed of the following steps, many of which are often, and inappropriately, omitted from discussions of analysis and interpretation:

Cross Reference: Book 5, chapter 4, for a discussion of the iterative nature of data analysis and interpretation

(a) planning and managing project/data;
(b) writing analytic memos;
(c) reading, marking, commenting on data;
(d) searching for specific words, phrases, content;
(e) developing the coding scheme;
(f) coding;
(g) revising the coding scheme;

(h) retrieving coded segments;
(i) recoding;
(j) organizing data based on a conceptual framework;
(k) hyperlinking (linking different types of data or codes/ concepts to specific data segments);
(l) searching the coded database to test ideas;
(m) mapping the data (creating visual/graphic depictions of themes, relationships among codes, etc.); and
(n) generating output (to examine current status of analysis-interpretation, for presentation and discussion, etc.).

The treatment of data analysis using qualitative software by Lewins and Silver reflects both the seamless process of analysis and interpretation and the capacity of CAQDAS to support such a process.

Definition: In a purely inductive approach, one permits the codes and themes to emerge from the data in order to yield an *emic* perspective that is most reflective of the views of participants

The framework for discussing data analysis–interpretation reflects an **inductive-abductive-deductive** continuum. Although pure qualitative researchers are more likely to approach analysis from an inductive approach, most researchers engaged in ethnography are likely to fall somewhere on the continuum from inductive to deductive (e.g., as in generating grounded theory). In practice, analysis and interpretation is more likely to reflect some degree of interaction between inductive and deductive approaches. This interaction is more appropriately labeled as "abductive" so as to reflect both an iterative process and the *blending of emic and emic perspectives*. To best reflect the potential variations in approaching data analysis–interpretation, we review inductive, deductive, and abductive approaches to "coding" or sense making in this section. This approach to sense making is based on both experience and accumulated knowledge within the social, educational, and health sciences. Readers are referred to resources in these fields including Books 1, 2, 3, and 5 in this series, that provide in-depth treatment of the range of approaches to data analysis and interpretation (in some cases referred to holistically as "coding").[2]

Definition: In a purely deductive approach, the researcher analyzes and interprets data from a preconceived theoretical or *etic* perspective that is less likely to reflect participant views

The data analysis–interpretation continuum essentially permits the researcher to move from "data" (e.g., text, video, pictures) to theoretically informed interpretations. For example, in **inductive approaches** such as generation of grounded theory, researchers move through a process of generating codes, categories, themes/concepts, and finally theory (see Saldaña 2009), with each level or step in the process representing progressively more abstracted, higher-order constructions. In a **deductive approach**, researchers start with theory-based codes that guide the process of analysis and interpretation of data (e.g., Bakeman and Gottman 1986), the goal of which is to test rather than generate theory. Whereas an inductive approach is open-ended and intended to capture the participants' conceptualization of phenomena under study, a deductive approach is directed toward interpreting experiences from the researchers' conceptualization (based in existing theory and research). Inductive approaches are more consistent with the philosophical underpinnings of ethnography and other approaches to qualitative research. The mixed method nature of ethnography, as represented in the *Ethnographer's Toolkit*, and the emerging models of research in social, educational, and health sciences, necessitate consideration of the full continuum of approaches. For those mixed methods (some combination of qualitative and quantitative) researchers, the **abductive approach** is much better suited to data analysis and interpretation. Thus, the range of approaches to research requires thinking about analysis and interpretation along the inductive-abductive-deductive continuum.

Definition: Abduction is an iterative process that blends emic and etic perspectives and represents an interaction between inductive and deductive approaches

Data Analysis (Coding)

The coding process, what researchers might consider the core of data analysis, involves:

- Making conceptual decisions about coding and "coding schemes" (i.e., what codes will be used and how will one approach the identification and operationalization of codes)
- Training reliable coders (data analysts)
- Coding the data in a consistent manner

Unless one operates from a purely deductive framework, the process of coding involves an iterative process in which initial coding is followed by the retrieval of

coded segments, recoding, and then reorganizing the coding scheme to delineate subcategories and/or superordinate categories. This process ultimately leads to the more
interpretive phase of identifying patterns and themes and
generating theoretical constructs and relationships, and
subsequent data representation (e.g., graphic depiction of
relationships). The discussion below begins with the conceptual decisions. As coding and data analysis are covered
in depth in Book 5, this section addresses issues particularly
relevant to the coding of multimedia data.

Conceptual Decisions about Coding

Decisions about how to approach coding start with
conceptual considerations: Do we approach the data
inductively, deductively, or abductively? What is the basis
for conceptualizing the coding scheme or framework? To
what extent do we rely on existing theory and research?
How do we balance this existing framework with views
and experiences of research participants? To a great extent,
these decisions are influenced by earlier conceptual considerations related to research questions, philosophical
and theoretical foundations of the study, and data collection techniques. In this section, we examine variations
in approaches to coding along the inductive-deductive
continuum. Issues related to decisions about coding are
likely to be similar across most forms of multimedia data.
Addressing analysis of each type separately is beyond the
scope of this chapter; unless otherwise noted, one can
assume that the subsequent discussion applies across most
data types (audio, visual, textual, graphic, etc.).

Deductive coding involves application of preexisting
theoretically or empirically derived codes (i.e., well-devel-
oped definitions of key constructs based on existing theory
and research). Alternatively, *inductive coding* involves the
identification of codes (meaning units) represented in or
derived from the data (e.g., in grounded theory) and development of a new coding scheme. As stated earlier, more
often, coding involves a combination of deductive and
inductive approaches (an *abductive* approach), in which the
researcher begins with the application of preexisting theo-

retically/empirically based major codes or constructs (e.g., depression or anxiety) and modifies the scheme through identification of additional codes (new categories or subcategories) to represent data that do not fit with preexisting construct definitions. For example, a researcher interested in stress and coping might initially code interview data collected from adolescents in Asia for instances of personal coping strategies that rely on the resources of the individual (e.g., problem solving and capacity for seeking social support; see Folkman et al. 1986) but discover that adolescents in the target culture also engage in communal coping (collective attempts at adaptation, response to adversity, or goal accomplishment; see Hobfoll 2002). The evidence of strategies that are different would lead to the identification of new types of coping and/or reformulation of our conceptions of coping. In summary, selecting or developing a coding scheme can involve adopting a preexisting scheme, modifying a preexisting scheme, or developing a new coding scheme (Nastasi 2008, 45–46).

Cross Reference:
Book 5, chapters 4, 5, and 6

The latter two approaches, modification or construction of a coding scheme, are most consistent with qualitative research methods, as they increase the likelihood that the findings reflect meaning from the perspective of participants. Given the individual and contextual variation of most human phenomena and the nature of ethnography, most preexisting schemes will require at least some modification.

The researcher may start with a general set of codes reflecting constructs derived from existing theory and research but recognize the potential limitations for application across populations and contexts. Although the general categories may guide initial analysis, coders will generate additional codes inductively to reflect the current data set.

EXAMPLE 7.4

DEVELOPING CODES IN TEAM RESEARCH WITH MULTIPLE SITES

In ongoing research with a team of partners from multiple countries, Nastasi and colleagues[3] were interested in capturing culturally specific conceptions of psychological well-being and psychologically healthy environments. Although existing theory and research informed the initial conceptual framework, we were skeptical about our coding schemes because we had used them only in work in Sri Lanka, and

researchers feared that what worked there might not be valid in other settings. As a consequence, the coding team became engaged in exploring alternative approaches to coding cross-country data sets, relying on an abductive strategy, which makes use of the conceptual model that framed the study while simultaneously examining the data inductively for alternative conceptual schemes or codes. The process is best described as iterative and varies from strict inductive analysis (making sense of the data based on the voices of participants) to constant comparison of new "codes" with the existing scheme. The challenge in such a data set is to distinguish between what might constitute "universal" codes or meaning units and what might better be represented as "culture-specific" codes. This initial "coding" of the data is followed by an interpretative process of depicting the relationships among codes, drawing both universal and country- or site-specific inferences about definitions of psychological well-being and psychologically healthy environments. Complicating the process are the multiple data sources (students, parents, educators, mental health professionals) within each site; thus a similar abductive process must be applied to examining cross-informant similarities and differences.[4]

Inductive development of a coding scheme is most likely to occur in the theory development process, when relatively little is known about the phenomenon of interest or when the target population or context is totally unfamiliar or recognizably different enough to question the validity of existing schemes. With an inductive or grounded theory approach, the categories (domains, codes) evolve or originate from the data. In such instances, the ethnographer/researcher sets out to define the phenomenon of interest purely from the perspective of those being studied (i.e., from the "emic" perspective). In contrast, when the researcher applies a preexisting scheme without modification, the phenomenon is interpreted from the perspective of the researcher (i.e., from the "etic" perspective). The researcher's approach to developing a new scheme may vary in terms of the influence of existing theory and research. For example, in the early stage of theory development, the researcher may approach the data in a highly inductive manner, with a minimum of preconceived ideas. In this situation, the researcher starts the process of scheme development by reviewing all of the recorded or transcribed data and identifying relevant categories for classifying behaviors, ideas, events, and more. These categories then become the basis for coding the data; that is, coders apply the code to the full set of data. Subsequent refinement of the coding scheme might involve identification of subordinate or superordinate categories to most appropriately represent the data and explain the phenomenon under study.

Preparing Reliable Coders

How the researcher approaches coding influences the preparation of coders and the establishment of a reliable coding process. Regardless of the approach to coding, there are a few general guidelines for preparing coders. First, inform coders about ethical issues such as the need to maintain the security of data and to protect the identity of informants. Second, provide an introduction to the purpose and methodology of the research. Third, make sure coders have an appropriate level of knowledge about research methodology and the conceptual basis of your work. Working with multimedia data also requires that coders are prepared in the use of the technology and medium. In particular, training in the use of CAQDAS programs for multimedia data is necessary (see the earlier section on data management and transcription).

Cross Reference: See Book 5, chapters 4 through 7, for more details on coding and preparation of coders

Coding Data in a Reliable (Consistent) Manner

Coding in a reliable manner (often referred to as intercoder or interrater agreement or reliability) refers to the consistent interpretation and application of codes to the data set by multiple coders. Although these terms have traditionally been applied to deductive coding approaches, the concept of reliability or consistency also is important across the deductive-inductive continuum. Initially, a common understanding must be established between/among prospective coders, which is part of the process of preparing coders. Subsequently, consistency checks across individual and multiple coders must be conducted throughout the process of coding. If the researcher is using an existing coding scheme, the process of establishing intercoder agreement involves teaching and practice so that multiple coders use the scheme in a consistent manner. Although application of the scheme to different contexts and individuals or groups may require some modification of the definitions of codes or categories, it is typically expected that such changes will be minimal. Thus, the focus is on establishing a consistent interpretation and application of preexisting codes. When using inductive coding, the process of establishing consistency involves the construction of categories and their definitions. Thus, coders are more active in constructing the meaning of codes, and establishing agreement becomes more of a collaborative process. With multimedia, establishing reliable coding also requires attention to the manner in which the media are used. The researcher needs to establish guidelines for inclusion of both verbal and nonverbal data. Important questions include: What is the basis for "coding"? Is it what participants *say* or *do* or *both*? How do coders balance the verbalizations and actions as the basis for coding? For example, if facial expressions contradict what the participant says (e.g., say "yes" but shake head "no"), how is this coded differently from congruent verbal-nonverbal segments? If using CAQDAS software, what are the rules for including video or audio clips in the coded segments? Do coders note where in the tape the segment occurs, or do they actually insert the clip during the coding process? And, how are contextual features handled? To what extent are these critical to consistent application of codes? Does it make a difference if the conversation between surgeon and nurse is observed in a surgery versus nonsurgery setting? How are these contextual variables recorded and reflected in the codes? In addition to the typical requirements related to the consistency of coding, researchers also need to attend to consistency in the way that the different types of data (audio, visual, textual) are used in the process of coding and subsequently in interpretation.

Data Interpretation

The primary purpose of interpretation is to make sense of the data in order to answer research questions, develop or inform theory, contribute to the body of existing knowledge, solve real-world problems, or contribute to practice and policy decisions. Thus, the goal is to transform data into information that can be shared with others and be applied in useful ways. As noted, analysis/coding and interpretation constitute an iterative process in which attempts to make sense of the data can lead to the need for further data collection or a reanalysis of the existing data. The value of multimedia is the capacity to review the audio or videotapes to reconsider the meaning of verbalizations, actions, contextual features; to reanalyze the data as new questions arise; to explore codes/variables in more detail; to address discrepancies in interpretation, and more. For example, based on coded data, researchers may disagree as to the meaning of codes related to communication between teachers during instructional team meetings. The researchers can jointly review the videotapes for the coded segments and discuss the discrepancies in meaning. These discussions can lead to the resolution of discrepancies or decisions to reanalyze data or reconsider interpretation of the data. The capacity to capture live action through videotape affords unique opportunities for researchers not possible in traditional approaches to participant observation. Of course, review of data requires reconsideration of other data forms as well (e.g., the observer's notes taken during videotaped observations). Interpretation ultimately involves the consideration of multiple sources and forms of data. Thus, one decision for researchers is the weight given to different forms of media during the analysis-interpretation process. Although multimedia can enhance the data collection and analysis process, researchers are faced with reconciling potential discrepancies afforded by these multiple data forms.

Data Representation and Dissemination

Multimedia data offer unique opportunities for data representation and dissemination that go beyond traditional scholarly written or oral textual formats. Multimedia data, especially in digital form, permits integration of written and visual media for presentations and facilitates naturalistic representation. Brown (2002) describes *digital convergence* as the integration of various forms of digital media (audio, visual, graphic) to facilitate analysis and representation of qualitative data, and he contends that digital convergence

> can preserve the original streams of consciousness that qualitative data so often reveals but is so difficult to carry through to representation. With data in common multimedia formats, it can be then edited together, quickly and easily, while retaining more (if not all) of the original context of its production. The linear word processed text remains a benchmark for qualitative research dissemination. However, the linking of these documents, as we know, provides a rich environment for qualitative writers. Of course, what I have just described is the strategy of using *hypertext*, a kind of writing that uses computer technologies to allow multiple pathways through a document through the use of hyperlinks. Sophisticated hypertext writing is rapidly developing into an art form in its own right, as well as a legitimate publishing format. (9)

Thus, "researchers can embed video clips, photography and other visual media into (hyper-) textual documents and also embed written texts and visual images into live performance events" (Miller-Day 2008, 4). HyperText Markup Language (HTML) and PDF formats support hyperlinking and multimedia presentations and permit online publishing of multimedia scholarly journals, such as *Forum Qualitative Sozialforschung/Forum: Qualitative Social Research (FQS*; http://www.qualitative-research.net/fqs/). For such journals, manuscripts are published online using HTML and PDF formats, which can include text, images, sound, graphics, and video. Brown (2002) describes the HTML manuscript as "a genuinely multimedia paper" (9). For examples of multimedia journal articles, see Miller-Day (2008) and Valentine (2008) published in *FQS*, which report on qualitative research using multimedia formats and represent findings through photographic images and hyperlinks to online audio and video clips (e.g., via www.youtube.com; www.video.google.com). In such publications, a picture of the web image is included in the document and can be accessed by clicking on the document or accessing the relevant web page online. In addition, video links are listed as a separate category of references.

The capacity to present findings in multiple formats facilitates dissemination to diverse audiences and for diverse needs, thus making research more accessible to practitioners, policy makers, and the public (Miller-Day 2008). For example, presentations in HTML or PDF format can be made available through researcher/agency websites or distributed on CDs/DVDs. Ziebland and McPherson (2006) describe DIPEx and its public informational website www.healthtalk online.org (personal experiences of health and illness), a medical education website for professionals and nonprofessional consumers (e.g., patients and their families):

> www.healthtalkonline.org is a website based on video and audio-recorded interviews about people's experiences of health and illness. Each condition specific module on the site has around 25 _Talking About_ summaries (each illustrated with 10–12 video and audio clips) on different topics from the interviews. Healthtalkonline has been used in many different teaching and learning environments, including problem-based learning, teaching communication skills and teaching research methods. (412)

Interviews contained on the website are derived through qualitative research using multimedia methods (i.e., interviews with individuals about their experiences with health and illness).

Multimedia formats also provide the opportunity to engage consumers/readers in an interactive manner with data. The work of Thøgersen (2009) is illustrative:

EXAMPLE 7.5

EXAMINING THE ATTITUDES OF ADULT DANES ABOUT ENGLISH LANGUAGE INFLUENCE ON THEIR MOTHER TONGUE

Thøgersen used qualitative research methods, structured (survey) and unstructured (open-ended questions) phone interviews with forty-seven adults from Denmark as part of a large-scale project to examine attitudes toward English language influence among speakers of Nordic languages. The interviews were audio recorded and subjected to discourse analysis. Data included both oral responses to structured questions from a Likert-scale survey and to open-ended questions. The researchers wanted to represent the data in a format that differed from academic tradition; that is, providing a presentation that was "pluri-linear rather than of [*sic*] uni-linear, simultaneous rather than chronologically progressing, multi-voiced rather than one-voiced, fragmentary rather than uniform, suspended rather than finished" (12–13). To accomplish this, they made use of computer-based interactive software, Macromedia Flash®, converting oral responses to audio (having one person read aloud excerpts from the forty-seven respondents) and text formats. The representation of the data (in the online published article) shows graphic depiction of text (inserted into the document), including both structured questions with response options and narrative responses. By clicking on the "text" graphic the reader has access to the audio format as well (oral version of the response), so the reader can both see and hear the "response." In addition, the graphics provide interactive links (e.g., between narrative and questionnaire data). Thus the reader is able to experience the complexity ("cacophony") inherent in the data.

One caveat, as noted by Thøgersen (2009), is that the presentation described requires accessing large files (audio and graphic) and may be less than universally accessible. One recommended solution is to write to the author for a CD version. Nevertheless, the approach is innovative and provides interactive access to findings in a way that brings research to life. With rapid advances in technology, researchers may find such modes of presentation more accessible in the future.

Multimedia presentations can also facilitate dissemination to and education of the public (e.g., medical patients), as illustrated in the work of Sandelowski, Trimble, Woodard, and Barroso (2006):

EXAMPLE 7.6   

USING MULTIMEDIA PRESENTATIONS TO MAKE RESEARCH FINDINGS ACCESSIBLE
TO RESEARCH PARTICIPANTS

To make research findings accessible to HIV-positive women, Sandelowski and colleagues developed a multimedia representation, written script and DVD, of the experiences of women who were HIV positive. The script, based on findings from ninety-three qualitative studies (of 1,700 women), was developed by an interdisciplinary team of academics and clinicians from nursing and communication studies. Qualitative findings (primarily interview data) were transformed into scripts that depicted fictional women (based on experiences of real women as reflected in qualitative data) sharing their experiences of managing stigma associated with HIV-positive status. Using professional actors depicting women from target demographic groups, DVD representations of the scripts were created. The intended use of the DVD, *HIV-Related Stigma in Five Voices*, was for viewing by HIV-positive patients waiting for clinic appointments.

Sandelowski et al. provide examples of the scripts and describe the process of script and DVD development. This work provides an excellent illustration of how research can be transformed into media that are accessible to the public.

Valentine (2008) provides an especially innovative application of multimedia in a project that combined action research with performative social science.

EXAMPLE 7.7

COMBINING ACTION RESEARCH AND PERFORMATIVE SOCIAL SCIENCE WITH MULTIMEDIA

The purpose of the project, *Our Story Scotland*, was to gather narrative accounts of the experiences of a marginalized group, the LGBT community of Scotland, using multimedia storytelling techniques, which would then be made available through media representations (for public) and museum archives (for researchers). Narrative accounts of members of the LGBT community were collected using a range of visual, graphic, audio, textual, and dramatic representations: oral histories collected through individual interviews in provided settings (often respondents' homes); written narratives—stories and poetry; narrative exchanges in which groups came together to share their stories; dramatic monologues performed at local theatres; visual narratives in the form of posters, comic strips, drawings, paintings, masks, mobiles, quilts, and caricatures generated by participants at LGBT community events; and storytelling through music, dance, and visual/graphic displays at an annual traditional festival (*ceilidh*) (Valentine 2008).

Riecken, Strong-Wilson, Conibear, Michel, and Riecken (2004) provide another example of multimedia participatory action research with marginalized populations.

EXAMPLE 7.8

MULTIMEDIA AND PARTICIPATORY ACTION RESEARCH WITH A CANADIAN ABORIGINAL SCHOOL

Researchers partnered with Aboriginal teachers and high school students in Canada in a health and wellness project. The students selected the specific health and wellness topics; collected data in the form of oral interviews, songs, written texts, and visual images, collected using digital video; and then transformed the data to video productions for dissemination. Riecken et al. (2004) describe the project using the multiple voices of research partners to depict the experiences of both university researchers and community participants.

In sum, the decision to use multimedia techniques in the collection of qualitative data has implications for all the phases of the research process, including data collection, analysis, interpretation, and dissemination. Moreover, multimedia techniques extend the capacity of researchers to understand and represent the experiences of research participants and to study complex phenomena in natural settings. Technological (multimedia) advances afford researchers opportunities to capture complex phenomena in real time and to permit examination and reexamination of verbalizations, actions, interactions, and contexts in ways that extend far beyond traditional ethnographic approaches.

APPLICATIONS OF MULTIMEDIA TECHNIQUES

Multimedia techniques can serve multiple purposes in research studies. These include facilitating interviewing by using video-cued recall/reflection, studying interpersonal communication and interactions, and studying professional practice in medical and education settings. Furthermore, multimedia data have been used for professional training of researchers and clinicians. Multimedia techniques have been used to facilitate qualitative data collection in its various forms, including interviewing, observations, portfolios, diaries, and field notes. In addition to ethnography, multimedia techniques have been applied to grounded theory studies (Bergman, Preisler, and Werbart 2006; Calandra, Brantley-Dias, Lee, and Fox 2009), as a technique for eliciting informed consent in medical trials (Henry, Palmer, Palinkas, Glorioso, Caligiuri, and Jeste 2009), and as an intervention tool in intervention studies (Calandra, Brantley-Dias, Lee, and Fox 2009; Long, Angera, and Hakoyama 2006; Sharry, Guerin, Griffin, and Drumm 2005).

In this section we have summarized the wide range of applications for multimedia techniques in qualitative research. Table 7.3 presents examples of these specific applications.

CONCLUSIONS

Since the publication of the first edition of the *Ethnographer's Toolkit* in 1999, technological advances have been responsible for expanding the potential applications of multimedia for qualitative data collection, analysis, and representation. The wide range of applications summarized in the preceding section and Table 7.3 exemplify the extent to which qualitative researchers have adopted the new technologies in ways that enhance the research process. Researchers must develop relevant technological expertise and continue to stay abreast of technological advances to use them effectively. They also should give serious thought to how these technologies can be integrated with their research projects in ways that enhance the research process, contribute to theory development, and facilitate translation of research to practice and policy.

Table 7.3 Applications of Multimedia Techniques to Qualitative Research

---

Data Collection

- Videotaped observation of sixth-grade classroom in Norway to explore relationship between exploratory learning and dialogue between students (Fottland and Matre 2004)
- Used video camera to conduct narrative observation of children (ages six to eight years) during peer interactions in after-school program in Sweden (Sparrman 2005)
- Provided adolescents with video camera to set up at home for recording daily (for one month) their feelings, thoughts, experiences related to living with a parent with cancer (Buchwald, Schantz-Laursen, and Delmar 2009)
- Set up a video camera in a "diary room" adjacent to the classroom where sixth-grade students could record at scheduled and unscheduled times (over seven weeks) their feelings, thoughts, views of learning, and mathematics (Noyes 2004)
- Provided children and adolescents with camcorders on which they documented their daily lives for four to eight weeks with particular focus on their experiences of "living" with asthma (Rich and Patashnick 2002)
- Used handheld computers to record field notes and researchers' personal journals (Brown 2002)
- Identified children's social networks by giving children digital cameras to photograph all their friends and contacts (Krensky 2002)
- Documented the daily activities of adolescent girls by giving them BlackBerrys upon which they send in periodic reports (Eisenhart and Allaman 2010)

Facilitated Discussion/Interviewing

- Students (ages six to sixteen, participating in music education program in rural school in Iceland) viewed edited "video portfolios" based on longitudinal documentation of their own musical performances and were interviewed regarding their perceptions of the meaning of music they had composed (Faulkner 2003)
- *Video-cued narrative reflection*—observations of videotaped interactions used to facilitate reflection by professionals (e.g., medical providers, therapists); reflection process also typically recorded
  - Used video clips (brief segments depicting incidents of blaming in family therapy sessions) to examine therapists interpretations of "blaming events" (Bowen, Stratton, and Madill 2005)
  - Used segments from videotaped footage captured via handheld video cameras during 24/7 observation of clinical practice of an intensive-care unit (ICU) in Australia to facilitate reflective interviews with clinicians on nature and quality of professional communications captured on tape (Carroll, Iedema, and Kerridge 2008)
  - Used videotapes of provider (doctor/nurse)-patient interactions for the purpose of professional development of providers in Sweden; supervisor viewed tapes with providers and facilitated reflection-learning process (Holmström and Rosenqvist 2004)
  - Used videotapes of classroom practices (recorded by teachers) to stimulate reflective dialogue (between researcher and teacher) about pedagogy (Powell 2005)
- *Interpersonal process recall interviewing (IPR)*—"immediate" viewing of videotaped interaction combined with interviewing participants to examine their experiences during the interaction
  - Use of IPR to investigate counselor and/or client perceptions of the counseling process (Larsen, Flesaker, and Stege 2008)
  - Use of IPR to examine therapist reflections on their approach in therapist-client sessions (O'Hara and Schofield 2008)
  - Used videotapes of therapy sessions to interview patients and nurse-therapists about their recall of experiences in the sessions (Raingruber 2003)
- Eliciting *career narratives* of prospective teachers by cocreating graphic novels (Campbell-Galman 2006)

Studying Interpersonal Communication/Interaction

- Videotaped simulated "problem identification interviews" between teachers and psychological-educational consultants in training to study communication patterns in consultation (Benn, Jones, and Rosenfield 2008)
- Videorecorded outpatient intake visits at pediatric clinics to study three-way interactions among clinician, parent, and child patient (ages ten to eighteen years) (Clemente 2009)
- Videotaped routine doctor (general practitioner)-patient interaction during medical visits to London clinics to examine potential sources of "miscommunication" between bilingual patients communicating with doctors in their nonprimary language (Roberts, Moss, Wass, Sarangi, and Jones 2005)
- Videotaped parent-adolescent conversations followed by separate cued recall interviews with parent and adolescent to examine respective perspectives on the communication event; conducted in Canada (Marshall, Young, and Tilton-Weave 2008)
- Videotaped caregiver-infant dyadic interactions over nine to thirteen weeks in childcare setting to study development of infant-caregiver relationship (Lee 2006)
- Intergenerational learning (Kenner, Ruby, Jessel, Gregory, and Arju 2007)
- Videotaped interactions of interdisciplinary medical team during staffing of patient cases on long-term care facility to examine communication practices (Bokhour 2006)
- Videotaped medical emergency teams in Australian hospitals to study communication patterns among medical staff and with ward staff (Santiano, Baramy, Young, Saggu, Cabrera, and Parr 2008)

Professional Practice

- Videotaped interactions in primary medical care and surgery settings to study the social interaction inherent in medical practice—illustrates use for research and medical education (Heath, Luff, and Svensson 2007)
- Videotaped interactions between call-takers and dispatchers in medical emergency call centers to study workplace collaboration (Fele 2008)
- Collaborative (researcher-teacher) analysis of videotaped performances by teachers in U K. (Hennessy and Deaney 2009)
- Videotaped teacher-student interactions in study of "team teaching" in Taiwan (Jang 2006)

Professional Training/Education

- Use of videotaped interviews by novice qualitative researchers to facilitate professional development of interviewing skills through structured review and reflection process (Uhrenfeldt, Paterson, and Hall 2007)
- Pedagogical use of CAQDAS in professional training of social workers, through use of videotaped sessions for demonstration or individual student evaluation of their own videotaped sessions with clients (Macgowan and Beaulaurier 2005)
- Use of qualitative analysis of video and audio recordings of interviews with patients about their experiences with health and illness to develop illustrative video/audio clips for medical education and professional development (Ziebland and McPherson 2006).

Note: The purpose of this table is to highlight the use of multimedia, particularly videotaping, in research. In many of these studies, however, videotaping was combined with other methods of data collection and recording such as interviewing, journaling, and field notes. In some cases both video and audiotaping were used to serve different purposes (e.g., videotaping to capture interactions with audiotaping of subsequent interviews).

NOTES

1. Multimedia includes video, audio, visual, and graphic, much of which can be digitized. This chapter focuses particularly on the use of digital video technology, although some references to other forms of media are provided.

2. Recommended sources on data analysis and interpretation (or coding) reflecting the inductive-abductive-deductive continuum: Bakeman and Gottman (1986), Leech and Onwuegbuzie (2008), Lewins and Silver (2007), Miles and Huberman (1994), and Saldaña (2009).

3. The transnational, transcultural project, *Promoting Psychological Well-Being Globally*, sponsored by the International School Psychology Association with partial funding from Walden University, USA, has research partners from the school psychology community in Brazil, Estonia, Greece, India, Italy, Mexico, Romania, Russia, Slovakia, Sri Lanka, Tanzania, and USA (Boston, California, New Orleans, Puerto Rico). Project activities are coordinated by Bonnie Nastasi through Tulane University. Each site researcher is responsible for transcription and translation of data to English and preliminary coding data; cross-site data analysis is being conducted at Tulane University by a team of doctoral students from the School Psychology Program. The project's purpose is to develop culture-specific definitions of psychological well-being and psychologically healthy environments, based on perspectives of key stakeholders (student, parent, teacher, school administrator, health or mental health support staff). The project is a first step in understanding psychological health from a cultural perspective and subsequently developing programs to promote well-being of students through individual and ecological change. Research partners conduct formative qualitative research, including focus groups, individual interviews, and elicitation activity to examine stressors and coping strategies of school-aged children. Data are recorded using a combination of written notes and audiotaping for back-up purposes and to facilitate accuracy checks. Qualitative data analysis examines cultural-specific definitions of constructs related to children's psychological well-being and the environments that can facilitate their well-being. Findings are expected to highlight culturally determined and universal themes and lead to school-based programming to promote psychological well-being.

4. Readers can contact the author for details on this ongoing research.

REFERENCES

Bakeman, R., and J. M. Gottman. 1986. *Observing interaction: An introduction to sequential analysis.* New York: Cambridge University Press.

Benn, A. E., G. W. Jones, and S. Rosenfield. 2008. Analysis of instructional consultants' questions and alternatives to questions during the problem identification interview. *Journal of Educational and Psychological Consultation* 18: 54–80. DOI: 10.1080/10474410701864115.

Bergman, H. F., G. Preisler, and A. Werbart. 2006. Communicating with patients with schizophrenia: Characteristics of well functioning and poorly functioning communication. *Qualitative Research in Psychology* 3: 121–46.

Bokhour, B. G. 2006. Communication in interdisciplinary team meetings: What are we talking about? *Journal of Interprofessional Care* 20: 349–63.

Bowen, C., P. Stratton, and A. Madill. 2005. Psychological functioning in families that blame: From blaming events to theory integration. *Journal of Family Therapy* 27: 309–29.

Brown, D. 2002. Going digital and staying qualitative: Some alternative strategies for digitizing the qualitative research process. *Forum: Qualitative Social Research* 3(2): 1–15. http://www.qualitative-research.net/fqs/

Buchwald, D., B. Schantz-Laursen, and C. Delmar. 2009. Video diary data collection in research with children: An alternative method. *International Journal of Qualitative Methods* 8(1): 12–20.

Calandra, B., L. Brantley-Dias, J. K. Lee, and D. L. Fox. 2009. Using video editing to cultivate novice teachers' practice. *Journal of Research on Technology in Education* 42(1): 73–94.

Campbell-Galman, S. A. 2006. *The Ariadne thread*. Doctoral dissertation, School of Education, University of Colorado, Boulder.

Carroll, K., R. Iedema, and R. Kerridge. 2008. Reshaping ICU ward round practices using video-reflexive ethnography. *Qualitative Health Research* 18: 380–90. DOI: 10.1177/1049732307313430.

Clemente, I. 2009. Progressivity and participation: Children's management of parental assistance in paediatric chronic pain encounters. *Sociology of Health and Illness* 31: 872–88. DOI: 10.1111/j.1467-9566.2009.01156.x.

Eisenhart, M. E., and E. Allaman. 2010. Circulating figured worlds of school, romance and family in teenage girls' mobile communications. Presented at the American Anthropological Association. New Orleans, Louisiana, November.

Faulkner, R. 2003. Group composing: Pupil perceptions from a social psychological study. *Music Education Research* 5: 101–24.

Fele, G. 2008. The collaborative production of responses and dispatching on the radio: Video analysis in a medical emergency call center. *Forum: Qualitative Social Research* 9(2): Article 40. [online journal] http://www.qualitative-research.net/fqs/

Folkman, S., R. S. Lazarus, R. J. Gruen, and A. DeLongis. 1986. Appraisal, coping, health status, and psychological symptoms. *Journal of Personality and Social Psychology* 50(3) (March): 571–79. DOI: 10.1037/0022-3514.50.3.571

Fottland, H., and S. Matre. 2004. Exploring researchers in dialogue: Linguistic and educational perspectives on observational data from a sixth grade classroom. *International Journal of Qualitative Methods* 3(3): Article 4.1. Retrieved from http://www.ualberta.ca/~iiqm/backissues/3_3/ pdf/fottland.pdf

Heath, C., P. Luff, and M. S. Svensson. 2007. Video and qualitative research: Analysing medical practice and interaction. *Medical Education* 41: 109–16. DOI:10.1111/j.1365-2929.2006.02641.x.

Hennessy, S., and R. Deaney. 2009. "Intermediate theory" building: Integrating multiple teacher and researcher perspectives through in-depth video analysis of pedagogic strategies. *Teachers College Record* 111: 1753–95.

Henry, J., B. W. Palmer, L. Palinkas, D. K. Glorioso, M. P. Caligiuri, and D. V. Jeste. 2009. Reformed consent: Adapting to new media and research participant preferences. *IRB: Ethics and Human Research* 31(2): 1–8.

Hobfoll, S. E. 2002. Social and psychological resources and adaptation. *Review of General Psychology* 6(4) (December): 307–24. DOI: 10.1037/1089-2680.6.4.307.

Holmström, I., and U. Rosenqvist. 2004. Interventions to support reflection and learning: A qualitative study. *Learning in Health and Social Care* 3(4): 203–12.

Jang, S. J. 2006. Research on the effects of team teaching upon two secondary school teachers. *Educational Research* 48: 177–94.

Kenner, C., M. Ruby, J. Jessel, E. Gregory, and T. Arju. 2007. Intergenerational learning between children and grandparents in east London. *Journal of Early Childhood Research* 5: 219–43. DOI: 10.1177/1476718X07080471.

Krensky, B. 2002. An act of hope: Developing social responsibility through issue-oriented community-based art education. Unpublished doctoral dissertation, School of Education, University of Colorado, Boulder.

Larsen, D., K. Flesaker, and R. Stege. 2008. Qualitative interviewing using interpersonal process recall: Investigating internal experiences during professional-client conversations. *International Journal of Qualitative Methods* 7(1): 18–37.

Lee, S. Y. 2006. A journey to a close, secure, and synchronous relationship: Infant-caregiver relationship development in a childcare context. *Journal of Early Childhood Research* 4: 133–51. DOI: 10.1177/1476718X06063533.

Leech, N. L., and A. J. Onwuegbuzie. 2008. Qualitative data analysis: A compendium of techniques and a framework for selection for school psychology research and beyond. *School Psychology Quarterly* 23: 587–604. DOI: 10.1037/1045-3830.23.4.587.

Lewins, A., and C. Silver. 2007. *Using software in qualitative research: A step-by-step guide.* Thousand Oaks, CA: Sage.

Long, E. C. J., J. J. Angera, and M. Hakoyama. 2006. Using videotaped feedback during intervention with married couples: A qualitative assessment. *Family Relations* 55: 428–38.

Macgowan, M. J., and R. L. Beaulaurier. 2005. Using qualitative data analysis software in teaching about group work practice. *Journal of Teaching in Social Work* 25(1/2): 45–56. DOI: 10.1300/J067v25n01_03.

Marshall, S. K., R. A. Young, and L. C. Tilton-Weave. 2008. Balancing acts: Adolescents' and mothers' friendship projects. *Journal of Adolescent Research* 23: 544–65. DOI: 10.1177/0743558408322143.

Mavrou, K., G. Douglas, and A. Lewis. 2007. The use of Transana as a video analysis tool in researching computer-based collaborative learning in inclusive classrooms in Cyprus. *International Journal of Research and Method in Education* 30: 163–78.

Miller-Day, M. 2008. Translational performances: Toward relevant, engaging, and empowering social science. *Forum: Qualitative Social Research* 9(2): Article 54. http://www.qualitative-research.net/fqs/.

Nastasi, B. K. 1999. Audiovisual methods in ethnography. In *Ethnographer's toolkit, Book 3. Enhanced ethnographic techniques: Audiovisual techniques, focused group interviews,* and elicitation techniques, ed. J. J. Schensul and M. D. LeCompte, 1–50. Walnut Creek, CA: AltaMira.

———. 2008. Advances in qualitative research. In *The handbook of school psychology*, fourth edition, ed. T. Gutkin and C. Reynolds, 30–53. New York: Wiley.

Nastasi, B. K., and D. H. Clements. 1992. Social-cognitive behaviors and higher-order thinking in educational computer environments. *Learning and Instruction* 2: 215–38.

Noyes, A. 2004. Video diary: A method for exploring learning dispositions. *Cambridge Journal of Education* 34(2): 193–209.

O'Hara, D., and M. J. Schofield. 2008. Personal approaches to psychotherapy integration. *Counselling and Psychotherapy Research* 8(1): 53–62.

Powell, E. 2005. Conceptualising and facilitating active learning: Teachers' video-stimulated reflective dialogues. *Reflective Practice* 6: 407–18. DOI: 10.1080/14623940500220202.

Raingruber, B. 2003. Understandings video-cued narrative reflection: A research approach for articulating tacit, relational, and embodied understandings. *Qualitative Health Research* 13: 1155–69. DOI: 10.1177/1049732303253664.

Rich, M., and J. Patashnick. 2002. Narrative research with audiovisual data: Video Intervention/Prevention Assessment (VIA) and NVivo. *International Journal of Social Research Methodology* 5: 245–61.

Riecken, T., T. Strong-Wilson, F. Conibear, C. Michel, and J. Riecken. 2004. Connecting, speaking, listening: Toward an ethics of voice with/in participatory action research. *Forum: Qualitative Social Research* 6(1): Article 26, http://www.qualitative-research.net/fqs/

Roberts, C., B. Moss, V. Wass, S. Sarangi, and R. Jones. 2005. Misunderstandings: A qualitative study of primary care consultations in multilingual settings, and educational implications. *Medical Education* 39: 465–75. DOI:10.1111/j.1365-2929.2005.02121.x.

Rostvall, A., and T. West. 2005. Theoretical and methodological perspectives on designing video studies of interaction. *International Journal of Qualitative Methods* 4(4): 1–28. DOI: 10.1080/17437270701383305.

Saldaña, J. 2009. *The coding manual for qualitative researchers*. Thousand Oaks, CA: Sage.

Sandelowski, M., F. Trimble, E. K. Woodard, and J. Barroso. 2006. From synthesis to script: Transforming qualitative research findings for use in practice. *Qualitative Health Research* 16: 1350–70.

Santiano, N., L. Baramy, L. Young, G. Saggu, R. Cabrera, and M. Parr. 2008. Problems and solutions arising during a study in visual semantics of the Medical Emergency Team System. *Qualitative Health Research* 18: 1336–44. DOI: 10.1177/1049732308322595.

Schnettler, B., and J. Raab. 2008. Interpretative visual analysis: Developments, state of the art and pending problems. *Forum: Qualitative Social Research* 9(3): Article 31, 1–29. http://www.qualitative-research.net/fqs/

Sharry, J., S. Guerin, C. Griffin, and M. Drumm. 2005. An evaluation of the parents plus early years programme: A video-based early intervention for parents of pre-school children with behavioural and developmental difficulties. *Clinical Child Psychology and Psychiatry* 10: 319–36. DOI: 10.1177/1359104505053752.

Sparrman, A. 2005. Video recording as interaction: Participant observation of children's everyday life. *Qualitative Research in Psychology* 2: 241–55.

Thøgersen, J. 2009. Cacophony: Ways to preserve the complexity of subjects in the research presentation. *Forum: Qualitative Social Research,* 10(3): Article 7, http://www.qualitative-research.net/fqs/

Uhrenfeldt, L., B. Paterson, and E. O. C. Hall. 2007. Using videorecording to enhance the development of novice researchers' interviewing skills. *International Journal of Qualitative Methods* 6(1): Article 3. Retrieved from http://www.ualberta.ca/~iiqm/backissues/6_1/uhrenfeldt.pdf.

Valentine, J. 2008. Narrative Acts: Telling tales of life and love with the wrong gender. *Forum: Qualitative Social Research* 9(2): Article 49, http://www.qualitative-research.net/fqs/

Young, M. F., B. K. Nastasi, and L. Braunhardt. 1996. Implementing Jasper Immersion: A case of conceptual change. In *Constructivist learning environments: Case studies in instructional design,* ed. B. Wilson, 121–34. Englewood Cliffs, NJ: Educational Technology Publications.

Ziebland, S., and A. McPherson. 2006. Making sense of qualitative data analysis: An introduction with illustrations from DIPEx (personal experiences of health and illness). *Medical Education* 40: 405–14.

8 ◆━◆•◆•◆•◆

CREATING PARTICIPATORY ETHNOGRAPHIC VIDEOS

Heather Mosher

INTRODUCTION TO PARTICIPATORY VIDEO-BASED RESEARCH

Participatory video is a dynamic research process that engages participants in using video technology as a tool for communicating and solving local problems. Rooted in democratic ideals, the goal of the participatory video process is to tackle an issue of local concern through participation, teamwork, and empowerment (White 2003). Participatory video has been widely used as a communication tool in community development initiatives (Lunch and Lunch 2006), but it has more recently emerged as an innovative methodology in ethnographic and other social science research.

The first participatory video project took place on a remote offshore island of Newfoundland known as Fogo Island, in the late 1960s (Crocker 2003; Quarry 1984). Outraged by the ineffective actions of the local government, Canadian academic and activist Donald Snowden wanted to help the impoverished fishing villages voice their concerns and organize to improve their situation. Snowden believed that media could help communities to develop at a grassroots level based on the direct efforts of local people, so he teamed up with filmmaker Colin Low to produce twenty-eight short documentaries made in collaboration with Fogo Islanders. In the 1960s when Snowden carried out this participatory video project, the film production process was more costly and technically complex. Therefore, Snowden and Low did not train Fogo Islanders in the technical aspects of the film production process, but instead provided a process that gave the community itself the decision-making control over how the community was represented. The process included a feedback loop for discussion and dialogue at all stages of the process. The films depicted Fogo Islanders talking about a range of local issues, including the lack of organization among fishing communities, the need for more communication, and the resentment and anger toward the government for making important decisions about their future with no community consultation process (Crocker 2003).

Screening the films across fishing communities on the island became an important part of the participatory video process. Snowden and Low noticed that people were not comfortable expressing their views to each other in face-to-face meetings but were comfortable voicing their concerns on film and having their opinions shown to other community members. Thirty-five screenings were held, reaching a total number of three thousand viewers (Williamson 1975). When islanders watched each other's films at community screenings, the impact of seeing other people like themselves experiencing the same struggles empowered the communities to coordinate their community development efforts. The films were also launched as a tool for communication between local government and the Fogo Islanders, which ultimately resulted in government support for an islandwide fisherman's cooperative that strengthened the local economy and enabled the cooperative to directly manage the fishing industry and keep the profits on their island (Crocker 2003; Quarry 1984). Snowden explained that the "films did not do these things: people did them. There is little doubt, however, that film created an awareness and self confidence that was needed for people-advocated development to occur" (cited in Quarry 1984).

The approach to participatory video varies from researcher to researcher. Some projects are like Snowden's, in which the community decides the content of the film through iterative cycles of feedback and dialogue at film screenings, and the researcher handles the technical aspects of the video production. On the other end of the continuum, researchers may choose to take a more back-seat role in the video production process, providing equipment and training for participants to take control over the video production process in its entirety, from concept stage to editing the final cut and distribution. Regardless of the methods used, however, a key feature present in all participatory video research projects is group or **community participation** in the video creation process (Lunch and Lunch 2006).

Definition: Community participation refers to the involvement of people from a community confronting a problem with ethnographic filmmakers to document it and use the results

PARTICIPATORY VIDEO METHODS

Participatory video is a research methodology intended to enhance communication, self-expression, and potentially broader social change around a particular issue, and to promote community development through a participatory process. The methodology focuses both on process and product, with the idea that the process of creating a video can be a vehicle for "horizontal communication" that occurs between groups or local communities (Lunch and Lunch 2006). Participatory video encourages two-way communication, or "mutual reciprocal learning" (Freire 1970), to sustain and improve the quality of the research process and the quality and impact of the video product. The video becomes part of the "action," an agent of change, and a mechanism for reflection and opening dialogue—not only for academics but also for the community in which the research originated. As the video product is distributed, the video advances the research process as diverse audiences view it. Through audience experience, the video sustains a process of learning and action with the goal of long-term transformation toward positive social change. At the end of the process, the video product becomes a tool for "vertical communication" between communities and policy makers or government authorities (Lunch and Lunch 2006).

Definition: Participatory video is a research methodology intended to enhance self-expression, communication, and potentially broader social change around a particular issue, and to promote community development through a participatory process

Some researchers use participatory video methodology because video can be a more accessible format to many people across a range of educational backgrounds and literacy levels. Everyday people can use storytelling as a vehicle for producing and communicating knowledge. People can create and view videos *together*, making use of the different combinations of skills that each person brings to the whole group and to the creative process. A video can thus become a useful tool for group activities, group reflection, community dialogue, and the development of future action. By producing, watching, discussing, and analyzing video material together, participatory video is an effective method for participants to learn how to work together, and to listen to and become aware of diverse perceptions on an issue. Similar to photovoice, many researchers use participatory video when the community's voices are unheard on a particular issue that directly impacts their lives.

In summary, participatory video offers a unique way to:

- Reach a wider audience
- Enhance vertical/horizontal communication
- Express the viewpoint/experience of participants
- Shift power dynamics
- Share, reflect, and develop critical consciousness

IDENTIFYING THE ISSUE(S)

The first step in participatory video is to identify the issue(s) of concern that the research is attempting to address. This step involves not only defining *what* issue(s) will be addressed by the research but also *who* is part of deciding this area of focus. Researchers may approach a community with a specific issue already in mind, with the understanding that this issue is of concern to the community. Even if the idea of the participatory video project did not originate in the community, the participant community should decide the focus of the research based on its needs. How this step is approached can be influenced by multiple factors, including available funding and specific community needs, among others.

Cross Reference: See Book 7 for more information on participatory action research

The researcher assists the group by facilitating supportive processes for dialogue and democratic decision making in whatever domain the group has a concern. The issue to pursue in research is identified over time, as it emerges through group dialogue around the community's strengths and needs. In effect, the researcher acts as a facilitator to ensure the evolution of the content of the video through group participation.

There are many benefits to using participatory video methodology, but readers should keep in mind that it is more time consuming and costly and requires more resources and potentially a larger investment by funders. Thus pragmatically, funding can be an influential factor in how the issue is identified. Funding can both provide opportunities and much-needed resources but at the same time can restrict the topics that are pursued.

In participatory video, the specific needs of a community are *always* considered when defining the issues pursued during the research. ***The participatory video process always involves the community in defining and carrying out the research.*** However, the degree to which the community con- **Key point** trols the selection of the issue can depend on some of the factors just described. The entire process of identifying the issue(s) of concern is interwoven among factors that include:

- Community interests, concerns, and resources
- Appropriate funding sources
- The amount of funding available

Thus the first step is both a critical and a complicated one for keeping the project focused.

DESIGNING THE RESEARCH

It is important to invest enough time to develop a strategic plan so that the research and video have the intended impact. Designing the research involves making decisions around critical choice points. Below is a list of topics and questions that the group might address when designing the participatory video research process and outcomes.

- Objectives
- Activities/data
- Participants

- Research process
- Management of power and conflict
- Process versus product oriented

Objectives

What are the objectives of the research? What is under-stood, or not understood, about the issue? What specific questions will be explored during the research? What is the purpose of the video being created? Who is the desired audi-ence, and what impact on them is desired? Simply picking up a camera and filming randomly without direction or purpose often results in the type of footage that you might see in your Uncle Carl's endless home movies, barf bag required. However, determining objectives and a focus for the filming should not limit creativity and self-expression. A critical first step in deciding *what to do with the film* is to keep the research project manageable, fun, and effective at achieving its objective. The process of actually asking these questions in a community setting often helps people to define more specifically their issue of concern, which in turn allows for an effective strategy for resolving those issues. It is difficult to solve a problem if the objective is not specifically defined.

Activities/Data

What activities or data would help clarify the issue to understand the root cause? Should multiple data types be col-lected? What is the time line for these activities? What is the cost/benefit of collecting different data types? Before crafting a communication or creating a video narrative, it is impor-tant to gain a deeper understanding of the issue, identifying the root causes and the multiple viewpoints and actors that affect, and are affected by, the problem. Different types of data can be collected as part of the research process and used to inform the creation of the video. For example, the research team can collect data by videotaping or taking photographs, collecting survey data, or conducting inter-views. Data also can be collected online through various local, state, and federal records. Figuring out how much data to collect and how to go about doing it is part of the research design process.

Good-quality research is grounded in experiences of ethical care, passion, communion, and social responsibility (Finley 2003). As of yet, research criteria to assess quality, authenticity, and credibility of research design have not been developed for participatory video methodology. However, Mosher (2010) adapted a set of criteria from various areas of qualitative inquiry to ensure high-quality participatory video research. This participatory video rubric was primarily adapted from Susan Finley's (2003) three interconnected commitments to assess the quality of an inquiry: (1) community, (2) action within community, and (3) visionary critical discourse. The rubric also incorporates concepts within the areas of qualitative inquiry (Fine, Weis, Weseen, and Wong 2000; Lincoln and Guba 1986), performance ethnography (Alexander 2005), arts-based research (Finley 2003), action research (Reason and Bradbury 1999; Reason 2006), participatory research (G. L. Anderson 1998), and social justice studies (Charmaz 2005). In the following box are criteria for evaluating the quality of research in the context of participatory video.

EVALUATING GOOD QUALITY RESEARCH INVOLVING PARTICIPATORY VIDEO (MOSHER 2010)

1. Community

- Is there evidence of *ethics of care* among the participants and the researcher-facilitators?
- Is the research performing a *useful*, local, community service?
- How does the research give *voice* to participants?
- Is the research an *emergent process*?
- How has the community *sustained the process* after the project has ended?
- How have community members been involved in *reviewing the material* with the researcher and challenged researcher interpretations and representations of them?

2. Action within Community

- How does the video create an *open space for dialogue* between community members and audience members?
- Does the research *provoke questions* rather than draw conclusions?
- Has the research helped people to understand and appreciate other *diverse views* in the setting?
- Does the research and video (or report) create opportunities *for empathy and communion* among participants and communities?
- Does participation in the research have *transformative potential* for those involved in the process and for the audience or viewers of the video?
- Did the research process or products create a space where *unjust systems were identified and interrogated*?

3. Visionary Critical Discourse

- How open and *accessible* is the video to different audiences?
- Does the video encourage the audience to learn and *engage in critical reflexiveness* in ways that could connect community experience to broader issues of social and cultural interaction?
- Is the audience likely to be *moved to some kind of action*?
- Does the research *spark further research* in other substantive areas, or contribute to the making of a better society?

Participants

Who is involved in the research? How much are they involved and in what phases? Some of the more technical aspects of production, like video editing and writing, can be cumbersome and technically complicated to carry out in a group format. Participant involvement in these processes requires more intensive training as well as relatively

expensive editing hardware and software. If participants are working more independently on their video products, then it might make more sense to provide this training so that each individual has the most control over their own video product. If a larger team is working on creating a community-focused video product, then it may be most efficient to have participants more heavily involved around screenings and video feedback sessions of rough cuts or drafts of the video throughout production.

EXAMPLE 8.1

LEVELS OF PARTICIPATION IN THE PARTICIPATORY VIDEO PROCESS AT DIGNITY VILLAGE

As part of her doctoral research at Portland State University during 2005 to 2010, Heather Mosher (2010) carried out participatory action research with a nonprofit called Dignity Village (www.dignityvillage.org) in Portland, Oregon, which is one of the longest-running and most-organized self-help housing communities in the nation. Dignity Village provides a transitional housing model built from the ground up by homeless people as a democratic society run entirely by its residents. The intent of this research was aligned with the larger goal of Dignity Village to provide conditions and processes that allowed unhoused people to organize for long-term social change. The specific aims of the doctoral research centered on increasing and sustaining quality participation and engagement critical to the healthy development of Dignity Village into an empowered community that could effectively engage in and inform public policies around homelessness and housing. A strategy identified by the community during the research process involved using participatory video methodology to cocreate a video action tool as an orientation video for newcomers, intended to build cooperative relationships and facilitate empowerment within the community.

When the research began in 2005, there were approximately thirty-five individuals who resided at Dignity Village; however, this number fluctuated between thirty and sixty residents throughout the duration of the research.[1] The community was too large to involve everyone in every step of the participatory video process, so it was important to cocreate a research process that would be:

- *Inclusive* to the multiple perspectives and membership roles in the community
- *Participatory and collaborative*, allowing for all levels of participation, including activities for individuals, pairs, small groups, and the larger community
- *Transparent*, providing regular communications between the core group and the broader community, and with ongoing recruitment for individuals to become involved at different stages of the research process

- *Flexible* and respectful of coresearchers' time and changing circumstances. As the research required a long-term commitment of at least one year, many coresearchers at Dignity Village moved out of the community to different housing, got jobs, went to school, or needed time and space to deal with other life demands.
- *Effective* at achieving shared goals within the anticipated time frame. Participatory video projects can take a long time, so it is important to create milestones against which the group and community can track their accomplishments.

In this participatory video project, participation was structured to provide the opportunity for every resident to be involved in the research process at some level. Coresearchers (researcher-facilitators and Dignity Village residents) recruited other coresearchers to participate in the participatory video process in one of two ways: (1) as part of the core research group, and (2) as community consultants, providing information and feedback to the research group at specific milestones throughout the project. These groups were established to provide some structure, but they remained flexible and open to allow for individuals to become more or less involved in the research over time as their circumstances or interests changed.

During the research, participation in the core group fluctuated but, on average, there were nine core researchers who participated regularly one day a week for about one year. An additional fifteen individuals participated periodically in core group activities, with most people becoming actively involved in the video production process. Drafts of the video were shown to the community at community screenings for discussion and feedback, in an iterative process.

The question of who will be involved in the research can be more complicated than it looks. While it is crucial to involve community leaders, it is equally important to encourage a good representation of the community in order to build trust and access, gather viewpoints, and to present an authentic and thorough representation of the issue. Encouraging the involvement of leaders and those with influence in the community will help to remove simple barriers such as access to space for viewing footage and obtaining feedback. But without the input of the full range of stakeholders—to whatever extent a researcher is able to get that—the video will not be seen as representative of the community. A video is only as effective as its sources. If it is perceived as biased or one-sided, people will discount the issues raised and see the video as an extreme view that can simply be ignored.

It is also critical to look beyond the community and to identify other stakeholders that are affected by or are affecting the problem and decide whether to recruit a few key players (policy makers, government officials, business leaders) from the broader community to become involved in the research. This is done by identifying who has the power to make decisions that can improve the situation and who can reduce some of the barriers that the research team may encounter during all phases of the project (research, production, and dissemination phases). The involvement of these "external" stakeholders can be as simple as forming guidance groups who provide advice and input for the project at specific stages. These groups also can function to test the impact of video messages, providing feedback from a broader audience at early stages to help understand potential reaction to the video. In other words, they can serve as gatekeepers to communicating to the intended audiences. This is one of the most difficult tasks in video production and is often neglected until the product is finished. Guidance groups can help the community reach their desired audiences effectively with the final video product, and avoid "preaching to the choir."

Research Process

How will people work together to carry out these tasks—as individuals, teams, groups, or as a community? Participatory video research projects vary on a continuum that ranges from a more independent, or individual-driven, creative process to an interdependent process. This could be called the "independent-interdependent art" continuum.

Think of **independent-art** as a creative process that is individual-driven. The process primarily involves the expression of an individual person that emerges from feedback and support from a group or community. Individuals work independently to collect video footage on a particular topic and then come together as a group to review and obtain feedback.

Definition: Independent-art is a creative process that is individual-driven

Definition: Interdependent-art refers to a creative work of art (like Interdependent-art refers to a creative work of art (like a video) that emerges directly from teamwork. Small groups may work together to capture footage and then reconvene to review and provide feedback on other groups' footage. In some cases, an entire community may decide to work together to create the video. This requires more organization and planning for decision making and finding different roles in the production for everyone in the community, whether it is filming, being recorded, or being the location scout, the production assistant, the clapboard person, sound person, graphics designer, or reviewer/consultant. The entire group or community owns the process and product. Table 8.1 summarizes the benefits and limitations to each approach.

Table 8.1   Benefits and Limitations of Different Approaches to Participatory Video

Approach	Benefits	Limitations
Individual (Independent-art)	• The ability to pursue more topics of interest • Less time-consuming • More intensive skill-building (to operate camera, sound, edit, etc.) • Can use basic and inexpensive equipment	• Need more support for individuals (will be doing all steps alone) • Lacks in team-building • Limited to videotaping shots that can be captured by only one person • Increases risk and harm to individual • Reduced access to groups/ communities (build trust through partnerships with groups, being part of a team) • May require more equipment depending on number of individuals involved
Community (Interdependent-art)	• Builds sense of community and cooperation • Process of creating video as a team becomes more central to research • Process itself can become an intervention in community, depending on specific problem/issue being addressed	• Often requires a focus on one topic due to time investment • The larger the group, the more time-consuming to gain consensus and understanding • Can require a greater range of filming equipment to allow for entire group to participate • Additional skills required from facilitator/filmmaker for training group in filmmaking

Management of Power and Conflict

Power dynamics are intrinsic to every relationship, whether thinking about couples, groups, communities, or politics. Because participatory research involves working with others, conflicts and power dynamics are inevitable. Participatory video originated as a way to give "power" to those who are unheard and to democratize control over the media by having a say in how a view is expressed or a community is represented. Power dynamics between the community and policy makers are the easiest to see and manage. Power dynamics among community members are sometimes more difficult to recognize and can create many challenges to the group video production process. The only way to manage these dynamics effectively is to be prepared for them and assume they exist in every group. Researchers should decide early on how to deal with conflict when it emerges in the group. Be clear about developing and following group ground rules. A clear and consistent group process will support effective communication and productive dialogue; it must be protected so that conflicts can be managed rather than escalated further. Tensions should not be allowed to fester; they should be brought to the surface for dialogue.

Process versus Product Oriented, or Both

In his review of research using participatory video methodology, Huber (1999) found a distinction between process- and product-oriented projects. As Huber noted, "A project can have its focus on the process of production or on the product, the actual video, or on both" (Huber 1999, 16). Both aspects are important in participatory video projects, but many differences exist in the extent of time and focus on each. Research is inherently focused more on process with a goal of producing knowledge that is reliable and valid. Conventional filmmaking is product-oriented—with a heavier focus on artistic expression, style, and audience reach. In participatory video, both aspects are important, and each project is unique in how it approaches these two dimensions. For example, some researchers use participatory video as a process of individual or community empowerment, focusing less on the artistry in the video and/or its potential reach. In this case, it is more about having the freedom to express a viewpoint—typically occurring among individuals/group who have been marginalized and whose voices have not been heard. It is also seen as process of gaining community control over how the group/community is represented as well as contributing to the dialogue on the issue and how it is addressed. Other participatory video projects may have a different level of focus: rather than individual-level empowerment or change, the goal is instead broader social change. Many times, these projects have a more product-oriented focus, with a goal of crafting a communication tool that will reach and influence policy change. Participatory video projects may also start out with an individual-level focus and eventually broaden the scope to affect social change more broadly.

EXAMPLE 8.2

PROCESS-ORIENTED PARTICIPATORY VIDEO PROJECT WITH YOUTH

The 2007 Project Youth Doc[2]—New Columbia program was a four-week intensive and hands-on filmmaking and youth empowerment program for thirteen-to-fifteen-year-olds in a predominantly African American and economically distressed community in Portland, Oregon. The New Columbia community was redeveloped to replace the deteriorated WWII Columbia Villa low-income housing during the Urban Renewal project in 2003 to preserve and develop affordable housing within an integrated housing mix of mixed income, race, and ethnicity.

The Project Youth Doc (PYD) project used a process-oriented approach. The purpose of the PYD project was to facilitate the transformation of the youth involved in the production process through skills building, increasing empowerment and leadership, developing critical thinking about issues that affect their lives, and becoming an active agent of change in their community. At the end of the PYD summer project, each small group or individual had created one short, edited video. All videos were shown to parents and the broader community at the community resource center in an effort to enhance support for the healthy development of the teens. The main focus for the screening was to provide a space for the teens to express themselves to adults and to build the teens' confidence and maturity as a result of the screenings.

DEVELOPING A STORYLINE

Once decisions are made around who is involved and how they are involved in the process, the next step is to develop a basic storyline before starting to shoot the video. A storyline can be illustrated by a simple **visual storyboard** that describes the style and the different parts of the story in sequence. A storyboard is essential for gaining consensus on the broad direction of a video's story and for determining a plan for the general steps to be taken in achieving the goal of making the video.

It is unnecessary to predetermine every part of the story (e.g., what will be said in interviews), but the collaborative activity of creating a storyboard helps to align the group's efforts and to create a clear and cohesive narrative structure or framework for filming. Creating a storyboard requires remaining open-minded about the outcomes of interviews and explorations; however, the existence of a blueprint keeps the main message from getting lost.

It is also important when developing the storyline to refer back to the defined objectives and the intended audiences on a regular basis. A good way to start this discussion is to work with the group to define the style of video, because the specifics of the storyboard often flows from the overall way in which participants see the film. A **film style** is a combination of conventional techniques and aesthetics that filmmakers use to appeal to the audience and enhance the meaning and depth of the storytelling. The style might be described, for example, as informational, persuasive, or visceral/emotional, and it can involve scripted scenes or a scriptless approach.

Participatory video does not use an entirely scripted approach. It follows a documentary style in which participants' voices are heard and new knowledge about a topic is inductively pursued. Some participatory video researchers, however, have found the most effective format to include a combination of scriptless and scripted scenes (Chowdhury, Odame, and Hauser 2010). Including scripted scenes in participatory video has several benefits. Some researchers have found the process of filming scripted video scenes to be useful for capacity building (Chowdhury, Odame, and

Definition: A visual storyboard is a blueprint that outlines the broad direction of the story and acts as a plan for moving forward with steps for video completion

Definition: A film style is a combination of conventional techniques and aesthetics that filmmakers use to appeal to the audience and enhance the meaning and depth of the storytelling

Hauser 2010) and increasing cooperation and teamwork among larger groups of participants (Mosher 2010). With scripted scenes, the story message and narrative structure is more clearly articulated and shared within the group before setting out to shoot the video. Scripted scenes are often challenging to carry out. They require serious planning and preparation, a larger set of people to carry out a variety of tasks, and high levels of teamwork (Chowdhury, Odame, and Hauser 2010). Participatory video projects can benefit from using both scriptless and scripted styles, since each style uses different methods to engage participants in its production, as well as engaging audiences through a variety of formats for self-expression and storytelling.

> **Definition:** A narrative story structure is a sequence of events that has a beginning, middle, and end that moves the story forward and illustrates a problem or conflict in a setting

Another important dimension in creating the storyline is to examine the narrative story structure itself. A **narrative story structure** is a sequence of events that has a beginning, middle, and end that moves the story forward and illustrates a problem or conflict in a setting. Generally, this is divided into three parts: set-up, conflict, and resolution, often referred to as the three-act structure. Researchers should work with participants to encourage them to think about how different ways of telling a story can change its impact and reach. One way to accomplish this is to bring short clips from a variety of popular movies, PSAs, TV shows, shorts, or other videos. These can be used to illustrate different styles of storytelling and assist with brainstorming the elements of a good story. Several concepts can be introduced to help participants critique a variety of clips and to discuss what worked and what did not. These include **character**, **point of view**, and **genre** (Cizek 2005).

> **Definition:** Character refers to the "cast" of people (or any invented or real beings) represented in the story

Character refers to the "cast" of people (or any invented or real beings) represented in the story. Point of view is the source of the storytelling, the perspective that provides the narrative thread throughout the story (e.g., first person or third person). Genre is the overall type or style of the film, such as horror film or musical or drama or comedy, based on a set of conventional stylistic criteria. Participants can use these concepts to create their own effective storyline.

> **Definition:** Point of view is the source of the storytelling, the perspective that provides the narrative thread throughout the story (e.g., first person or third person)

The creation of the storyline will vary depending on the group's developmental age and level of literacy. For example, adults often think in words and will develop a

storyline narrative that is detailed, lengthy, and wordy. Children, on the other hand, think more visually and may not have the skills to write out their narrative in words. They may describe scenes with simple drawings to convey the story, which can translate more easily to visual storytelling. While younger children may find this task to be enjoyable, they are likely to need assistance in the technical aspects of capturing these scenes with the use of a camera. The two case studies below constitute samples of storyboards and exercises used with children and adults during this phase of the participatory video process.

Definition: Genre is the overall type or style of the film, such as horror film or musical or drama or comedy, based on a set of conventional stylistic criteria

EXAMPLE 8.3

CHILDREN'S STORYBOARD EXERCISE TO PRODUCE A PUBLIC SERVICE ANNOUNCEMENT

The storyboard example in Figure 8.1 is from a participatory video research project that was part of a month-long summer environmental education program for children and youth called AHAS Outdoors.[3] The environmental participatory video project was led by Susan Finley, associate professor of education at Washington State

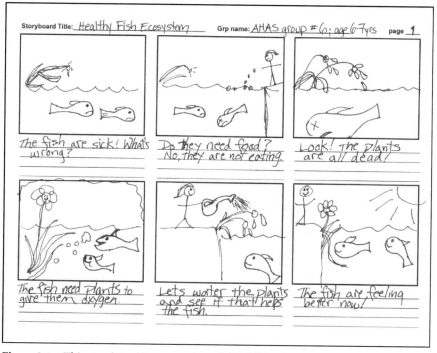

Figure 8.1 This storyboard is a recreation of the children's storyboard for the "Healthy Fish" public service announcement.

University, Vancouver, and founding director of the At Home At School (AHAS) program (www.athomeatschool.org). The idea was to facilitate a process in which youth, ages seven to sixteen years, worked together in small groups to create their own Public Service Announcement (PSA) on an environmental topic of their choosing, following four weeks of daily, hands-on instruction about nature and environmental issues.

The first exercise involved watching PSAs so the youth could get a sense of the type of short video story they were going to create. Several PSAs were shown to the class, including the classic environmental PSA from the 1970s called "Keep America Beautiful (Crying Indian)" (this PSA can be seen on YouTube), and PSAs that were created by youth at schools around the country. After showing the sample PSAs, AHAS teachers handed out a storyboard that depicted the story frames for each PSA. These were used to facilitate a brief and engaging discussion among the kids about what they liked about the PSA, how they understood the message of the story, and the story structure that formed the beginning, middle, and end of the story.

The youth formed groups of three to five students, and each group was given a blank storyboard handout, which they used as a template to create their own storyboard. With one teacher for each group of youth, the groups set out to explore their surroundings (within the Colombia Springs Environmental Education Center complex) and to decide on a story to tell that emerged directly from their immediate environment.

In one group of the youngest children, the children explored around the Center, calling out their observations of plants, insects, and more to their teachers. The role of the teacher was to assist this young group in figuring out which topic really excited them, the questions they had about the topic, and the message they wanted to tell the world in relation to the topic. The teacher also had the role of gently guiding the children to topics and stories that could be filmed in one day and told simply in no more than two minutes of video. This particular group chose to tell a story about the fishpond at the Center. The group noticed that there were few fish, and several of them had bent and droopy top fins, and they wanted to understand the environmental causes for that problem. Was this a sign of an unhealthy environment? What could they do to improve the health of the fish in the fishpond?

With the assistance and guidance of the teacher, the group sat down and sketched out the beginning, middle, and end of their stories, scene by scene, and then researched the problem by talking with one of the Center's staff. The children also explored the plants in the environment and gathered some information on healthy and unhealthy environments for fish in ponds. Once they defined their story and message, the children collected the props for filming and negotiated among themselves about who would be actors and who would be directors. Then the group used about a half-day to film their narrative based on their storyboard. One of the teachers did the actual editing under the direction of the group of students, since there was only one editing station and not enough time to teach students how to

edit. Also, children of this age range often do not have the attention span necessary for editing. At the end of the program, the PSAs from each group were screened to the entire class, and then they were distributed on a local cable access station.

The initial stages of creating the Dignity Village community-based orientation video (introduced in Table 8.1) involved discussing the purpose of the video, the main message to communicate, and the intended audience for the video. The first activity in this process used a video critique exercise in which the core research group viewed three short videos and then discussed the elements of the videos that made them powerful and effective in having an impact on their audience. Through this exercise, coresearchers became aware that different audiences may respond differently to specific styles of storytelling, and the group learned how to craft their message and artistic style to the defined target audience. The exercise also helped coresearchers to understand basic story structure—rising action, conflict, climax, and so on. This activity developed coresearchers' skills for constructing the storyboard.

The core research group identified the primary audience for the orientation video as newer residents of the community who were absent during the initial struggle in establishing Dignity Village. The purpose of the video was to "light a fire under people, and get people connected to Dignity Village" by communicating how residents could be active and socially responsible members of their community. The research group wanted this message to be less information-driven and more passionate and visceral to promote a connection to Dignity Village through an empowering and motivating message.

   **EXAMPLE 8.4**

ADULT STORYBOARD EXERCISE IN PARTICIPATORY VIDEO PROCESS AT DIGNITY VILLAGE

In the storyboarding process, the research group discussed how to communicate the message by showing, rather than telling, and brainstormed the types of visual and audio content that would have the most impact on intended audiences. The storyboard was divided into three main sections (introduction, main story, and ending) that described the purpose, length, and specific messages to convey for each of these three sections while keeping in mind the overall purpose of the video (Figure 8.2). Through extensive discussions, the group created a rough outline of individual

Storyline Script

(Excerpt)

(*completed July 9, 2006*)

Purpose: To light fire under people, and get people connected to Dignity Village
Audience: Newcomers (and other Villagers – internal use)
Length: 30-60 minutes

Section	Time	NARRATIVE STRUCTURE	VISUAL IMAGES
INTRO:	[10-min]	**Purpose:** *"we know what you've gone through" / "this is where we came from" / "power of community in action"*	
	[2-min]	Street scenes	**Video/photographs:** Dumpster diving, padlocked restrooms, sleeping in doorway with Ghetto blanket, police harassment, sleeping in tents, bushes, or in dumpster, raining downtown, panhandling, fight on street, Laura's photos?, downtown welfare office – accessing services **Sounds:** sirens, street sounds **VO/audio:** sound bites of diverse reasons why individuals are homeless (record at Village membership meeting)
	1:30 sec	Introduce Dignity Village though POV of Cami (camera), a newcomer who just came out of the doorways	**Video:** • Person on street, "now what the hell do I do?" (in response to cycle of homelessness and barriers) • B-roll of persons walking in DV front gate, meeting security who greets and escorts to TNP • Show front title credits over entrance video (produced by... title of video, etc) • TNP greets and individual asks, "what's this place about?" or "how did this get started?" or "Is there room for me?" (transition to showing history and context of DV

Figure 8.2 Example of a text-based storyboard created by adults at Dignity Village.

scenes that would build on previous scenes and progress the story toward the climax or main message of the video.

The main goal of the orientation video was to connect members to Dignity Village through shared goals and experiences, so it was first necessary for the core group to identify exactly what those goals and experiences consisted of. The group decided that the purpose of the introduction in the video was to identify with newcomers and to get them "hooked" and connected to the story immediately. The group wanted to communicate that members of Dignity Village also came off the streets and out of the doorways, just like the viewers, by showing the historical struggle to create the Village from the original band of homeless "soldiers" to the current urban village. For the main story, the purpose was to shift a newcomer's perspective from an "I" to a "we" mentality. The group wanted the main section of the narrative to convey that Dignity Village is a place where people are supported and often successful in reaching their personal goals, through teamwork and cooperation in building a home and village. The purpose of the ending was to open dialogue about how to work together as a community toward shared values and a vision of future possibilities for Dignity Village.

The storyboard stage was one of the most time-consuming and challenging phases in the process. Good facilitation was necessary for the group to think that they were making progress and that everyone had contributed to creating the story. Sometimes the biggest challenge was to stay on task and include everyone in the group dialogue. It was very easy for vocal and longer-term members of the group to dominate the dialogue, leading to dissension in the group.

Despite the challenges, there were long-term benefits from taking the necessary time to carry out the storyboarding stage. For one, the process was central to building a group experience that laid the foundation to realizing a shared vision and identity, as well as creating an appropriate and inclusive representation of the community in the video. Thus, taking time to create the storyboard in a participatory and empowering manner not only provided communication and collaboration skills but also facilitated ownership of the tool in a way that increased its longer-term effectiveness and use in the community.

PREPARING FOR VIDEO PRODUCTION

Preparation is key to a successful video project. Laying the groundwork will not only result in a higher quality video but will also ensure the safety and enjoyment of those involved in the process.

Equipment and Expertise Considerations

 Key point ***It is important to determine the kinds of video equipment necessary for capturing the scenes depicted in the storyboard.*** Weigh the costs and benefits of different types of cameras, light kits, and sound equipment. Can the story be filmed outdoors so that extra lighting is not needed? Natural outdoor lighting generally works well, and the use of a basic reflector can reduce harsh contrast from bright sunlight and shadow, creating a softer, more even light. A fold-up reflector is relatively inexpensive to purchase, or a roughly similar product can be created in a pinch by covering a piece of cardboard in aluminum foil. If filming in noisy conditions, using higher-quality audio equipment such as lavaliere microphones may be necessary to obtain clear and crisp sound. For example, documentary filmmakers Heather Mosher and Wendy Kohn chose to interview members of a homeless encampment in their own living space, which was directly under a noisy interstate bridge in Oregon. Lighting was not a problem because interviews were carried out during the day, but getting good-quality sound was a huge obstacle because of the constant sound of traffic overhead. The filmmakers built a low-cost sound barrier out of PVC, cheap foam padding, and duct tape and used lavaliere microphones to interview subjects underneath the sound barrier. It was not the prettiest solution, but as the sound barrier was not in the shot, it worked well enough. Another consideration is electricity. To be safe, bring along enough charged batteries to run all of the video equipment for the entire video shoot on batteries alone.

The available equipment or budget constraints should have informed the development of the storyboard. For example, children may want to create a storyboard with a crime-fighting superhero animation and special effects. Unless researchers happen to know an animator who is willing to help or a studio that can teach them to animate, researchers will need to work with the children to brainstorm alternate ways of getting their story across without the use of animation. One option may be to have the children act out scenes in superhero costumes. Another option may be to learn how to use Claymation effects. There are many resources and instruction guides on the web for doing simple Claymation films in classroom settings.[4] Regardless of the age or abilities of the community or group involved, researchers will need to work together with participants to determine how to transform the storyboard into a realistic video production. It is important to be creative! The key is the story or message; expensive equipment or access to professional actors or special-effects gurus really is unnecessary. A little imagination and creativity can go a very long way.

And finally, plans should be made for how to disseminate the film. Higher-quality video for broadcast will require more expensive equipment and more intensive participant training than video to be shown on standard-definition DVD or YouTube.

Access to People and Locations

It is critical to lay the groundwork for gaining access to people and locations. Researchers must leave enough time for participants to build trust in a community and establish contacts to gain consent for interviewing and videotaping (K. Anderson 1988). It is crucial to establish clear protocols for gaining consent from subjects to film them and for staying safe and ensuring the safety and identity of those filmed. Institutional Review Boards will take special note of these factors in considering protection of human subjects—especially minor children. Researchers and participants should talk with community members (the subjects of the film) on how best to approach people about videotaping them. Should film subjects be approached before or after capturing the shot? What are the possible consequences of each approach? If filming in one's own community, it can be easier to access people during the production process, but be sure to consider safety issues for *after* the video has been disseminated (Cizek 2005). Involving the community in feedback sessions of the video is important so that the community members have a say in how they are represented. Feedback sessions are a useful process to enable researchers and participants to identify and assess the potential long-term impact of the video on the safety of those individuals and communities portrayed in the film. After discussing technical, ethical, legal, and safety issues, it is finally time to pick up the cameras!

Cross Reference: Book 1, chapters 1 and 2, and Book 3, chapters 1 through 3

Cross Reference: See Book 1, chapter 10 and Book 6 for more information on IRBs and protection of human subjects

TRAINING IN FILMMAKING

Before actually shooting the video, participants need to learn basic filmmaking skills and techniques. These are generally taught through hands-on training using games and exercises. Some skills that are gained during training include how to:

- Operate a camera using both a tripod and handheld (e.g., pan, tilt, zoom)
- Frame a shot (e.g., long shot, wide shot, close-up, rule of thirds)
- Set up and use lighting appropriately
- Record audio
- Keep production logs to manage video tapes
- Interview subjects
- Form a production team (define and designate crew roles)

Training involves an iterative cycle in which participants shoot, view footage as a group, evaluate each other's footage, and then shoot again to test out new techniques and build skills. This cycle is repeated until participants feel ready to start production. Training time depends on the experience of participants and the plan for distribution. Higher-quality video requirements (TV broadcast or theaters) may increase the reach and impact of the video but will require more extensive training and specialized equipment. For examples of participatory video training curricula, see Gregory, Caldwell, Avni, and Harding (2005), Harding (1997), Lunch and Lunch (2006), and Shaw and Robertson (1997).

Training in filmmaking is a crucial step in the participatory video process, not only because it builds video production skills but also because it facilitates leadership development (Menter, Roa, Beccera, Roa, and Celemin 2006), supportive interpersonal relationships, and project management skills. Training through participatory video builds confidence and promotes empowerment through exercising voice and control over self-expression. It provides participants with a means to improve their situation and their community.

SKILLS REQUIRED OF RESEARCHERS

Participatory ethnographic video research makes use of a combination of skills, many of which interact or are complementary. While it is not necessary for a researcher to be highly skilled at every field listed, it is very helpful to have some capabilities in and knowledge of the following areas:

- Ethnography
- Filmmaking
- Facilitation
- Collaborative and democratic learning
- Empowerment
- Application of multiple perspectives
- Self-reflection
- Communication and dissemination of research in nontraditional outlets

While ethnographic research skills and filmmaking are clearly important in participatory video research, the other skills listed may need more explanation. Participatory video research usually involves working in groups, and it can often be on topics with significant emotional importance to the group and community. For these reasons, facilitation is arguably one of the most critical skills to have within the group or to develop, in order to conduct research effectively using participatory video. Capable facilitation provides structure and processes that are necessary for cocreating (with participants) an empowering, collaborative, and democratic learning environment.

Empowerment is a process of gaining control and power based on principles of equality and democracy (Rappaport 1990; Riger 2002). Empowerment can appear to be a fairly simple concept on the surface, but it is one of those ideas that is not so easy to implement in practice. The process of empowerment is quite complex, particularly when applied to research with groups and communities. A process that seems empowering, or is empowering for a time, can unintentionally become disempowering. Navigating the complex terrain of empowerment requires a deep ability for self-reflection and a strong willingness to adjust one's perspective. Social dynamics in a group and in a community often change over time, and an "empowering process" will be one that is adaptable to the context.

Multiple perspectives is a systems concept developed by Harold Linstone (1984, 1999) that is based on the idea that complex real-life problems cannot be solved by the limited view of a single dominant perspective. Applying this concept to a research process means the inclusion and valuing of multiple points of view in order to develop a more complete multidimensional view of the complex issue. Particularly in participatory video, it is important to include a balance of multiple perspectives in how the story is represented in the video. It can be easy to exclude unconsciously some perspectives in the narrative, so it is important to reflect on the specific viewpoints that have *not* been included as well as those that have. The person who has a "voice" in the story may reflect and reinforce existing power relations in the represented group or community. The role of the facilitator is crucial in addressing these unequal power relations to provide a more balanced set of perspectives in the final product (Wheeler 2009).

One of the goals of participatory video may be to facilitate communication and social change on an issue. Therefore, skills in a wide range of communication and dissemination channels will broaden the video's reach to the intended target audiences.

PARTICIPATORY DATA ANALYSIS

"In the Field" Analysis—During the Production of the Video(s)

At various points throughout the production phase of the research, video footage of interviews, outtakes, or scripted scenes are shown and discussed as a group to look for emerging themes related to the research questions. This group analysis process informs the videotaping process and facilitates a deeper exploration of the main issues that emerge. The final storyline is constructed as a result of this experiential learning process.

The same iterative process applies whether video footage or photographs are being collected. The number of iterations depends on the same factors that influence the initial decisions for the entire project, including researcher and participant skills, budget, space, and timing constraints. In general, a minimum of two iterations will be needed to provide participants with enough time to discuss the themes fully and refine the concepts into ideas for a final product, and/or to deepen their understanding of the issues and perspectives related to the issue of concern.

The format for sharing and discussing footage depends on final goals for the video as well as practical constraints within the group. The group process can be facilitated as an open- ended brainstorming session, or a more defined process can be used to identify and discuss themes. Wallerstein and Bernstein (1988), for example, developed a model for dialogue called SHOWeD, which has been adapted by Caroline Wang and Mary Ann Burris (1994) for use in photovoice projects. SHOWeD can easily apply to participatory video as well. As the footage or photographs are reviewed, the group answers the following questions: "What do you See here? What's really Happening here? How does this relate to Our lives? Why does this situation, concern, or strength exist? What can we Do about it?" (Wang 2006, 151).

The process of sharing and reviewing each other's video is a critical stage, where participants begin to see the relevance of the process and the impact associated with video-based storytelling. Viewing footage, particularly interviews with other community members, greatly increases reflection and awareness of the complexity of factors involved in the issue. Multiple perspectives may be discovered that might not have been evident during the storyboarding phase, especially through comments and insights of quieter members of the community who might not be as forthcoming in a group setting. Footage taken of other groups or more external stakeholders (government officials, for example) might also provide a new or different perspective, calling for adjustments in the storyboard as the community recognizes the potential impact

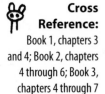

Cross Reference: Book 1, chapters 3 and 4; Book 2, chapters 4 through 6; Book 3, chapters 4 through 7 and Book 5, chapters 4 and 5

of horizontal communication between groups. This process is similar to the development of formative, iterative, and final research models as described in Books 1, 2, 3, and 5. The actual *creation* of the video can be a means to understanding, and not an end in itself, because deepening understanding takes place through iterative cycles of filming, sharing, and analysis.

Finally, sharing footage in this way is also an excellent peer-based teaching tool, providing immediate feedback for learning what works and what does not work visually. A TV or projector should be available for these group sessions so that groups can easily view footage together as quickly as possible after collecting it.

EXAMPLE 8.5

"IN THE FIELD" ANALYSIS OF A PARTICIPATORY VIDEO PROJECT WITH YOUTH

In 2007, thirty Hartford High School students from across the city came together in the Institute for Community Research's (ICR) annual Summer Youth Research Institute. Youth are employed as members of the ICR research staff during the annual six-week summer program. Using a Participatory Action Research approach, Institute staff and graduate student interns train the youth in research methods, which they use to conduct research and to develop action strategies on an issue that they determine to be of importance to themselves and their community. During this summer the youth decided to look into the issue of racism experienced by Hartford teens, and one of the three research methods selected for their inquiry was participatory video. ICR was able to offer this methodology because one of the student interns was a PhD student from Indiana University, who was well grounded in PAR and had extensive experience in participatory video with youth in California and Texas. The participatory video curriculum was divided into three sections: Issue-mation, digital autobiographies, and the creation of a research-based youth documentary.

The objective of the *Issue-mation component* was to have youth researchers understand animation, layering, and motion. Through the process youth were introduced to fundamental concepts including character development, setting, plot, storyboarding, and the basics of stop motion animation. Step one involved creating a flipbook. Youth researchers used one inch by one inch squares of paper to create thirty to fifty "frames" of a simple picture (e.g., a stick figure that was slightly altered on each page). When all of the pages were put together into a flipbook, thumbing through the drawings gave the illusion of motion for the figure. Step two engaged youth in the process of creating a two-character storyboard by drawing out the story, designing the backgrounds and scenes, and laying them out. They then moved their characters through the background, taking numerous pictures of them at each step. During the final step, the youth imported the images into Adobe Premiere, placed them on a time line, incorporated voiceovers with a digital video camera, and learned how to "chop-n-screw" (the art form of videography, painting digital images, forming messages, and producing counterhegemonic media by learning the essential tool kit of Adobe Premiere).

The next component involved youth in creating a *digital autobiography*. Starting with a short "Who am I?" poem, the youth took photographs to illustrate each line. The images were then imported into Adobe Premier, and the youth read their poems and selected songs to play as background underneath their recorded words. Again they lined up the sound, music, and images on a time line, reinforcing their skills and preparing them with both technical skills as well as the increased awareness and the critical reflection needed to create the documentary.

The *documentary* itself required designing and conducting video-based interviews with youth and adults to gather data on the independent variables (adult and youth attitudes and behaviors, the educational system and the media) as factors contributing to their dependent variable domain (racism as experienced by Hartford youth). These interviews were supplemented by the examination of statistics, legislation, review of related secondary materials, and reports. As data were collected, they were reviewed by the group and used to facilitate discussion and reflection as well as to determine collectively which segments of the video footage to use and how to intersperse data and images from other sources. This iterative process of viewing, discussion, and reflection was crucial to the development of individual and group critical consciousness as well as the creation of the collaborative product "Docn' da Beat," which was disseminated by the youth activist–researchers as an incorporated component of a seven-by-twenty-foot mural with related workshops on race. As summed up by one young Jamaican student— "Before this program I had never done research, nor did I feel that I had personally experienced racism—I really didn't think too much about it . . . My eyes were "opened" . . . I saw that racism was everywhere: in the movies, in the video games, in the media, at school, in society. Not only did I learn and teach others about racism in my community and how to work to erase it; I learned vital technological skills that will help me create cultural products that will have a lasting influence on my family and friends."

Summative Analysis of Collection: After the Production of the Video(s)

The "summative" analysis refers to the participatory analysis process that occurs after the end of the video production process. "Summative" analysis offers an opportunity to look at the collection of the videos as a whole and to identify linkages with other types of data that were collected during the research. The summative analysis phase allows for identifying broad themes that emerge from the videotaping and other data gathering, and then "tagging" bits of data (video clips) with these themes and subthemes in order to formulate the story that accurately reflects the issues of concern. This phase of attaching metadata to clips of footage is essential both as a process for group reflection and as a necessary practical step for locating appropriate footage to use in creating a final video product.

Transcribing the video footage is highly recommended as a first step in order to more systematically analyze the data and increase the quality and credibility of the research findings. *Video transcription* is a specific kind of data-entry process that involves transforming audio recordings and visuals into written form. A *video transcript* is a detailed written description of visuals, dialogue, and audio of a video recording in relation to the video time code on the tape. A *time code* is basically a marker of time at each video frame that facilitates logging, synchronization, and the management of video files. A time code is expressed as "hh:mm:ss:ff," which represents the hours, minutes, seconds, and frames of the video.

Because video transcription is a tedious and time-consuming process that involves minimal decision making and creative/editorial control, researchers should consider hiring outside transcriptionists (if the budget allows) or doing it as part of their researcher's role. Transcription involves additional training and a prerequisite level of comfort and knowledge of technology, so be sure to allow for this if the task is to be done in a participatory manner involving the research participants. On average, transcribing one hour of videotape can take six to eight hours of time, depending on the type of footage. This time can be cut nearly in half with the use of specialized video transcription software and newly emerging technology that increases the efficiency of the process. Many online resources also exist for outsourcing audio/video transcription to companies that can do this fairly cheaply and quickly. These companies often provide only a transcription of the actual voices heard in the footage, so outsourcing is best for interview tapes or group meetings, and not for footage with a lot of visuals and little talking. The choice of how best to transcribe the footage will depend on budget, the time frame for transcription, researcher skills, and available technology. A combination of outsourcing and researcher review can be a good way to keep costs relatively low without sacrificing completeness and quality.

While transcription is not an absolutely necessary step in the participatory video process, there are some significant benefits to having a transcription available for analysis and editing. First, having a complete transcript of the research data allows for different modes of analysis that can increase the credibility and reliability of the findings, and it provides a complete record for auditing.

Second, transcription with time codes can greatly speed up the editing process. If a small amount of footage is collected (less than five hours), it is difficult but possible for the researcher or editor to remember in general most scenes or interview segments of importance. But with a larger amount of footage, it is nearly impossible for any one person to have a clear memory of all that was actually captured during the production phase. By transcribing the footage into a database or even into a spreadsheet, it is much easier to assign thematic codes to specific clips, and then later to find exact footage that might have been reviewed but did not seem to be directly relevant at that time.

Third, transcribing the video data provides a more complete archive of the research. Documentary film projects and participatory video projects often involve anywhere from a 6:1 to a 20:1 ratio of *collected* footage to *footage actually used* in the final product. Since collecting data using participatory video may be more expensive as compared to other research formats, having the ability to easily access the data for other research projects or community work is a good way to leverage the costs into multiple uses, as well as important for additional collaborations on the topic. Transcribing and organizing the transcription and footage into accessible archives allows the data to be more easily selected for use in a variety of future projects.

Producing a visual text or video product does not preclude using text or other written materials. Other data sources can be used to inform the story and script during rewrites. And there may be creative ways to integrate and weave the different data sources and formats into the visual narrative. For example, the image of a written letter or a newspaper headline can be used within the video, while a community member narrates the onscreen text. In cases where there is insufficient footage or images to illustrate an important concept, incorporating onscreen text into video clips might be the best way to get the point across succinctly. Again, being creative is key to developing the story, concepts, and messages that the community wants to convey. The group will often come up with a lot of creative ideas gleaned from movies they have seen or from other experiences.

After all data are entered and the video has been transcribed, the research team (including participants) starts the "summative" analysis of the data. If the group decides to skip the transcription step, they can use notes from the "in the field" analysis instead of written transcripts to analyze the data as a whole. There is no standard recipe for the "summative" data analysis. However, a participatory analysis process with video typically involves the basic video postproduction steps listed below, which are used to gain a deeper understanding of the issue and to decide which video clips or other media to include or exclude from the overall narrative. The participatory analysis process of video involves:

 Cross Reference: See Book 4, chapters 1 and 7, for brief discussions of how to use content analysis to identify themes; see also Book 5 for an extended discussion of thematic and other forms of coding

- Thematic analysis of the video by reviewing both the written transcription and the video footage several times to identify overall themes
- Notes to indicate which video clips are emotionally or visually powerful and best communicate a part of the message and story arc

- Analysis of other data types, if multiple formats of data are collected and comparing and contrasting the findings from different data sources in order to map out and demonstrate the complexity of the issue from multiple viewpoints and modes of inquiry
- Expansion and development of the original story-board with specific findings based on thematic analysis of video footage
- Preparation of a more detailed "paper edit" by selecting specific sections of the transcript and organizing them based on themes and story flow (This is called a paper edit because it is often done by printing out the transcripts and physically cutting up pieces and moving them around as desired to form the story, often on a big corkboard or wall, or even on the floor. This can also be done using basic word processing software to reorganize pieces of the written transcript.)

Each step in the analysis process is participatory, but a range of factors influences exactly how much involvement by the participants is feasible. If the group is small enough or there is sufficient time and funding, the entire analysis process can be done as a group. If the group is large, or the data set (amount of footage or other media) is quite extensive, or the group's time is limited, it may be best for the group to provide input at a number of decision points throughout the analysis phase, with the researcher doing more extensive analyses and bringing summarized findings back to the group in an iterative process. At a minimum, it is important for participants to be involved in specific stages of the analysis process where critical decisions are made to guide the direction of the story development. Table 8.2 showing levels of decision making provides a framework for reflection on stages in the process when participation may be more crucial as well as more feasible.

If it is impossible for participants to be involved at every step in the analysis process, then it is important to consider the trade-offs in varying levels of participation in the process and how this may impact the research process and collaborative partnership, as well as the quality and

Table 8.2 Framework for Reflection on Critical Stages for Participation in the Analysis Process

Analysis Process	Level of Decision Making	Level of Training	Time Involved	Ease as a Group Activity[a]
Video Transcription/Data Entry	Low	Moderate to High	High	Low
Thematic Analysis of Video	Moderate	High	High	Moderate
Video-Clip Notes (rating of relevance, impact, etc.)	High	Low	Moderate	High
Collective Analysis of All Data (if more than one data type)	Moderate	High	*Depends*	Low
Storyboard Revision	High	Low	Moderate	High
Paper Edit	Moderate	Moderate	High	Low

[a] "Group activity" refers to the level at which a particular step in the analysis process can be carried out as a group activity. "High" reflects the ease in which such activities can be implemented in a larger group. A "low" rating indicates the activity is typically a solo activity and would be more difficult to apply to group work. Activities that are listed as "moderate" are ones that can be moderately participatory, with some aspects of the process able to be conducted in a group setting.

authenticity of the story. For example, video transcription requires training, a lot of time, and involves very little creativity and decision making. How much would the research process, partnership, and product benefit from participant involvement in the video transcription phase? Participation is hard to sustain in any research project, so it is important to consider the value of participants' time and interests and where ownership of the research process and final product will best be maintained.

The thematic analysis of all of the video footage can take a lot of time. If a thematic analysis of the video was carried out during the "field" analysis, then it might be reasonable to involve the group as consultants or advisors to this postproduction analysis process. Researchers can code the video data based on acknowledged themes, while keeping notes on questions or issues that emerge during the coding process. The questions and related video clips could then be brought to the group for clarification, discussion, and guidance in the analysis process.

The "video-clip notes" step in the analysis process can easily be carried out in a group setting. Watching video clips together can be fun and a great group-building exercise (particularly if only a small selection is shown based on the "field analysis" notes). The process of rating and analyzing the clips for content relevance and impact can stimulate productive discussion, guide the storyboard development, and generate ideas for editing techniques.

If the participatory video research involved collecting more than video data, analyzing the different data types may be a simple task, or a very challenging one. If it is not practical to involve participants in this step of the analysis process, it is useful to create engaging and effective ways to share data "summaries" with the group. For example, in a group session, the researcher can involve participants in interpreting summarized findings, making connections between summary data sets, and raising questions and developing conclusions about the range of data findings at this stage.

The storyboard revision step is another critical point for group dialogue and reflection. It is important for participants to be actively and fully involved at this stage since it involves integrating the collected video findings into the original story narrative in a way that is engaging, informative, and representative of the complexity of the issue. It may not always be feasible to involve the entire research group in the "field analysis," so the storyboard analysis step is an important decision point where video can be shared and reviewed, providing a chance for ongoing reflection on the issues and increased awareness of other viewpoints among the larger group.

If it is impossible for participants to be part of the paper edit, one solution is for researchers to organize the clip selections (based on group decisions and analysis from the storyboard revision step), and then involve the group in decisions around the final story structure and the broad range of video clips to include. Although this step is important to begin the process of selecting clips, it is nowhere near the final selection of clips for the video. The paper edit is a first step in cutting down the collection of footage to a manageable amount, and it is typically a selection of clips that together are from five to ten times longer than the planned final product. The main goal at this stage is to remove from consideration all of the clips that are clearly not relevant to the chosen themes of the storyboard, or that are so technically poor from a visual or audio perspective that they should not be included. Any clips that seem relevant to the selected themes and developed storyboard should be retained in the paper edit for further review in the editing phase.

EXAMPLE 8.6

TIME REQUIRED AND DECISIONS AROUND PARTICIPATION FOR SUMMATIVE ANALYSIS

The secondary goal of the collaborative research with Dignity Village (as part of Heather Mosher's doctoral research) was to document the impact of the participatory research process on empowerment and participation of individuals in the community as a whole. Due to the context of the research within a doctoral research program and the intensive time requirements (over one year) for the research process, the summative analysis phase of the dissertation research was primarily carried out by the researcher-facilitator (doctoral student) and focused on assessing the quality of the research process and the impact of the research on the Dignity Village community.

To accomplish this, Mosher collected data during the research process from multiple levels (individual, group, and community) and from multiple modes: (a) video record of individual interviews, core group research meetings, and community meetings/activities, (b) field notes, and (c) Dignity Village organizational documents. Data were analyzed using an inductive approach to identify key themes and processes that influenced participation and empowerment in the community.

With the sheer magnitude of data collected throughout this yearlong research (data included over two hundred hours of video footage, fifty documents of field notes, and two years of organizational meeting minutes), each step in this process involved a significant time commitment. For example, capturing all digital tapes to a hard drive required 205 hours (more than five weeks full time), basically one hour of time to capture sixty minutes of tape. Importing digital files into a custom database required an additional ten minutes per tape (about thirty-four hours).

The process of transcribing video footage was a particularly arduous process. On average, transcription of one hour of interview and group research video footage took between four to six hours. Transcription of b-roll (outtakes) was less time consuming, about two to three hours of time per hour of tape. Obtaining an accurate transcription of data was important since these transcriptions were then thematically coded and analyzed as original data. In total, for this project, the transcription stage required over 950 hours of time to complete (approximately six months, full time).

From a practical standpoint, it was not possible for the coresearchers at Dignity Village to be heavily involved in the transcription or video-clip notes process of such a large data set. Therefore, in addition to the thematic analysis of the video, Mosher also carefully evaluated visuals for inclusion based on "ethics of care." She assessed the meaning of the visuals, and the ethical implications of including certain visuals for possible inclusion in the final report. She selected potential clips based on the analyses and transcripts, and then assembled them into a general storyline, choosing the best and most representative clips for final inclusion. As this project was part of a doctoral dissertation, Mosher framed the dissertation report from her own critical reflection of the research, based on her experience as researcher-facilitator in the group process. She wrote an outline of the basic story structure for a video-based "visual results" section of her dissertation. Mosher deliberately chose video as the format of her dissertation results section to increase the accessibility and usefulness of the research to community partners and other nonacademic audiences.

EDITING VIDEO TO COMMUNICATE RESULTS

At the editing stage of the participatory video process, numerous questions emerge regarding who will edit the video, how the editing process will be managed in a practical sense, and who will make the broader editing decisions, among other issues. *Video editing* is the process of assembling a collection of video clips into a cohesive story using creative and technical elements of visual storytelling. The video editing process involves two main roles: (1) the editor(s), a more technical role, and (2) the director(s), a more conceptual role that involves providing feedback on the edited sequences and rough cuts, and having ultimate decision-making control over the story. Of course, the editor role is not just a technical role; a good editor will also have creative storytelling skills that can complement the directors' vision and bring powerful pacing and rhythm to enhance the storytelling and message. Each role is important and complementary in cocreating the video.

One of the biggest challenges in participatory video is to make the editing process as participatory and collaborative as possible. The technical side of video editing (the "editor" role) can be collaborative but is inherently more "solo" work. This role is similar to writing a paper. There can be multiple authors of a paper, but authors usually take turns writing the paper, tracking changes, and collaboratively building on each other's work. In addition to the solo nature of the editor role, this role also requires advanced skills and training in a range of video editing software and editing techniques. For these reasons, it is helpful to revisit decisions about this phase of the research with the group, so that informed decisions can be made or revised regarding how the editing will occur and how much participation is feasible or necessary.

If a participatory video project is to involve teaching participants the technical side of editing, be prepared for challenges in participant retention while training individuals in advanced editing techniques. Despite challenges, it is certainly possible for a participatory video project to provide training in very basic editing skills to those participants who are interested in the technical side of editing,[5] depending of course on the available resources and time. If, however, the goal of the participatory video project is to have additional impact by reaching and influencing a broader range of audiences, then it is worthwhile to invest resources in more advanced editing. Because this level of editing requires a more extensive skill set and experience, the editor is less likely to be someone from the participant community group. The editor may be a researcher or research partner, or even an outside professional editor. Regardless, research participants remain involved in the overall editing process through the director(s) role. Communication and feedback on multiple drafts of the video is essential to maintain the integrity of the message and the community's goals and vision for the video. The pacing of a scene, the timing of the narration, or the selected background music all can change the tone or feeling that the film conveys, which may in turn inadvertently alter what the participants meant to convey in the video. For this reason, it is essential to make sure that participants are in agreement with the community representation in the video and that the editor is responsive to requests for changes.

There are a number of iterative steps in the editing phase that often follow a fairly standard documentary film workflow for generating the final product. Each major step is an effort to cut out footage that does not contribute to the story flow, and to add in visuals and pacing that enhance the message, refining the film with each step into a more concise and powerful story that accurately conveys the community's message. This refinement process may require numerous feedback sessions with the research participants to review the editor's drafts during the editing phase, until the research group is satisfied with the community representation in the product.

The first step in the editing phase is to create a rough assemblage of more narrative-based video clips to tell the story. This **assembly cut** is a sequenced order of clips based on the "paper edit" and the story arc, and it is often three to five times as long as the intended final product or video report. The clips are simply "assembled" into a sequence, without transitions in between or any outtakes or other visuals. The assembly cut step is intended to form the narrative backbone of the story, to decide how the thematic concepts that were collected fit together in a way that conveys the desired message. If this step is intended to be participatory, one way to accomplish this is for a small group of participants to sit around the computer and take turns organizing clips, or efforts can be more coordinated by dividing up scenes or sequences for individuals or teams to work on independently, if sufficient computer resources and software are available. The sequences are then combined to make an assembly cut, either as a group around a computer (or perhaps using a projector) or by the editor alone. In either case, once the assembly cut is complete, this is a good time to get feedback from the larger group of participants or the community that is represented by the story. The membership of the specific group providing feedback depends on who is involved in the participatory video project and how their involvement was defined in earlier stages of the process. There may be several rounds of revision and resequencing of clips based on group feedback within the assembly cut phase.

Once an assembly cut is agreed upon, the editing group or the editor creates a "rough cut" version of the video. A **rough cut** is the first stage at which the film begins to somewhat resemble the final product, but it might still be

Definition: The assembly cut is a sequenced order of clips without transitions that form the narrative backbone of the story

Definition: A rough cut is the first draft of a film without transitions, dialogue, narration, or graphics as much as twice the length of the final film. Some initial outtakes and onscreen text are included, and the clips are trimmed to their approximate intended length. The sound and color is left untreated, with no transitions or smoothing, and simple place markers are used to indicate where dialogue, narration, or graphics will be included later. The rough cut is reviewed in iterative steps as in the assembly stage, to determine the impact of the story, to test out various visuals and music and narration or onscreen text, and to begin crafting the final film.

RESULTS FEEDBACK, LOCAL SCREENINGS

Definition: A fine cut is a film draft of intended length, sequencing, sound, and narration, ready to be screened for feedback

Once the editing process is nearly complete, and the rough cut has been modified based on the iterative feedback of the research participants, the editor(s) produce a near-final version of the video, often called a "fine cut." A **fine cut** is a version of the film that is trimmed to the intended final product length, with the entire sequence of images and sound in place, including at least an initial recording of any narration. The fine-cut stage is the point at which the film is first shown outside the research group and brought to other relevant groups and the larger community for feedback through numerous local screenings and focus groups. The specific audiences for these feedback screenings will depend on a variety of factors, including the specific issue of concern in the participatory video project, but for the sake of clarity, there are generally speaking three groups in the broader community who should provide some feedback before the film's release to the general public:

1. Film subject review
2. Direct community review (those directly affected by the issue of concern)
3. Sample target audience/external stakeholder review

The facilitator and research participants should discuss which specific community groups would provide needed feedback before the final release of the film, as there is a balance between too little and too much feedback. Issues of budget and timing will also affect this decision, as will the intended final audience for the film. Some of the feedback steps may be eliminated for films that are created for viewing within a small and narrowly defined group, such as the orientation video at Dignity Village intended only for new people entering the Village and not for the general public outside the Village.

Depending on the structure of film, it is best to start with a screening for a small group of just those people who are subjects in the film. The film subjects might also be research participants who have been part of the video production process already, but all of the film subjects should be included in the focus group screening. It is important to give film subjects a private screening area and a quiet, reflective space to watch themselves in the film, with a chance to process the video conceptually and the space to talk with others represented in film.

After screenings with these small groups and implementing appropriate changes to the film from these sessions, the next step is to get feedback from the people in the community who are affected by the problem, or the broader community that the film is representing. This group can be quite variable depending on the research project and issue of concern, but it might involve the community in which the issue is embedded, a community or group within a certain geographic location, or a broader group of people who are affected by the problem portrayed in the film. The direct community feedback screening consists of showing the fine cut version and then facilitating a critical discussion of the video and its representation of the issue. Generally, the community groups will not ask for significant reedits at this stage, but sometimes additional filming (pick-up shots, interviews) will be recommended to fill a gap or capture a missing perspective. The process is similar to "member checking" in that it is soliciting feedback from the local community regarding the validity and meaning of the research result.

Researchers should be aware that this point in the feedback process can be very challenging and entangled with many heightened emotions. The production group or individuals who are filming are often anxious about receiving feedback on their work and can easily feel overwhelmed at the thought of "publically" screening their video(s) and receiving criticism, particularly as screening typically is perceived as the end of the project. On the other hand, the community may not have been as involved in the process, and it may be the first time that community members really engage with the material. Everyone loves to be a film critic, and the community may be excited about providing comments and being part of the process, but the emotions around this excitement can sometimes be misinterpreted as overly negative criticisms of the video. Community members who have not been as involved also may not know the demanding work involved in the video production process and the constraints faced by the video team in doing its work. It is well worth taking time at the beginning of these screenings to educate the audience on the process and time involved in creating the video and to set up ground rules that will facilitate effective communication and supportive dialogue between the community groups and the research participants. When all sides become aware of the value of each other's perspective in the video creation process, the process is much less anxiety-provoking and conflict-laden.

The intent of these direct community screenings is to create a context where each person's feedback and skill in creating the video is valued and respected. This is again a situation in which the process itself is just as important as the actual feedback obtained for the final product. In this screening process, community members learn how to provide constructive criticism in a respectful and supportive way as well as to listen to feedback in an open and respect-

 Key point ful manner. *In this sense, participatory video is more than a vehicle for self-expression, skills-building, and vertical communication to policy makers or to "outside" audiences. Through sharing diverse perspectives and experiences, participatory video also becomes a tool for promoting a sense of community, as well as building the skills and capacity of the community to develop productively.*

The direct community feedback phase is also a way to extend the participatory video process toward bridging any divide that may have occurred during the production of the video between the core research group (those involved in actually producing the video) and the rest of community that is affected by the issue being explored. Even when the process of creating the video remains open and inclusive, the production group will likely become more cohesive through their shared experiences and teamwork. On the positive side, this may create group solidarity; however, on the negative side it can produce an "us versus them" mentality on the part of both the production team and other community members who, despite their involvement in producing and deciding upon the storyline, footage, and other data content, may have been less involved in the video production process. A carefully facilitated feedback session will help to open dialogue and dispel any tendencies toward divisive groupings.

If the video is intended to be shown more publically to affect broader social change, the next step in the feedback process is to screen the fine cut to smaller groups of sample target audience members or external stakeholders. These might include government officials or policy makers, heads of organizations that have a stake or impact on the issue of concern, or other groups or locations that have similar concerns. The fine cut is shown to the sample target audience members to test the effectiveness of the message, again through screenings with feedback sessions following the film. Regardless of whether the intended target audience is more external to the community producing the video, it is critical to obtain feedback from the identified target audiences to determine the clarity and effectiveness of the video message. This screening and feedback may be incorporated into the direct community screenings from the previous step or a separate screening for additional sample target audience members.

The dialogue during the feedback screening should reveal a deeper understanding of how the video had impact on the audience. It is important to consider three main areas of discussion on the impact of the video:

- *Emotion*: How well does the video resonate or emotionally connect with the audience?
- *Cognition*: Does the video inform or increase the audience's knowledge on the topic?
- *Behavior*: Does the video provoke the intended response? How much does the video encourage the

intended action? For example, the purpose of the video may be to promote critical thinking on the topic or to take a specific action to address the issue.

The "impact" of the video can be assessed in a variety of ways, by using interviews, focus groups, and surveys, among other measurement tools. An example from the collaborative participatory video research with Dignity Village illustrates one way to assess the impact of a video on an audience.

EXAMPLE 8.7

ASSESSING IMPACT THROUGH FEEDBACK SCREENINGS, INTERVIEWS, AND OBSERVATIONS

In the Dignity Village participatory video research, the goal was to collaboratively produce an orientation video that would "light a fire under people," raise critical consciousness, and energize individuals within the Dignity Village community to take action in the community as well as to participate in broader political discussions on homelessness in the Portland area.

Since the video was intended to be used solely within the Dignity Village community, there were no screenings for the general public. The impact and effectiveness of the video was assessed through community screenings within Dignity Village and feedback sessions on the "fine-cut" version of the video, as well as interviews with individuals and observations of community-level changes for up to four months after the first screening of the orientation video. When the "fine cut" was screened for the community, the coresearchers developed a question guide for eliciting feedback from the audience on the effectiveness of the video. The screening and feedback session was videotaped, while a coresearcher also took field notes of the responses. The example of the question guide used during the community screening is provided in Table 8.3.

In addition to what people said in their responses to the video during the community screening, coresearchers used nonverbal indicators as indicators of "emotional connection" and impact. During the video, coresearchers observed how peo-

Table 8.3   Example of a Question Guide for Community Feedback

1. What is your overall impression of the video?
   a. What do you like about the video?
   b. What do you dislike about the video?
2. What is the message of the video?
3. Does the video answer questions that you might have as a "____" (target audience) to the group?
4. Did the video story flow well?
5. Is the video too long, too short, or okay as is?

ple viewed the video. For example, did the audience seem bored? Did the audience leave the room or talk to individuals sitting next to them? Did the audience laugh or cry in the spots where it was intended for them to laugh or cry? Were individuals quiet and pensive at appropriate spots in the video? When the video finished, what was the activity level of the room? Was the room quiet, full of laughter, conversation, or active with individuals leaving before the credits were finished? These behaviors are just a few examples of possible indicators to assess the audience's "connection" and response to the video.

On the night of the community screening of the orientation video at Dignity Village, the common living room area was completely packed, with people even standing in the back to watch the video. Despite the core research group's expectations, nearly every individual living at Dignity Village showed up. Because this was not a mandatory meeting, coresearchers thought that this indicated a deeper sense of engagement by the community. After the screening, coresearcher Laura Brown, a member of Dignity Village, commented to the community, "What I really liked seeing was how many people showed up tonight and it was kind of same amount that shows up for a membership meeting that is mandatory. This wasn't mandatory so kudos for everybody who came. And the humor in [the video] that we saw, [the experience of watching the video] was different from a membership meeting where sometimes we are fighting and arguing . . . everyone was laughing and smiling and looked around afterwards and it is one of my favorite moments tonight at Dignity Village for 2½ years I've been here. [People clap]."

In a packed room of about forty people, not one person left the room during the video screening. This was an unusual occurrence at Dignity Village. It was almost a custom for individuals at Dignity Village to "take bathroom or smoke breaks" during community meetings, or even while watching a Hollywood movie or TV show. During the fine-cut screening, the room was quiet, except for moments of laughter at points the coresearchers had anticipated. The impact of the orientation video far exceeded their expectations. It seemed to immediately reenergize the community. The orientation video also seemed to have an empowering effect on newcomers in the community, with many of them more actively participating in the discussion and feedback.

To assess the long-lasting effect of the video on empowerment and participation, the researcher-facilitator interviewed individuals in the community and documented community-level changes over a four-month time period after the video screening. Overall, after the creation of the orientation video the state of the community appeared to have a more engaged and reenergized feel, an increased sense of community, an awareness of politics around homelessness, and an increase in collective action. For example, newer members seemed to get more involved in leadership positions. Even after the mandatory meeting rule was overturned, members came to meetings and actively participated in decision making on ways to improve the community. The community seemed to be providing more supports for new-comers, and newcomers seemed to be responding to those supports by getting more involved in the community. In addition, the community as a whole was more active at strengthening networks with other nonprofit organizations in Portland and began participating in outreach events to raise awareness and to advocate for changing policies around homelessness. Years later, the video is still being shown to new residents as they first arrive at Dignity Village.

The orientation video may have "lit a fire" in the belly of the people in the community, but the video was not intended to be a tool to sustain that fire. Changing community practices to support this new energy and momentum became a new responsibility for the people and the community itself.

After receiving feedback from the community, the research team usually meets again as a group to evaluate the feedback as a whole and to decide which feedback to act upon and which to save for future versions. The **final cut** or master video is when the picture is "locked" (no more changes to images), all graphics, special effects, or animations are complete, and both the image/coloring and sound quality are adjusted to their final optimum levels, depending on how the video is to be disseminated. When reviewing feedback, the research group should not dismiss feedback simply because the group did not plan enough time and resources for this feedback and improvement process. Special care should be taken to ensure accurate and multidimensional representation of the community based on the feedback provided. This is not only related to the ethics of care between researcher and participants but is also important to ensure that the video has the community's support for distribution and impact.

> 🕸 **Definition:**
> The final cut locks the film after researchers respond to community feedback, after which no more changes are possible

DISSEMINATING RESULTS

In participatory video, the purpose of dissemination is to break down the communication barriers between academic institutions and the public, with the goal of inclusion and participation in dialogue and decision making around issues that directly impact people's lives. Participatory video creates knowledge that is useful, relevant, and readily applicable to local solutions; it therefore can have great impact for positive change. In more traditional academic reports, the purpose of dissemination is to make research results available to other researchers, to advance science and share knowledge. *Dissemination in participatory video is less focused on sharing knowledge with other academics and more focused on communicating with other communities and policy makers.*

Key point

In deciding on the dissemination plan for participatory video research, several questions discussed in the initial planning sessions should be revisited. For example, what is the dissemination plan for the video? Who are the intended audiences, and how can they be reached? What are the research objectives, and how will disseminating the video help to further those objectives? The dissemination phase calls for creating a plan with participants that addresses how to share the video with policy makers, community leaders, or government officials in a way (or multiple ways) that amplifies the impact of participant's voices, stories, and recommendations to policy makers. For example, in a participatory video project carried out in Turkmenistan, Central Asia, participants left copies of the video with key people in the villages and with local video-lending shops. At the same time, they arranged a screening at the British ambassador's residence for high-level representatives from a number of international donor agencies, embassies, and local organizations active in the agricultural sector (Lunch 2006).

There are many ways that the final video can be distributed. Parts of the video (or the entire video, if short enough) can be streamed on the Internet, or shown within a PowerPoint presentation to government, corporate, or nonprofit decision makers. If the video has a human rights objective, the video can be presented as evidence before a national court, regional body, or international tribunal, like the United Nations (Caldwell 2005). Other formats and settings include public service announcements and longer-form documentaries shown in community settings, public places, or in theaters. Some short videos or longer films might be appropriate for submission to film festivals, depending on the topic and intended reach. Regardless of where it is shown, the video may have more impact if accompanied by other forms of data and modes of communication. For example, participants might hold a Q&A with the public after a screening, or create a text-based report or one-page fact sheet that summarizes findings and desired actions after viewing the film.

The dissemination phase of the research can be just as time consuming and complicated as the production phase, so wise planning is necessary. If the research involved guidance groups (or involved other stakeholders in the process), they can be extremely useful at the dissemination phase. The stakeholders can function as gatekeepers to increase accessibility to the intended audiences and decision makers that are often hard to reach.

A final question that is likely to be raised at some point as a project winds down is "Who 'owns' the data and the video product?" Ultimately, the video should belong to the community of engaged partners that produced it. This is not automatically the case, however, and to avoid confusion and problems at a later date, ownership of the video and data should be clarified at the *beginning* of the project rather than at the end. It is best to consult with an intellectual property attorney at the start of any research project to clarify these rights and to assist in drawing up agreements, so that future use of the video is not constrained. The legal constraints can be somewhat complicated with video products, particularly if there is a chance that the video might be broadcast or shown more broadly to a larger community, external stakeholders, or the general public. The effective reach or impact of the research should not be limited by neglecting to clarify these legal issues; it is much, much cheaper and easier to have the proper agreements in place at the beginning than to try to manage a disintegrating situation legally and emotionally after problems arise.

SUMMARY

Participatory ethnographic video is a research methodology full of benefits and challenges. One of the main challenges is affordability, given the increased time, expense, and skills required of participants and researchers. Another set of challenges relates to ethical and methodological dilemmas that are heightened with the use of video. One the one hand, participatory video broadens the reach of a research report to a wider range of audiences, but on the other hand, private discussion of issues becomes more public, which heightens the risk of harm for individuals and communities who are represented in the video. In addition, the public nature of video can limit what people say on camera, raising questions about its credibility and authenticity. In essence, the potential for both harm and positive change are significantly enhanced.

Putting media and research in the "hands of the people" using democratic and participatory methods is the key aspect of what makes participatory ethnographic video so powerful and unique as a research method. Armed with the power of knowledge and an effective communication tool, social change and social justice becomes more possible for those who have been historically silent and misrepresented. The video production process and iterative cycle of viewing, communicating, and filming, builds cooperation and teamwork as well as critical consciousness. Joanna Wheeler comments on the more unique aspects of participatory video in research for working in violent contexts (Wheeler 2009). She explains, "People were more willing to listen to what others were saying when they watched it on video than they would have in face to face encounters. This kind of listening in such settings is not something that is easily achieved by other methods, even given the limitations" (13). Through sharing diverse perspectives and experiences, participatory video also becomes a tool for promoting a sense of community, as well as building the skills and capacity of the community to develop productively.

NOTES

1. Because of the city of Portland restrictions, Dignity Village provides services for up to sixty individuals residing in the community at any one time.

2. Project Youth Doc is an annual summer documentary filmmaking program for teens by the nonprofit organization The Hollywood Theatre in Portland, Oregon. See www.hollywoodtheatre.org.

3. This program was funded by the No Child Left Inside grant program administered by the Washington State Parks and Recreation Commission.

4. For more information on Claymation for classrooms, see https://sites.google.com/site/movies2bmade/home and http://instech.knox.k12tn.net/training/claymation/quickguidecm.htm.

5. In her doctoral research, Mosher (2010) found that most community members were interested in learning how to operate a camera, and very few were interested in developing video editing skills. Several participants were interested in gaining a basic understanding of the technical side of the editing process, but most participants were more comfortable with participating in the director role of the editing phase.

REFERENCES

Alexander, B. K. 2005. Performance ethnography: The reenacting and inciting of culture. In *The SAGE handbook of qualitative research, third edition*, ed. N. K. Denzin and Y. S. Lincoln, 411–42. Thousand Oaks, CA: Sage.

Anderson, G. L. 1998. Toward authentic participation: Deconstructing the discourses of participatory reforms in education. *American Educational Research Journal* 35(4): 571–603.

Anderson, K. 1988. Participatory video in community development. *Media in Education and Development* 21(4): 163–68.

Caldwell, G. 2005. Using video for advocacy. In *Video for change: A guide for advocacy and activism*, ed. S. Gregory, G. Caldwell, R. Avni, and T. Harding, 1–19. London, UK: Pluto Press, in association with WITNESS. Retrieved on May 30, 2011, from http://www.witness.org.

Charmaz, K. 2005. Grounded theory in the 21st century: Applications for advancing social justice studies. In *The SAGE handbook of qualitative research, third edition*, ed. N. K. Denzin and Y. S. Lincoln, 507–36. Thousand Oaks, CA: Sage.

Chowdhury, A. H., H. H. Odame, and M. Hauser. 2010. With or without a script? Comparing two styles of participatory video on enhancing local seed innovation system in Bangladesh. *Journal of Agricultural Education and Extension* 16(4): 355–71.

Cizek, K. 2005. Safety and security. In *Video for change: A guide for advocacy and activism*, ed. S. Gregory, G. Caldwell, R. Avni, and T. Harding, 20–73. London: Pluto Press, in association with WITNESS. Retrieved on May 30, 2011, from http://www.witness.org.

Crocker, S. 2003. The Fogo process: Participatory communication in a globalizing world. In *Participatory video: Images that transform and empower*, ed. S. A. White, 122–44. Sage: Thousand Oaks, CA.

Fine, M., L. Weis, S. Weseen, and M. Wong. 2000. For whom? Qualitative research, representations and social responsibilities. In *The handbook of qualitative research*, ed. N. Denzin and Y. Lincoln, 107–32. Thousand Oaks, CA: Sage.

Finley, S. 2003. Arts-based inquiry in QI: Seven years from crisis to guerilla warfare. *Qualitative Inquiry* 9(2): 281–96.

Freire, P. 1970. *Pedagogy of the oppressed*. New York: Continuum.

Gregory, S., G. Caldwell, R. Avni, and T. Harding. 2005. *Video for change: A guide for advocacy and activism*, 20–73. London: Pluto Press, in association with WITNESS. Retrieved on May 30, 2011, from http://www.witness.org.

Harding, T. 1997. *The video activist handbook*. London: Pluto Press.

Huber, B. 1999. Communicative aspects of participatory video projects: An exploratory study. Unpublished masters thesis. Swedish University of Agricultural Sciences, Department of Rural Development Studies. Uppsala, Sweden.

Lincoln, Y. S., and E. G. Guba. 1986. But is it rigorous? Trustworthiness and authenticity in naturalistic evaluation. In *Naturalistic evaluation: New directions for program evaluation, no. 30*, ed. D. D. Williams, 73–84. San Francisco: Jossey-Bass.

Linstone, H. A. 1984. *Multiple perspectives for decision making: Bridging the gap between analysis and action*. North-Holland, NY: Elsevier-Science Publications.

———. 1999. *Decision making for technology executives: Using multiple perspectives to improve performance*. Boston: Artech House.

Lunch, C. 2006, March. Participatory video as a tool for documentation. *LEISA Magazine* 22(1): 31–32. Retrieved on May 30, 2011, from http://www.agriculturesnetwork. org/magazines/global/documentation-for-change/participatory-video-as-a-tool-for-documentation.

Lunch, N., and C. Lunch. 2006. *Insights into participatory video: A handbook for the field*. Published by Insight. Retrieved on May 5, 2011, from www.insightshare.org.

Menter, H., M. C. Roa, O. F. Beccera, C. Roa, and W. Celemin. 2006. Using participatory video to develop youth leadership skills in Colombia. *Participatory Learning and Action* 55, 107–14. Retrieved on May 21, 2011, from http://www.st-otherwise.org/wp-content/uploads/IIED-Using-PV-to-develop-youth-skills.pdf.

Mosher, H. I. 2010. Participatory action research with a Dignity Village: An action tool for empowerment within a homeless community. Unpublished doctoral dissertation, Portland State University.

Quarry, W. 1984. The Fogo process: An interview with Don Snowden. *Interaction* 2(3): 28–63.

Rappaport, J. 1990. Research methods and the empowerment social agenda. In *Researching community psychology*, ed. P. Tolan, C. Keys, F. Chertok, and L. Jason, 51–63. Washington, DC: American Psychological Association.

Reason, P. 2006. Choice and quality in action research practice. *Journal of Management Inquiry* 15(2): 187–203.

Reason, P., and H. Bradbury, eds. 1999. *Handbook of action research: Participative inquiry and practice*. London: Sage.

Riger, S. 2002. What's wrong with empowerment. In *A quarter century of community psychology: Readings from the American Journal of Community Psychology*, ed. T. A. Revenson, A. R. D'Augelli, S. E. French, D. L. Hughes, D. Livert, E. Seidman, M. Shinn, and H. Yoshikawa, 395–408. New York: Kluwer Academic/Plenum Publishers.

Shaw, J., and C. Robertson. 1997. *Participatory video: A practical approach to using video creatively in group development work*. London and New York: Routledge.

Wallerstein, N., and E. Bernstein. 1988. Empowerment education: Freire's ideas adapted to health education. *Health Education and Behavior* 15(4): 379–94.

Wang, C. 2006. Youth participation in photovoice as a strategy for community change. *Journal of Community Practice* 14(1): 147–61.

Wang, C., and M. A. Burris. 1994. Empowerment through photo novella: Portraits of participation. *Health Education and Behavior* 21(2): 171–86.

Wheeler, J. 2009. "The life that we don't want": Using participatory video in researching violence. *IDS Bulletin* 40(3): 10–18.

White, S. A. 2003. Participatory video: A process that transforms the self and other. In *Participatory video: Images that transform and empower*, ed. S. A. White, 63–101. Thousand Oaks, CA: Sage.

White, S. A., and P. K. Patel. 1994. Participatory message making with video: Revelations from studies in India and the USA. In *Participatory communication: Working for change and development*, ed. S. A. White, K. S. Nair, and J. Ascroft, 356–86. New Delhi: Sage Publications.

Williamson, H. A. 1975. The Fogo process in communications: Training for agriculture and rural development. In *Communication in development: A multinational perspective*, ed. F. L. Casmir, 93–98. Norwood, NJ: Ablex Publishing.

INDEX

Note: Page numbers in italics refer to figures and tables.

ABOUT THE AUTHORS, ARTISTS, AND EDITORS

Jean J. Schensul, founding director, and full-time senior scientist, Institute for Community Research, Hartford, is an interdisciplinary medical/educational anthropologist. Born in Canada, she completed her BA in archeology at the University of Manitoba and her MA and PhD in anthropology at the University of Minnesota. From 1978 to 1987, as deputy director and cofounder of the Hispanic Health Council in Hartford, Connecticut, she built its research and training infrastructure. In 1987, she became the founding director of the Institute for Community Research, an innovative, multimillion-dollar community research organization, conducting collaborative applied research in education, cultural studies and folklore, participatory action research, and community intervention research in the United States, China, and India. Dr. Schensul's research cuts across the developmental spectrum, addressing contributions of ethnography to disparities and structural inequities in early childhood development, adolescent and young adult substance use and sexual risk, reproductive health, and chronic diseases of older adulthood. She is the recipient of more than twenty National Institutes of Health research grants, as well as other federal, state, and foundation grants. In addition to conferences, workshops, over eighty peer-reviewed journal articles, many edited substantive special issues of journals including *Anthropology and Education Quarterly, AIDS and Behavior, American Behavioral Scientist*, and the *American Journal of Community Psychiatry*, her collaborative work in research methodology is reflected in a book (with Don Stull) titled *Collaborative Research and Social Change*, the widely celebrated seven-volume series, the *Ethnographers' Toolkit*, with Margaret LeCompte, and in other articles and book chapters on ethnography and advocacy, community building, and sustainability of interventions. She has served as president of the Society for Applied Anthropology and the Council on Anthropology and Education and is an elected board member of the American Anthropological Association. In recognition of her work as a scholar-activist she has been awarded two senior anthropology awards, the Solon T. Kimball Award for anthropology and policy (with Stephen Schensul) and the Malinowski Award for lifetime contribution to the use of anthropology for the solution of human problems. Dr. Schensul holds adjunct faculty positions in the departments of Anthropology and Community Medicine, University of Connecticut, and is codirector, Qualitative Research and Ethnography, Interdisciplinary Research Methods Core, Yale Center for Interdisciplinary Research on AIDS.

Margaret D. LeCompte received her BA from Northwestern University in political science, and after serving as a civil rights worker in Mississippi and a Peace Corps Volunteer in the Somali Republic, she earned her MA and PhD from the University of Chicago. She then taught at the Universities of Houston and Cincinnati, with visiting appointments at the University of North Dakota and the Universidad de Monterrey, Mexico, before moving to the School of Education at the University of Colorado-Boulder in 1990. She also served for five years as executive director for research and evaluation for the Houston Independent School District. She is internationally known as a pioneer in the use of qualitative and ethnographic research and evaluation in education. Fluent in Spanish, she has consulted throughout Latin America on educational research issues. Her publications include many articles and book chapters on research methods in the social sciences, as well as her cowritten (with Judith Preissle) *Ethnography and Qualitative Design in Educational Research* (1984, 1993) and coedited (with Wendy Millroy and Judith Preissle) *The Handbook of Qualitative Research in Education* (1992), the first textbook and handbook published on ethnographic and qualitative methods in education. Her collaborative work in research methodology continues with this second edition of the *Ethnographer's Toolkit*. Dr. LeCompte is deeply interested in the educational success of linguistically and culturally different students from kindergarten through university, as well as reform initiatives for schools and communities serving such students. Her books in these areas include *The Way Schools Work: A Sociological Analysis of Education* (1990, 1995, and 1999) with K. DeMarrais and *Giving Up on School: Teacher Burnout and Student Dropout* (1991) with A. G. Dworkin. Her diverse interests as a researcher, evaluator, and consultant to school districts, museums, communities, and universities have led to publications on dropouts, artistic and gifted students, school reform efforts, schools serving American Indian students, and the impact of strip mining on the social environment of rural communities. Her most recent research involves explorations in the politics and finance of public universities. A Fellow of the American Educational Research Association, the American Anthropological Association, and the Society for Applied Anthropology, she has been president of the Council on Anthropology and Education of the American Anthropology Association and editor of the journals *Review of Educational Research* and *Youth and Society*. A founding member and the first president of the University of Colorado-Boulder chapter of the American Association of University Professors, she also served as vice president of the Colorado Conference of the AAUP and was active in faculty governance at the University of Colorado. As professor emerita, she continues to use action research strategies in the service of improving the intellectual life in higher education.

Stephen Borgatti, PhD, is a sociologist and professor and Endowed Chair at the University of Kentucky in the Management Department of the Gatton College of Business and Economics. His research is focused on social network, and he also has an interest in cultural domains and knowledge management. He is a senior editor at *Organization Science* and an associate editor at *Computational and Mathematical Organizational Theory*. He also sits on the editorial boards of *Administrative Science Quarterly* and *Field Methods*. He also was a board member for the *Journal of Management* and *Sociological Methodology*. Dr. Bortatti was a two-term president of INSNA, the professional association for social network researchers, and he founded the SOCNET listserv as well as the UCINET support group. An innovator in cultural methods research, he is one of the founders of the NSF-funded Methods Camp, which provides instruction on cultural analysis to new faculty in the social sciences.

Ellen Cromley is a medical geographer with a PhD in geography from the University of Kentucky. She coauthored *GIS and Public Health* (2002, 2011 2nd edition) with Sara McLafferty. After more than two decades as a professor in the department of geography, University of Connecticut, she left to conduct independent research and spent four years as senior research associate at the Institute for Community Research in Hartford, Connecticut, as an investigator on grants funded by the National Institute of Alcohol Abuse and Alcoholism, the National Institute on Drug Abuse, and the National Institute on Mental Health. Dr. Cromley has mentored researchers at M.D. Anderson Cancer Center and the University of Connecticut Center for Health, Intervention, and Prevention, who are seeking to integrate geographic methods and GIS into their work. She served as a member of the NIH Community-Level Health Promotion study section and has conducted a number of national workshops on GIS and spatial analysis for federal research agencies.

Daniel Halgin, PhD, is assistant professor of management at the LINKS Center for Social Network Analysis at the University of Kentucky. He completed his doctoral studies in the Management and Organization Department at Boston College. His research focuses on social network theory and identity dynamics and how these concepts influence firm and individual behavior. He uses a network perspective to study the process by which individual, group, and organizational identities are formed and the ramifications of these identities on competitive behavior, performance, and labor market activity. In addition, he investigates the effect of cultural sentiments on the portrayal and performance of organizational leaders.

Sheryl A. Ludwig, PhD, is an associate professor in Educational Foundations and Teacher Education at Adams State College, Colorado. She obtained her a doctorate from the University of Colorado after a thirty-one-year, award-winning career as a public school teacher. Her research focuses on strategies used by indigenous and immigrant students to survive and flourish in the United States. During her dissertation research in Guatemala, she explored differences in indigenous teaching and learning among Maya women weavers and their children in the home and in the village public school. She also focused on the struggle for identity among Maya women who defined themselves as artists but saw their persons denigrated by racist policies and their work commodified in global markets. At Adams State College, she continues her work with the Maya immigrant community in southern Colorado and their village counterparts in Guatemala; she has developed an exchange program linking Adams State with these communities.

Heather Mosher, PhD, is a community psychologist and research associate at the Institute for Community Research with a doctorate in Systems Science-Psychology. In her work, she aims to facilitate the development of healthy communities through rigorous multilevel research that uses cutting-edge digital media methods and innovative modes of disseminating research findings. As a mixed-method applied researcher and a professional filmmaker, she has conducted community-based research using video with economically disadvantaged communities in the United States and East and southern Africa and Latin America. She has worked with a diverse range of marginalized populations, including women, low-income, homeless, minority, youth, and LGBTQ communities. Her primary areas of research include research methods, social processes, and social/structural inequalities, with a particular focus on poverty, homelessness, and housing.

Bonnie K. Nastasi, PhD, is associate professor and codirector, School Psychology Doctoral Program, department of psychology, Tulane University. Her research focuses on culturally appropriate health promotion and health risk prevention programming for child, adolescent, and adult populations. Her prior appointments were as faculty in the schools of education, University of Connecticut; State University of Albany, New York; and Walden University. She spent seven years as director of interventions at the Institute for Community Research, Hartford, where she was coinvestigator on two large, multilevel NIH grants that included a systemwide social development intervention in the New Haven Schools and a multilevel intervention to reduce HIV risk among married men in Mumbai, India. She has published extensively on qualitative and mixed-methods research as well as culturally specific intervention approaches in schools.

Stephen L. Schensul, PhD, a medical anthropologist, is professor of Community Medicine and Health Care, University of Connecticut School of Medicine, and director of the Center for International Community Health Studies. He is an internationally recognized community-based HIV researcher, with more than two decades of funded research on sexual risk, sexual health, and HIV in South Asia. For the past ten years, he has guided two collaborative, large-scale, multilevel NIMH studies on HIV risk among married men (2001–2007) and married women (2008–2013) in India, based on cultural factors as markers of risk for sexually transmitted infections. Dr. Schensul teaches global health and mixed-methods community-based research, including the use of secondary and archival data sources to develop, guide, and confirm field studies, and since 2000 he has taught and provided methodological guidance to MPH, MPhil, and PhD students in the United States and India. In 2010 Dr. Schensul received the Career Achievement Award given by the Society for Medical Anthropology.

Merrill Singer, PhD, is a professor in the department of Anthropology and senior research scientist at the Center for Health, Intervention, and Prevention at the University of Connecticut. He is a member of the executive committee of the Center for Interdisciplinary Research on AIDS (CIRA) at Yale University. While deputy director of research at the Hispanic Health Council in Hartford, he received a number of NIH and other grants for research on alcohol use, drug use, sexual risk, community and interpersonal violence, and AIDS prevention. An expert in community-based research, his focus has been on structural factors contributing to health disparities in hard-to-reach populations. His current research focuses on both drug use and HIV risk and environmental health issues, including a growing focus on the impact of global warming on international health. His research spans the globe, including the United States, Brazil, China, and Haiti.

Robert T. Trotter II, PhD, is an Arizona regent's professor, department of Anthropology, Northern Arizona University, Flagstaff. His work in medical anthropology addresses cross-cultural issues in health care delivery and prevention, focused on cancer, HIV prevention and intervention, disabilities, and addiction studies. He also designs and conducts evaluation programs for complex partnerships (industry-university, government-university-community, community-scientist), creating cultural models of collaborative systems, ethnographic explorations of institutional dynamics, and organizational network analysis. He applies new ethnographic research methods, research design, computer-assisted ethnography, and international training in rapid ethnographic assessment as well as anthropological research ethics. His publications include books and articles on Mexican American traditional healing, cross-cultural alcohol and drug studies, migrant farm worker health and education, HIV/AIDS,

alcohol and drug prevention studies, partnership design, diagnosis and intervention, and anthropological ethics.

A fiber artist, quilter, teacher, curator, and lecturer, **Ed Johnetta Fowler-Miller** is
acknowledged to be one of the most creative and colorful improvisational quilt-
makers in the United States. Widely exhibited in the United States and internationally, her quilts can be found in many important museums, corporate and
private collections including The National Gallery of the Smithsonian Institution in Washington, D.C.; Nelson Mandela's National Museum in Cape Town,
South Africa; Wadsworth Atheneum Museum of Art in Hartford, Connecticut;
and the Rocky Mountain Quilt Museum in Golden, Colorado. Her home state
of Connecticut awarded her its most prestigious artistic award, The Governor's
Art Award, as well as the Wadsworth Atheneum Museum of Arts first Presidents
Award; Leadership of Greater Hartford's Arts and Cultural Award, Vision Award
for Arts; and Cultural and Capital Community College Heritage Award. The
Home and Garden Station featured Ed Johnetta on the Modern Masters series;
she appeared on Debbie Allen's series *Cool Women*, Public TV, Tokyo, Japan; and
her woven creations were worn by actress Phylicia Rashad on *The Cosby Show*.
The Sunday *New York Times* featured her in the Best of the Best series, and most
recently, she appeared on HGTV's *Simply Quilts*. In 2009 Ed Johnetta represented the United States and the Women of Color Quilters Network at the largest quilt festival in the world in Yokohama, Japan, and in 2010 she represented
the United States in Costa Rica where she lectured and taught workshops. She
has exhibited her work across the United States and lectures and offers workshops in New England, elsewhere in the United States, and worldwide. More
information can be found at http://www.edjohnetta.com.

Graciela Quiñones-Rodríguez is a gourd carver/lutier/multimedia artisan/
performer and master teaching artist. She draws most of her inspiration from
indigenous and traditional Puerto Rican imagery and symbols to create *higüeras*
(gourds), clay/wood figures, and folk string instruments (*cuatros, tiples,* and *bor-
donuas*). Quiñones-Rodríguez has been a resident artist in numerous schools
and libraries throughout Massachusetts, Connecticut, and New York. She has
received fellowships and awards from the Commission on the Arts, the New
England Foundation for the Arts, and the National Endowment for the Arts. Her
works have been on exhibit in Puerto Rico; the Smithsonian Institute; University
of Massachusetts, Wisconsin; New York; and several exhibit sites throughout
Connecticut. She is a member of Urban Artists Initiative and the Connecticut
Cultural Heritage Arts Program. She is a licensed clinical social worker, currently working at the Storrs campus of the University of Connecticut.